Rustic Warriors

WARFARE AND CULTURE
General Editor: Wayne E. Lee

*A Rabble in Arms:
Massachusetts Towns and Militiamen
during King Philip's War*
Kyle F. Zelner

*Empires and Indigenes:
Intercultural Alliance, Imperial Expansion,
and Warfare in the Early Modern World*
Edited by Wayne E. Lee

Warfare and Culture in World History
Edited by Wayne E. Lee

*Rustic Warriors:
Warfare and the Provincial Soldier on
the New England Frontier, 1689–1748*
Steven C. Eames

Rustic Warriors

Warfare and the Provincial Soldier on the New England Frontier, 1689–1748

Steven C. Eames

NEW YORK UNIVERSITY PRESS
New York and London

NEW YORK UNIVERSITY PRESS
New York and London
www.nyupress.org

© 2011 by New York University
Paperback edition published 2025
All rights reserved

References to Internet websites (URLs) were accurate at the time of writing.
Neither the author nor New York University Press is responsible for URLs
that may have expired or changed since the manuscript was prepared.

Library of Congress Cataloging-in-Publication Data
Eames, Steven C., 1954–
Rustic warriors : warfare and the provincial soldier on the
New England frontier, 1689–1748 / Steven C. Eames.
p. cm. — (Warfare and culture)
Includes bibliographical references and index.
ISBN 978-0-8147-2270-1 (hardcover)
ISBN 978-1-4798-4317-6 (paperback)
ISBN 978-0-8147-2271-8 (ebook)
ISBN 978-0-8147-2287-9 (ebook)
1. New England—History—Colonial period, ca. 1600–1775. 2. New Englanders—
Warfare. 3. Soldiers—New England—History. 4. Massachusetts. Militia—History.
5. New Hampshire. Militia—History. 6. New England—History, Military. I. Title.
II. Title: Warfare and the provincial soldier on the New England frontier, 1689–1748.
F7.E119   2011
974'.02—dc23   2011028153

New York University Press books are printed on acid-free paper,
and their binding materials are chosen for strength and durability.
We strive to use environmentally responsible suppliers and materials
to the greatest extent possible in publishing our books.

The manufacturer's authorized representative in the EU for product safety is Mare Nostrum
Group B.V., Mauritskade 21D, 1091 GC Amsterdam, The Netherlands.
Email: gpsr@mare-nostrum.co.uk.

Manufactured in the United States of America

10 9 8 7 6 5 4 3 2

To Kathleen,
Many years ago we took a walk up the road—
this is but another step in that wonderful journey.

Contents

List of Maps	ix
Preface and Acknowledgments	xi
Introduction: The New England Provincial Soldier: A Problem of Perception	1

PART I: WARFARE ON THE NEW ENGLAND FRONTIER

1	The Initiation of War and the New England Military System	21
2	Garrisons: The First Line of Defense	35
3	Provincial Forts: The Magnet	51
4	Scouts: Patrols, Probes, and Raids	69
5	Expeditions: The Anglo-American Partnership	91
6	Stores of War: The Logistical Nightmare	110

PART II: THE PROVINCIAL SOLDIER

7	Recruiting: Gone for a Soldier	131
8	Officers: Chosen to Lead	153
9	Battle Drill and Fighting Spirit	172
10	Battle Experience: Facing the Enemy	198
11	The Wounds of War	217

Afterword	242
Notes	245
Index	302
About the Author	306

List of Maps

Frontier Towns, 1698	20
Forts in King William's War, 1689–1698	53
Forts in Queen Anne's War, 1704–1712	54
Forts in King George's War	56
Targets for Expeditions, 1690–1748	93

Note: Modern state and international boundaries have been included on maps to allow easier orientation.

Preface and Acknowledgments

Historical research rarely proceeds in a straight line. The historian boldly pursues an embryonic thought or notion down a path filled with so many turns, forks, and dead ends that the final result often has little connection to the original destination. So it went with this project. John Shy's provocative article "A New Look at the Colonial Militia" provided the initial idea.[1] At the time the article was written, Shy believed that although the "evidence gathered so far is not full nor does it admit of any quantitative conclusions, . . . it does indicate that a growing number of those who did the actual fighting were not the men who bore a military obligation as part of their freedom."[2] This thesis prompted an analysis of soldiers from Dover, New Hampshire, who performed active duty in 1745, which in turn led to the present study. But what began as a relatively straightforward and simple quantitative test of Shy's thesis has twisted and turned and grown so much since that beginning, the final form bears little resemblance to the incipient concept.

During the course of my research I found considerable inspiration from the work of the "new" military historians such as John Keegan, Sylvia Frey, and J. A. Houlding.[3] They have examined in intimate detail the effects of war and army life on the soldier and have provided new insights while destroying old stereotypes. Encouraging this approach in 1981, Richard H. Kohn recommended that historians studying the social history of the American soldier should reconstruct "the life and the environment of the enlisted man in much greater detail and depth than has ever before been attempted." As Kohn suggested:

> By first asking the most basic descriptive questions and using the methods of other disciplines, military historians can recover the fullness of the military experience. Initial research might concentrate on the assumptions that the military has brought to the acquisition, training, and government of soldiers, then the regulations of armies and navies,

the uniforms and the equipment, the drill and fatigue duty—in short, the minutiae of military life in its entirety. . . . historians could create so realistically the physical and mental world of the enlisted man that the time-honored reliance on literary sources and on the artistry of fiction could be diminished.[4]

This, then, is the direction my research has taken. The intention to conduct a quantitative analysis of colonial soldiers has blossomed into a social history concentrating on the impact of war and military life on the New England provincial soldier.

So many people have influenced and assisted in this work it is hard to single them all out. Early on, Robert Gilmore encouraged me to explore where my heart and mind led me. Vincent Capowski graciously read a few chapters and provided valuable suggestions and encouragements. Our many discussions concerning military history at St. Anselm College were not only enjoyable but provided an important sounding board for my ideas. I must also mention the influence of Darrett Rutman. He was a hard task master to be sure, but one who expunged naiveté and fostered a respect and love for the writing of history.

Service and teaching at Mount Ida College over the years distracted me from writing for too long. Over those years there were individuals who encouraged me to publish this work and get on to other projects. In particular, Emerson W. "Tad" Baker has been persistent in his nudging, and I have appreciated every nudge. I also appreciate Guy Chet's acknowledgment. Guy and I are almost diametrically opposed in our interpretations, but he still expressed appreciation of the work, and his appreciation meant a great deal. Kyle F. Zelner also provided encouragement at a time when I needed it. Finally, I greatly appreciated the kind words from Fred Anderson.

Then there are those in your personal life who provide support and understanding, friends and family who provide that timely pat on the back. I wish I could thank them all individually but the names are too many to list without the risk of leaving out someone. I will mention and thank Tom Nesbitt for continuing to provide me with research material. I also want to thank Ellen Goldberger for enduring my constant kvetching during the rewrite process: man nor beast knows no better friend.

Best of all, there is my family. The raising of my three children, Mairi, Kelsi, and Jonathan, certainly added to the service and teaching at my college to steal time from bringing this work to completion; however, to paraphrase Clark Gable, frankly, I don't give a damn. They provided experiences that I will always treasure and all three turned into wonderful, caring human beings. And my wife, Kathleen, has always been a rock of support, through graduate school, adjunct teaching, and the climb to tenure. None of this would have happened without her love and support. There is no better "looker afterer" in the world and she is *my* wife.

"There was not a moment of doubt as to the choice of a commander, for Phips was imagined to be the very man for the work. One John Walley, a respectable citizen of Barnstable, was made second in command with the modest rank of major; and a sufficient number of ship-masters, merchants, master mechanics, and substantial farmers, were commissioned as subordinate officers. About the middle of July, the committee charged with the preparations reported that all was ready. Still there was a long delay. The vessel sent early in spring to ask aid from England had not returned. Phips waited for her as long as he dared, and the best of the season was over when he resolved to put to sea. The rustic warriors, duly formed into companies, were sent on board; and the fleet sailed from Nantasket on the ninth of August."
—Francis Parkman, *Count Frontenac and New France under Louis XIV* (1896)

Introduction:
The New England Provincial Soldier

A Problem of Perception

Scattered around northern New England are a few garrison houses that have withstood the attack of age and the elements. Altered by their various owners and hemmed in by modern construction, they nevertheless remind us of a time when Native-Americans and Europeans sought to destroy each other, when it was worth a life to harvest a crop or walk to a neighbor's house. Such remnants of the French and Indian wars run through the texture of New England like a fine linen thread. Appellations like Ambush Rock, Fort Hill, or Garrison Street dot the regional geography, and even the names of the towns themselves, such as Goffstown, New Hampshire, and Westbrook, Maine, provide a direct link with those colonial conflicts.[1] The legend of our sturdy Puritan ancestors, muskets in hand, fighting off hordes of screaming Indians continues to hold a strong position in local mythology, even if it owes its existence more to nineteenth-century romanticism and Hollywood than reality. In the latter half of the nineteenth century, a period now known as the Colonial Revival, the Centennial celebration, the final defeat of the western Indian tribes, and the apparent closing of the frontier recalled to New Englanders their own Indian wars, and they assiduously recorded the legends and stories of those early years in their town histories.

Everywhere, local historical societies preserved the relics of their heroic age—an Indian war club, a collection of powder horns, a musket or sword that belonged to some long-forgotten Indian fighter were all carefully laid out in viewing cases with the appropriate labels, now yellow and faded. Perhaps the most startling artifact was preserved in the Memorial Hall Museum in Deerfield, Massachusetts. Housed in an old school building whose several floors overflow with memorabilia, the museum is an antiquarian paradise. As you pass among the shoes, farm implements, carriages, spinning wheels, and pewter mugs, you suddenly confront a door standing by itself in the middle of the floor—a witness to the night of February 28, 1704, when over three hundred Canadians and Indians sacked the village of Deerfield, killing thirty-eight and capturing 111 of the inhabitants. During the course of that attack the Indians chopped a hole through the door of the Sheldon house and, thrusting a musket through the hole, shot Mrs. Sheldon as she rose from her bed. The solitary object in the Memorial Hall Museum is that very same door. Faced with this venerable portal, the hole miraculously unrepaired, the mind endeavors to imagine the village on that night—the bitter cold of a New England winter, the hideous shouts of the raiders, the sound of musket fire, the blows of the hatchets on the door, and the terror of Mrs. Sheldon as she started out of her bed. But in the end the imagination fails because this door, stripped of its supporting framework and original environment, stands by itself in an old school building amid the shoes, the farm implements, the carriages, and the spinning wheels.[2]

Historians attempting to understand the French wars and the soldiers who fought in them have had to cope with the mythology of this period. Their interpretations and the observations of many contemporaries generally contradict the heroic image of the colonial soldier. British officers serving in the last French war and government officials in particular viewed the provincial as ill-disciplined, unprofessional, and incompetent. General John Forbes called colonial soldiers "a gathering from the scum of the worst people . . . an extream bad collection of broken Innkeepers, Horse Jockeys, and Indian Traders." James Wolfe found the troops provided by the colonies "in general the dirtiest most contemptible cowardly dogs that you can conceive. There is no depending on them in action. They fall down dead in their own dirt and desert by battalions, officers and all. Such rascals as those are rather an encumbrance than any real strength to an army." Other officers believed the Americans to be an "Obstinate and Ungovernable People, and Utterly Unacquainted with the Nature of Subordination in Generall . . . There's nothing to be found among them all but Laziness, Neglect Disobedience and Disorder, all ill and eating Constantly . . . [they are] the lowest dregs of the People, on which no dependence can be had, for the defense of any particular Post by themselves."[3]

While obviously less acerbic in their reaction, the opinions of many historians who have examined the history of the early French conflicts concur with the notions of these professional military men. The story, as frequently told, is a familiar one, and it easily leads to the conclusion that the New England war effort was not so noble and her soldiers not so heroic. In the fall of

1688, after months of friction and confrontation, Edmund Andros, governor of the Dominion of New England, declared war on the Eastern Indians and led a force of seven hundred provincial soldiers into the province of Maine. However, the ascension of William and Mary to the English throne altered the course of this war and, indeed, the history of New England itself. This Glorious Revolution expanded Andros's Indian war into the major conflict known as King William's War, the first of several struggles that pitted the English colonies against their French neighbors to the north.

Thrown into political limbo by the Revolution and the overthrow of Andros in the spring of 1689, an unprepared New England felt the destructive power of the Eastern Indians at Dover, New Hampshire, in June, and residents suffered the loss of the village and fort at Pemaquid, Maine, later that summer. During the following winter and spring Count Louis de Frontenac, governor of New France, launched a three-pronged attack that resulted in the destruction of Schenectady, New York; Salmon Falls, New Hampshire; and Fort Loyal in Casco Bay. Although William Phips did capture the French fort at Port Royal, Nova Scotia, in the spring of 1690, the subsequent failure of the Quebec expedition that fall brought New England to the brink of financial disaster. Events proceeded from bad to worse during the rest of King William's War. York, Maine, was decimated in January 1692; Oyster River, New Hampshire, suffered a similar fate in the summer of 1694; and in February 1696, the stone fort at Pemaquid, rebuilt at great expense by Governor William Phips four years earlier, was captured by the French and subsequently destroyed.

In 1697 the Peace of Ryswick brought only a temporary halt to this string of disasters. The renewal of bloodshed occurred in early August 1703, when five hundred Abenaki Indians under French leadership struck several towns on the Maine frontier, initiating the war named for Queen Anne. Thirty-nine inhabitants were killed or captured at Wells alone, and over one hundred from the other communities added to the toll. The following winter witnessed the destruction of Deerfield and the sad march to Canada of over one hundred captives, a march so eloquently described by the Reverend John Williams. Throughout Queen Anne's War, as in the other French and Indian wars, New Englanders on the frontier were subjected to constant attacks by small parties of Indians who ambushed men working in the fields or women and children in their homes. The provincial forces seemed incapable of preventing these incursions.

In 1707 Massachusetts twice attempted to capture Port Royal but both efforts were frustrated by the apparent incompetence and dissentious behavior of the officers. Three years later they finally succeeded in taking the

Introduction | 3

French fort; however, the effort to capture Quebec in 1711, this time with the assistance of British troops and naval support, ended in disaster when several transport ships struck shoals at the mouth of the St. Lawrence River, resulting in the loss of over nine hundred British redcoats, sailors, and regimental women.

Queen Anne's War came to a merciful end in 1713, but nine years later a minor war with the Eastern Indians erupted on the Maine-New Hampshire frontier. Named for Lieutenant Governor William Dummer, it is remembered chiefly for the death of the Jesuit Sebastian Rale and the battle known as Lovewell's Fight, in which the English commander and most of his men were killed. Following the end of Dummer's War in 1725, a period of peace allowed New England to catch its breath and even increase its borders with the establishment of new towns on the frontier. The start of King George's War in 1744 brought New Englanders their greatest victory when they captured, with the help of the British Navy, the fortress of Louisbourg on Cape Breton Island. But the reduction of Louisbourg proved to be the high point of the conflict, as this triumph was followed by more lost opportunities to capture Quebec and the usual bloody raids by the French and Indians, including the loss of Fort Massachusetts in 1746.

Through four wars with the government of New France and her Indian allies, the New England colonies had precious little to show for it. Two minor victories at Port Royal (in 1690 and 1710), and one major victory at Louisbourg in 1745 that was subsequently reversed by the Treaty of Aix-la-Chapelle, did very little to offset the catalog of bungled expeditions, fruitless raids, and the death and destruction along the frontier. Chronicling the disasters of Quebec in 1690, the destruction of York and Deerfield, and the debacle of Port Royal in 1707, historians have branded colonial government officials and military leaders as inefficient bunglers and the provincial soldiers as undisciplined amateurs. No other answer seems to explain the reason why the more populous and prosperous New England colonies (not to mention the rest of Anglo-America) could have so much difficulty defeating the smaller and weaker colony of New France, and, in fact, seemed to proceed from one military disaster to the next. "It seems incredible," wrote historian I. K. Steele, "that it could take seventy years to settle the military contest between Canada and her English-speaking neighbours to the south, since the population figures for 1689 suggested odds of nearly twenty to one against the Canadians."[4] Richard Marcus agreed with Steele, observing that "in view of the preponderance of manpower, wealth, and material enjoyed by the English North American colonies in their struggle with New France, the historian cannot but be impressed by the failure of the English to protect their frontiers adequately and master their northern enemies sooner then they did. This embarrassing disparity between means and accomplishment was early evident."[5]

Most historians blame this "embarrassing disparity" on inefficiency and lack of professionalism within the colonial military structure. The nineteenth-century historian Jeremy Belknap believed that "a confusion of councils, and a multiplicity of directors" had led to "frequent changes of measures, and delays in the execution of them" underscored the incompetence of the provincial military establishment. Logistical support was appalling, "forts were ill supplied with ammunition, provisions, clothing and snowshoes. When an alarm happened, it was necessary, either to bake bread, or dress meat, or cast bullets, before a pursuit could be made."[6] At the turn of this century John Fiske agreed with Belknap that the government of Massachusetts seemed to be its own worst enemy. During the initial phase of Dummer's War, the legislature interposed "obstacle after obstacle" in the path of Governor Samuel Shute in his effort to wage war against the Eastern Indians. "Its blundering conduct was not unlike that of the Continental Congress in the War for Independence."[7]

However, the most serious indictment has been made against the officers and men who constituted the colonial military forces. Their inadequate training and civilian ties prevented them from achieving the status of a true soldier. "Massachusetts had made her usual mistake," wrote Francis Parkman. "She had confidently believed that ignorance and inexperience could match the skill of a tried veteran, and that the rude courage of her fishermen and farmers could triumph without discipline or leadership. The conditions of her material prosperity were adverse to efficiency in war. A trading republic, without trained officers, may win victories; but it wins them either by accident or by an extravagant outlay in money and life."[8]

Recent studies of colonial military history have supported this traditional view. John Ferling found the "inadequately trained and frequently utilized militia forces had acquired an appalling reputation by the eighteenth century . . . [this] disgraceful reputation was probably deserved."[9] Edward P. Hamilton elaborated on this point even more. "The average provincial was a poor soldier," he wrote. "He could not well be anything considering his background and lack of training. Farm boys, sailors, fishermen, apprentices, and the jobless, all these were what the hurriedly raised armies drew upon to a large extent. Those who led them generally had little or no military qualifications . . . he was merely the leader in civilian life, the squire, the tavern keeper or the merchant, translated overnight into the military leader."[10] Guy Chet was more pointed in this criticism. "The unprofessionalism that characterized colonial armed forces," he wrote, "made them uniquely inept and unreliable."[11] Chet concluded that the "tactical ineptitude of provincial troops and their commanders has been attributed to the insurmountable challenges posed by the North American wilderness and by the offensive prowess of Indian combatants. A closer analysis indicates that colonial armed forces deserve a greater degree of responsibility for their failings and failures."[12]

This inefficiency and lack of professionalism on the part of provincial soldiers has yielded two conclusions: first, the French were obviously superior in waging war in the New World, and, second, British regulars were needed to bring the wars to a close. The concept of French preeminence was advanced very early by historians. Jeremy Belknap observed that "there was a striking difference between the manner in which [war] was managed, on the part of the English and on the part of the French. The latter kept out small parties continually engaged in killing, scalping and taking prisoners . . . on the other hand, the English attended only to the defense of the frontiers; and that in such a manner, as to leave them for the most part insecure. No parties were sent to harass the settlements of the French. If the whole country of Canada could not be subdued, nothing less could be attempted."[13] Pervading this interpretation is the image of the Canadian *coureurs de bois*. "The Canadian yeomanry being mostly hunters, boatmen, or wood-rangers, and always in the woods, were about as skilled in forest warfare as the savages with whom they fraternized," wrote the nineteenth-century historian Samuel Adams Drake.[14] "Every attempt to reach and destroy these vigilant foemen in their own fastnesses proved worse than futile. New England was losing ten lives for one; and in property more than fifty to one."[15]

In the second half of the twentieth century, the strongest exponent of the theory of French superiority was the Canadian historian W. J. Eccles. According to Eccles, New France held out so long against overwhelming odds because they were "vastly superior to the Anglo-Americans in forest warfare . . . [their success] was more a measure of New England's military ineptitude than of French strength . . . it was not the Anglo-American frontiersmen or the provincial troops that ultimately conquered Canada . . . Canada was finally conquered, after six years of hostilities, by the Royal Navy and British regular soldiers."[16]

Since the colonies could not provide adequate troops for their defense, indicated by the evident superiority of the French and their Indian allies, British regulars were the obvious solution to the colonial military problem, according to British officials and many historians. "In the French wars the bulk of the important fighting was done by European troops," wrote Harold L. Peterson. "American troops in general lacked discipline and training in European tactics, and aside from a few brilliant exceptions they were considered unreliable by the English commanders."[17] In an article published in 1958 investigating "Anglo-American Methods of Indian Warfare" during the seventeenth and eighteenth centuries, John K. Mahon believed that "an analysis of colonial Indian warfare reveals a simple truth which our folklore has tended to obscure: that trained regular soldiery, first the redcoats and then their American counterparts, were more important than unorganized frontiersmen in breaking the power of the Indians."[18] While frontiersmen "kept up a constant attrition," in the end it was the regular soldier in the ranks, armed with a musket and bayonet, who broke the power of the Eastern Indians.[19]

Taking this theory to its natural conclusion, historians believe that in dispatching regulars to America, both British and French, the Europeans forced their form of warfare on the New World. The provincial soldiers had failed through four wars to settle the Anglo-French colonial rivalry due to incompetence and their inability to fight the French and Indians on their own terms. The question would be settled by European troops in a European manner. I. K. Steele put this argument succinctly when he observed that,

> North American pride in the ways of the New World has often led to the assumption that, in warfare as in everything else, the new men of the New World were better than the history-laden men of the Old. The defeat of General Braddock or the later success of the American Revolution can, with some misrepresentation, be seen as evidence of this superiority. Yet, it is obvious that, in the climax of the Anglo-French struggle, the Europeans came and forced their kind of warfare on the wilderness . . . in the Anglo-American army there was relatively little struggle over adoption of the essentials of European warfare. As long as the Americans fought like guerrillas, they were wasting their major advantage—manpower. The large influx of British troops after 1755, as well as more direct control of the fighting from Britain, ensured complete acceptance of conventional warfare.[20]

This debate between those who argue that war in colonial North America became more "American," or "Native," and those who argue that war became more European has continued, with the latter focusing on the incompetence of provincial military efforts and the growing involvement of English regular forces.[21] Armstrong Starkey wrote that "during the course of the seventeenth and eighteenth centuries, warfare in North America became increasingly Europeanized."[22] Starkey indicates that this may have been a deliberate choice. "Necessity and familiarity drew the Canadians to the Indian way of war, but Anglo-American militias and provincial troops remained rooted in the European military tradition."[23] Guy Chet was more pointed. Chet argued that "it was the poor performance of colonial forces in King Philip's War and King William's War that led eighteenth-century colonial magistrates to address the short-comings of their military forces through a greater reliance on British forces and imperial administration."[24] Further, "only when Britain involved itself in the planning and execution of these offensive campaigns were the colonies able to effectively threaten French centers of military and administrative power."[25]

The logical progression contained in this view of colonial military history is difficult to ignore. Provincial soldiers were simple farmers who lacked training and discipline, and, therefore, with a few exceptions, they exhibited a remarkable degree of incompetence and inefficiency in their martial efforts. The settlers and soldiers of New France and their Indian allies displayed great superiority over the New England farmers in waging war in the New World, thus forcing the British government to send regular troops who finally conquered New France by the use of European military methods. But if the initial notion of provincial incompetence is false, then the assumed preeminence of Canadian-Indian forces and British regulars needs to be reexamined, and I will show that the concept of the New Englander as a poor soldier, proven by his performance in the early French wars, is an erroneous impression fostered both by a focus on parts of the story and by the nature of the warfare itself.

The opinions of contemporary British officers contain the most obvious erroneous view of provincial soldiers. They initially pronounced that the New Englanders were poor soldiers, and as the only military experts who observed the provincials firsthand, their opinion is valued, even if their choice of adjectives is considered caustic. Despite the excessive style, their credentials as experts are rarely challenged. John Ferling wrote that "the American officers were 'People totally Ignorant' of military skills, according to one British witness."[26] John Shy believed the opinions of British military men would later "have disastrous consequences for them," but he never doubted the truth of their observations. Instead, he proposed a theory that the provincial units observed by the British were poor because the disfranchised, the dregs of colonial society, filled their ranks. According to Shy, military service had ceased to be a part of colonial social responsibility, and thus the British did not view the best soldiers America had to offer.[27] Other recent studies concur with this analysis. Historians have attempted to explain why the provincial soldier was ineffective and thus seek to justify British observations, instead of suggesting the possibility that the regular officers were wrong, that their prejudices ran so deep they were unable to recognize the truth.[28]

Douglas Leach correctly points out that "rarely could a regular officer bring himself to utter words of praise for colonial troops, who, when measured by European professional standards, continually seemed to fall far short."[29] Leach also emphasized the aristocratic background of many British officers who viewed provincials as "crude, uncultured, undisciplined, and largely untrained in the science of civilized warfare." Though not all British officers were aristocrats, they were all professionals who "prided themselves on the smartness of their appearance, the quality and uniformity of their accouterments, and the mastery of complex evolutions."[30] When Admiral Peter Warren sent Marine Captain James MacDonald on shore during the siege of Louisbourg in 1745, the New Englanders soon tired of his finicky criticisms of their troops. Provincial commander William Pepperrell wrote "we were glad to get rid of him, for the most he did was to find fault that our encampment was not regular, or that the soldiers did not march as handsome as old regular troops, their toes were not turned enough out, etc."[31]

The observations of British officers are best placed in context by understanding that they viewed their own troops in the same way. James Wolfe may have referred to provincial soldiers as "the most contemptible cowardly dogs," but when he wrote to his father in 1755, he had the following comments to make about British regulars. "I have but a very bad opinion of the infantry in general. I know their discipline to be bad, and their valor precarious. They are easily put into disorder, and hard to recover out of it; they frequently kill their Officers through fear, and murder one another in their confusion."[32]

Unfortunately, although historians have spent a great deal of time attempting to explain the observations of British officers and government officials, these opinions are of almost no value in understanding the provincial soldier. The British viewed the world with the unshakeable bigotry of class, nationality, and European military experience. Anything outside their vision of the world was suspect and inadequate, and thus only soldiers trained in a European, and preferably British, manner could be considered ideal. When the British government decided to commit British troops to America in the last French war, the extensive role of the regulars should not be used as an indication of incompetence on the part of colonial soldiers. Once the British army became involved, the provincials were shoved aside, used as laborers or beasts of burden, and this represents only the natural consequences of the deep-seated prejudice of British officers.[33]

Some historians have consciously, or unconsciously, adopted this prejudice. Provincial soldiers are compared to their concept of the ideal soldier, a soldier modeled on modern military concepts, but whose origins date back to European standing forces of the eighteenth century, and specifically the army created by George Washington and Revolutionary leaders during the War for Independence. The concept is vague, centering on strict discipline and extensive training, but it is the yardstick used to measure all colonial military efforts. According to Lawrence Delbert Cress, the militia was "ill prepared for the hardships of camp life and the discipline required for effective military operations."[34] John Ferling agreed, saying that military operations such as a siege "required time and was best conducted by a well-disciplined body of regular troops."[35]

The inference of a universal ideal for soldiers is plain, although undefined. The bonding of "successful military campaign" and "effective military operation" with soldiers "requiring" extensive training and continuous service underscores this notion of the ideal soldier. However, there is no universal ideal soldier, for the concept must also presuppose that all wars and all battle conditions are universal as well. In reality, while the value of military discipline should not be underestimated under normal conditions, soldiers are ideal only if their training and motivation anticipate the kind of war and combat conditions they will encounter. Therefore, before condemning the provincial as a poor soldier, historians need to compare him to soldiers fighting a similar enemy under similar conditions. Otherwise, like the opinions of those British officers, the comparison is worthless.

But the erroneous impression of New England provincials as poor soldiers originates from far more than a misinterpretation of the notions of British officials. The enormous difficulties of waging war in the New World have been underestimated. The economic strain on the colonies was tremendous and has been well documented by Gary Nash and Douglas Leach. The Quebec expedition of 1690 alone increased the taxes in Massachusetts twenty times the normal rate and forced the first, but by no means the last, issuance of paper currency. Throughout the French wars, New England would experience various blows to its economy, including unremitting inflation and the almost constant depreciation of the currency.[36]

But beyond the overall stress to their economies, provincial governments (and this includes both New France and the English colonies) were hampered by economic realities and deliberate mercantile policies of their home governments. Arms, artillery, and most of the powder and lead used by provincial forces had to be obtained from England or other sources. British soldiers, unlike their colonial counterparts, had a plentiful supply of arms, ammunition, and, perhaps most important of all, the full support of the British navy. Under these circumstances, success came easier to the British army in the Seven Years' War, while during the previous four wars provincial governments had to constantly beg for such logistical and naval support because they did not have it.

Even more important, as John Brewer has revealed in *The Sinews of Power: War, Money, and the English State*, the British government was not capable of committing such resources until the Seven Years' War. Certainly they were not able to commit such direct military aid in King William's War because the means to do so did not exist. The growth of the British army really began with the Glorious Revolution and the ascension of William III. From there the British government had to develop the administrative and tax structure, not to mention overcome English prejudice against standing armies, to gradually increase military commitments throughout the so-called Second Hundred Years' War. That they committed such regular forces to North America in the 1750s, and did not do so earlier, perhaps reflect the ability to commit such forces and the desire of William Pitt to expand the empire more than incompetence of provincial forces.[37]

Another factor involved in any evaluation of military performance that is not only underestimated, but often ignored entirely, is the element of chance, or, if you prefer, the fortunes of war. Historians are uncomfortable with the concept of chance or luck. They fear (and often this fear is justified) that it will lead them into the murky depths of "if only" speculation. If New Englanders failed in most of their major military operations then there has to be a reason that can provide the basis of analysis and comparison, a reason that fits historiographic norms. Samuel Adams Drake concluded that during King William's War "great enterprises had turned to great failures . . . not so much from faulty conceptions, as from the want of organization, discipline, command, and of that kind of confidence which comes with them."[38] Edward Hamilton believed the expeditions against Montreal and Quebec in 1690 failed because "they were both led by amateurs, capable and well-meaning men but utterly unskilled at warfare, and they were composed of untrained farmers and tradesmen, commanded by inexperienced officers. The French on their side had a great leader, skilled officers and some trained regular troops. It is small wonder that the English were repulsed."[39] The New Englanders failed because they were ignorant, inefficient, and undisciplined.[40]

However, the military theorist Carl von Clausewitz wrote "war is the province of chance. In no sphere of human activity is such a margin to be left for this intruder, because none is so much in constant contact with him on all sides. He increases the uncertainty of every circumstance, and deranges the course of events . . . all action in war is directed on probable, not on certain results. Whatever is wanting in certainty must always be left to fate, or chance, call it what you will."[41] A large part of the failure of the 1690 campaign came from the inability of the forces at Albany to attack Montreal and tie down Frontenac, and from William Phips's delay in arriving at the walls of Quebec with his fleet, a delay that enabled Frontenac to reach the city with heavy reinforcements just as the New England ships were anchoring in the river. However, an outbreak of smallpox in the army gathered at Albany partially explains their inability to attack Montreal, and one of the main causes of Phips's delay was the necessity to wait for a shipload of powder from England (he eventually sailed without it). Thus chance (the outbreak of smallpox) and logistics (the powder from England) played major roles in the defeat of provincial forces in their bid to reduce New France. Neither of these reflects negatively on the ability of provincial soldiers, yet the interpretations given above indicate the reason for failure was the inefficiency and lack of professionalism on the part of New England military forces.[42] As Clausewitz correctly observed, "we cannot suppress an inward feeling of satisfaction whenever expectation realizes itself, and if it disappoints us our mind is dissatisfied."[43]

While logistics and chance assist us in understanding the reason for some of the reverses suffered by New England in the early French wars, the principal cause of the misconception that provincials were poor soldiers can be attributed to historical methodology and to the peculiar characteristics of the type of warfare involved. It is the concentration on major events and on major disasters that has given the impression of incompetence. Traditional historical research often duplicates the methods of modern news reporting in that the ordinary escapes detection while the spectacular captures the eye. An airplane crash gives the impression that air travel is unsafe because the hundreds of flights that take off and arrive each day without incident do not make headlines. The recitation of disastrous occurrences in the early French wars (i.e., Quebec 1690, Salmon Falls, York, Pemaquid, Deerfield, Port Royal 1707, and so on) gives the impression of incompetence, but it ignores the constant military service and protection provided by patrols and garrison troops and also the disruption of the Eastern Indians by numerous raids conducted by provincial soldiers. As Richard R. Johnson observed, the emphasis placed on the disasters detracts from the service provided by soldiers on patrol and the string of garrison houses and forts along the frontier. "Such was the pattern of the frontier war, with the enemy battering, and occasionally breaking, the links of the chain of the frontier towns but with reinforcements always close at hand and backed by the central government's determination never to abandon a threatened town."[44]

The difficulty in appraising defensive tactics involving guerrilla-style warfare is that when the tactics are successful, nothing happens. Although there is evidence that it did occur, we can never know how many lives were saved or how many towns escaped destruction by diligent patrols or alert garrisons that discouraged Indian war parties. The Indians left no records, they filed no reports, and they granted few interviews. Therefore, their successes are magnified because nothing counterbalances the slate.

Dismissing the efforts of provincial soldiers involved in *"la petite guerre"* as "short-term emergency duty" performed by "haphazardly trained and poorly disciplined militia,"[45] historians studying the colonial soldier have concentrated on the soldiers' involvement in major expeditions such as Quebec in 1690 and 1711 or Louisbourg in 1745. This superficial examination of the early French wars has encouraged the interpretation that provincial war efforts were inept. But theories based on superficial examination are only valid when supported by deeper analysis. The concentration on the major events ignores the complexity of war on the northern frontier. Like the Sheldon door in Deerfield, emphasis on just the major events rips away the structure and foundation without which the New England military effort loses its reality and its vitality.

This emphasis on the major disasters is also responsible for promoting perhaps the biggest myth of all: that the French were superior in conducting war in the New World. Closer analysis reveals that the tactics of the French and English were remarkably similar and their success rates overall were about the same. Both had to defend against that most difficult form of warfare—the surprise guerrilla attack—in which all the advantages as to time and place of the strike lay with the attacker. For New France, the soldiers' foe was the powerful Iroquois of New York while New England soldiers initially dealt mainly with war parties from the Abenaki tribes in the east and later from native groups in Canada. To defend against such surprise attacks, the French and English built fortified houses and forts along the frontier, which served as both a sanctuary for local inhabitants and as garrisons for soldiers posted there.[46] In addition, the English and French governments organized scouting parties to constantly patrol on the outskirts of these frontier towns, as well as guard the inhabitants at their work. Due to the success of the Abenaki war parties in attacking New England, historians have branded this form of defense as totally inadequate. W. J. Eccles observed that "smaller parties harried the New England frontier continually without the Anglo-American settlers being able to defend it successfully," yet the French, employing the same methods, had as much trouble stopping the Iroquois as the English did the Abenaki.[47] In actuality, this method of defense proved very effective when used properly, with the understanding that no static defense can totally stop the guerrilla surprise attack.

The English and the French realized that the best way to stop the raids was to send their own raiding parties into Indian territory. With small numbers and a fragile economy, the American Indian, though terrifying, was essentially a vulnerable adversary. The destruction of their grain supply or the capture of their families or chiefs could quickly bring about a truce. The French used the same strategy on the English colonists to discourage their expansion east and north, and it was this sort of large offensive raid involving the French and Indians that caused the major destruction of towns such as York and Deerfield.

Historians often suggest that New Englanders were incapable of conducting similar raids against Canadian villages. W. J. Eccles believed that the English colonies "had no body of men capable of traveling through hundreds of miles of trackless wilderness at any time of the year, let alone in mid-winter, to attack New France."[48] However, the New England colonists throughout the early French wars conducted raids against Abenaki villages deep in New Hampshire and Maine both in summer and in winter. As the majority of Indians used by the French on their raids came from the villages of Norridgewock or Pequawket, it made more sense to attack villages that actually provided the warriors for French raids rather than to waste Canadian villages.

The governments of Massachusetts and New Hampshire had to defend a long frontier while mounting offensives against two enemies: the French in Canada and the Eastern Indians. While they willingly conducted raids against the Eastern Indians, the New Englanders felt the best answer to the French menace was the capture of Canada itself. Therefore, they preferred to put their energies into major expeditions and never seriously considered emulating the French strategy.[49] But here again, W. J. Eccles claims that "the attempts of the English colonies to conquer Canada all ended in failure; several large-scale expeditions had to be abandoned before they made contact with the foe owing to poor organization and general ineptitude. Only part of Acadia, very weakly defended, was lost by the French in all this time."[50] True enough. Between 1690 and 1748, New England participated in the planning and execution of nine major expeditions.[51] Of those nine, three were successfully completed (Port Royal in 1690 and 1710, and Louisbourg in 1745); in two the English forces arrived at their destination but were unsuccessful in their attack, and the rest involved cancellation for various reasons. However, during that same time period, although rarely discussed, the French also contemplated major expeditions against military targets or population centers in New England. One French expedition never passed the planning stage, another had to be cancelled, and two others, designed to recapture Louisbourg and devastate the coast of New England, ended in disaster.[52] Through three wars, only one French expedition aimed at the New England colonies accomplished its purpose (the capture of the fort at Pemaquid in 1696). If the failure of major expeditions was caused by poor organization and general ineptitude, there is no indication that this was restricted only to the English colonies.

This study focuses on the beginning of the Second Hundred Years' War when the English colonists fought wars with minimal help from the mother country. There have been many studies of the last French and Indian War (often referred to by its European name, the Seven Years' War), most notably works by Fred Anderson.[53] In particular, his work presents a valuable study of the provincial units that served alongside British regiments in that "Great War for Empire." Similarly, King Philip's War in the 1670s has been covered from every conceivable angle.[54] The period in between, from King William's War through King George's War, represents very different circumstances from those other two conflicts. The Indians in King Philip's War were an internal enemy and within easy reach (although not necessarily easy to find), and they were not supported by a European government. In the last French war, the great weight of the British (and French) military descended on America, completely changing the rules and circumstances.[55] From 1688 to 1748, New Englanders fought a foe at some distance and, for the most part, without major help from England.

A complete understanding of early American warfare cannot be gained by concentrating on the major events by themselves; the subject is far too complex. War in the New World assumed its own patterns and offered its own set of problems to be overcome by all participants. Through decades of conflict, the New England military system became tuned to the rhythm of frontier war. Juggling a commitment to families, communities, and themselves, the New Englanders who performed active duty in the French wars learned and adopted the tactics of "*la petite guerre*" while never losing sight of their ultimate strategic purpose—the reduction of Canada.

In this respect, Guy Chet places me squarely on the side of those who see an "Americanization" of war in North America, or in other words, a growing adoption of "native" approaches to war. This is a legitimate interpretation: one that I espoused at one time, but now I don't see the provincial approach to war becoming more "native" or more "European." As John Morgan Dederer wrote in *War in America to 1775: Before Yankee Doodle*, "The colonists were eminently sensible, resourceful people who sought useful knowledge from any source. They borrowed only what they thought they needed: if it did not work, it was discarded; if it worked, it was improved and adapted for their new environment. They could not transport European institutions whole to the New World, so they borrowed extensively but selectively."[56] And so they also borrowed from native ways of war. It was not either/or: it was a merger of approaches, truly an *American* way.

Part I will reveal that what developed in North America was a way of war that blended preserved elements of European war and adopted native approaches. It is essentially an operational study of defensive (garrison houses, forts, patrols) and offensive strategies (raids and expeditions) used by Massachusetts and New Hampshire. Chapter 1 describes the coming of war, in both the formal sense as a declaration between nations or people, and the intimate manifestation of that war in the form of an attack. The chapter also introduces the military system of New England, delineating the administrative militia from the active provincial service, and discusses the initial response to war—pursuit of enemy raiding parties. The preparation of frontier communities to defend themselves, and the use of fortified or "garrison" houses follows in chapter 2. Warfare involving primarily provincial forces begins with a description of provincial forts (discussed in chapter 3), including their construction, garrisons, and their usefulness in drawing the fury of large enemy forces away from frontier towns. The conduct and the development of effective scouting techniques, both defensive and offensive, are explained in chapter 4, and chapter 5 explores the Anglo-American cooperation that was necessary to attempt the reduction of Canada itself. Finally, the last chapter in part I details the logistical problems associated with the procurement of weapons and ammunition without which the war could not have been fought.

While part I focuses on how war was conducted, part II focuses on the *experience* of provincial soldiers. Recruiting practices, including both incentives and compulsion, and an analysis of what type of individual actually performed active service begins part II. Provincial officers, how they were chosen, and their dual responsibilities of leadership and the enforcement of military regulations are discussed in the next chapter, followed by an examination of training and discipline and the source of fighting spirit. Chapter 10 depicts the physical experience of combat and the tactical response to Indian warfare. The final chapter presents a review of wounds, accidents and illness, medical care, and the psychological impact of war, manifested primarily in a bitter hatred of the Eastern Indians.

I do not attempt to portray New England provincials as completely heroic or as completely inept. As with all armies, the ranks of New England provincial soldiers included a wide spectrum of ability; they were neither all heroes nor all bunglers. They had to compensate for the curves thrown at them by chance, and, like their Canadian and Indian counterparts, they had to conduct war under enormous handicaps, especially in the area of logistical support (a handicap they would have to overcome again during the War for Independence). Only by examining the total military effort on the northern frontier, only by understanding how war was conducted and experienced, and only by restoring the whole Sheldon house to the shattered door, in other words, the structure and the foundation to the traditional framework, can we hope to present a balanced view of the New England provincial soldier.

PART I

Warfare on the New England Frontier

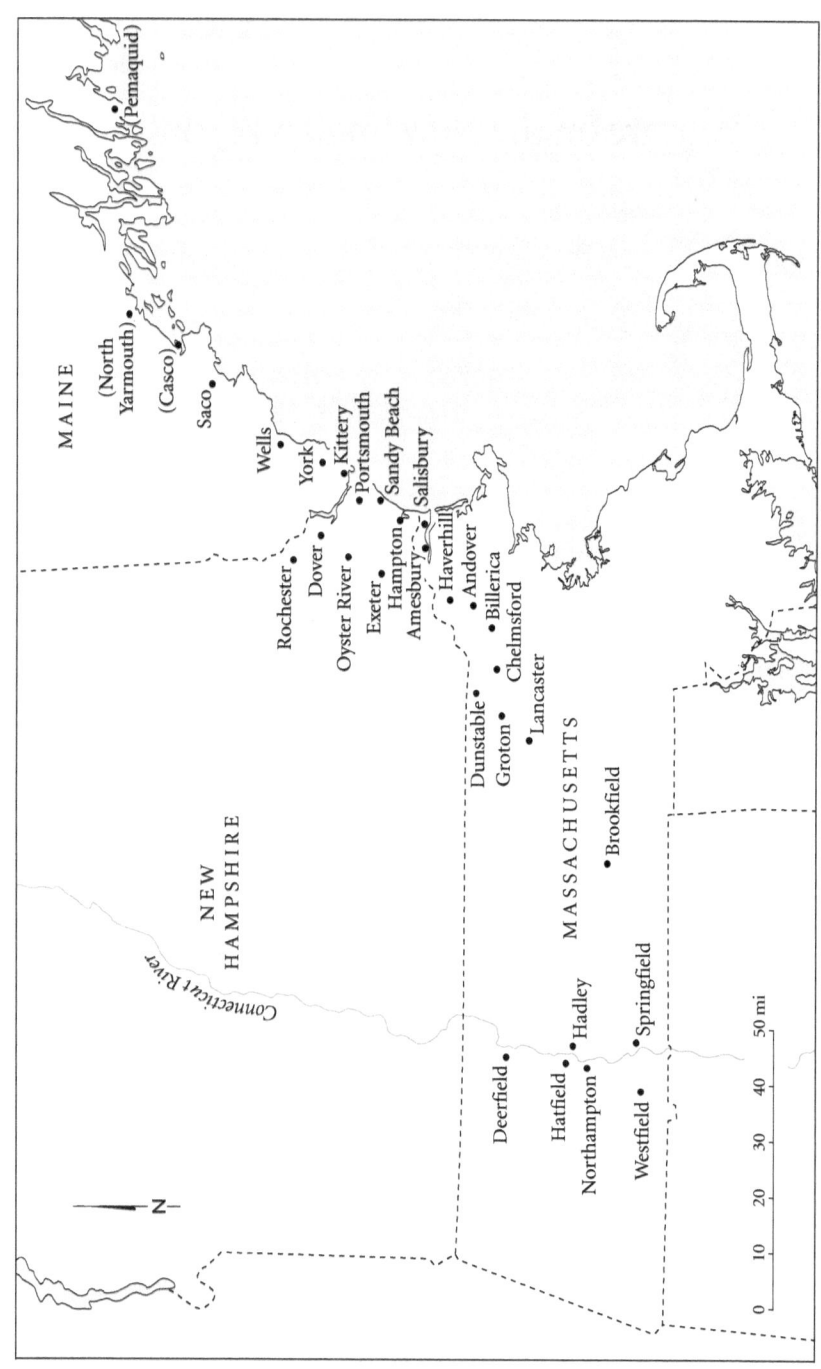

Frontier Towns, 1698

1

The Initiation of War and the New England Military System

On the evening of Tuesday, September 29, 1691, Henry Dow, a member of the Committee of Militia for the town of Hampton, New Hampshire, wrote a few hasty lines to Major Robert Pike, the commander of the militia for the county of Norfolk, to inform him that war, with its death and destruction, had descended again upon the coastal communities of New Hampshire. At approximately noon that same day a force of about forty Indians attacked homes on the outskirts of Sandy Beach, burned one or two buildings, and killed or carried away at least sixteen people belonging to the Brackitt and Rand families. Messengers had slipped away from the garrisons in Sandy Beach to alert the neighboring towns, including Hampton. When two of the messengers returned to Sandy Beach that evening they saw the Indian party, with canoes over their heads, apparently heading toward Hampton, and so the messengers quickly ran back to raise the alarm. As Hampton prepared to defend itself against this imminent assault, Dow sent a messenger to alert higher authorities concerning the depredations at Sandy Beach and the "sad condition" of Hampton now threatened by an "inemy so violent."[1]

Dow's letter reached the home of Robert Pike in Salisbury, Massachusetts, around eleven that same night. Awakened from his sick bed, Pike added his own postscript concerning another attack in Berwick, Maine, resealed the letter, and gave instructions that it be carried to Captain John March. March sent the message to a Captain Mosely, ordering him to forward it to "the Magistrate at Ipswich cort." The magistrate, Nathaniel Saltonstall, awakened "neere to break of day" by the messenger, penned his own postscript, and forwarded the letter to the "Governor & Council In Boston Haste post hast." Sometime that morning, Wednesday, September 30, as a party of Hampton men left to succor their neighbors in Sandy Beach, the government of Massachusetts finally received word that once more the French and Indian enemy had infested the northern frontier.[2]

Stretching from the Kennebec River in Maine, through New Hampshire and the Massachusetts counties of Essex and Middlesex, and terminating in the Connecticut River Valley, the northern frontier of New England in 1689 was a thin line of settlements separating the English colonies from their adversaries to the north and east.[3] A list of Massachusetts frontier towns drawn up in 1698 included Wells, York, Kittery, and Saco in Maine; Salisbury, Amesbury, Haverhill, Andover, Billerica, Chelmsford, Dunstable, Groton, Lancaster, and Stow in eastern Massachusetts; and Deerfield, Brookfield, Hatfield, Northampton, Hadley, and Westfield in the west. To this list we can add the New Hampshire towns of Dover, Rochester, Durham (Oyster River), Exeter, Portsmouth, Rye (Sandy Beach), and Hampton. At the beginning of King William's War the frontier in Maine also included Pemaquid, North Yarmouth, and Casco, but they were abandoned or destroyed in the opening attacks of that war. During the years of peace these areas would be reoccupied and the frontier pushed out everywhere with the founding of new communities, especially in the period between Dummer's War and King George's War.

War came to this frontier on two levels: the commencement of hostilities between governments or people and the actual intrusion of that war on the local level. The first was formal in nature, involving the people of Massachusetts and New Hampshire as a whole, and lasted several years before peace treaties could be affirmed. The second brought war in a very personal way to communities on the frontier. It was sudden and lasted only a few brutal hours. But both triggered activity or a response from the New England military system.

New England fought New France as the result of a formal declaration of war between their mother countries in Europe. The notification of such a declaration took about a month to reach the colonies—any longer could possibly leave them unprepared for attack. When William of Orange brought his new kingdom into his quarrel with Louis XIV in May 1689, Boston did not learn of the declaration of war until the following month, and when war was declared by the government of Queen Anne against France and Spain on May 4, 1702, the news arrived in Boston on June 19.[4] However, notification of the formal commencement of what later became known as King George's War in March 1744 did not reach Boston for two months, a delay that enabled the French at Louisbourg to launch a surprise attack against the fishing station at Canso, Nova Scotia.[5]

The formal declaration of war against hostile Indian tribes usually occurred after a gradual buildup of tension and even bloodshed. Disputed boundaries between the settlements in Maine and the Eastern Indian tribes came to be the root cause of these conflicts, exacerbated by the greater Anglo-French rivalry. In 1688 the variance centered on North Yarmouth and illustrates the gradual escalation that led to formal declaration of war against the Eastern Indians. Irritated by the plundering of Baron St. Castine's trading post by Governor Sir Edmund Andros, the destruction of crops by cattle, and the continued building on disputed lands by the English, the Indians began to kill cattle around North Yarmouth. Judge Benjamin Blackman took sixteen Indians into custody at Saco to intimidate the tribes from further mischief, but the infuriated Indians seized English hostages of their own. When Governor Andros attempted to quiet the situation by arranging a conference, the Indians failed to appear. Prompted by the heightened tension, the settlers at North Yarmouth began the construction of several garrison houses. After the Indians abducted a few of the workmen and held them overnight, the people of North Yarmouth asked for the protection of soldiers while they completed the garrisons. In September the Indians snatched two more workmen, and an attempt to free them led to an all-day battle in which several were killed on both sides. Further attacks and seizures of English settlers led Andros to issue a proclamation on October 20, demanding that the Indians return their prisoners and surrender anyone who had participated in the murder of an Englishman. Although Andros released all Indian prisoners in English custody as a gesture of goodwill, the Indians made no reply to his proclamation. The governor raised a force of 700 men and marched into Maine to wage war on the Eastern tribes.[6]

Although tensions existed before the start of Queen Anne's War, the commencement of killing and depredations was not gradual but began with a massive coordinated attack on all the communities in Maine on August 10, 1703. However, the pattern of a gradual escalation of tension, and even death, before the formal declaration of war would be repeated in Dummer's War and King George's War. Heightened anxiety led the Bay government to send 200 men to Maine to guard the frontier in 1720. Apprehension and anger between the English and the Eastern Indians grew until the summer of 1722. The Indians would launch two major attacks against Fort St. George in Thomaston, Maine, and over fifteen Indians would be ambushed and killed by the English before Governor Samuel Shute formally declared war on July 25.[7] Over twenty years later, repeated attacks throughout the summer of 1745 eventually prompted Governor William Shirley to declare war on the Eastern Indians on August 23, two months after the fall of Louisbourg and seventeen months after the declaration of war between England and France.[8] In all of these conflicts, the declarations of war against the Indian tribes were separate from the corresponding European struggle and had to be ended by treaties similarly distinct from the European peace treaties. The New England colonies fought two foes from two separate conflicts at the same time, although they are usually lumped together as the "French and Indians."

The initiation of war on the local level was neither delayed nor formal, but was sudden and always potentially devastating. Often the notification that war had arrived emanated from the noise of the attack itself—the war cry, musket fire, and screams of the victims.[9] On other occasions an all-too-brief warning alerted inhabitants to the presence of the enemy. Dogs now and then signaled the approach of a foe by barking or growling.[10] The strange behavior of other animals could warn of the proximity of enemy raiding parties. In May 1690 the suspicions of the people of Falmouth, Maine, were correctly aroused when they observed the cattle staring at the woods, refusing to go near the fence that lined the field.[11] The warning that a Captain Jones of Oyster River, New Hampshire, received was more explicit and abrupt. Thinking that the barking of his dogs might be caused by the presence of wolves, Jones sat on a flanker at his garrison one evening in July 1694. As he surveyed the surrounding woods his eye caught the flash of powder from the pan of a musket in the woods, and he instinctively threw himself backward just as the ball struck the spot where he had been sitting.[12]

Warning or not, once an attack began it was necessary to alert other members of the community to their danger and also notify neighboring towns. Again, sometimes the notification came from the noise of the attack itself; the sound of firing or an ominous cloud of smoke usually indicated that the enemy had struck again. Francis Hooke of Kittery heard the sound of firing toward York during the attack on that town in 1692,[13] and Charles Frost reported that Wells was alarmed "by the shotting of Many guns in the woods nere the garisons" in September 1695.[14]

In 1642 Massachusetts Bay stipulated the official method of notification should be the firing of three muskets, sending a messenger, beating a drum, or firing a cannon. Later the law would be amended with the addition of a burning beacon and increasing the first method to four muskets. New Hampshire passed similar laws calling for the firing of four muskets, a cannon and two muskets, or the beating of drums. To prevent the spreading of false alarms, statutes prohibited the firing of muskets after dark, the offense carrying a penalty of a 20-shilling fine or two hours in the stocks.[15]

Cannons in frontier communities, usually in the form of swivel guns (small cannons mounted on a wall), provided warning and communication more than actual defense. As the French wars began, signal cannons had been used to report a variety of activities and thus the firing of a signal cannon could cause momentary confusion. John Gyles remembered that when the men in the fields heard the report of the signal gun at Pemaquid in the summer of 1689, his father hoped the sound meant the arrival of a ship bearing good news, a hope immediately shattered by the volley of forty Indian muskets.[16] As King William's War progressed, the sound of a cannon shot came to mean one thing: the presence of the enemy and the need to gain the safety of a fort or garrison. In one incident during King William's War the deliberate firing of a false alarm saved the lives of some stubborn women in Exeter, New Hampshire, who insisted on picking strawberries in the woods. Their frustrated husbands and fathers in the garrison fired the signal cannon to scare them into returning. Later they discovered that Indians had been waiting to ambush the party of berry pickers when the signal gun scared them off as well.[17]

The sound of the signal cannon, musket fire, or the beating of drums served as signals of immediate danger to inhabitants and as distress calls to neighboring communities. Those neighboring towns would beat drums and fire their cannons to alert other towns and assemble a force to aid the beleaguered community. Francis Hooke in Kittery wrote of "allarams round about us" in 1691, and the distant roll of drums and trumpets probably saved Lancaster in 1704 and Haverhill in 1708 from complete devastation when the enemy forces, hearing that the countryside was aroused, hastily withdrew.[18]

The most common method of ensuring that other towns received notification, not to mention alerting higher provincial authorities, was to send a messenger, a method obviously hazardous to the individuals who volunteered to leave the safety of a garrison and travel through the woods known to be full of Indians. During the attack on Salmon Falls, New Hampshire, in 1690, William Plaisted "made his Escape from Captain Wincols house which was twice assaulted by the Enemy but they were beaten [off] by six or seaven English men whome he left in possesion of said house when he came away from thence to give this advise."[19] Cotton Mather recounted the story of Ebenezer Babson of Gloucester, which provides a vivid illustration of the hazards of being such a messenger. "Bapson went, to carry the news [of enemy activity] to the Harbour; and being about Half a mile in his way thither, he heard a Gun go off, and heard a Bullet whiss close by his Ear, which Cut off a Pine bush just by him, and the Bullet lodg'd in an Hemlocktree. Then looking about, he saw Four men Running towards him . . . so he ran into the bushes, and turning about, shot at them, and then ran away and saw them no more."[20] Though hazardous, the messenger system remained an important method of alarm and a vital source of intelligence that enabled the New England military authorities to form the proper response.

In responding to war, whether a formal declaration or an actual attack, New England governments drew on their inhabitants to perform as soldiers. With the exception of the few Indian forces raised, no thought was given to hiring foreign mercenaries to fight New England's wars. The well-documented English aversion to standing troops discouraged that option to a certain degree, but more significantly, the cost was prohibitive. The British government's focus was firmly set on continental Europe and really had no substantial land army until the mid-eighteenth century; thus England would not or could not protect the colonies with professional soldiers.[21] Therefore, New Englanders would have to perform that function, and it was the militia system that enabled the colonial governments to put together the military forces necessary to respond to war.

The role of the New England militia in the colonial wars has been the subject of some controversy among historians. The most prevalent interpretation, in its most cynical form, depicts the militia as selfish citizens who mouthed platitudes for defense but against standing armies, then when actual duty called, they forced those outside the mainstream of the community into service. They craftily constructed laws that exempted the privileged from duty and excluded the "have-nots" in their society from participation in the militia, then passed legislation that prohibited the use of that militia outside the colony, thereby guaranteeing they would not have to fight.[22]

However, it is questionable if the New England militia, as constituted by law, was ever intended to fulfill an actual combat role. Although some historians have tried to make a claim that the militia served an active role in the seventeenth century,[23] the use of New England militia companies, *as conceived by legislation*, for active duty would have stripped communities of every able-bodied man between the ages of fifteen and sixty who were capable of defending the town and supporting the local economy. Even the earliest military operations in Massachusetts, the various exploits of Myles Standish, the Block Island expedition, and the Pequot War were undertaken by volunteers or pressed men from the communities of Plymouth or the Bay Colony, not by militia companies themselves.[24]

As the militia was not used for active service, the laws prohibiting the employment of a militia outside the colony were purely political in nature. The Massachusetts Charter of 1693 gave the governor "full power by himself or by any Chief Commander . . . appointed by him from time to time to . . . assemble in Martiall Array and put in Warlike posture the Inhabitants of Our said Province ... and to lead and Conduct them and with them to Encounter Expulse Repell Resist and pursue by force of Armes ... within or without the limitts of Our said Province." Of course the Act further stated that the governor could not send soldiers "out of the Limitts of the [province] without their Free and voluntary consent *or* the Consent of the Great and Generall Court or Assembly of Our said Province,"[25] but the Massachusetts Assembly regularly gave its governors virtual *carte blanche* to transport or send its soldiers "to the relief of the neighboring provinces or colonies" while the Assembly was between sessions.[26] In effect, the provincial forces "detached out of the militia" with their own government-appointed officers in command were then sent pretty much wherever provincial authorities desired.[27]

The rare occasions when this statute was invoked usually involved political jealousies between colonies or internal disruption that extended beyond the military emergency. After the destruction of Oyster River in July 1694, Lieutenant Governor John Usher of New Hampshire appealed to the government of Massachusetts three times in two weeks for troops. Governor William Phips, who was technically the governor of New Hampshire as well, replied to the first request by invoking that section of the law that prevented the sending of militia beyond the border. "I cannot order," he wrote on July 19, "the detaching or impressing men to serve in your province."[28] Phips, mired in the political controversy that soon led to his recall to England, was not overly concerned with the fate of his northern colony, and thus the statute provided him an excuse to ignore Usher's appeal. In addition, Usher had been critical of Phips's conduct as it concerned New Hampshire and Indian relations.[29] Three days after Phips's reply to Usher, Lieutenant Governor William Stoughton informed the government of New Hampshire that one hundred men would be sent to their relief, although he later insisted New Hampshire pay at least part of the expenses. The one hundred men were not easily raised, however, but not because of English militia traditions and colonial laws. Relating part of a conversation he had with Stoughton in October, Usher told the New Hampshire Council that "many [Massachusetts] soldiers whoe had been in the Province to serve itt, were very ill treated; the Which I am altogether ignorant of."[30] The ill treatment apparently referred to the men from Newbury who had eagerly volunteered to chase the Indian raiding party that had devastated Dover, New Hampshire, in 1689. During that service their unfavorable impressions of the inhabitants of New Hampshire, and the fact they were forced to stay longer than they planned, left a bad taste.[31] In the midst of that crisis in the summer of 1694, Usher received a letter from the town of Newbury indicating there were few men willing to volunteer for service in New Hampshire.[32]

Throughout the early French wars, Massachusetts scouting parties regularly went into the mountain and lake region of New Hampshire, and pursuit forces from New Hampshire frequently succored their neighbors in Maine without any thought to statutory limitations. The crisis in the summer of 1694 is one of the few instances where that section of the militia law prohibiting the use of the militia outside the colony was employed, and the reasons did not involve institutional theory and tradition, but politics and pique.

Although it was not meant for active service, the New England militia served two important functions—it provided administration, or a military bureaucracy, for the provincial governments, and it furnished a defensive structure for local communities. The administrative function of the militia actually mirrored the regimental system within the British army during the late seventeenth and eighteenth centuries. Like the New England militia, British regiments consisted of companies that were commanded by captains and lieutenants. But the regiment and its companies served only an administrative purpose. They enabled the British government to survey their soldiers through company rolls, to issue uniforms, arms, ammunition, food, and to dispense the meager pay. For the purposes of combat, the "regiment" became a "battalion" (or two or three battalions depending on the size of the regiment), and the men distributed into equal firing platoons, subdivisions and grand-divisions, each commanded by the captains and lieutenants and all without regard for the original composition of the administrative units called companies.[33]

As the "regiment" and the "company" provided for administration within the British army, and not a tactical or combat role, so the New England militia provided an administrative capability for the governments of Massachusetts and New Hampshire. In the words of Morrison Sharp, the duties of militia officers "were limited to drilling their men, keeping their muster rolls, and inspecting the home-stored supplies of powder, lead and guns."[34] The company clerks and officers, and the field grade officers in the county regiments through whom they reported, provided a network of military bureaucrats that enabled the provincial governments to find soldiers and assess the colony's military capabilities.

The second function of the militia, especially for the officers, focused on community defense. The supervision of arms, ammunition, and supplies played a part here, but responsibilities also included keeping garrisons in repair, providing for watches and wards, and preparing a list of members of the militia to pursue enemy raiding parties or aid neighboring communities.[35] Although the tactical role of the militia in the defense of towns has been emphasized by some historians, during actual attacks there was little semblance between the militia as delineated by statute and the regular community fighting for survival. The control of a militia officer extended over only those who managed to get into his garrison, and sudden attacks left little time for the legalities concerning membership in the militia, the list and exemptions which have so enamored social historians. During an Indian raid everyone—the privileged, the militiaman, the "have-nots," and even women and children—became soldiers to a certain extent.

In his article "Persistent Localism: English Social Change and the Shaping of New England Institutions," Timothy Breen has correctly emphasized the parochial nature of the militia. "The colonial government could dispatch an army against the Indians, but the militia itself was a local institution." Breen compared the militia with Congregational churches and town government. "All of them stressed local control, even if that meant an unprecedented degree of popular participation in the selection of the leaders." Reacting to the political and social disruption in England caused by the crown-appointed militia officers, "the immigrants . . . restored the trainbands to community control. Once the militia had been transformed into a local structure, it became highly unlikely that it could be used to oppress the settlers."[36]

The militia of northern New England, then, was what Fred Anderson called a combination "Home Guard, draft board and supply network."[37] Despite the attempts of John K. Mahon to devise the categories "standing militia," "volunteer militia," and "war volunteers" for military service,[38] only two general groupings were recognized in New England during times of war—soldier and inhabitant. Every man who volunteered or was pressed for active military service, every man "in His Majesty's pay," was a provincial soldier. Everyone else was an inhabitant, including members of militia companies who might be involved in local scouting or involved with alarm lists and the pursuit of the enemy. Indeed, it could be argued that even in these circumstances men came under the control of the provincial government. As early as 1630, all soldiers in Plymouth wounded in action became the responsibility of the province, not the local community,[39] and those inhabitants pursuing Indian raiding parties were rewarded by the provincial government for any Indians who were killed.[40]

Provincial soldiers stationed in frontier towns also came under the command of local militia officers, and this led to an overlapping of jurisdiction, which can be difficult for modern scholars, and even contemporaries, to understand. Soldiers assigned to garrison houses were under the orders of the garrison owner, often a militia officer, as well as their provincial commanders, who may or may not be present. For example, when Daniel King and John March returned from their raid into Maine in 1691, the two commanders were released from service, but their soldiers were stationed in garrisons "under the care of their Inferior Officers with the advise and assistance of the chiefe Officer of the respective places whereto they are assigned." The arrangement caused a "great murmering among the souldiers."[41]

However, provincial officers (officers with commissions from the provincial governments) took precedence over the militia in all military concerns. The Bay government ordered all "sheriffs, Marshals, Constables and other officers, military and civil" to aid Benjamin Church in his 1689 raid into Maine.[42] When the province of New Hampshire authorized Captain Nathaniel Mesharvy to "beat his drums" in a regiment of militia for volunteers to take Louisbourg, they commanded the "Colonel, with the other Officers in the said Regiment . . . not to give the said Nathaniel Mesharvy any Obstruction or Molestation herein, but on the Contrary to Afford him all the necessary encouragement and Assistance."[43] Provincial officers carefully preserved this distinction and separation, and statutes exempted "all such as have had commissions, and served as field officers or captains, lieutenants or ensigns" from militia training.[44]

Administrative duties and the overlapping jurisdictions could produce an adversarial relationship between local militia leaders and provincial officers. Colonel Thomas Westbrook, provincial commander in Maine during Dummer's War, had several problems and confrontations with community leaders. "I proposed to some of the Commission officers of the Militia," wrote Westbrook in April 1724, "that when our Scouts are lodged, that they rally together the Inhabitants, and that with the remainder of the Soldiers and part of them they range the woods on the backs of the Towns . . . but I have received no Answer from them."[45] A few days later an obviously frustrated Westbrook sent the following to Lieutenant Governor William Dummer. "The Enclosed is a Coppy of an Impertinent Letter from Mr Peter Nowell, Representative of York, which I am almost ashamed to trouble your Honour with, neither should I have presumed to have done it had it not seemed to have reflected on your Honour, he asserting that your Honour promised the men should be dismist in Convenient time to help to put their seed into the ground. His daily declareing he has brought a presumed dismission for the men has Created a great deal of uneasiness among the people."[46]

One area in particular that irritated provincial commanders was the frequent inability of militia officers to force their communities to observe elementary defense precautions. When Westbrook consulted with the militia officers and town officials of Biddeford, Maine, they admitted they had not followed the government's instructions concerning defense measures.[47] On another occasion, he informed Dummer that his "advise to the Inhabitants and orders to the officers has always been not to go out with less then fifteen or eighteen men or more as the occasion may require but the inhabitants are so obstinate they will go out not above two or three at a time two or three miles from their garrisons if they cannot all have a guard in one day and the Officers of the Militia in each town do not take any care to regulate them, they refuse to help in watching in their garrisons at night where soldiers are . . . especially the inhabitants at Perpooduck point I acquainted them it was your Honors orders but they refused to comply. There lies this difficulty with me which I can't tell how to get over."[48]

Much has been written about the process of electing militia officers in the seventeenth century. The freemen of the town elected men for their nomination as officers, and these nominations were sent to the government who had final approval.[49] This system changed with the arrival of the new charter in 1693–1694, which granted more power to the governor. The governor now appointed all military officers with no mention of a community nomination process, but the selection of the militia officers was both crucial and controversial due to the definition of their function in the community. Militia officers exercised their power as members of the local Committees of Militia. These Committees of Militia consisted of the local magistrate and all the leading officers of the militia (for example, the captain of every foot company and troop of cavalry were members), with any three providing a working quorum.[50] The committees exercised a great deal of control over their communities, including deciding who would become a soldier if sufficient volunteers were not found, assigning inhabitants to garrisons, and making economic decisions concerning the tilling of fields and the impressment of supplies and their distribution. The militia officers and committee members decided whose cattle would be confiscated for the war effort, who would be pressed as a soldier, and when homes and crops would be abandoned for the discomfort of garrison living. These decisions affected the economic well-being, and even the lives, of the inhabitants of the frontier communities, and thus the social standing and the political and religious affiliations of these men were an important consideration if their orders were to be followed.

In *A Respectable Army: The Military Origins of the Republic, 1763-1789*, James Kirby Martin and Mark Edward Lender reiterated a common observation about the constitution of militia companies: "militia law by the early eighteenth century rather systematically excluded the indigents and the unprivileged (a mushrooming proportion of the population by the 1750s) from service." Martin and Lender believed this trend proves that communities were discriminating against the lower classes in order to force them into military service.[51] However, if militia companies did exclude nonproperty holders from their rolls, and this trend involves the slave-owning southern colonies more than New England, it was because the decisions made by militia officers, including confiscation and abandonment, directly concerned the owners of property. Therefore the owners of that property were very concerned about the standing of those officers. It was not a conspiracy to separate the poor from the community in order to draft them for military service, but it had more to do with the basic issue of property rights.

Indeed, when no immediate danger threatened, militia officers had difficulties prodding their fellow citizens to observe precautions, and if any political or religious dissension split the community their job became almost impossible. In particular, the provincial officers sent to the eastern frontier at the start of King William's War found the communities torn apart by political fighting resulting from the Glorious Revolution, and the militia was in disarray. Sylvanus Davis, commanding Fort Loyal in Falmouth, Maine, asked the government in July 1689 for someone to regulate the militia of the town in order to control the inhabitants.[52] At the same time, Jeremiah Swain found the people of Berwick "in as much Danger of Some among them as of the Enimy for want of a well Settlement of the Militia." Swain met with the leading men in the community, as well as some from New Hampshire just across the river, got them to agree on the placement of garrisons and appointed commanders over the militia, but "not without great Opposition by some."[53] When Swain was ordered to dissolve his command the following November, he informed the government he had left a provincial officer in charge of the area. Although he had urged that some of the local officers take control of defense measures, he was told the local government "was so lame that they could scarce command each man his family," and it would be the undoing of the frontier not to leave one of the provincial officers in charge because the soldiers in garrison and the inhabitants feared the Bay government more then they did their own officers.[54]

Despite frustration and animosity between provincial soldiers and inhabitants, they usually managed complete cooperation when pursuing the enemy. As an almost instinctive reaction, pursuit of enemy raiding parties was an attempt to rescue captives and punish the perpetrators, and it could involve inhabitants, provincial soldiers, or a combination of both.[55] This cooperation was quite common and encouraged by the provincial governments. Part of provincial officer Simon Willard's instructions in 1689 commanded that "upon notice of the Enemyes approach to make out a party or partys against them if by the advice of your Officers, and the Officers and cheife persons of the place with the assistance of the Inhabitants it shall be judged you have a sufficient strength to issue forth against them."[56] In November 1711, when three Indians and a Frenchman stole a fishing sloop, Ensign William Hilton and four others from York, Maine, joined with a sergeant and eight soldiers from the garrison and sailed in pursuit, recaptured the sloop, and executed the thieves.[57] During the spring of 1746, a Sergeant Trott and nine soldiers were joined by twelve inhabitants in order to chase a party of Indians who had killed a man near North Yarmouth, Maine. Trott had to call off the pursuit when the inhabitants ran out of provisions. The next day twenty-six more local men joined the force and they tracked the raiding party for several miles, finding many traces of the enemy, but once again, as Trott recorded in his journal, "the inhabitants that went with us having no provision would go no further."[58]

Often such pursuit accomplished nothing; the Indians slipped away leaving little trace.[59] Other times provincial soldiers faced running into the prepared and hidden enemy they were pursuing. Jeremy Belknap recounted one such ambush that occurred in what is now Nashua, New Hampshire, in September 1724. When two men who were making turpentine failed to return in the evening, "a party consisting of ten of the principal inhabitants of the place started in search of them, under the direction of one French, a sergeant of militia. In this company was Joseph Farwell, who was the next year lieutenant under [John] Lovewell." From signs at the work site, they concluded the men had been taken by Indians only a short time before, and so they decided to pursue immediately. "Farwell advised them to take a circuitous rout, to avoid an ambush. But unfortunately he and French had a short time previous had a misunderstanding and were then at variance. French imputed this advice to cowardice, and called out, 'I am going to take the direct path; if any of you are not afraid, let him follow me.' French led the way and the whole party followed, Farwell falling in the rear." Firing from ambush at a brook crossing, the Indians killed most of the men instantly, then overtook and destroyed the rest as they tried to flee, all except Farwell, who led them a merry chase until he plunged into a thicket and eluded them.[60]

Pursuers also placed any English captives in the hands of the enemy in jeopardy.[61] In 1695 nine captives from Newbury, Massachusetts, were clubbed by their captors when a pursuit force came too close.[62] One of the four children taken from Cape Neddick, Maine, in 1705 was executed in revenge when pursuers shot one of the raiding party.[63] Another captive suffered the same fate two years later when a pursuit party engaged the raiders so closely they forced the Indians to leave their packs behind, which "exasperated their spirits."[64]

With the constant threat of ambush and the very real danger to captives, it may appear to have been counterproductive to continue pursuit activities. But the records indicate that the rescue of captives, or punishment inflicted on raiders, occurred frequently enough to encourage pursuit, especially with the added incentive of a financial reward for enemy killed.[65] In 1692, pursuers chasing a raiding party that had struck Brookfield, Massachusetts, trapped the Indians in a swamp, killed most of them and recovered all captives and plunder.[66] In June 1696, a pursuit force from Dover, New Hampshire, found the Indian raiding party that had just struck Portsmouth Plain cooking breakfast on a hill in what is now the town of Rye. As the captives were between the Indians and the top of the hill, the rescuers charged from the reverse slope, released the captives, and drove the Indians into a swamp, recapturing all their plunder (the site has since been called "Breakfast Hill").[67]

Numerous other examples could be given to justify the pursuit of enemy raiding parties despite the risks.[68] More than anything else, pursuit was an impulsive, emotional reaction to the intrusion of war on local communities. It fulfilled a need to strike back, to undo the hurt, and to save neighbors from the anguish of captivity. The cooperation between inhabitants and provincial forces involved in pursuit underscores the emotional involvement. Often at odds under normal circumstances, this cooperation lasted at least as long as the adrenaline flowed.

As an instinctive impulse, the reaction to the intrusion of war on the frontier was brief and relatively simple; however, the reaction to war on the provincial level was far more complex and deliberate. The formal involvement in war by the governments of Massachusetts and New Hampshire signified the beginning of economic hardship, personal and collective sacrifice, and death and destruction. Although some support came from England, the initiation of war forced the provincial governments to activate their military systems to defend the frontier communities as well as carry the war to the enemy. The administrative backbone of that system on the local level was the militia companies and committees. The officers and committee members enabled the provincial governments to gather and distribute supplies, prepare the inhabitants for their immediate defense, and raise soldiers for provincial service. But it was the provincial soldiers, separated from the inhabitants and the militia by virtue of their active service, who actually waged war for the colonies.

2

Garrisons

The First Line of Defense

In the 1760s Thomas Hutchinson, reviewing the recent history of the Indian wars in New England, concluded that "the settlement of a new country could never be effected, if the inhabitants should confine themselves to cities or walled towns. A frontier there must be, and nothing less than making every house a fort, and furnishing every traveller with a strong guard, could have been an effectual security against an enemy, as greedy after their prey as a wolf, and to whom the woods were equally natural and familiar."[1] As it was impossible to turn every house into a fort and provide every traveler with an armed escort, Douglas Leach has correctly interpreted this statement as meaning "a man who undertook to be a pioneer had to accept as an occupational hazard the possibility of being scalped."[2] Despite the difficulties, the governments of New Hampshire and Massachusetts were committed to defend their frontier line because its collapse would have exposed the older, more established communities to the ravages of the enemy. As the Bay government stated in 1715 in granting the establishment of Brunswick and Topsham, Maine, "a Strong Settlement there will greatly tend to dislodge the Indians from their Principall Fishery, keep them from chief carrying Places, and be possibly a Means of removing them further from us, if another War should happen."[3] In addition, the government of Massachusetts was most anxious to maintain communities in the eastern areas of the District of Maine because the title to that land, especially around the Kennebec River and eastward, was disputed, and in any land dispute, possession is nine-tenths of the law. Therefore the best interests of the Bay government, and the older communities in Massachusetts, lay in giving full support to the towns on the frontier.

While all the communities along the frontier line were potential targets during the early French wars, especially vulnerable were those towns that were contiguous with the major invasion routes—particularly the Kennebec, Saco,

Merrimack, and Connecticut rivers—as well as those whose geographic locations reduced potential support from neighboring towns. Among the latter were all the towns along the Maine coast and in the province of New Hampshire. With the sea at their backs and removed from the population centers around Boston and along the North Shore, residents in those towns had to rely on their own resources and direct aid by sea from the provincial governments. Lancaster, Massachusetts, which was located on the western flank of the eastern war zone, also suffered from similar handicaps. Although the inhabitants on the frontier organized themselves for their own protection and enrolled their men on the militia rolls and constructed fortified sanctuaries, they ultimately had to depend on provincial aid and soldiers to bolster their defense.

The communities on the frontier needed the support of their governments because the strife of the French wars struck at their very existence. The incidents of destruction, loss of life, captivity, and separation that were experienced by communities on the frontier, "the Hazards and Sorrows," as Cotton Mather wrote, "which you suffer by lying so near unto a Barbarous Enemy," are too familiar to mention in detail.[4] But beyond the immediate consequences of desolation and death, warfare on the New England frontier meant the almost total disruption of economy in the area.[5] All business activities—agriculture, masting, fishing, and milling—were at risk in time of war. As Charles Frost informed the government of Massachusetts in 1747, the people on the Maine frontier "cannot pretend without the utmost hazard, to plant or sow, or carry on any other business, especially on the most out and exposed parts. And unless immediate succor or assistance I cannot perceive how Gorham Town, Marblehead, and Sacarappy can subsist."[6] The inability to produce food and maintain an economy and the constant threat to life and property convinced many people on the frontier that they needed to leave their homes for more secure settlements. Whether by individuals or whole communities, this abandonment resulted in the loss of territory and the gradual erosion of the frontier line.

The effects of abandonment on individuals involved personal tragedy— the loss of valuables and property, and sometimes the splintering of families. In 1690 Abraham Collins of Casco Bay, "drawn off from thence in to these parts by the Distress of Warre with a Child a bout 18 monthes" put the child in the care of a wet nurse in Boston, but, dissatisfied with the arrangement, he later removed it to another nurse in Milton. The town of Milton ordered that the child be returned to his father, who refused to have anything to do with it, and in fact he "left said Child in the street." The child eventually ended up in the care of Collins's employer, who petitioned the General

Court to cover his expenses because the child, and indeed the Collins family, had become a victim of the war.[7] According to Jeremy Belknap, the New Hampshire families forced to abandon their homes along the Connecticut River during King George's War "deposited in the earth, such furniture and utensils as could be saved by that means; they carried off on horseback such as were portable; and the remainder, with their buildings, was left as a prey to the enemy, who came and destroyed or carried away what they pleased."[8]

Although safer from Indian attacks, the refugees often found their circumstances no better than on the frontier. Driven from their home in Maine "by the Enemy," John Ryly's family resided in Charlestown "where they had nothing to maintaine them but the dayly labour" of the husband and father. Unfortunately, John Ryly was pressed and sent back to Maine as a soldier, leaving the family "in extream want, having nothing wherewith to feed and cloath them." Jane Ryly petitioned the General Court for assistance for her and her children, requesting either the return of her husband or some sort of grant so her and "her two young Children may not perish for lack of bread."[9] Similar stories and petitions are spread throughout the records of Massachusetts and New Hampshire. Many of these refugees never returned to their frontier holdings, preferring the security of the settled areas, and they or their heirs sold their lands to others. The proprietors of the Pejepscot Company, who resettled the lands around Brunswick and Topsham, Maine, purchased many tracts of land from war refugees or their descendants.[10]

Beyond the personal tragedies involved, the abandonment of frontier communities constituted a serious blow to the war effort of the New England colonies. To halt the erosion of the Maine frontier at the beginning of King William's War, and the loss of control over disputed territory, the Bay government issued orders to the inhabitants to stay in their communities, but simple directives had little effect as all communities above Wells, Maine, were soon deserted.[11] Alarmed at the drain of able-bodied men from their town, the people of Wells petitioned the government that "there be an effectual care taken that the Inhabitants of this province may not Quit thiere places with out liberty first obtayned from Leguel Authority."[12] In 1693 the General Court passed laws prohibiting the settlers from deserting their lands without permission of the legislature, and the court threatened to enact specific punishments for those who did so, principally the forfeiture of their holdings.[13] Eastern men caught in the older settlements were forced to return to their frontier communities, and orders for the impressment of supplies specifically mentioned that the committees of militia in Maine had the right to seize any cattle, but "Especially from such persons as Desert the Province."[14]

In order to alleviate their economic distress and obtain direct military aid, settlements sought official designation as a "frontier town."[15] Such a designation brought financial support in the form of subsidies to pay the minister's wages and an abatement of provincial taxes. It also meant direct military aid from the province in the form of supplies and soldiers.[16] The number of soldiers posted in towns along the frontier varied according to need and proximity to the enemy. A proposal by the Massachusetts government in 1698 called for twenty to twenty-five men in each of the communities remaining in the district of Maine, and anywhere from two to eight men assigned to the frontier towns within Massachusetts (with the exception of Deerfield, which would have sixteen).[17] When Suncook applied to the New Hampshire Legislature in 1747 for military aid, they voted that "four good effective men to be posted at Suncook to guard the same until the twentieth of October next, said men to be shifted once a month."[18] On at least one occasion, financial aid and military assistance were combined by hiring some of the inhabitants to be posted as soldiers in that town. During King George's War the Bay government allowed up to eighteen men from New Marblehead (Windham), Maine, to draw full pay as soldiers. They stood watches with the "western men" stationed in the town but were not required to join in scouting, and they were to be protected by the "western men" when they worked in the fields. The pay they drew was divided among all the families in the community. Despite grumbling from the provincial soldiers and their officers, the use of this unusual financial arrangement prevented the desertion of another frontier town.[19]

Another community requested military assistance but then changed its mind when the soldiers arrived. The Isles of Shoals, situated off the coast of Maine and New Hampshire, was a raw, independent, and Godless community of fishermen who had little respect or use for the organized governments on the mainland, except when the Indian wars struck too close to home.[20] When the nearby town of York was destroyed in January 1692, the citizens of the Isles of Shoals realized just how vulnerable they were, and in their panic they requested military aid from Massachusetts the following day. "We beseach and intreat your honours that we may not be left to the favour of our enemies . . . please send us a man of strict and good conduct . . . that may joyne with the heads of this place to bare Rule and keep ordour amongst us." They also requested forty soldiers "whose charge both for meat drinke and wages we will att our own cost freely disburse and discharge."[21] Three weeks later the request was repeated and the officer and forty soldiers were sent. However, when they arrived they encountered a distinct hostility from the residents and a refusal to provide the promised quarters and food. Many of the fishermen were employees of wealthy businessmen on the mainland, and these businessmen specifically ordered that support be withheld. The chagrined authors of the original petition wrote to the governor and council, complaining about "those who like Bullocks unaccustomed to the yoke are exceedingly loath to be ruled they being many of them persons, who came here for an employ, only because they would be ungoverned and free from all manner of publick charge."[22] The government finally informed their commander that if the support was not forthcoming that he should "draw off and leave them to stand upon their own defense,"[23] and they informed the inhabitants of the Isles of Shoals that "it may occasion no small Sorrowful Reflections, when your Selves and Estates become a prey to the Enemy, that you rejected the Assistance readily offered you upon your desire."[24]

It is unknown if the residents of the Isles of Shoals finally provided the promised support; however, soldiers sent to the more exposed areas of the frontier line generally had fewer problems finding accommodations. Usually constituting part of a larger offensive or defensive force, the provincial soldiers destined to bolster exposed towns were marched to the frontier and distributed among those communities.[25] The soldiers were assigned to garrison houses within each town, although complete coverage was rarely possible. For example, of the sixteen garrisons in Berwick, Maine in 1711, only nine had soldiers assigned.[26] Provincial governments ordered their officers to post soldiers in garrisons on the outskirts, or "most exposed parts," of the town where they were more likely to do the service they were supposed to do.[27]

The garrison houses where these provincial soldiers found themselves posted were the first line of defense on the northern frontier.[28] These ubiquitous structures, whose numbers varied from town to town, either were private dwellings either owned by local officials (officers of the militia and ministers being the most common) or were simply strategically located.[29] In addition to being the center of military activity, they often served as public houses and taverns as well.[30] Some of these structures consisted of a single house built of squared logs laid horizontally on top of each other.[31] The Clark garrison in Cape Neddick, Maine, was forty feet long and twenty-two feet wide with a kitchen extension. The walls were made of squared timbers twenty inches wide and five inches thick, dovetailed at the corners and built without a frame. The lower floor had three rooms plus the kitchen and the second floor, which projected out over the first, had four rooms.[32] The windows and doors were strengthened as well. The Gilman garrison in Exeter, New Hampshire had a heavy covering door that was raised or lowered in front of the regular door by use of a pulley system.[33]

As the French wars progressed it became common to turn these fortified houses into small forts by erecting a palisade or outer wall of upright logs set into the ground. A fortified gate permitted entry, and flankers, or log towers, built at opposite corners of the palisade served as watchtowers and covered the outer walls in case of attack. These larger garrisons had smaller houses built either within the palisade or around the outside to accommodate the other families seeking shelter.[34] The Larrabee garrison in Kennebunk, built in 1720, had a fourteen-foot-high palisade, with corner sentry boxes and a large projection over the main gate, surrounding five single-story buildings: two were to accommodate local families, two for provincial soldiers posted there, and the Larrabee dwelling itself, the largest and strongest, in the center.[35]

Families within the community were assigned to the nearest garrison, and the numbers involved combined with the length of stay could create intolerable living conditions. "We Consider your uneasy condition," observed Cotton Mather in his sermon *Frontiers Well-Defended*, "when you are thrust and Heaped up together in Garrisons, where the Common Comforts of your Lives must needs have an Extreme Abridgement brought upon them."[36] The word "heaped" is very appropriate. After the Indian attack on York in 1692, the survivors took shelter in three garrisons, and Captain John Floyd of Kittery, arriving to succor his neighbors, reported that "there is a hundred souls in Captain Alcock's house that have their whole dependence upon him for bread."[37]

Garrisons, depending on their size and situation, regularly housed one to fourteen families and averaged twenty-five to thirty "souls." A list of twenty-one garrisons in York in 1711 reveals that six had thirty or more individuals assigned, and the Preble garrison, listed as the "Store House," had sixty-four.[38] At the same time, over in the Berwick area of Kittery, of fifteen garrisons occupied, the Neal garrison had ten families and seventy souls; Plaisted's had fourteen families and seventy-four people; and the Spencer garrison sheltered one hundred.[39]

Such close quarters created uncomfortable situations and unusual social behavior, especially when evidence of enemy activity precluded extensive absences from the protective walls. Charles Clark, in *The Eastern Frontier*, related the story of Alice Metherel, who found the Curtis garrison in Wells "a happy frolicking place." Alice's husband had disappeared to parts unknown, and she had borne the child of one of the few black slaves in the district five years previously. During the confinement Alice shared a room with a soldier from Kittery named John Thompson, even though "most of the people that did belong to the garrison did Lie in there Litle houses nere the garison."

The arrangement bothered some of the other soldiers and two or three older women, not because of the way the room was shared but because Alice got pregnant and named Thompson as the father.[40]

The provincial soldiers assigned to bolster the defenses of the frontier towns added to this cramped, uncomfortable "heap" of humanity. Normally, twenty to thirty soldiers were assigned to the exposed towns, with one to four being posted in individual garrisons.[41] The soldiers operated under the dual command of the provincial officers and the militia officer who commanded the garrison, although the provincial officers took precedence. The men had to obey the commands of the masters of the garrisons where they were posted and were not to absent themselves without official leave. Their principal duties were to guard the inhabitants as they performed their daily labors and to add their weight to the defense of the garrison if attacked.[42] The overlapping command situation could create difficulties. In 1690 Simon Willard was forced to leave his command in Falmouth to discuss the war effort with the government in Boston. He placed various provincial sergeants in command of the soldiers in local garrisons, including Sergeant Richard Hicks at Ingersols, with the overall command of troops outside of the fort, and Sergeant Joseph Huit at Lawrence's garrison. Willard admonished Huit to be "always advising with sergeant Hicks as ocasion may be, not changing of Souldiers without the consenting of both officers concerned," meaning the militia officers Ingersol and Lawrence.[43]

The issues of military protocol and the effects of close quarters, as well as other irritants such as differences in religion, could lead to animosity between the inhabitants and the provincial soldiers. Cotton Mather addressed the potential for hostility between inhabitants and soldiers when he wrote that "Possibly, The Souldiers from other parts Quartered sometimes among you, may occasion some Disorder; For, a Resort of many People to any places, is usually attended with some Disorderly and Exorbitant Behaviors. We assure our selves, that the Souldiers which are sent to your Assistance, will find all possible Civility, in your way of treating them . . . But, if any Souldiers that come among you, should be Wild, and Vain, and Lewd, God forbid, that your Children should learn their wayes, or that your Manners ever should be Corrupted by their Evil Communications."[44]

Mather emphasized the need to work together, and to understand that God may have sent the wild soldiers to be taught the Christian way by example, although he pointed out that pious soldiers should not have cause to complain about frontier families. Sometimes the solution to this kind of irritation was not the Christian ethic but was a request for transfer by either party. Elisha Andrews, a provincial officer, wrote from Wells in the autumn of 1690 to the Bay government that "I Crave of your Honours that if Souldiers Must be kept here, that we might be Relived and others Sent in our Room: for their is such Anamossity betwixt the souldiers and the inhabitants; that their is Little hopes of us Doing any thing that tends to gods honor or the good of the Country."[45] Similarly, in May 1725, David Parsons wrote the governor of Massachusetts from Leicester that he had "met with some difficulty with one of [the soldiers] who is not pleased with my family orders, and his capt being at some distance, takes more liberty then is very pleasing to me (I do not enter a complaint) but if it might be agreeable to your honor a well qualified man 50 miles distant is willing to take his place, and this affair to be quiet."[46]

Another reason for this animosity often grew out of the fact that while the soldiers provided a degree of safety for the frontier communities, they also presented a very real strain on limited supplies of provisions and clothing. In 1690 Elisha Andrews acknowledged the arrival of "a hundred bushells of indian Corn and rye: 30 Wastcoats: 30 pair of Drawers and a hogshead of salt," but felt this a "Small Supply Considering the poverty of the inhabitants; and the nesessity the Souldiers are in Respect of Cloathing Shirts shoes and stockings that I have a great deal of trouble to keep them here the Inhabitants not Caring for our Company; they not Desiring above twenty; if any."[47] The destruction of crops and livestock by Indian raiding parties, and the obvious physical dangers involved in the further cultivation of their fields diminished the amount of food available on the frontier, and the restriction of all business activity, agricultural or otherwise, hampered trade for essential goods, especially clothing. The presence of provincial soldiers only aggravated this situation.[48]

The inhabitants provided for the soldiers, and themselves, as best they could, working their own fields under the protection of provincial guards or working on land in the immediate area of the garrisons allotted to the families living there. The government informed the owners of these garrisons that they were compensated for this by the increased defense offered by the presence of these other families.[49] All contributions by the inhabitants to the maintenance of the provincial soldiers was to be indemnified by the provincial governments, although this compensation could be delayed, which only increased the level of animosity.[50] In 1689, Joseph Prout reported from Falmouth that the inhabitants were "not willing to bring in any [food] without redy payment,"[51] and Abram Preble of York sent in a petition proving that he "by himself and others his Neighbors Expended Considerably on the Countrys Service by Billitting of Soulders in the Years 1690: 91 and 94." Preble proceeded to list every meal provided, every horse fed, every night spent by a soldier, every sick soldier tended (including the "winding Sheate" for the one who died), by himself and his neighbors over the course of those three years.[52] Although few are as detailed as Preble's, numerous petitions from inhabitants exist that requested compensation for provisions supplied to provincial soldiers.

When provisions were not forthcoming voluntarily, military officials often had to impress what they needed, although in most instances the inhabitants were compensated for these goods as well.[53] As part of their administrative duties, and to make such seizures perhaps more acceptable, local committees of militia were usually "Impowered to Impress and take any fatt Cattell (for the suply of Country Soldiers) from any person whatsoever,"[54] although provincial officers could press food and cattle if necessary. However, whether voluntarily given or impressed, there often came a time when the supply of food simply gave out, especially after raids or during periods of high enemy activity. "They have allready Killed So many Cattle for the Souldiers," wrote William Vaughn from Portsmouth in 1691, "that they have hardly left where with to Sustain their [own] family's this winter and that many famylyes have hardly bread to eat."[55] At these times it was necessary for the frontier communities to call on their provincial government for supplies.[56]

Early in King William's War the governments of New England collected supplies for the "reliefe of the garrisoned souldiers Imployed against the comon enemie in the eastern partes and the poore famelyes yet remaining there or forced away from their habitations in distresse and want" through "free and voluntary contribution," or impressment, in the older settlements.[57] Sent to the eastern frontier by sea and to the west overland, the goods were placed in the care of "some Suitable person to be appointed by the said Committee [of Militia] in each towne" who was responsible for the equitable distribution of the supplies.[58] This "faithful person" had to keep a "distinct and particular account" of provincial supplies, and usually took charge of the impressment of local provisions.[59] Because the position of distribution officer in frontier communities involved complicated paperwork, control over compensation, equitable distribution and impressment of supplies, and constant letter writing to provincial governments, the job often became one continuous aggravation, with very little reward or acknowledgement.

Beyond the obvious need for food, the most serious problem for the inhabitants and the soldiers posted on the frontier involved an adequate supply of clothing. While some food was produced on the frontier, very little clothing was made, especially in the early years of the French wars. Frontier areas had to rely on the older communities where textile production—spinning, weaving, and tailoring—was protected from the disruption of war, and where cloth and clothing could be imported from England. Inhabitants on the frontier used their agricultural products to provide a means of exchange to obtain clothing and other necessaries. As supply officer for the town of Falmouth in 1689, Joseph Prout impressed a "parcell of beef which was on board a Shallop bound westward, belonging to One Wallace which he was [carrying] to purchase cloathing for his family . . . I promised him that he Should be Speedily paid."[60] In fact, clothing supplied by the provincial government became a means of payment for local provisions. Thus the overworked Joseph Prout complained to Governor Bradstreet that the shipment of clothing barely met the needs of the soldiers so that "little of it can be Spared towards the paying for or purchasing of meat."[61]

The provincial soldiers sent to garrison the frontier towns were particularly affected by clothing shortages. Whether volunteers or pressed men, they generally wore one set of clothes—coat, waistcoat, breeches, and shoes—with perhaps some spare shirts and socks. Hard or extended service would eventually wear out this initial wardrobe, and if the soldier's family could not provide for replacements, which was often the case, then the provincial government had the obligation. In addition, soldiers raised in the summer months who were forced to extend their tour of duty into the winter then needed clothing suitable to the climate. Therefore, distribution officers constantly requested clothing to supply the provincial soldiers on the frontier. "Some fall Shoes are desired and expected by some of the Soldiers," wrote the diligent Joseph Prout, "as also Some Stockings and Some more Shirt cloath, as also Some more coats, breeches, Neckcloaths &c."[62]

At the beginning of Queen Anne's War, just a few days after the massive attack on the communities in Maine on August 10, 1703, the Bay government ordered the provincial commissary officer, Andrew Belcher, to raise provisions in anticipation of the extensive employment of soldiers on the eastern frontier, the "stores and magazine for the Eastern Parts be lodged at Mr. Peperel's garrison in Kittery."[63] Belcher had to provide "for the use of the forces raysed for H.M. service, hatchets, powder-hornes, belts and snapsacks of each 500, large shoes and stockens of each pair, and that they be delivered to the souldiers as they shall have occasion to be charged therewith upon request."[64] In order to assemble these stores it was necessary to impress the items themselves or the labor necessary to make them. On August 23 the Massachusetts Council "Ordered that a warrant be made out to impress six or eight shoe-makers to be employed by direction of Mr. Joseph Bridgham forthwith to make shoes for the supply of the forces."[65] Despite these efforts, however, deficiencies in supplies and provisions would continue to complicate the war effort.

Critical shortages of food and clothing could impair the ability of the frontier towns to maintain their defenses and even their communities. A lack of food could lead to sickness. Provincial officer James Converse wrote the Bay government from Portsmouth in 1690 "to Informe your Honors of the miserable Condetion that we are in for want of bread and cloaths . . . our Soldiers are sick some of the small pox and others of A feaver, I have borrowed bread for the Hospetall, and the sick in severall places, and I am not Able to provide for so many people upon my own account, for severall Gennerous Gentlemen of the place are weary with doing for the publique."[66] In Gorham, Maine, during King George's War an outbreak of black tongue killed four, and affected so many men, including the eleven soldiers stationed there, that the women had to stand guard.[67] One of the families in Gorham was so destitute that the woman of the house rode alone to Falmouth at night, purchased Indian corn, took it to a mill to be ground, and then waited until dark to make her journey home.[68]

Such shortages of food and clothing could force the provincial soldiers to abandon their posts. After an attack on Portsmouth in 1695 the garrisons throughout New Hampshire were reinforced, but the six men sent to Dover were discharged after a short time as the town was "destitute of all manner of provision for the subsistence of said soldiers, as the law directs in that kind."[69] Soldiers stationed in Wells in 1691 complained in September to the governor and council that "wee Humbly Conceive it is not unknown to your Selves that wee have ben in the servis a long time: and as farr as wee Can understand are like to Continue longer: which wee are not Capable to doe; being maney of us aledy almost naked; we are willing to Serve your Honors in what we are Capable of, but not with out Cloathing."[70] In October, Richard Buckley, another government commissary officer, wrote from Portsmouth that "I Cannot understand of any Cloathing to come for the Soldiers without which I conclude it Impossible for the most of them to subsist, therefore I expect e're long to be called home . . . the Soldiers as yet as far as I can perceive continue in reasonable good order but I fear they will no longer than till they shall understand there are no supply's comeing."[71]

On one occasion soldiers used a lack of supply, or at least an alleged shortage, as an excuse to desert. In April 1690, three soldiers, William Williams, Thomas North, and Richard Warren, left their assigned posts in Berwick "under the pretence they wanted shirts to chang." Although the inhabitants in the garrison offered them shirts, North announced he was heading for Boston and "would not be stopd nor hindered as long as hee had any powder and shott, And that it was little odds to him to kill [one] of us as an Indian." Their sergeant, apprised of their intention, and the offers of shirts, tried to persuade them to stay, but Williams, North, and Warren left anyway, promising to return that night, a promise no one believed. The report of this affair concluded with a list of witnesses to the soldier's "opprobious highe and wicked speeches slighting of command, only Warren was sober butt other Two sordid fellows full of Rascality in word and actions."[72]

As indicated by the story of Williams, North, and Warren, the animosity between inhabitants and the provincial soldiers went beyond the problems of cramped quarters and minimal supplies; the inhabitants were not always impressed with the caliber of their defenders. In reality, provincial officers retained their best men, the most physically fit and the most enthusiastic volunteers, for scouting and raids, and they posted those incapable of marching and the pressed men in garrisons. When provincial forces were reduced after a campaign, the pressed or hired men were left behind in garrisons; the enthusiasm of these pressed men for the service of their country was less than could be desired, at least in the opinion of the inhabitants of the frontier.[73]

The practice of posting the less desirable soldiers in garrisons would continue throughout the early French war period. In July 1691 Daniel King and John March reported from Portsmouth that of 108 soldiers available for their raid into Maine, "Not above sixty . . . are fitt for any Service but to Keep Garrison."[74] William Vaughn found King's and March's men to be in a "shattred Condition" on their return from the east in August. He found them "uncapable of any further Service att present, then strengthening the frontiers," and so posted them in garrisons along the Maine coast and New Hampshire.[75] In 1724, Colonel Thomas Westbrook reported a request by the residents of Kittery to have five or six men posted at a new garrison they were constructing. "It being so great a Service to so many people," wrote Westbrook, "I have presumed to lodge five or six Ineffective men that were not fitt to march, till your Honors pleasure be known in that affair."[76]

The poor behavior of these soldiers often raised the ire of the inhabitants and even their own officers. The disruption of the Glorious Revolution probably contributed to poor behavior in 1689. Joseph Prout reported that "those soldiers left here are most of them men of Ill behavior and take little notice of their Commander, many of them do often Swear that they will march away home."[77] Sylvanus Davis, the commander of Fort Loyal in Falmouth in 1689, described his attempts to hold the soldiers who, along with the inhabitants, had abandoned North Yarmouth. Davis showed them the orders from Boston requiring them to stay, but this made them all the more obstinate; "laffing and Shouting," they told Davis they would stay over their dead bodies "for thay had dun thaire Duty that they was hired for."[78] Although not all garrison soldiers were unhealthy, disabled, pressed, and expendable, enough of them irritated the inhabitants whom they were trying to protect. After his experiences with deserting soldiers, Sylvanus Davis was convinced that the practice of hiring soldiers would be the ruin of the country.[79] Elisha Hutchison agreed with Davis's sentiments and suggested in 1692 that the defense of the Maine frontier would be enhanced by "Maintaining a garrison at Pegipscott or about Kenibeck, with a sufficient force of Stout able men (and not such Children as usually are sent for Souldiers)."[80]

Beyond the presence of provincial soldiers, the garrisons proved to be more a psychological defense than an actual military strong point in two respects: one negative and one positive. The proximity of the garrison houses and the presence of the provincial soldiers, no matter what their quality, led to overconfidence. The strength of the building itself seemed to be a sufficient safeguard so that in many cases sentries and watches were not posted. During one attack on Northampton, Massachusetts, the Indians found a garrison that had no guard, and so they simply thrust their muskets through the loopholes and shot the inhabitants as they emerged from their rooms.[81] In Dunstable twenty troopers returning from a patrol turned their horses out to graze and entered a garrison where they had a "carousal." No guard was posted and so the Indians shot the owner as he left the palisade, rushed through the gate and into the house before the troopers could reach their weapons. Grabbing chairs and clubs they finally forced the Indians out of the house but not without losing half their number.[82] In both cases the security of the strong house created an impression of safety.

Such carelessness would continue throughout the French wars whenever people tired of their cramped garrison existence. Lieutenant Governor John Usher reported to the Board of Trade in February 1704 that he had "visited the out-garrisons, [and found] all families at their respective houses, not in garrison, and secure as if no war."[83] In 1723 the people of Dover, New Hampshire, tired of garrison living, began to return to the safety of the strong walls only at night until eventually even this precaution was abandoned with fatal consequences.[84] Despite laws requiring all persons to abide in their assigned garrisons or be fined,[85] the inhabitants needed to get on with living, planting, milling,

Garrisons | 47

and masting—all the work that was to be protected by the provincial soldiers posted in the town. But when this work became extensive, tired men neglected simple precautions. They became reckless and careless, such as the hunter in New Hopkinton, New Hampshire, who departed from his garrison before dawn while the other occupants were asleep—and he left the door open.[86]

The negligence and laxity on the part of the inhabitants of frontier communities, which emanated from this false sense of security represented by the garrisons, created nothing but anxiety and aggravation for the provincial officers assigned to protect them. Captain Elisha Andrews wrote to the Bay government in 1690 that the inhabitants of Wells were at present in garrisons, but "several are desirous of going home to their own houses, and the most part of them is for keeping little or no watch, for there is no command amongst them, which makes them incapable of defense, that if the enemy comes upon us I am afraid their carelessness will be both their destruction and ours also."[87] Echoing Andrews's concerns thirty-four years later, Colonel Thomas Westbrook recommended that scattered garrisons be called in or they will be surprised by the enemy as "the people generally preach up peace to themselves if the Indians do not knock some in the head in six or seven days."[88]

However, in addition to the negative aspect of false security, the garrisons could provide positive benefits from a purely psychological standpoint by deterring some Indian attacks and saving the lives of people who had no actual defensive capabilities. In 1706 some women caught alone in a garrison during an attack fired the alarm gun, loosened their hair, put on hats, and fired muskets out of the loopholes. Their bluff was successful and the raiding party quickly withdrew.[89] Thomas Bickford saved his Oyster River garrison singlehandedly by firing muskets from several loopholes, changing hats and shouting orders to imaginary defenders.[90] Similarly, a woman in Dover, New Hampshire, during an attack in 1712 saved herself by shouting orders and alarms throughout the garrison, even though she was alone, convincing the Indians that the garrison was well guarded.[91] In 1705 two men from Amesbury, Massachusetts, caught in the open without weapons during an Indian raid, took shelter in an abandoned garrison where they found two broken guns without ammunition. Thinking quickly, they thrust the muzzles through the loopholes and kept shouting, "Here they are, but don't fire till they come closer!" and the Indians obligingly kept their distance.[92] Douglas Leach has doubted the veracity of this and other stories, and no doubt the truth was stretched in some cases; however, such accounts of successful bluffs are numerous and run throughout the early French wars. It is doubtful they are all fabrications. In each of these cases, the apparent strength of the buildings and outworks provided a psychological defense where no real military deterrent existed.[93]

Of course, when called to, and prepared, larger garrisons could prove quite adequate for defense against a determined attack.[94] Perhaps the best example occurred at the Storer garrison in Wells, Maine, during June 9–11, 1692. The Storer garrison had a palisade and flankers with small shacks outside for local families and it sat on a small rise just above Wells Harbor.[95] The garrison was commanded by Captain James Converse, who had fifteen provincial soldiers and an unknown but apparently small number of inhabitants. In addition there were fifteen men on two sloops anchored close to the garrison in the harbor. Bleeding cattle running from the woods warned of the presence of the enemy and on the morning of June 9 a force of five hundred Indians under French command stepped out of the woods, brandishing their weapons, hurling shouts of defiance and musket balls at the garrison. Although they captured one hapless fellow outside the walls, the brisk fire from Converse's men soon drove them back into the woods.

The enemy next concentrated on the sloops, shooting fire arrows in an attempt to set them ablaze. Eventually they attached boards to the front of a cart, a crude sort of mantlet or shield, and pushed it toward the sloops.[96] The cart soon became bogged down in the mud and the men behind slowly picked off as they tried to free it. The Indians spent the night dropping random shots into the garrison, although Converse dispersed some of them by sending six men out to ambush the snipers. Another major assault was threatened the following day and Converse ordered his men to withhold fire until the enemy closed the range. One of the defenders had his nerve fail at this point and suggested the garrison consider surrendering, but Converse simply said he would shoot the next person who raised that issue, and he then ordered them to open fire. With Converse running from flanker to flanker directing the fire, and with the women not only loading weapons but firing them as well, the garrison held off the attack.

A final attempt was made against the sloops with a fire raft; however, the wind drove it ashore before it reached its objective. Under a flag of truce the French and Indian force attempted to cajole the English into surrendering but Converse would not succumb, so the Indians mutilated and killed their one prisoner out of frustration and departed. Forty-eight hours after it began, the siege of Storer's garrison was over.[97]

This siege represents the ultimate example of the military effectiveness of the garrison house. They were a necessary component of frontier defensive strategy, a first line of defense used on the frontier of New France.[98] The northern frontier of New England was a thin line of communities under siege, but each town's survival depended on more than garrison houses alone. Its survival depended on a healthy economy or the ability to plant and harvest, mill grain, fish, and cut lumber and masts. Without the ability to maintain the economic foundation, the French and Indian threat became overwhelming to the inhabitants, and the option of abandoning their communities all the more inviting.

Committed to the preservation of the frontier line, the governments of New Hampshire and Massachusetts had to bolster their frontier with economic aid in the form of grants, tax abatements, and contributions of food and clothing. They also stationed soldiers in the towns to protect the inhabitants at their daily labor and augment the defensive capabilities of the local militia, even though the immediate defense of the communities and the garrisons within them was a serious drain on provincial military manpower, a drain that provincial officers tried to compensate for by employing their least competent soldiers for that duty.

In some respects the garrison houses were a dubious blessing. Beyond the diffusion of manpower, the effectiveness of the garrison system, like all the endeavors of mankind, depended so much on the human factor. Garrisons defended by individuals with the fortitude of a James Converse could withstand enemy attacks, and quick-witted individuals in seemingly hopeless situations could use the obvious strength of the garrison to bluff the fragile Indian psyche, but the presence of the garrisons could also lead to a false sense of security and could result in carelessness, negligence, and ultimately death or captivity. The garrison was an important part of the New England military strategy; it was a first line of defense or a last resort for the inhabitants of the frontier towns, but the war effort of New Hampshire and Massachusetts had to consist of more than garrison houses if it was to be successful. That greater effort would involve provincial forts and the offensive capabilities of provincial soldiers.

3

Provincial Forts

The Magnet

Although garrisons provided a sanctuary and a modicum of protection for the inhabitants and the soldiers, forts symbolized a permanent military presence on the northern frontier. They not only provided a strong defensive structure, but also served as headquarters for the provincial forces in the area and as barracks for scouting parties. To the Eastern Indians the forts embodied the power and the presence of the English government by providing a site for the negotiation and signing of treaties, and, when built on their major invasion routes, by disrupting their normal operations in time of war. Both the symbolic and very real threat posed by English forts made them special targets for French and Indian raiding parties and expeditions, especially after the expansion of the frontier line and the accelerated fort-building program during the 1720s and 1730s. Because of the special attention focused by the larger enemy raiding forces on the frontier forts, it could be said the forts became a magnet that drew the fury of the enemy on themselves and away from the exposed communities.

As the French wars began only a few forts existed on the northern frontier. When Governor Edmund Andros took his small army into Maine during the fall of 1688, he constructed several small forts to house his soldiers during the winter; however, the majority of these structures were quickly abandoned during the subsequent Glorious Revolution the following spring.[1] In 1689 the principal forts on the frontier line included one at Pemaquid, one called Fort Loyal at Falmouth in Casco Bay, a fort on the Merrimack River at the "upper plantations," and another fort similarly situated on the Connecticut River.[2] Of those four major forts, two, Pemaquid and Fort Loyal, were destroyed by the fall of 1690. During the course of King William's War, numerous small forts, like Fort Mary at Saco, Maine, in 1693 and a small fort at Newcastle at the mouth of the Piscataqua, were built to protect the surrounding regions.[3] In 1692 Governor William Phips replaced the destroyed fort at Pemaquid with a substantial, and expensive, stone structure, which he named William Henry, but this fort was subsequently captured by a French expedition and destroyed in 1696.

By the beginning of Queen Anne's War, and during the course of that conflict, several forts were added to the defenses of New England. The English military engineer for the colonies, Wolfgang W. Romer, rebuilt the fort at Falmouth, Maine (sometimes referred to as the "New Casco Bay Fort"),[4] and in New Hampshire, Fort William and Mary, first proposed in 1697 as a replacement for the small bastion protecting Portsmouth Harbor, gradually took form under Romer's supervision. The building and maintenance of this fort would be a constant source of controversy throughout the history of provincial New Hampshire. Although Romer would dispute his contentions later, Lieutenant Governor John Usher reported the fort completed in 1705 and he asked Whitehall for the cannon to mount in its emplacements.[5] Under the administration of Governor Joseph Dudley, the Bay government completed work on Castle William in Boston Harbor, erected fortifications around the trading house at Dunstable,[6] and replaced Fort Mary at Saco, considered to be "ill-placed and ill-built," with a fort at Winter Harbor.[7] Fortifications also existed at Marblehead and Salem.[8]

At the conclusion of Queen Anne's War, the frontier in Maine began to push eastward, and with it came the need for protection. The Company of Pejepscot Proprietors, using land at the mouth of the Sagadahoc River, which had been purchased from the Indians as well as the heirs of the settlers who had abandoned the region in 1689, established the towns of Brunswick and Topsham in 1715.[9] As part of that settlement the company refurbished and enlarged one of the abandoned Andros forts, calling it Fort George.[10] Four years later they sponsored the construction of Fort Richmond a few miles up the Kennebec to further protect their new settlements.[11] At the same time, the Bay government constructed Fort St. George in present-day Thomaston, adjacent to Penobscot Bay. In 1729 a small fort, called Frederick after the Prince of Wales, was built at the site of the old Fort William Henry at Pemaquid.[12]

The extended period of peace after Dummer's War encouraged the continued expansion of the frontier line, which created a virtual boom in the building of forts. In the 1730s the government of Massachusetts attempted to block the northern invasion route into its growing western frontier by constructing two forts along the Connecticut River: Fort Dummer in present-day Brattleboro, Vermont, and a fort at Number Four (Charlestown, NH), and in the 1740s covered the western approaches with Forts Shirley (Heath,

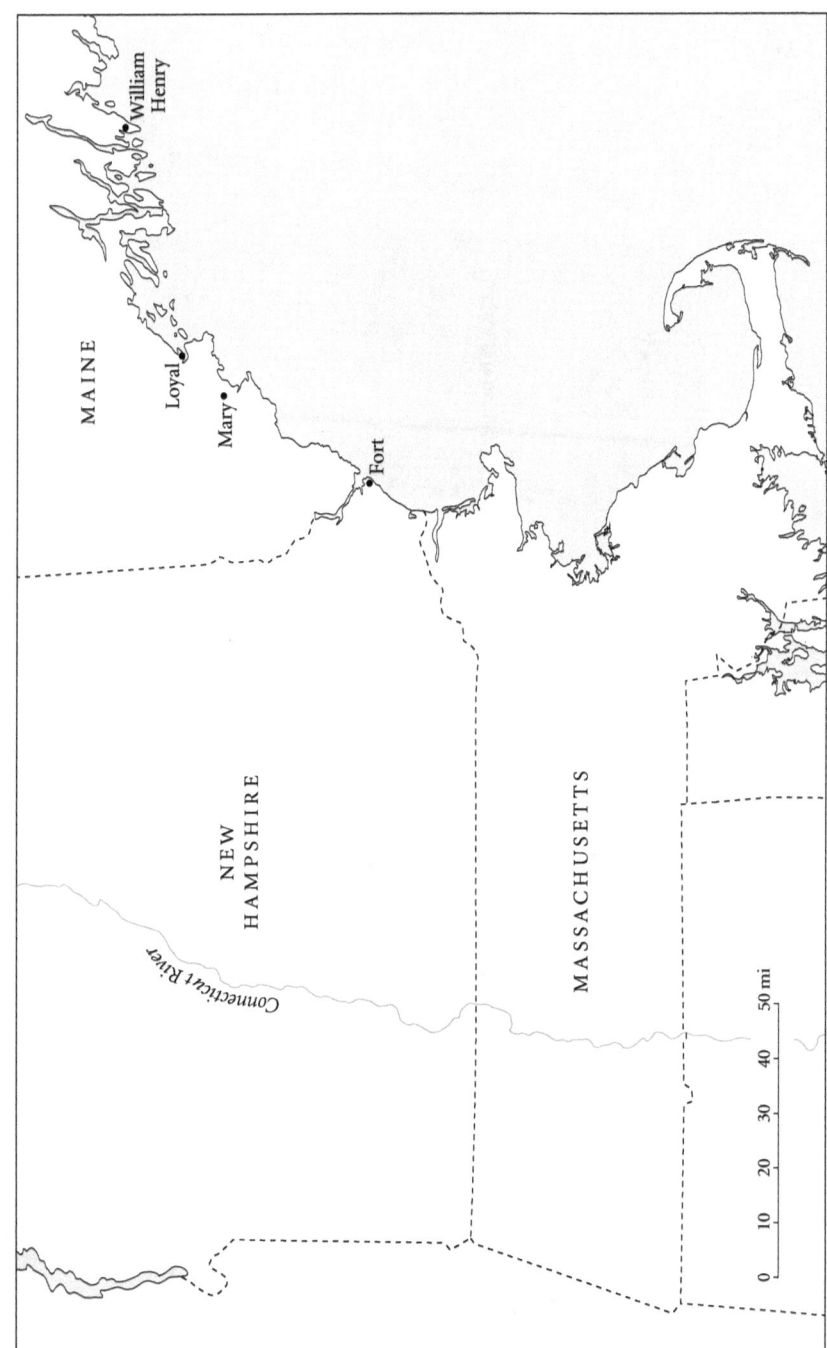

Forts in King William's War, 1689–1698

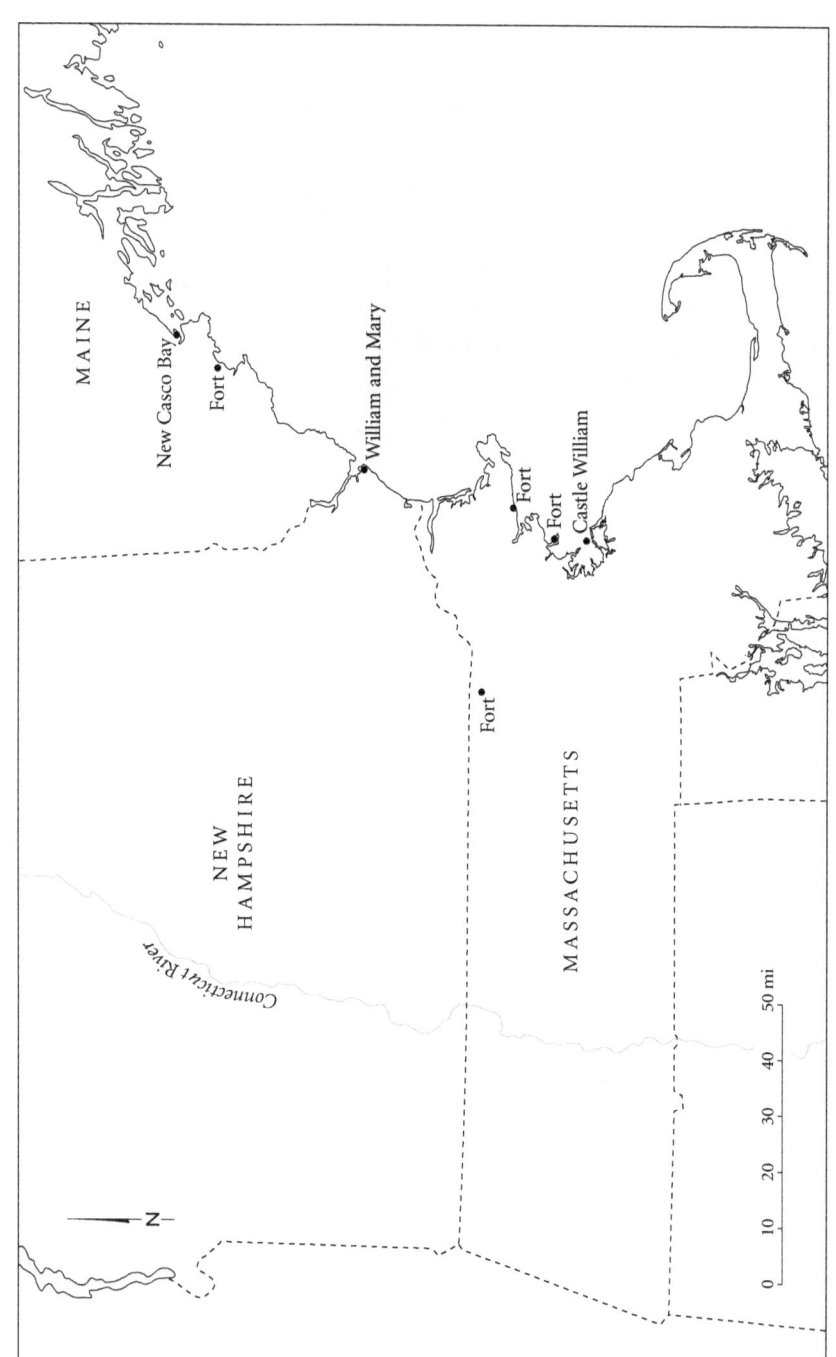

Forts in Queen Anne's War, 1704–1712

MA), Pelham (Rowe, MA), Massachusetts (North Adams), and a small post on the West Hoosic River (Williamstown, MA).[13] Number Four was the most northern post; Massachusetts was situated on the Hoosic River, which flowed into the Hudson River above Albany; and the small West Hoosic post was the most exposed fort on the western approaches to Massachusetts. During King George's War New Hampshire forces also constructed a temporary fort on Lake Winnipesauke.[14] Throughout this period, numerous small forts built by communities or other interests, were erected along the northern frontier, including Lovewell's fort built on Ossipee Lake, the defensive structure built by Scotch-Irish settlers at Penacook, New Hampshire, and a small fort built at Gorham, Maine.[15]

The provincial forts presented almost a myriad of designs and sizes. Most used wood as their main construction element, but some forts, especially those near the coast, were substantial structures made of stone. Fort George in Brunswick and Fort Mary in Saco were stone forts, as was Fort William Henry at Pemaquid. William Henry had an outside circumference of 737 feet and the wall fronting the sea was twenty-two feet high and six feet thick at the gun ports.[16] A round tower near the western side stood twenty-nine feet high. The fort had twenty-eight gun ports and eighteen guns mounted, including six eighteen-pounders, and it usually had a garrison of sixty to one hundred.[17] But lime was scarce and thus the mortar tended to crumble, so the fort looked impressive but had substantial weakness.

Forts built in the interior, such as the fort at Number Four and Fort Massachusetts, used logs as their main defense. The structure at Number Four had large connecting buildings of horizontal hewn logs built almost in a square shape. A palisade of upright logs extended around most of the fort. Palisades built in this manner often did not have the logs touching each other with firing platforms as our folklore commonly depicts, but were actually planted several inches apart. In this case the palisade only kept the enemy at a distance, while the defenders fired from the buildings within.[18] The palisade of Fort Massachusetts had logs laid horizontally over a foundation of stone, and the northeast angle was protected by a watchtower. Inside the fort a large log house and several smaller structures served both as barracks and blockhouses.[19]

Fort Shirley was a small structure, about sixty feet on a side (about the size of a softball diamond) with eleven-foot-high walls and two eleven-foot-wide barracks rooms that formed two opposite sides. The walls were made of horizontally placed squared timbers. Squared timbers also covered the floors of the barracks and the parade area in the middle. According to Michael D.

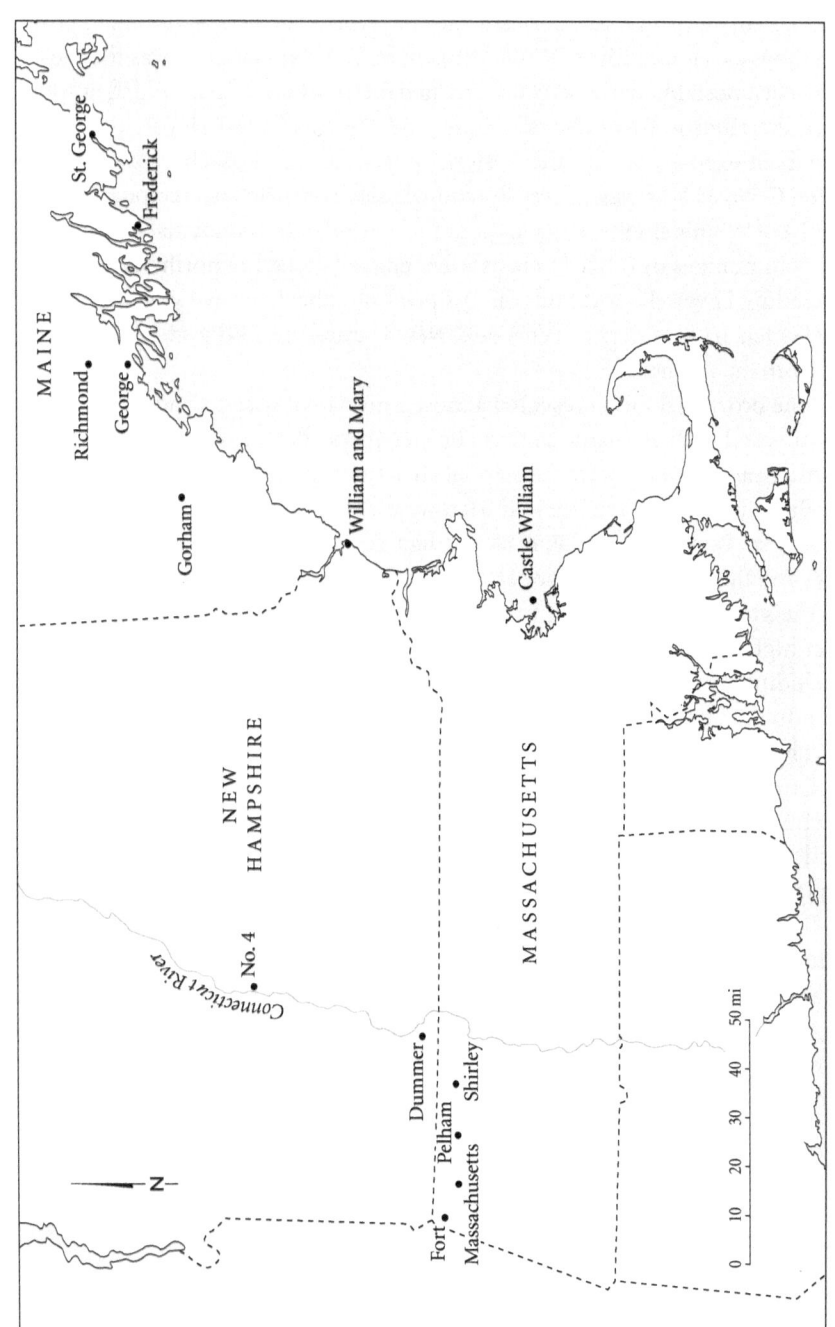

Forts in King George's War

Coe, despite being a modest structure in size, Fort Shirley used 12,000 shingles and 16,000 shingle nails for the roofs, 2,000 board nails, and 500 weight of 20 penny nails.[20]

Similar in construction, the fortification at Gorham, Maine, typifies the small community fort. Built on the highest point of land, the principal structure was a building fifty feet long made of hewn logs, surrounded by a palisade of timber with two flankers or watchtowers. An excellent description of the palisade was provided in 1757 when the proprietors of the town voted to have it repaired. "Voted money, per foot for stockading the fort where the walls are defective, supposed to be one hundred feet, and to be done with spruce, pine, or hemlock timber, and the bark peeled off, and to be thirteen feet long and ten inches in diameter, to stand three feet in the ground and ten above, where the rocks will admit of digging three feet; and to be lined with six inch stuff, peeled as the other timber."[21] The difference in appearance between these small forts and the larger garrisons was very small, distinguished only by the fact that garrisons were privately owned, and the forts belonged to the community or the province. One unusual community fort was the large palisade constructed at Deerfield, Massachusetts. It was unusual in that the palisade encompassed most of the central area of the town, including the meeting house, the town common, and fifteen houses (running 40 by 60 rods, or 560 by 840 to 640 by 960 feet, depending on which rod length is indicated). Rather than a sanctuary, this fort attempted to preserve the heart of the community. Its long walls probably were not meant to be defended (such a structure would take a large garrison) but existed as an impediment to any enemy. However, even this large palisade failed to defend Deerfield, as drifting snow enabled French and Indian raiders to clamber over the wall and unhook the gate in February 1704.[22]

As the French wars progressed, and the frontier began to expand, it became the practice of the proprietors of new communities and the provincial governments to build a fort for the protection, not to mention the encouragement, of the settlers.[23] The cost of construction of frontier forts, as well as the maintenance, could amount to a considerable burden. When the Pejepscot Company proposed to settle the communities of Brunswick and Topsham, Maine, they were ordered by the government not only to provide a fort for the safety of the settlers, but "for travelling backwards and forwards, for transporting Cattle &c, but most especially for facilitating the March of Forces to their relief in Time of War, A Road be made passable for Horse and Foot by Ferries, Bridges &c."[24] Arrangements for building the road and fort would be made by the proprietors, and the cost would be borne by the

Bay government; however, despite the fact the shell of a stone fort built by Andros in 1688 remained, the proprietors understood the "House [of Representatives] inclinable to a Wooden Fort on account of the cheapness of it."[25] The directors of the Pejepscot Company estimated the cost of a wooden fort, based on a similar one built a few years earlier at Winter Harbor, to be £500. "Rather than the Said Fort should be made of Wood, and so liable to be consumed by Fire," wrote the proprietors, " . . . We offer, that if the General Court will please to allow Five Hundred Pounds, and let us have the Fifteen Men, which are designed for that Garrison, we will enter into Engagements to repair and finish the aforesaid Stone Fort."[26] The fort, to be named "George," would be fifty feet square with four bastions or blockhouses, two made of wood "at our own charge," and barracks to house the garrison. The proprietors only asked that £300 be advanced to pay for materials.

The General Court agreed to this proposal and work commenced on the fort. The final costs included labor charges for masons, carpenters, smiths, laborers (mostly the fifteen provincial soldiers), and "Mr. Watts Boy cooking the pot"; materials such as shell lime, stone lime, over 10,000 feet of boards, pine plank, oak plank, glass casements, hinges, and a "large lock for the Gate"; provisions and drink; the hiring of sloops to transport materials; and "small expenses" including "1 horse lost," "loss and wear of tools," and £30 "allowed Mr. Watts his trouble."[27] The total cost for the completion of Fort George came to £688 of which the government of Massachusetts contributed £500 for the fort and £12 for the subsistence of the soldiers.[28]

Of course, Fort George was only a small installation; the cost of the larger provincial forts caused even more controversy, pitting colonies against the British government and against each other. After the close of King William's War the British government insisted that Massachusetts replace Fort William Henry at Pemaquid, which had been destroyed by the French in 1696. They believed the presence of a fort at Pemaquid helped to reassert the British claim to disputed territory and would discourage Indian incursions by covering the Kennebec, Damariscotta, and Sheepscot rivers. The fort would thus become another strategic and political card in their dealings with the French.[29] The Bay government balked at this order, however, as they felt the site offered little strategic advantage to justify the frightful cost involved. Lieutenant Governor William Stoughton wrote the London government on June 3, 1701, to voice the General Court's reservations. "As to the erecting of a Fort at Pemaquid, it is the general opinion of all who know the place that the Situation thereof is such as renders a Fortification there of very little or no use for the securing of our Plantations, nor can it be a bridle to the

Indians, being far remote from any present Settlement of the English and lies much out of the Common road of the Indians the greatest numbers of which, that usually annoy us, having their Plantations and settlements on this side thereof."[30] Two months later the Governor's Council amplified their position by pointing out that Fort William Henry had cost £40,000 to build and maintain, and, even though they had not been sure it accomplished anything, the government of Massachusetts had kept the fort supplied and garrisoned, only to have it fall into enemy hands and be destroyed. They could not now support the cost of a fort so removed from the frontier.[31] The government of Massachusetts won this fight. Although Colonel Romer drew up plans for a new fort in 1699 and his successor, Colonel John Redknap, did likewise in 1705, neither fort was ever built (a smaller fort called Frederick was built on the site in 1729).[32] The British government even tried subtle blackmail by insinuating the further support of the colony as regards stores of war would not be as freely provided unless the Bay government rebuilt Pemaquid, but the tactic failed as the rebuilding effort got lost in other political controversy.[33]

Fort William and Mary in Portsmouth Harbor caused similar friction between governors and assemblies. When Governor Bellomont urged the building of a fort on Great Island in 1697, the New Hampshire Assembly agreed to listen to proposals, but they were astonished when Romer presented his construction estimate of £6,000. The assembly pleaded poverty and with the death of Bellomont the project was put on a back burner until the commencement of Queen Anne's War.[34]

At that time the assembly voted to provide £500 in grain and other supplies, and £500 in labor provided by inhabitants pressed on a rotating basis who worked for their subsistence only. Unfortunately, the grain did not realize the price originally thought, and so the contribution was devalued to £450. In addition, Romer reported that the laborers provided consumed far more than they worked. In November 1703 he wrote that "they had already consumed upwards of £26, and had not done £8 worth of work."[35] Though reported completed in 1705, the fort required constant repair and became a continuing source of friction concerning its maintenance costs. In July 1708, George Vaughn, agent for New Hampshire, reported that the fort had never really been completed and was decaying because the province could not afford to pay for its upkeep.[36] Vaughn said the fort was "builded and made of turff and saltmarsh sodds, which in a little time moulders and cannot endure the stormy weather and searching frosts of that countrey." In answer to a query from the Board of Trade, Romer agreed that the fort had never been completed. He said that fishermen who were anchored off the island had stolen the protective lead aprons off the cannon, and if they could do it the French certainly could. Romer said the garrison usually consisted of four men even though close to thirty cannons were mounted, "and in my time upon application made to the Governour there was ordered for a few days 16 men in time of some danger, then did the People universally complain ... and the fort was againe guarded as before by 4 decrepid men."[37]

The controversies and arguments over the support of William and Mary would continue throughout the French wars. In early February 1740, Governor Jonathan Belcher upbraided the assembly for its lack of financial support for William and Mary. "Fort William & Mary the only Fort of the province is in a poor condition for defense and I shall in a few days lay the particular state of it before you when I hope you will do what may be necessary on your part that it may be sufficiently repaired and furnished with all warlike stores and with men and thereby render it capable of protecting the people and trade of the province. You are sensible, gentlemen, I have often recommended this matter to former assemblies whose answers have been that the people were not able to support this fort nor defray the other necessary charge of government."[38] In its reply the assembly pointed out that this was "the first opportunity we have had of making any supply to the publick treasury or repair of the fort, since that ample supply made in the year 1737, in as much as your Excellency was pleased to dissolve the last General Assembly before the House had finished the Treasury accounts." However, they reiterated their contention that to support the fort to the extent that the governor wished, "we fear ... would be an insupportable burden to the people and we should bring upon ourselves a greater or more certaine misery than that which we pretend to remedy."[39] When Belcher sent his report on the condition of William and Mary, the assembly sent its own inspection team to the fort a few days later to refute his contentions.[40]

At one point the British government attempted to have the state of Massachusetts pay part of the cost for William and Mary because the fortification protected the town of Kittery across the harbor as much as it did Portsmouth, but the Bay government flatly refused, citing New Hampshire's failure to support the defense of other areas.[41] The controversy here concerned the upkeep of another frontier fort, Fort Dummer on the Connecticut River. Built in a disputed area between New Hampshire and Massachusetts, Dummer was found to be in New Hampshire territory when the border was finally settled, so the Bay government naturally felt New Hampshire should pay for the fort.

However, the New Hampshire Assembly refused, pointing out, with some justice, that Dummer gave very little protection to their communities, and, in fact, was designed to cover the Massachusetts towns to the south. In the end Massachusetts had to garrison and maintain both Fort Dummer and the fort at Number Four to its north.[42]

The governments of Massachusetts and New Hampshire kept soldiers posted in their forts even in times of peace, although in most cases this involved only a token force.[43] Some forts, like St. George, became important trading posts, or "truck houses," which required the presence of men to handle the lucrative Indian trade. Like those posted in garrison houses, however, soldiers stationed in forts between the wars tended to be pressed or hired men because few volunteered for such service.[44] Of course, during declared wars the number of soldiers at provincial forts increased substantially and often included not only the men in the garrison but also men assigned to patrols and raiding parties.[45]

The normal tour of duty in a provincial fort was one year.[46] If soldiers served longer than that, the government would begin to receive complaints and petitions from the soldiers, their families, or their communities demanding their release.[47] But other soldiers became long-term residents of the fort and even permanent members of the local community. For example, as part of its "Encouragements to enlist," the Pejepscot Company promised that any soldier who served at least six months at Fort George and desired "to become Inhabitants, we will endeavor to obtain a General Order from His Excellency the Governor to release them, they finding another man in their room, and when so dismist they shall have One Hundred Acres of Land granted to each of them equall with the other Inhabitants."[48]

For most that stayed, however, the lure was less spectacular. Their extended tour was simply the natural consequence of their chosen profession or particular assignment. The commanders, interpreters, gunsmiths, blacksmiths, and even chaplains all had the potential for extended service at frontier forts—to become as gunsmith Ebenezer Nutting did while stationed at Casco Bay during Dummer's War, a "resident of Falmouth in the King's service."[49] Another gunsmith, Mark Rounds, had previously served at Falmouth during Queen Anne's War, and he settled in the town after 1715.[50] John Gyles, a former captive of the Eastern Indians during King William's War, was stationed at the fort in Falmouth from 1700 to 1706, where he was the chief interpreter for the Massachusetts government. Gyles later directed the construction of Fort George in 1714 and commanded that post until 1725 when he was commissioned for Fort St. George.[51]

Provincial Forts | 61

When John March was appointed "Commander of Her Majesty's Fort at Casco-Bay, and Manager of the Trade for the Publick with the Indians there," he knew his stay might be protracted so "in Order to attend that service forsook his own habitation in Newbury and Removed his family, stock of Cattle and other Estate to the said fort." March would lose most of his possessions, including almost forty head of cattle, thirty-six pigs, twenty-five sheep, and almost twenty acres of crops, including "As good pese as ever I saw," in the Indian attack of August 10, 1703, although he and his family would remain safe within the walls of the fort.[52]

The presence of March's family in the fort at Falmouth was not unusual. Although certainly not an extensive practice, it was not uncommon for soldiers to bring their wives and children when posted at frontier forts. Women and children were present at Fort William Henry when it fell in 1696 and at Fort Massachusetts in 1746.[53] In assessing the disaster at William Henry, Francis Parkman concluded that "the government of Massachusetts, with its usual military fatuity, had . . . permitted some of the yeoman garrison to bring their wives and children to this dangerous and important post" and thus concern for the safety of the families led to the fort's quick capitulation.[54] However, although it certainly entered into the garrison's discussions, the failure of both William Henry and Massachusetts to withstand a siege involved far more compelling reasons than the presence of families.[55]

In addition to easing the pain of separation and reducing the problems of subsistence for poorer families while the husband was serving on the frontier, wives and children may have helped the soldiers endure garrison life, which consisted mainly of fatigue duty, watches, and boredom.[56] The journal of Lieutenant John Burk chronicling his stay at the fort at Number Four in New Hampshire from March 10 to May 14, 1748, provides an insight into the typical activities associated with garrison duty. The cutting and hauling of firewood from the surrounding forest proved to be the most constant chore, and the most dangerous. On March 11, 1748, the men had brought in eight loads of wood; on the 14th they hauled in or cut twelve loads; and on the following day they "got nine Load of wood and was out nine men of us for the tenth and last load which proved one two many for we was attacked by the Indians." The resulting ambush left one killed, one wounded, and one captured, but the cutting of firewood had to continue.

Other chores proved less dangerous and more mundane. They brought in and installed a grindstone, repaired the hospital, built a privy and an oven, boiled soap and planted a garden, and made dugout canoes. On a more personal level, Burk made himself a chest "to put my things in" and on March

24 "made a pair of Indian shoes that was my days work." When not working or standing watch, diversions included wrestling, storytelling, and, for at least one man, heavy drinking, as Burk recorded that "Old father Sumers got Drunk." Three weeks later, "Sumers" "broke" his back "playing ball"—unfortunately, the exact nature of the game is unclear.[57]

Like garrisons, forts, especially those in the more remote areas, experienced shortages of food and clothing.[58] The fort at Number Four was supplied by canoe from Fort Dummer, but occasionally the men rotated back to Massachusetts towns to replenish their supplies. In April 1748, Burk and seventeen others went to Deerfield and Northampton where they bought forty pairs of shoes for the garrison and recruited another soldier. On a more personal level, Burk had his gun mended and purchased material to make seven shirts, three locks for his chest, and a new rammer, or "gun stick," for his weapon.[59]

Michael D. Coe reveals that Elijah Williams in Deerfield had a substantial part of his store's business dedicated to supplying the forts and soldiers in that area with supplies, and this store was probably the place Burk and the others went for their needs. Such articles included eating utensils and other personal items, shoes, clothing, and, perhaps most important, food. The soldiers assigned to western forts in Massachusetts were supposed to be issued one pound of bread, one-half pint of peas or beans per day, two pounds of pork for three days, and one gallon of molasses for forty-two days. Getting this to outlying forts was a difficult undertaking. Soldiers supplemented this ration with gardens for vegetables and livestock (to provide fresh meat as a respite from the salted meat provided by the government).[60] Hunting did not provide a large portion of food. Joanne Bowen found from archaeological evidence at Fort Pelham that 90.2 percent of the usable meat came from domesticated sources and only 9.8 percent came from wild animals.[61] Still at times food could be plentiful, especially in the summer growing season. Coe relates how Seth Pomroy wrote to his wife from Fort Massachusetts in August 1748, "I Shant want any Thing Sent to me: we live at This Fort well; my Diner yesterday was a Bisquitte Suitt whertleberry Puddin & a good Peace of Corned Beef with Squashes & Turnip: no Syder, But a good appitite."[62]

Bad sanitation, and perhaps spoiled food, caused serious outbreaks of dysentery, or "bloody flux." During the siege of Fort Massachusetts in 1746 half the meager garrison was down with dysentery. Of course, concepts of sanitation were rudimentary compared to the methods of food preparation in the twenty-first century. They could not prevent what they did not understand, but the government of Massachusetts did provide different food items for the comfort of the afflicted, particularly oatmeal and rice. And the copious amounts of rum and tobacco provided to garrisons could help ease distress and anxiety.[63]

Soldiers at forts near population centers could moonlight, or take jobs in the community to supplement their income and fill the time. Usually these were odd jobs, cutting firewood or splitting shingles and clapboards, but soldiers with specific skills, such as gunsmiths or cordwainers could employ these skill sets for the benefit of the communities and their own pocket books.[64] For the forts removed from frontier communities, there was no chance for moonlighting, and for a soldier stationed there time could weigh very heavy. In the summer of 1746 a regiment, commanded by Colonel Theodore Atkinson, was raised in New Hampshire to participate in a planned assault on Canada, but the threat of a French invasion kept them close to home. Atkinson's regiment was stationed at William and Mary where they spent their time repairing the structure. With the collapse of the French invasion threat in October, the men of Atkinson's regiment were sent to Lake Winnipesauke to build a fort, which they named Fort Atkinson. Jeremy Belknap related that the soldiers were "plentifully supplied with provisions, and had but little exercise or discipline."[65] The men and officers were not allowed to disperse until orders came from England, which did not arrive for a year. Offenses were not punished; some hunted, some scouted, and some, sick and tired of the soldier's life, deserted.[66]

Long tours of duty and the inevitable boredom of garrison life always made desertion a problem for post commanders. Faced with holding together a garrison rocked by the events of the Glorious Revolution, Sylvanus Davis had his share of troubles at Fort Loyal in 1689. When a pirate ship appeared in Casco Bay, seven men deserted for a life they felt would be more profitable and exciting, taking with them powder and shot from the fort, and various personal items belonging to other soldiers. Among the deserters was the fort's gunsmith, who took three guns and all his tools.[67] Wholesale desertions such as this were rare, however, because soldiers usually exercised more discretion by simply slipping away, or they used more imagination like Benjamin Dower of Norwich who forged discharge papers in his commander's absence before he left Fort Mary in 1725.[68]

It should be emphasized that the problems associated with garrison duty were not restricted to New England provincial soldiers but affected all armies of the eighteenth century. J. A. Houlding discovered that for British regiments "extended stay on a distant station was bound to have the most serious effect upon a unit."[69] Commanding officers in remote British forts were reluctant to discharge worn-out men because replacements were rare, and they also relaxed punishments and fatigue duty for fear of driving the men to desert. However, allowing the soldiers to moonlight, while good for morale, decreased significantly the drill proficiency of the unit. In 1768 the Eighth Regiment of Foot arrived in Canada with 500 officers and men, and the men were dispersed to various forts on the frontier. In 1785 the regiment returned to England with 150 "very old men" and would not recover from its garrison duty for four years.[70]

Of course, the presence of the enemy increased activity and certainly eliminated the problem of boredom. Local alarms, attacks on work parties, or other evidence of enemy raiding parties resulted in increased watches and not a little anxiety. Sylvanus Davis kept his scouts out by land and water during the tense August of 1689, and they "beat to arms" three times a day to prevent surprise.[71] When the new fort at Falmouth came under attack in 1703, the commander, John March, divided his command into three shifts of twelve men each and rotated them every two hours, and the soldiers at Number Four doubled the guard whenever the behavior of their dogs indicated the possible presence of the enemy.[72]

Naturally one of the primary purposes of the forts was to defend against attack, and on numerous occasions throughout the early French wars provincial soldiers had to withstand sieges. Only one, the capture of Fort William Henry by Pierre Le Moyne d'Iberville in 1696, could be considered a formal siege in the European style. For the French, according to d'Iberville's biographer (who apparently agreed with the British government), Fort William Henry "was a powerful structure, capable of overawing the Indians and keeping them loyal to the English."[73] D'Iberville had at his command three warships, 200 French soldiers and sailors, over 500 Indians, and several pieces of artillery, including at least two mortars and five field guns.[74] When asked to surrender, the fort's commander, Pasco Chubb, replied that he would not yield the fort though "the sea was covered by French vessels and the land with Indians."[75] D'Iberville established his batteries on the islands in the harbor and on the landward side of the fort, setting them with such skill that the defenders could only use one gun in reply, the others having no targets in their line of sight.[76] After one day of bombardment, Chubb surrendered William Henry.[77]

Most sieges on the northern frontier were not so elaborate. They were informal affairs flavored by *la petite guerre* and involved large Indian raiding parties who employed no artillery. Three principal methods of attack were used. The first tactic was intimidation. Usually, the enemy would display a show of force outside the walls to convince the defenders they had no hope.

At Fort Mary in 1695 the enemy force came into the open, planted the French colors, and opened fire, but as the fort commander John Hill reported, "our bullets sune apoynted a new Ensigne for them: and [forced] thire Cullers to Retreat."[78] At Fort Massachusetts in 1746 "there appeared an Army of French and Indians, eight or nine Hundred in Number," related the Reverend John Norton, "who having surrounded the Fort on every Side, began with hideous Acclamations to rush upon the Fort, firing incessantly upon us on every side . . . we suffered them to come up in a Body 'till they were within twenty Rods of us, and then we fired; upon which the Enemy soon betook themselves to Trees, Stumps and Logs."[79] This psychological pressure continued throughout the siege. John Norton wrote that the French and Indians "continued thus to fire upon us, until between eight and nine at Night; and then the whole Army (as we suppose) surrounded the Fort, shouted, or rather yelled with the most hideous Out-cries all around the Fort; this they repeated three or four Times: We expected they would have followed this with a Storm; but were mistaken."[80]

Once the besiegers believed they had presented the hopelessness of the situation, an invitation to surrender was issued, and duly answered by the English defenders in the negative. Expressed in heroic and colorful language, at least as recalled after the fact, these intrepid retorts did not normally come back to haunt and embarrass the speaker as did Pasco Chubb's hasty remarks at Fort William Henry. John Hill at Fort Mary recalled that "About two a'clock: Cam two men with a flag of truce, I demanded thire bisnis thay answered Mounsere Capt demanded a surrender of the fort and that he would give boon quartier: and If we would not hee would battalle all night: I told them If that ware thire bisnes I should discors them onely with the musels of our guns."[81] Colonel Thomas Westbrook, in describing the siege of Fort St. George in 1722 to Lieutenant Governor William Dummer, wrote that the Indians repeatedly demanded the surrender of the fort, but the garrison shouted "they wanted no quarters at their hands. Daring them Continually to Come on and told them it was King Georges Lands and that they would not Yield them but with the Last Drops of their Blood."[82] When a French officer demanded the surrender of the fort at Number Four in 1747, the commander, Phineas Stevens, refused, saying the fort had been entrusted to him and he would defend it with all his means.[83]

When intimidation failed, the besiegers sometimes attempted to mine under the palisade in order to collapse a section of the wall. This tactic never worked as planned. The Indians, under French supervision attacking the fort at Falmouth in 1703 spent two days and nights tunneling from the shore of the bay toward the walls of the fort. In this instance the timely arrival of the provincial galley lifted the siege.[84] Almost twenty years later a similar attempt at undermining the palisades of Fort St. George was defeated when rains caved in the tunnels.[85]

The third tactic employed the use of fire against the wooden palisades of frontier forts, accomplished either by setting fire to out-buildings in hopes the flames would spread to the fort, or by pushing combustibles up to the walls.[86] In 1690 Sylvanus Davis finally surrendered Fort Loyal when the Indians managed to place a barrel of tar and other flammable material against the palisades.[87] The Reverend John Norton related that their sergeant prepared the defenders of Fort Massachusetts for possible fire attacks by ordering "that all the Tubs, Pails and Vessels of every Sort, in every Room, should be filled with Water, and went himself to see it done."[88]

During the attack on the fort at Number Four in 1747 the Indians set fire to a deserted cabin and the flames spread to the grass, which in turn threatened the fort itself. Half the garrison maintained a covering fire while the other half fought the flames and doused the walls. They accomplished this feat by digging eleven trenches to the outside deep enough for a man to stand in and throw buckets of water on the outside walls. They not only stopped the threat from the grass fire but kept the walls wet all night to prevent further incendiary attacks.[89]

In most cases these tactics failed and the provincial forts defended themselves quite adequately. In fact, between the fall of William Henry in 1696 and the end of King George's War, only one major fort was lost to the French and their Indian allies, and that fort, Massachusetts, beset by several hundred French and Indians, was defended by twenty-two men under the command of a sergeant, and half the command had been struck down by illness before the enemy arrived. Massachusetts held out for two days and only surrendered when the ammunition supply, which had been low when the siege began, reached critical levels.[90]

The historian John K. Mahon believed the provincial forts were not effective because "it was simple for the savages to pass between the strong points, raid the territory beyond, and slip away unharmed."[91] In one respect what Mahon said is true: The forts could not stop all the raids on the frontier, but then no defense could totally stop the small Indian raiding parties. However, to dismiss forts as ineffective does not agree with the overall picture. The provincial forts on the northern frontier provided a military presence and represented the authority of the English government, and thus they provided an obvious political target for the French and Indians. They also threatened the line of retreat for larger raiding parties, especially those built on major invasion routes, such as the fort at Number Four. As a result, the French and Indians began sending their larger raiding forces against the provincial forts rather than the New England communities. With the large parties expending their energies against forts like St. George, Number Four, and Massachusetts, and the increased vigilance of English scouts, there were far fewer large-scale attacks on New England towns after the destruction of Deerfield in 1704. Thus, though expensive to build and maintain, even in defeat and destruction the provincial forts were a magnet that drew the fury of large enemy raiding forces away from the frontier towns.

4

Scouts

Patrols, Probes, and Raids

Provincial forces did not remain stationary in garrison houses and behind fort walls. Units of provincial soldiers performed defensive patrols, intelligence-gathering probes, and offensive raids. The governments of northern New England referred to any armed force moving beyond the frontier line as a "scout."[1] Although the title "ranger" has been prevalent since the Seven Years' War, especially with the fame of Rogers Rangers (the British military apparently promoted the use of that term during that last French war). There are a few scattered references to provincial soldiers "ranging" the woods, but in all official documents the term "scout" is used as a designation. Scouts varied from local patrols marching among the towns to extended raids striking deep into Indian territory. Among the latter we can include the large forces striking at Indian villages or French settlements around the Bay of Fundy. Although sometimes referred to as expeditions, they were really no more than reinforced raiding parties—the scout in its ultimate offensive form and the principal weapon used against the Eastern Indians.

The number and effectiveness of scouts did not remain static during the early French wars. The aggressive use of raiding parties, with a few exceptions, found limited success during King William's War because provincial officers had to master the procedures and logistics of long-distance marches. But by Queen Anne's War the use of scouts, both defensive and offensive, increased rapidly. Winter raids when the Indians were most vulnerable became routine, and increased patrols and scouts all year long kept the enemy off balance. During Dummer's War the aggressive use of large provincial forces marching against the Indian villages of Norridgewock and Pequawket eventually broke the power of these Eastern tribes, and the officers who led these raids became heroes to the frontier communities struggling for their existence. Scouts were the cardinal element of warfare on the northern frontier, the essence of *la petite guerre*, and provided provincial soldiers, both officers and men, with their most significant martial education.

To "scout" means to observe the motions and obtain intelligence concerning an enemy,[2] but war in the New World added a combat emphasis as well. Scouts can be identified as defensive or offensive by their primary goal and scope of operation. Defensive scouts operated "on the backs of the towns,"[3] or close to the frontier communities, and their mission involved four major objectives: first, they had to "observe the motions of the Enemy and give notice of danger to the Towns or farmes adjacent" (usually revealed by their tracks or campsites);[4] second, protect the inhabitants while they performed their labors;[5] third, pursue the enemy after they had struck; and finally, ambush known trails and fords used by enemy raiding parties as well as "visit the Enemys usual fishing places where in probability they now are And upon your discovery . . . you are to attack fight take kill and destroy them."[6]

These patrols on the backs of frontier communities were often thankless tasks involving much fatigue and even more frustration. All officers commanding provincial scouts were required to submit a journal chronicling their activities to ensure they had done their jobs correctly. While most journals are succinct and provide little detail on the methods employed and the experiences of the soldiers, a few relate in great detail the difficulties associated with scouts' lives, and from them we can understand the frustration of patrol duty. In April 1746, a Sergeant Trott led a patrol operating between North Yarmouth and Brunswick, Maine. Trott and his men guarded the inhabitants while they brought in timber, then investigated three alarms but could not discover their meaning. At one point his patrol, reinforced by the local militia, pursued an enemy raiding party, and Trott recorded the typical signs of Indian activity found in the woods beyond the frontier. After picking up the reinforcements from North Yarmouth, they "followed the enemies tracks into the woods and came to their camps made with sticks covered with bark and marched upon their tracks about two miles further and found their fire place where their [sic] had lately been a fire, we marched about two miles further and found where they had had a fire, we marched on still about three miles further and came to the place where we supposed they camped the night before and saw three large fire places, and fifty-three spits to roast meat upon." Trott continued on the trail for a few more miles but ended the pursuit when the inhabitants ran out of provisions.[7]

Naturally, weather could play havoc with patrols, causing extreme discomfort and even dangerous conditions. In May 1724 Allison Brown led a patrol around Saco and encountered problems with inordinate amounts of water. Brown reported that "the River is so overflowed and the woods so full of water that ther was no going unless the men waded to their middles over many brooks which wee were obliged to pass over some were so great that several men were obliged to swim over and cutt trees on each side to meet so that the rest might bring their provision over dry, the Swamps and Interval land was so overflown that 'twas leg deep as wee marchct."[8]

One year earlier Jeremiah Moulton of York led a patrol of provincial soldiers covering all the towns in southern Maine, and his journal provides perhaps one of the best descriptions of the constant marching and countermarching, ambushes, protection, and frustration involved with defensive patrols. Leaving Falmouth on May 6, Moulton's men marched to Wells, where one man sprained his ankle and had to be left behind. On the 9th they marched through the woods on the "back of Wells," scouted around York on the 10th and at Berwick on the 11th when they heard two men had been killed by Indians. Moulton reported that "while I was after those Indians another scout of Indians killed a man at Wells and burnt a saw mill and 50,000 [feet] of boards, we pursued them till night designing to pursue them the next day, but a violent storm of rain prevented it." On the 12th they waited out the rain, then Moulton divided his scout by sending ten men to patrol on the back of Salmon Falls while he marched the rest above Berwick. On the 14th of May, Moulton took his half of the scout to Kittery to protect the judges of the Superior Court then sitting in session. On the 16th they took provisions and rested, then scouted around York the following day. On the 18th they headed to Ogunquit and then on to Wells.

> [we] scouted on back of Wells in hopes to find some of the Lurking Enemy lurking to take the people as they went to meeting but we found none of them allthough four of them was discovered by the Inhabitants while we were in the woods . . . on the 22 day we marched from Wells through the woods on the back side of York. Whilst we was in the woods we heard an alarm at Cape Neddick. We immediately struck through the woods to Cape Neddick expecting to have came upon the Enemy, but we missed of our Expectations for they told me they took the alarms from Wells. Immediately we marched to Wells when came there they told us the alarms came from Saco falls, and some of the inhabitants had seen two Indians. On the 23rd day we through the woods to York: on the 24th we Scouted on the heads of out fields while the inhabitants mended their fences: on the 25th Guarded and Scouted at the out mills while the Inhabitants hauled their Lumber. The 26th Sabath day: on the 27th we took provisions and sent a Scout of men

to Kittery to guard an Express that was going to his honor . . . on the 4th [of June] scouted on the back of Wells. The Inhabitants . . . having a Great number of board at their mill at Merriland, which Lyeth between Wells and Berwick, and thinking ever day . . . the Indians would burn them, and [so] by their Request and it being a very likely place for to meet the Enemy we Lay in ambush about said mills while the Inhabitants wrought with about Two hundred men till the 14th day of June. We discovered where eight of the Indians had placed themselves by the road to have shot on the teams, but our Scouts which went on each side of the same Some distance from the road for fear of surprise. Thay coming on, said Indians start up and Run. Our Scout pursued them but the woods being so thick we could not have a shot at them: . . . on the 19th we divided our Scout into three parts and waylaying in the Edge of the woods above Salmon Falls, the Inhabitants of Berwick went to work in their out fields while we Lay in ambush. Made no discovery but tracked ten of them which had gone a few days before: on the 20th we also divided in to three parties, Two parties of them waylayed on the heads of the fields while the inhabitants wrought in their out fields about their corn: myself with the other party Lay in ambush about three miles above Berwick where the Indians used to pass from Berwick to Dover . . . on the 25th Captain Harmon Took the Scout . . . Sir Since this I have been Constantly Scouting with Captain Harmon, his Lieutenant being sick.

Despite the obvious exertions required in this type of patrol, and despite the frustrations of missed opportunities to strike the enemy, Moulton was able to conclude his report by stating unequivocally "I choose marching Rather then Lying in garrison."[9]

While defensive patrols may seem complicated, with their simultaneous objectives of warning, protection, pursuit, and ambush, offensive raids can be viewed in rather simple terms—they were either intelligence-gathering probes or search-and-destroy missions. The New England governments received intelligence from various sources. Some information was gleaned from casual conversations with Indians at truck houses, which reinforced the importance of having interpreters always posted at those trading establishments. In July 1703, Indians visiting the truck house at Dunstable mentioned they had observed 150 Indians assembled in Canada along with a force of Frenchmen. Other Indians reported the Pequawket and Penacook Indians had brought together their warriors and only waited for a force from Norridgewock before they made a massive attack on the English settlements. In this particular instance the news was all too accurate. Despite the fact that scouting parties were dispatched to "make discovery of the approach of the enemy and observe their motions," a large force of French-led Indians launched a massive attack on the Maine settlements in early August. In addition to these chance conversations, the government of Massachusetts occasionally sent friendly Indians to Canada as deliberate spies.[10]

Intelligence concerning major French operations also came from London and from other colonies. For example, Peter Schuyler of New York, taking advantage of his close relations with New York and Canadian Indian tribes, passed along any information that might affect New England. In June 1708, Schuyler reported to Governor Joseph Dudley of Massachusetts that a large force of French and Indians was preparing to descend on the towns along the Piscataqua River. With this information corroborated by Indian scouts, Dudley raised 2,000 soldiers for the frontier in garrison and on patrol, and he put half the militia on alert. In this instance, half the Indians deserted the French before they left, and another large number of Abenakis never arrived at the rendezvous at Lake Winnipesauke. The reduction of their numbers forced them to change targets and attack Haverhill.[11]

In addition to the reports of friendly Indians and other outside sources, intelligence concerning the Eastern Indian tribes was gathered by small companies of soldiers sent on deep probes into Indian territory.[12] Provincial soldiers scouted the lands of the Penacook Indians around Lake Winnipesauke, the Pequawkets at the head of the Saco, and the Norridgewocks on the Kennebec. They sought signs of large Indian parties on the move, evidence of planting activities, and the location of fishing and hunting areas. Early in Queen Anne's War frequent probes sent by Governor Dudley revealed that the Indians had apparently abandoned their villages and removed their tribes to the protection of the French in Canada.[13] Dudley believed the Eastern Indians left their lands principally because of the frequent raids sent into their territory by the New England governments.

These offensive raids were nothing less than search-and-destroy missions, and their purpose was threefold: to disrupt the economy of the Eastern Indians; to intimidate the raiding parties with the presence of provincial soldiers on their invasion routes; and to destroy warriors through ambush and battle. The commanders of these raids were apprised of these goals through simple but explicit instructions. In 1725 Captain Samuel Willard was ordered to scout to Pequawket and then down the Kennebec and Androscoggin rivers. Willard was to "Kill, Take and Destroy to the utmost of your power all the Enemy Indians you can meet in your March, and Search for their Corn, destroying all you can find."[14]

Of course strategies are generally easier to devise than to execute, and so it was in the case of the provincial raids. Of the three major goals the disruption of the Indian economy proved the easiest to achieve.[15] The Eastern Indians depended upon hunting and fishing to provide for their subsistence, and specific locations within the tribe's territory became associated with water fowl or shellfish.[16] Through casual conversations with the Indians, the observation of previous scouting parties, and the experience of their own hunters and fishermen, the provincial governments knew the locations of these areas and regularly ordered their commanders to scout and ambush them "to keep the Indians from their fishing and planting, to distress them farther against winter."[17]

Provincial raiding parties also sought to discourage French and Indian forces by their presence. The old raider Benjamin Church often attempted to intimidate the enemy. During his 1690 raid into Maine, Church left messages at one destroyed village, telling the Indians who had done the deed and threatening his return if they did not reform. His force also killed several Indians and took captive the wives of some important chiefs.[18] Church's bravado probably had little effect, but the capture of the sachems' wives may have been instrumental in forcing the Indians into a temporary truce that November.[19] However, such opportunities for direct intimidation were rare. At the very least the English hoped the evidence of large parties scouting the woods would create second thoughts among enemy raiders.

Determining if these efforts accomplished their purpose can be difficult. When intimidation succeeded, there were no attacks, but there is no difference between successful intimidation and simple inactivity on the part of the enemy. In both cases nothing happens. Despite this perception issue, there is tenuous evidence to indicate provincial presence in the woods achieved results. Samuel Penhallow related that in 1704 when a French deserter warned of an approaching force, "Expresses and Scouts were every way sent to observe their motions." A large part of the enemy party fell to arguing and turned back, and when the reduced force sent their scouts ahead, they found the English "as thick as the Trees in the Woods." This news discouraged the party, causing most of the remainder to desert.[20] Eight years later a scout of New Hampshire soldiers found where bark had been peeled off of trees, and continuing along the trail "Imediately came upon the Wigwams in a very obscure place," numbering seventeen in all. However, the Englishmen were convinced the Indians had been scared off by the presence of so many scouts in the woods because the wigwams had never been occupied.[21]

Of course, the reports of the enemy intimidation may represent an overly optimistic conclusion on the part of the New Englanders. In assessing the results of Church's raid along the coast in 1704 for the Board of Trade, Governor Dudley reported that "we are every day advised that what the forces of this Province did there against the enemy was of great value, and hath been such a discouragement to the French and Indians that for 5 moneths past my marching partys in the desert can find no footsteps of them."[22] How much of this statement is true or how much is wishful thinking on the part of Dudley is impossible to know.

The final purpose of the raiding parties, the killing of Indians through ambush, proved to be the most difficult as well as the most hazardous. Indian fishing and hunting grounds, fords and warrior paths, as well as the villages themselves were all targets for ambuscade or attacks, but the provincial forces rarely found their foe where they expected.[23] Although provincial soldiers experienced some success in this regard, to "search out and destroy the enemy" was indeed easier said than done.[24] In addition, like defensive patrols, the very real possibility existed that the English scouts themselves could be ambushed. In 1690 a scout under Captains Floyd and Wiswell were following a trail when they ran into an ambush near Wheelright Pond in present-day Lee, New Hampshire. An engagement ensued that lasted several hours and cost the lives of fifteen Englishmen, including Captain Wiswell.[25] Numerous other examples of such ambushes exist throughout the history of the period.[26]

The success or failure of raids into enemy territory depended on many factors, including the quality of the commander and the soldiers, the weather, logistical support, and the guides or "pilots" who led the scouts into the mountains and forests. The provincial governments used local inhabitants, hunters, Indians, and former captives to pilot their raiding parties. A Maine hunter who guided provincial raiding parties was Richard Hunniwell. Listed as the pilot for the March-King raid in 1691, he was wounded in the famous beach fight that ended that disastrous scouting expedition.[27] Four years later he appeared "ready and willing" to pilot a scout commanded by Pasco Chubb.[28] In 1722 Colonel Thomas Westbrook used four redeemed captives for guides and intelligence concerning location of the enemy.[29] Two years later he employed Stephen Hardin as pilot, "an Expert one on Saco Kennebunk and all the rivers as far as Winipeesiaucut Ponds he having hunted on that ground for many years past, He was Pilot to Lieutenant Johnson Harmon on his last march who says he never saw a man have more Judgment in the woods than he."[30]

Friendly Indians were also frequently used as guides.[31] One Mohawk named Christian guided many scouts during Queen Anne's and Dummer's Wars, including the great raid on Norridgewock in 1724.[32] Of course, being a hunter,

Indian, or former captive did not guarantee a pilot could always find the destination, as John March found out in 1703 when his massive raiding force of 360 men never approached their target due to the confusion of the guides trying to follow overgrown trails.[33] Thomas Westbrook experienced the same disappointment in 1724 when the ineptitude of his pilots ruined his designs.[34]

In addition to the quality of the pilots, difficulties in the procurement of provisions could create serious problems for long-range scouts. Food and replacement clothing had to be gathered and prepared, and then transported by the soldiers, usually in "snapsacks" or knapsacks. Smaller scouts could also hunt as they marched, and, like their French and Indian counterparts, New England soldiers became adept at procuring game.[35] A company under John White and Seth Wyman, which left Lancaster, Massachusetts, in July 1725 and scouted in New Hampshire for about a month, augmented their stores with several bears and a black moose. They also killed "divers Rattle snakes, which pestered us very much in our march."[36] Earlier that same year a scout under the command of John Lovewell reportedly "were well entertained with Moose, Bear, and Deer; together with Salmon Trout, some of which were three feet long, and weighed twelve pounds apiece."[37] Apparently "fish stories" have not changed much over the centuries.

While hunting and fishing did supplement the food supplies of smaller parties, success was haphazard at best. Game animals can prove scarce during certain times of the year and under some weather conditions, and larger groups of men moving through the woods had a tendency to drive the game away before them. Under most circumstances, therefore, raiding parties had to husband their supplies for the duration of the scout. But even with strict frugality and careful conservation unforeseen shortages could force the termination of a scout and endanger the health of the soldiers. Raiding parties and scouts could return to the settlements in a ragged, starving, and sick condition. The soldiers from the March-King raid of 1691 arrived in Portsmouth in a "shattred Condition (some haveing lost their Guns and maney their Shoes and stockins)," and were thus considered fit only for garrison duty.[38] A raiding party led by Thomas Westbrook in 1724 had to be terminated early when some of the men lost their bread while wading through the rivers and streams swollen by recent rains.[39]

Food shortages were hazards that all soldiers experienced when they marched into the woods of New England—the New Englanders were not exceptional in this respect. A major French raid against the western Iroquois in 1684 found their provisions to be inadequate due to mismanagement in transportation, and as a result many of the soldiers fell dangerously ill.[40] In

1747 a force of apparently starving French and Indians laid siege to the fort at Number Four. After several attempts to burn the walls, the French called a parley and the French officer demanded that food be gathered for his men even before asking for the fort's surrender. When refused, the French officer became quite agitated and began shouting threats about taking the fort by storm and the likely consequences of that action. The fort commander, Phineas Stevens, broke off the talks and the siege resumed. After a while the French called for another parley and suggested to Stevens that if he sold them some food they would go away. Stevens declined this business transaction and after firing a few more shots in frustration, the French force moved off to find provisions elsewhere.[41]

Weather obviously also played a role in the success or failure of a scout. A heavy downpour forced soldiers to halt their march in order to protect their food, powder, and weapons, and the prolonged rain not only created swollen rivers, as in the Westbrook raid, but often produced illness among the men.[42] The White-Wyman scout in July 1725 encountered heavy rain on the 17th, which forced them to halt their march, then another rainstorm hit them on the 20th, by which time several of the men were ill. Two days later White reported that "Several more of our men were taken ill with a Bloody Flux, which we Suppose was occasioned by Excessive Rains and Immoderate Heats." The march continued, despite the prevalence of sickness within the company, until the 26th, when rain once again forced a halt, "our men continuing sick." The next day found "the Storm continuing, and our men growing worse we lay still all day." When the storm passed, White and Wyman led their men home.[43]

Because of the physical demands placed on offensive scouts, officers employed only the best soldiers available to them. In 1695 Major Charles Frost of Kittery informed the Bay government that the raiding party he had dispatched up the coast of Maine "are well fixt with armes: and are the best of all souldiers,"[44] and Johnson Harmon, returning from a scout up the Saco river in 1723, reported that "the 120 men that I have the Honour to Command [are] most of them Old Experienced Souldiers."[45] Benjamin Church recommended that soldiers employed on raids "be men of good reason and sense . . . for bad men are but a clog and hinderance to an army, being a trouble and vexation to good commanders, and so many mouths to devour the country's provision, and a hinderance to all good action."[46]

Offensive scouts varied greatly in size, from a handful of men to large companies numbering several hundred. But all operated on the march, or at least were supposed to operate, in a similar manner. As the main party followed a trail or a river, smaller scouts would be constantly detached to investigate signs of enemy activity and to prevent ambush.[47] The provincial governments often explicitly ordered that raiding parties and probes "take special care to avoid danger by ambusments, of being drawn under any disadvantage by the enemy in your marches, keeping out scouts and a forlorn hope before your main body."[48] The journal of a scout led by Captain John Cagon in September 1722 provides an excellent example of how scouts were conducted. The purpose of the scout was to probe for signs of enemy activity on the Merrimack River and up into the lands of the Penacook and Pequawket Indians.[49] Leaving Dunstable, Massachusetts, on September 18, the scout traveled in canoes up the Merrimack River. On the 19th they overturned a canoe and lost two cooking kettles and one gun; although "with much difficulty" they managed to recover the weapon. On the 20th they continued up the river, sending scouts along each bank to look for signs and possible ambush.

Every day they continued this same pattern, the main body on the river in canoes with flanking scouts on each bank. On the 22nd they camped at the mouth of the Contoocook River where the returning scouts reported that they had heard Indians "hallowing" nearby. The next morning Cagon sent out three parties; one of seven men up the Contoocook, another seven to the "Wenopessocket" river, and two men sent "about the mountains." All the scouts reported finding no sign. That night they heard a gunshot up the Contoocook, and, quickly seizing their weapons, left camp to investigate but found nothing. Cagon spent the next day camped at the Contoocook as well, sending scouts up the rivers again with the same negative results.

On September 25 they left the Merrimack and headed up the "Wenopessocket" River. As they neared present-day Laconia, their scouts found the tracks of some Indians who had been hunting a bear. Cagon immediately dispatched more scouts but they found no further sign. On the 28th they put their canoes in Lake Winnipesauke and crossed to the northeast side where they proceeded on foot toward Ossipee and the trail to Pequawket. At Ossipee Pond they discovered the tracks of another force of Englishmen, and "being discouraged" because this party was ahead of them, they retraced their steps back to Winnipesauke. High winds buffeted their canoes as they crossed the lake "(but by the goodness of God) we all got safe over a little before it was dark." They passed down the river (at present-day Weir's Beach) and camped on an island. On their return to the Merrimack they discovered more tracks that appeared to be hostile, but on closer examination Cagon and his men determined they were English. On October 2 they camped at Suncook Falls and arrived in Dunstable on the 3rd.[50]

A similar scout in 1707, using the same techniques, encountered much different results. In early February, Lieutenant Seth Wyman led his men into New Hampshire to the area around Monadnock Mountain. When they awoke on the morning of the 6th, the company gathered wood for fires to cook breakfast and warm themselves in the winter air. Wyman ordered two scouts of four men each to check for signs, sending one to the right and one to the left. He admonished them to be particularly careful not to confuse the sounds of their own company's hatchets with the enemy. "After they had bin upon the Scout about an hour, [he] Saw both Scouts returning together, running towards our Camp as men affrightened, and called to me at a distance to put out our fires, for they had discovered a Body of the Enemy." The right scout had indeed heard the sound of hatchets and, making a wide circle to make sure they were not their own men, came on a camp. The corporal approached the unknown force hidden in the smoke of their fire and heard voices that he believed were French and Indian. The corporal pulled his men back and, meeting up with the other scout, ran to warn their company. As Wyman conferred with his officers over a plan of action he found his anxious men crowded around him. "He bid them move off, Scatter, and stand on their own Guard, upon which three quarters of our men ran away homewards." The end result was a court martial for "a false report . . . of the discovery of the Indian Enemy . . . and for their returne home, in a mutinous disorderly manner."[51]

The ability to perform long-range offensive scouts was a skill honed throughout the early French wars, but Queen Anne's War proved to be pivotal in the development of those techniques that produced efficacious offensive raids and probes. During King William's War the ineffective use of deep probes and large raids can be attributed largely to inexperience. The employment of defensive patrols easily carried over from the earlier Indian wars, especially King Philip's, but the large raids undertaken in those earlier conflicts had been against adjacent targets. The experiences of King Philip's War did not anticipate the military complications of the French wars, and as a result the initial martial efforts of Massachusetts and New Hampshire achieved little success. For example, in 1690 Jeremiah Swain brought several hundred men to the Maine frontier but spent his time marching back and forth as a kind of giant patrol. The provincial governments of New England and their soldiers found that offensives against enemy targets in the French wars would require longer marches and greater logistical problems. Learning new strategies and tactics for this new kind of war would prove painful and frustrating.

In particular, the large raiding party led by John March and Daniel King in 1691 ended in disaster largely because of ignorance and misfortune. Ordered to clear the area north of the Merrimack River of the enemy before heading east "in search of the said Enemy French or Indians,"[52] the raid almost immediately encountered difficulties. As March and King led their company from Haverhill through Exeter to Portsmouth, they were forced to leave a considerable number of their men at Greenland due to sickness and poor firearms. This loss threatened to end the raid before it really started, but they were able to make up their losses by enlisting men in New Hampshire and Maine, including a company commanded by Captain Samuel Sherbourne of Hampton.[53]

However, this inauspicious beginning only presaged further difficulties. As the force was leaving Portsmouth Harbor they were fired on and detained by two alleged pirate ships. After providing depositions concerning the "herleburley with the Privateers,"[54] they finally sailed to Saco but found no evidence of enemy activity. March and King then took their company to Macquoit (Freeport, Maine) and marched to Pejepscot. Finding no sign of the enemy once again, they returned to Macquoit and their waiting vessels. During the embarkation, a large party of Indians opened fire from ambush, killing or wounding many of the soldiers remaining on shore, including, among the slain, Captain Samuel Sherbourne. March and King managed to retrieve the remainder of the shore party and, after a long firefight with the Indians on shore, brought their shattered command back to Portsmouth.[55]

The exploits of Benjamin Church provided an exception to the rather bleak record of offensive scouts during that first French war. Church was one of the few veterans of King Philip's War who was able to use his previous experience and adapt to the new larger kind of conflict. Using a combined force of about equal numbers of Indians and whites mostly recruited from Plymouth, Church participated in four major raids. The first in 1689 consisted principally of his arrival "in the nick of time" to help drive away an enemy force attacking the settlement at Casco Bay, an engagement known as the Battle of Brackett's Woods.[56] During the second raid in the fall of 1690, Church landed at Macquoit, marched to the abandoned Fort Andros at Pejepscot and then up the Androscoggin to an Indian fort where he killed several Indians, captured some important Indian women, and destroyed the structure. His officers at a council of war convinced him to end the raid so they returned to Macquoit and sailed to Casco Bay, now deserted after the French capture of Fort Loyal earlier that summer. While at Casco Bay he allowed his Indians to sleep on shore, where they were attacked by a force of French

Indians. Church disembarked the rest of his command and drove the attackers away. On returning to Portsmouth he wanted to enlist more soldiers and continue the raid, but the Bay government, shocked at the debts incurred over the Quebec expedition, begged poverty and disbanded his command.[57]

The third raid in 1692 attempted ambushes around Penobscot Bay, and then proceeded up the Kennebec to Teconnet (Waterville, Maine). The Indians burned their village at his approach but he did manage to destroy considerable stores of corn. Four years later his fourth raid went along the coast of Maine and into the Bay of Fundy where he plundered and burned some French settlements. Superseded in command by a Lt-Colonel Hathorne, Church wanted to raid the principal Indian village at Norridgewock but Hathorne refused. The raid ended with a half-hearted attempt to take a small French fort and truck house on the St. John River.[58]

In all these raids Church used techniques that would become common in later wars. When he attacked the Indian fort on the Androscoggin in 1690, he had his men drop their knapsacks to free their movements and then ordered "the captains to draw out of their several companies sixty of their meanest men, to be a guard to the Doctor and knapsacks."[59] Unattended packs invited ambush, as John Lovewell would later discover. Church also made extensive use of whaleboats in his raids. "Being farr nimbler then any pinnace, able to carry 15 men each being about 36 foot long, yet so light that two men can easily carry one of them," in the hands of his Plymouth men and the "whaling Indians" of Cape Cod they were an effective means of transportation for raiding parties along the Maine coast and on the waterways of the northeast, and "of so great use for surprizing of places and vessels in the night, their padles making no noise as oares do."[60]

While Church's raids achieved variable results, it is significant that he consistently put together forces and engaged in long-distance offensive raids. Of course, it helped that Church had companies of Indians as they were the real experts. With the exception of James Converse, who accompanied Church on his second raid and conducted an offensive scout to Teconnet in May 1693, few English raiding parties penetrated far or accomplished much. In addition, military coverage of the frontier lacked consistency as fiscal pressures compelled the drastic reduction of provincial forces during the winter to a handful of soldiers posted in garrisons.[61] Both the provincial governments and their officers had a great deal to learn, but enlightenment would come during Queen Anne's War.

That war began with the same inefficiency and misfortune that had dogged most provincial raiding efforts in the previous conflict. In late September 1703

John March led 360 men on a raid to Pequawket "but through the difficulty of the Passage, and the unskilfulness of the Guides, they returned without Discovery."[62] Although March returned in November with four hundred men and managed to kill six Indians and destroy some corn,[63] Governor Joseph Dudley reported to the Board of Trade in December that the distance to the Indian villages "is such that our provision is spent before we can get to their headquarters; the forces were out 12 daies each time and necessarily carried all their provisions in theyr snap-sacks, being unpassable for horses, and so were forced to return before they could come to Pequawkit."[64] Yet two years later Dudley informed that same body he had kept out constant scouts and that "the people are so sensible of the benefit they have by these hard marches, wherein no souldier has more subsistence for 25 dayes than he carrys out on his back besides his arms, that they are very patient of the service."[65]

Several developments in provincial strategy and tactics produced this change. First, the governments of Massachusetts and New Hampshire greatly increased the number of soldiers involved in patrols, probes, and raids compared to King William's War. These "constant marches" kept the Indians away from their territories, forcing them to remove to Canada and thus increase the travel distance to the English frontier. By 1706 some of the leading citizens of New Hampshire and Maine involved in the mast trade were able to report to Whitehall, somewhat optimistically perhaps, that "the Indians in all the parts near us are beaten and burnt out of their forts, and their hunting and fishing destroyed to that degree that the husbandry and masting of this Province is secured and proceeds to as good effect as in time of peace."[66] In addition, the increased presence of provincial soldiers in the woods apparently forced a change in French and Indian tactics from the larger forces of Frontenac's day to smaller parties that were less easy to detect. Finally, the augmented use of scouts provided much-needed experience for provincial officers and men.

One of these "constant marches" in 1704 saw the last appearance of Benjamin Church in command of a field force. Church drew up a list of recommendations for the Bay government concerning this raiding party and long-range scouts in general, which provides some insight into his methods. He suggested that all whaleboats be fitted with leather loops and poles so they could be lifted over rocks, that two brass kettles be sent with every boat to cook food, and that all soldiers wear "Indian shoes" to protect the whaleboats and canoes. Church further suggested that leather, hemp, and wax be brought along to replace worn-out shoes. The raiding party should also take hatchets or light axes, "made pretty broad," to widen carrying places for the whaleboats. Church felt whale men should be hired to run the boats, as long as they could be released for whaling in the fall.[67] Samuel Penhallow reported that it was the custom of the men under Church's command "to rest in the Day, and row in the Night; and never fire at an Indian if they could reach him with a Hatchet, for fear of alarming them."[68] On this occasion Church again raided along the Maine coast and into the Bay of Fundy, the principal damage done being the burning of Grand Pré, the destruction of the dykes in that area, and the capture of French settlers to exchange for English prisoners.[69]

A second development that enhanced the effectiveness of offensive scouts was the inauguration of winter raids. In December 1703, when he reported the inconclusive results of John March's raids of the previous fall, Dudley informed the Board of Trade that he was preparing his forces for a winter march on the enemy. According to his reports, both the Assembly and Council of Massachusetts showed reluctance to support his design, preferring to disband most of the provincial soldiers for the winter as they had always done in the past to save the cost.[70] Dudley pushed forward his plan, however, and found some support in his northern colony. The New Hampshire Council and Assembly urged the use of winter marches as "it ever hath been judged the best season in the winter to go to the enemy's headquarters; they cannot be pursued so well in the spring."[71]

On February 9, 1704, Winthrop Hilton of New Hampshire led a force of provincial soldiers on snowshoes to Pequawket. Winthrop arrived at the village on the 16th and found it had been deserted for about six weeks, then brought his forces home again.[72] From the standpoint of the enemy killed and crops destroyed, the raid accomplished very little, but the psychological impact was tremendous. Hilton ended his journal of the march by concluding that "the winter time is the onely time ever to march against the Indian Enemy—both for their discovery and the health and least danger of our People."[73] Dudley was so pleased with the result he sent a copy of Hilton's journal to the Board of Trade, adding in a postscript that "this march was made upon the snow a yard Deep, every man in snow shoes with twenty dayes provisions upon small hand [sleds] carrying each four Mens provisions and of three hundred men in the Expedition no man returned sick."[74]

Acts were now passed in both New Hampshire and Massachusetts, ordering frontier communities to provide snowshoes for the use of the provincial soldiers posted there. "This season," observed Samuel Penhallow, "which before was dreaded as most hazardous, was now the time of greatest safety, and of less difficulty in travelling."[75] There is evidence that indicates the Eastern Indians had long feared the New Englanders might adopt this strategy.

The party, which devastated York in January 1692 had been out scouting the woods for soldiers, "haveing been (as they say) advised by some of Sandy beach Captives that the Bostoners were provideing Many Snow Shoes and Designed a Considerable army out this winter to Disrest them at Some of their head quarters which has made them Very uneasy this winter."[76]

Now Winthrop Hilton had proved it could be done. Dudley wrote in April 1704 that he had "given this Country as well as the Indians conviction that we can beare the frost and travell with our Victuals as long as they."[77] Winter raids became common, with Hilton out almost every winter until his death in 1710.[78] His most successful raid occurred in January 1707, when soldiers under his command surprised and killed more than twenty Indians near Black Point, Maine.[79]

Although winter raids would continue throughout the rest of the early French wars, care had to be taken that early thaws did not ruin the design. Winthrop Hilton's original plan for his 1707 raid had to be curtailed when the "mildness of the winter prevented his going so far as expected."[80] Johnson Harmon, an officer with considerable raiding experience, returned exasperated from a scout that had been ordered for late February 1723. Harmon led 120 men with snowshoes and moccasins up the Saco River but found that the ice in the rivers had already broken up, forcing him to terminate the raid early. "It's a great grief to the perticular officers and no less to my Selfe," wrote Harmon, "that wee were Obliged to march into the woods in such a season when we had not a rational prospect of doing our Countrey service."[81]

A third important innovation commencing simultaneously with the winter marches was the encouragement of scalp hunters. Bounties for Indian scalps had been offered in previous wars, but the governments of Massachusetts and New Hampshire now offered a larger reward for those who "maintain themselves free from the Province charge."[82] The initial rate was £40 per scalp, £8 pounds higher than volunteer provincial soldiers in "Her Majesty's Pay," and the scale would increase as the wars progressed.[83] Both Dudley and the parsimonious provincial assemblies seized on the concept of soldiers who would be paid only if successful, but Dudley was not without reservations. Essentially they would be freebooters recognizing little government control. As Dudley observed to Lieutenant Governor John Usher of New Hampshire in late November 1703, "I am fearful the volunteers when they please will expect to disband and break in upon the right of the Government how to use them when we please. Here has been a great noise of volunteers in these parts, but are not the least benefit, and the souldiers must know wee can march them when we please without the word volunteers writt upon them."[84]

But two weeks later he urged Usher to "encourage the bussness of Volunteers."[85] The concept of scalp hunting would prove popular and increase the number of soldiers in the woods. The Reverend Thomas Smith of Falmouth recorded in his journal in 1745 that the "People seem wonderfully spirited to go out after the Indians. Four companies in this town and many more in other towns are fitting for it; the government offer four hundred pounds for the scalp of a man to those who go out at their own expense, and three hundred and ten pounds to those who have provision from the province."[86]

Eventually the government exerted some control on scalp hunters by regularizing their position. Companies of "snowshoe men" were raised in frontier communities commanded by officers with provincial commissions.[87] Unlike scouts taken from provincial forces posted on the frontier for months at a time, snowshoe companies drawn from men living on the frontier received wages only when they were actually on a raid but were paid for scalps as volunteers. Thus the government subordinated some of the scalp hunters through the commissions and wages.

The use of offensive scouts reached its ultimate expression during Dummer's War. The Eastern Indian tribes had never really been satisfied with the peace arrangements that ended Queen Anne's War, and the Massachusetts government accused French ambassadors in their midst, especially traders like St. Castine and Jesuit priests like Sebastian Rale at Norridgewock, of encouraging this discontent.[88] At the first sign of trouble, the Bay government sent two hundred men under Shadrach Walton to the Maine frontier. Walton's mission was essentially to "show the colors" through active scouting and thus discourage the Indians from further trouble.[89] Tensions gradually increased, however, over the next two years with the Indians venting most of their frustration against Fort St. George and the English increasing the number of both defensive and offensive scouts. In July 1722 the Indians conducted a half-hearted siege against St. George while a provincial scout under Johnson Harmon and Samuel Moody killed eighteen Indians near Pejepscot.[90] Governor Samuel Shute acknowledged the obvious and declared war on the Eastern Indians.

But there was a major difference in this conflict. Although the French government encouraged the animosity between the Eastern Indians and the English, there could be no direct involvement because Great Britain and France were not at war, thus depriving the Indians of French officers for their larger raiding parties and logistical support. Also, there would be no expensive expeditions to mount against Canada. The results would be disastrous for French policy and for the Eastern tribes.

The most successful raid conducted against the Eastern Indians in any of the wars occurred in August 1724, when a force of provincial soldiers destroyed the village of Norridgewock and the principal promoter of French policies on the eastern frontier, the Jesuit Sebastian Rale. The raiding party, numbering 205 white men and three Mohawk Indians, including the old scout Christian, and commanded by Johnson Harmon and Jeremiah Moulton from York, Maine, left Fort Richmond on August 8 in seventeen whaleboats. Arriving at Teconnet on the 9th, they left the whaleboats under the protection of an officer and forty men and proceeded on foot. As they approached the village, Harmon took sixty men to destroy the cornfields while Moulton, after ordering ten men to guard the packs, attacked the village with the remainder of the force. After a brief firefight they charged through the village, driving the Indians across the river.[91] The raiding party returned to Fort Richmond on the 16th and Johnson Harmon was in Boston to make his report on the 22nd.[92]

The provincial forces suffered no casualties. They returned with twenty-six scalps, and they estimated that fifty to eighty more Indians died in the river.[93] Among the slain were at least seven principal chiefs of the Norridgewocks and Sebastian Rale. Samuel Penhallow called the raid on Norridgewock "the greatest Victory we have obtained in the three or four last Wars; and it may be as noble an Exploit (all things considered) as ever happened in the time of King Philip."[94] Besides the loss in lives and Indian leadership, the elimination of the influence of Rale proved the greatest blow. The village of Norridgewock did not disappear, but after the blow struck that August its inhabitants never were the threat they had been in the past.[95]

A second stroke against the Eastern Indians, this time the Pequawkets on the upper Saco River, involved the rise and fall of the King of the Scalp Hunters—John Lovewell. With a bounty of £100 for soldiers not in the government's pay, scalp hunting had become popular among the more adventurous on the frontier. Raising companies mainly from communities along the Merrimack River, Lovewell led three raids into Winnipesauke-Ossipee-Pequawket region. In December 1724 his first raid netted him one scalp and a captive boy, but in February 1725 he and his men took ten scalps and returned in triumph to Dover, New Hampshire, waving the bloody trophies. On April 16 he left Dunstable with a force of forty-seven men, three of whom turned back and another became so sick that Lovewell was forced to build a simple fort at Ossipee Lake where he left the sick man, the doctor, and eight others. Lovewell then pushed on to Pequawket where his company was ambushed and fought an all-day battle with seventy to eighty Indians in which Lovewell and fourteen others died and several others were wounded.

The Indians broke off the action late in the afternoon and the surviving Englishmen made their way home.[96]

Apparently Lovewell's earlier successes generated an overconfidence that resulted in an unaccountable neglect of elementary precautions. Lovewell did not post a guard over the knapsacks when he and his men went to investigate the report of a gun. The Pequawkets found the packs and laid an ambush. Ironically, Lovewell had left such a guard over the knapsacks when he killed the ten Indians in February, but the omission of this elementary precaution on his later raid probably cost him his life.[97]

Like that other overconfident Indian fighter, George Armstrong Custer, John Lovewell became a greater hero in death than he had been in life. Eulogies and songs were composed in his honor and for the men who accompanied him.[98] The war itself was often referred to as "Lovewell's War" due to the fame of this slain scalp hunter. The impact on the Pequawkets was also profound. No accurate account of their casualties is known, but they did lose at least one principal chief and many warriors.[99] Historian Charles Clark believed the defeat of the Pequawkets opened the interior of New Hampshire, and the bloody results of Lovewell's fight contributed a great deal to this.[100] Like the Norridgewocks, the Pequawkets did not disappear, but their military significance diminished greatly after Dummer's War.

With the power of the Eastern Indian tribes weakened, the provincial governments placed less emphasis on major raids during King George's War; however, the use of defensive patrols and small probing offensive scouts continued to be quite extensive. So extensive, in fact, that the Committee on Scouts of the New Hampshire Assembly reported "that from the 23rd of May 1744 to the 24th of August following we find Grants for men to be kept in his Majesty's service on the frontiers and at the fort [William and Mary] to the amount of 11,270 days."[101] John Goffe and Eleazer Melvin were only two of many men who led the small probing, offensive raids into enemy territory.[102] Both men had been part of Lovewell's company during his ill-fated raid to Pequawket. Goffe was very active in scouting on the New Hampshire frontier. In January 1746 he led twenty men on snowshoes, in May he was out again with fifty, and in June he went with thirteen.[103] Melvin, while stationed at Fort Dummer, led a particularly harrowing raid to the shores of Lake Champlain in 1747.[104]

The use of larger raiding forces in King George's War was also inhibited by other military considerations. With the French once again involved in the conflict, the governments of Massachusetts and New Hampshire were all the more determined to conquer New France. Thus the men who would have been used on major raids volunteered for expeditions. They went to Louisbourg in 1745, and the following summer joined another force raised for an intended assault on Canada, which never materialized. In October 1746 news arrived of a French fleet sent to attack New England and more soldiers were enlisted to defend the coast. When the French fleet met disaster, the provincial governments kept this army together for one year in anticipation of an assault on Montreal. Eleazer Melvin, who served as a lieutenant at Louisbourg, enlisted in the latter force and spent most of 1747 drilling, marching, and waiting in vain to attack Canada.[105] Although he had been active in scouting during 1746, John Goffe also enlisted in the provincial forces raised that October; as part of Atkinson's regiment he spent the next year cooped up in the small fort at Lake Winnipesauke.[106]

The scouting system as part of the military strategy of New England was not without its critics. Both contemporaries and subsequent historians have questioned the value of the patrols and raids and of the competency of the soldiers participating in them. The nineteenth-century historian Samuel Adams Drake, in particular, diminished the efforts of the provincial soldiers. "It being worse than useless to play at hide and seek with these vigilant foemen," wrote Drake, "who first showed themselves in one place and then in another, far distant, the authorities persevered in the plan of hunting them down in their own villages. Usually it was next to impossible for white men to approach them undiscovered, and after long and frightful marches a few deserted wigwams would be all that the disappointed rangers could find."[107] Time and again the New England governments sent their soldiers into Indian territory only to find no trace of the enemy, or even worse, to have that enemy sweep in behind to kill and burn at will. Jeremiah Swain's "march [in 1689] . . . disclosed the weakness of the whole system of defense; for Swain had no sooner uncovered the towns in his rear, after taking with him every available man that could be spared, than the Indians swooped down upon Durham."[108]

Drake saved his most acerbic comments for his evaluation of Benjamin Church. In Drake's opinion, "his ill-fortune dogged him like his shadow." His 1696 raid along the coast of Maine ended "like the others that had gone before it, in disappointment and disgrace,"[109] and in 1704 he failed to take Port Royal when the opportunity presented itself. In Drake's view Church, "with a force at hand fully competent to the task before it," failed to take advantage of his strength and contented himself "with a mere idle demonstration." "This ridiculous affair," wrote Drake, " . . . looked in the main as a failure, and if adaption of means to ends be looked to, it was one."[110]

Drake's criticisms only echo some contemporary observers. Benjamin Church's raids, especially his last one, produced mixed reactions. "Notwithstanding the Fatigue that this worthy Gentleman had undergone," wrote Samuel Penhallow, "and the Dangers he had run; the Spoil he had done, and the Victories he Wan, yet he could not escape the Censures of many. Some indeed extoled his Valour and Conduct even to an Hyperbole, while others endeavoured to lessen it With as much Disgrace and Infamy. Some thought he did too much, others too little."[111]

Drake and the other critics of provincial scouting efforts seem to gauge success by one criterion—body count. Raids were only successful if they resulted in a large number of enemy killed, thus the expense of increased scouts during Queen Anne's War led to that often quoted observation "that every Indian we had killed or taken, cost the Country at least a Thousand Pounds."[112] But attrition, not scalps, proved to be the real purpose of the raids and patrols. It was not a separate strategy as Guy Chet implies, but it was one real purpose of the raids. "We may . . . destroy their corn and houses," wrote Governor Dudley to the Board of Trade, "but no likelihood of seeing them, who will have their scouts out, and march off as we approach them . . . however the experience of the best men that have at any time been here can advise to no better method then by constant marches, especially in the winter to dislodge and starve them."[113] Samuel Penhallow observed that "although the Number [of Indians] that we destroyed . . . seems inconsiderable to what they did of ours, yet by Cold, Hunger, and Sickness, at least a third of them was wasted since the War begun . . . which made the Old Men weary of the War, and to covet Peace."[114]

Chet agreed with this assessment. "The English owed their victories in these wars, "he wrote, "not to their tactical effectiveness of their fighting forces against Indian troops but to their commitment to a campaign of attrition against Indian agricultural fields, grain stores and fisheries."[115] But Chet also indicates that this lack of success, namely body count, reveals incompetence, or at least "tacitical ineffectiveness" on the part of New England provincial soldiers.[116] Proffering a familiar theme, the Canadian historian W. J. Eccles believed that the British army conquered New France only after it was proven that the English colonists had been bested in *la petite guerre* by the French and their Indian allies. "The English colonials [could not] wage this type of warfare. For success it required men who could live in the wilderness and strike swiftly like Indians; who could march great distances on snowshoes in the bitter, morale-destroying cold, carrying their meagre supplies; and who could go into the attack at the end of a journey that in itself was a severe test of a man's endurance."[117] In particular the mystique of the *coureur de bois* dominates this interpretation. The *coureur de bois* were Frenchmen involved in the fur trade. Acting as agents and middlemen between the

Indian tribes and the French government, they acquired an intimate knowledge of Indian customs and language, as well as the ability to lead Indian raiding parties against English targets. According to the traditional interpretation, the economy of New England, based on agriculture, naval stores, fishing, and trade, did not produce an equal to the "woods runners" of New France. As John Ferling wrote, provincial raids "were often carried out with considerable zeal—though precious little skill."[118]

However, it should be noted that the Canadians *accompanied* Indians on these raids, and they did *not* do this on their own. The difference may only be in the English lack of Indian allies, not in capabilities. Under the leadership of men such as Benjamin Church, Winthrop Hilton, Johnson Harmon, John Lovewell, and John Goffe, the provincial soldiers were able to traverse great distances even in winter, carry their meager supplies, and attack the enemy at the end of their journey when they could be found. In order to wage the war of attrition that Chet focuses on, the New England provincial soldiers had to learn the skills to traverse the wilderness to destroy those Indians' supplies. John Grenier, in *The First Way of War: American War Making on the Frontier*, pointed out that "the most important lesson to emerge from the campaigns to the Eastward [in King William's War] was the realization that Americans, if necessary, could alone be effective rangers."[119] Grenier also correctly asserts that over time certain individuals and families became attuned to the way of woods war. Speaking of the careers of John Gorham and his descendants, Grenier wrote "that ranging was a way of life for successive generations of New Englanders among whom a 'corporate knowledge' of ranger warfare passed down from generation to generation."[120]

While the blows struck against the Norridgewock and Pequawket tribes during Dummer's War were the most conspicuous achievements of the provincial scouting parties, it is unknown how many lives were also saved by diligent patrols and raiding parties. The tactical adjustment made by the French and Indians during Queen Anne's War from the larger raids to smaller parties may have been forced by the growing numbers of provincial soldiers in the woods. This development was a mixed blessing. While preventing the wholesale destruction of communities, the smaller parties were less easy to detect, and thus, in the words of Samuel Penhallow, "did much more mischief then in larger."[121] Small groups of ten to twenty could slip in undetected to kill unwary inhabitants, and this sort of incursion could not be totally stopped by the English any more than the French could stop the Iroquois, as even W. J. Eccles admits.[122] The provincial governments of New England knew the solution to this problem was the reduction of Canada itself.

5

Expeditions

The Anglo-American Partnership

To critics of the New England provincial soldiers, nothing illustrates the chasm between the soldiers' ineffectiveness and the superiority of the French more than the inability of the English to emulate their enemy and assault French communities. "They had no body of men," wrote W. J. Eccles, "capable of traveling through hundreds of miles of trackless wilderness . . . to attack New France."[1] Jeremy Belknap observed that "the [French] kept out small parties continually engaged in killing, scalping and taking prisoners . . . on the other hand, the English attended only to the defence of the frontiers; and that in such a manner, as to leave them for the most part insecure. No parties were sent to harass the settlements of the French."[2] Some contemporaries agreed with Belknap's observation and lamented that the New England governments concentrated too much on defense, and "being onely on defencive, we waste away."[3] But as far as can be determined, the provincial governments never considered raids against French villages as an efficacious form of offensive strategy. Thus it is unreasonable to assume the provincial soldiers of New England were incapable of emulating their Canadian counterparts when they never attempted, or even contemplated, such an action. Whether they were capable or not will never be known because they never attempted it. From the beginning of the French wars the people of New England agreed with the sentiments of Governor Joseph Dudley that "all this unspeakable Trouble and Cost would be saved by rooting out the French at Quebeck and Mont Real."[4] The solution to the French and the Indian problem was the reduction of Canada itself and that would involve European military methods of siege achieved by major expeditions of men, artillery, and naval support.

The story of the New England expeditions against New France has been frequently told. The expeditions under consideration here include the attacks led by Sir William Phips in 1690 against Port Royal and Quebec (the former a success; the latter, a disaster); the double assault on Port Royal in 1707, and the more fruitful siege in 1710; the Walker expedition of 1711 against Quebec; Louisbourg in 1745; and the planned (and prepared for) expeditions against Quebec in 1709 and 1746, and Montreal in 1747, which never materialized. Provincial soldiers also participated in Admiral Edward Vernon's expedition against Cartagena, but unlike the attacks on Canada, colonial leaders were not involved in the conception and planning of this attack, and their soldiers only served as warm bodies to flesh out an essentially English operation.

To provincial strategists, the reduction of Canada meant the capture of Quebec. Serving New France both as capital and principal port, its capture would not only be a crushing symbolic and political blow, but it would cut the colony off from French supplies and military support. While the first major attempt to capture the city in 1690 failed, the strategy employed the well-known simultaneous two-pronged assault on Montreal and Quebec; this was sound and ultimately would be successful. But the failure of the 1690 expedition also proved that the New England governments did not have the logistical or naval capabilities, or even the financial base, to reduce Canada on their own.[5] The French problem in the New World would have to be settled in partnership with the London government.

Beyond Quebec itself, the French strongholds in the Maritimes seemed at first to be a reasonable target for provincial forces. From their ports in Nova Scotia, and later Cape Breton, the French dispatched privateers to attack New England commerce and fisheries, and they supplied their Eastern Indian allies with military stores. The New England governments understood that the capture of Nova Scotia and Cape Breton would not reduce Canada, but the elimination of these privateers and the weakening of the French alliance with the Eastern Indians were important secondary objectives. Because of their close proximity to New England and their remoteness from the center of French power in Canada, the provincial governments felt confident that the maritime targets were well within the capabilities of their military forces, and certainly the victory at Port Royal in the spring of 1690 seemed to confirm this judgment. However, that victory only delayed the inevitable conclusion underlined by the subsequent double failure to retake Port Royal in 1707—the colonies could not undertake expeditions on their own. After 1707 all colonial attempts to assault Canada, including the Maritime provinces, required the assistance of the British government.

Military expeditions in the eighteenth century consisted of many essential components. The successful expedition required soldiers for the investment and/or assault; soldiers for a garrison after reduction of the objective; artillery to reduce fortifications; powder and shot; engineers to conduct the siege and gunners to lay the artillery; provisions to feed and clothe the army during and after the attack; transport for the soldiers and provisions; warships

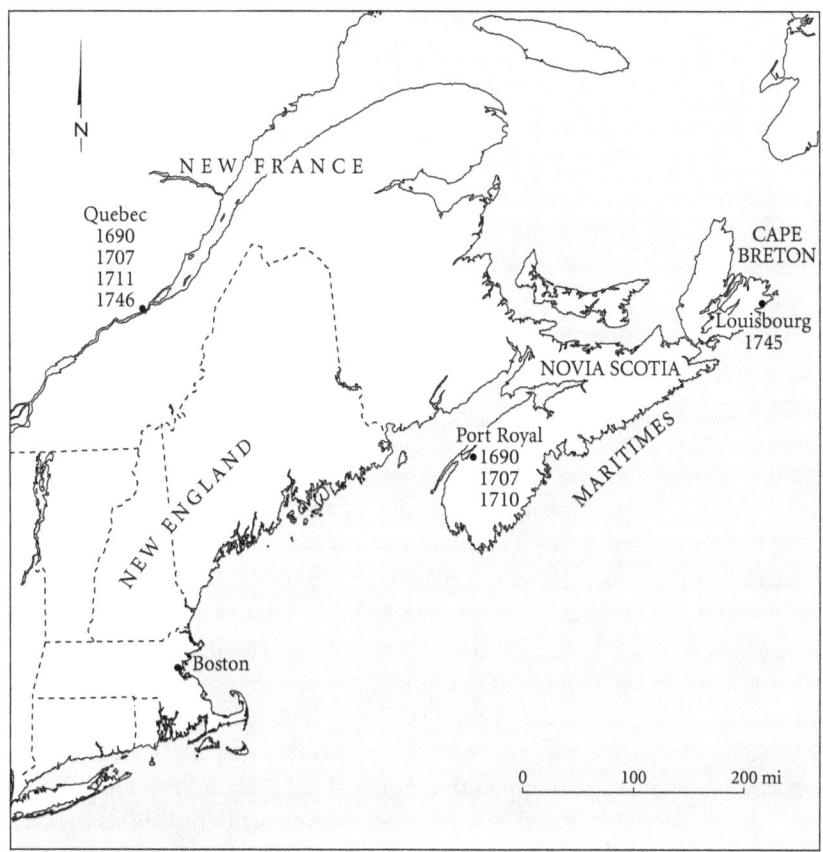

Targets for Expeditions, 1690–1748

to aid in the siege and protect the transport fleet from counterattacks; and, finally, the money to pay for it all. In 1690 the governments of New England twice attempted to provide all the components for major attacks on Canada and came up short both times. The disaster at Quebec is well known, and although the early assault on Port Royal was successful, the provincial army lacked a key ingredient for ultimate success, namely, the troops to garrison the fort. While, as an anonymous member of the Quebec expedition recorded, "the New Englanders are not discouraged by one repulse,"[6] they were discouraged by the cost and their own inadequacies. Thus a military partnership developed between the provincial governments and London in which the latter provided all the components for expeditions that were difficult or impossible for the colonies to contribute.

Having said this, England's willingness and ability to participate in this partnership developed over time. The historian John Brewer has illustrated how England's ability to wage war, particularly on land, was minimal in 1688 at the time of the Glorious Revolution; he found that England had been "sheltered" from the "increased scale of war" on the continent.[7] The Glorious Revolution and the war with Louis XIV changed all that. Still, England had to gradually increase its commitment to a large military establishment. Brewer wrote that "Britain was able to shoulder an ever-more ponderous burden of military commitments thanks to a radical increase in taxation, the development of public deficit finance (a national debt) on an unprecedented scale, and the growth of a sizable administration devoted to organizing the fiscal and military activities of the state."[8] It is a mistake to think of the English military in 1690 as the same that dominated during the Seven Years' War period. Through all the intervening wars the English gradually increased their military commitment and machinery, and the growth of the Anglo-American partnership reflects England's increasing ability to wage war as much as, or more than, developments in the colonies.

The first New England contribution to the Anglo-American partnership was of provincial soldiers for the main assault or fighting force. "There are men Enough in New England," observed one member of the 1690 Quebec expedition, "that will offer themselves as Volunteirs."[9] Enlistment quotas established for each colony were usually filled, although not without effort, especially when recent disappointments remained fresh in the public's memory. The ill-fated Port Royal expedition of 1707 created great difficulties for the Province of New Hampshire in raising troops for the intended assault on Canada in 1709.[10] And the tremendous disappointment accompanying that aborted affair caused problems for recruiting officers the following summer, as did the alleged mistreatment of the soldiers at Louisbourg following its surrender in 1745. In addition to previous disappointments, the normal strain of conducting a war hurt the effort of recruiting. Jeremy Belknap reported that New Hampshire managed to raise one hundred men for the Walker expedition in 1711 despite the fact that half of the available manpower was already serving on the frontier.[11]

As their second major contribution, the colonies provided provisions for both their own soldiers and any forces sent from England. A two- to three-month supply was considered a minimum initial allocation, and food that could be easily preserved was preferred.[12] Salted meat, hard biscuits, and grain were the staples of a military diet, although troops were fed fresh victuals while waiting for embarkation.[13] If the provisions were not available from public sources, the assemblies instructed their commissary agents to purchase or impress food from private individuals. The Louisbourg expedition created a considerable strain on public supplies of foodstuffs due to the size of the force being raised. When New Hampshire found that no pork was available in Boston, the council instructed that warrants be issued "for impressing such and so much pork as shall be necessary for the present emergency from those persons that have any to spare more than what is necessary for the use of their respective families."[14] During the second half of Queen Anne's War and throughout King George's War, annual preparations for major expeditions, whether realized or not, drained the colonies of foodstuffs. Because provincial soldiers spent the summer of 1709 drilling and eating while waiting in vain for British support, colonial leaders found provisions, especially pork and beef, to be scarce the following summer when raising the expedition for Port Royal.[15] In preparing for the Walker expedition in 1711, the New England governments discovered that after three years of providing for major military campaigns it was "impossible to provide pork and pease, etc. sufficient for the fleet and forces, [and] proposed there be two fish days in a week for the forces coming from Great Brittain," and they asked New York to supply the fish.[16]

In the end, the middle colonies offered to provide the bulk of the supplies for the expedition. However, the governor of New York would not let the ships carrying the foodstuffs sail without an armed escort, so when the British arrived in Boston, they found no provisions waiting. The disaffected British Quartermaster General, Richard King, pressed the Bay government to provide food for his soldiers and sailors. Local communities around Boston began to send in fresh provisions, mostly on the hoof, but King discovered the amounts were "not sufficient for a quarter of our troops. And all other things to be provided, were brought us with that sloath and indifference." A "diligent search was made for all the provisions in town that were proper to carry to sea," and King secured quantities of wheat, rye, and Indian corn to make bread. The provision ships from New York arrived two weeks later.

When he found the colonial transport ships not prepared or provisioned, King vented his frustrations in his journal. "The reluctancy and ill nature that these people shewed to serve us and forward the Expedition upon all occasions before: did not near so fully demonstrate their preverse and wicked intentions as this great neglect: it being evident to anybody that has seen this country, that they could fitt out and man twice the number of vessels they were to furnish for this Expedition in much less time than they had to do it in." Like most British officers in the eighteenth century, King believed the needs of the King's troops came first, and he had little compassion or understanding for colonials or their problems.[17]

The withdrawal of these foodstuffs from the stores of New England communities created both hardships for the inhabitants and for the opportunity for profiteering.[18] In *The Urban Crucible*, Gary Nash described the tension created by war shortages and the clash between the traditional duty of government to ensure minimal subsistence at a just price and the new economic theory of supply and demand. In particular, Nash related the story of Andrew Belcher, one of Boston's largest grain merchants, who was appointed Commissary General for the Bay government. Contracted to supply provisions for the four hundred Royal marines coming to aid the 1710 Port Royal expedition, Belcher, as a grain merchant, bought up all available grain supplies and, when the price had risen accordingly, he sold the grain to himself as Commissary General for a tidy profit. The frustrations of the general population over the shortage of bread and high prices exploded when Belcher attempted to export the surplus rather than reintroduce the grain into the local economy, an explosion that included mob attacks on Belcher's ships and warehouses.[19]

When the duration of expeditions became extended, or their commencements were delayed, the depletion of the initial allocation of provisions increased logistical difficulties. In addition, as the soldiers' personal wardrobes wore out, clothing and shoes added to the problems of provincial commissary agents. The length of the Louisbourg campaign exacerbated the problem of supply as the forces raised at the end of February 1745 began to exhaust their provisions by April, weeks before they made their landing at Gabarus Bay.[20] On April 10, William Pepperrell wrote to John Osbourne, Chairman of the Committee of War, that the army had no more than thirty days' provisions, and that it would be a shame to "fail in our attempt, for want of the necessaries of life with which our country is so richly supplied."[21]

After the fall of Louisbourg the shortage of provisions and clothing continued. The commissary agent for the New Hampshire regiment in particular earned the censure of the soldiers whom he served. A group of officers complained to the New Hampshire Assembly that there had been "a general cry of injustice and oppression against our Commissary throughout the regiment, during the greater part of the siege; and that, besides the great uneasiness occasioned by the soldiers being denied their just allowance, the discontent was increased and aggravated by an uncompassionate refusal of necessaries to the sick." The officers desired a committee be established to investigate the commissary, and they were convinced "there was a just ground for the general discontent and uneasiness, [and] that his tender mercies were cruelty." Because of his "fraud, injustice and oppression," the New Hampshire soldiers "endured hazard and hardships with intrepidity, when almost naked and quite lousie, without flinching from shot or shell, and being on duty twenty-four hours at a time . . . without one morsel of meat, or one drop of spirits . . . (and nothing better to drink than ill tasted, purging water) during the greater part of the siege."[22]

Pepperrell informed Governor William Shirley in early August that the provincial forces on the whole were destitute of clothing and for all intents and purposes were naked and barefoot. He wrote that the shoes that had been sent were too small and the shirts too short.[23] In replying to Pepperrell's complaints, John Osbourne indicated that the Committee of War was trying to supply the soldiers' needs, but procurement was difficult. The Bay government had impressed tailors to make more clothing and cordwainers to make shoes, and Osbourne reported that his committee was "daily picking up all that we can lay our hands on, yet do not expect to send full supply till some woolen goods arrive from England."[24]

Once the soldiers had been mustered and the provisions gathered, they had to be transported to the target, and that required the impressment or hire of provincial merchant and fishing vessels. Sir William Phips's Quebec fleet in 1690 consisted of thirty-two such craft, of all sizes and descriptions,[25] and the Port Royal expedition of 1710 numbered twenty.[26] Perhaps the greatest colonial fleet accompanied William Pepperrell to Louisbourg. It contained ninety-odd transport vessels and about a dozen assorted small warships.[27] As provincial authorities closed their ports until expeditions actually sailed to prevent disclosure of their intentions to the French, owners willingly loaned their vessels to the governments so they would continue to earn money.[28] But like the consumption of provisions, the lack of trade hurt the general economy, and a delay or extended operation only aggravated the situation. For example, even after the capture of Louisbourg, many vessels had to remain in government service to transport further shipments of supplies and replacements and thus were unable to return to trade or fishing.[29]

As noted earlier, while generally confident in the capability and enthusiasm of their people to support major expeditions, the New England government officials knew they could not undertake the reduction of Canada totally on their own.[30] However, convincing British government officials, whose eyes were firmly fixed on European affairs, that it was in their best interest to assist the colonies in the capture of Canada proved to be difficult at best. The colonial lobby used none-too-gentle prodding to shift the gaze of Whitehall across the Atlantic and provide the necessary support by approaching the subject through the London government's Achilles' heel—the pocket book. Provincial agents and leaders emphasized that beyond the elimination of the cost of the war itself, the French colony would provide England with an unlimited source of furs and fish, and, most important, masts, hemp, pitch, and tar for the British navy.[31]

Even after convincing the British of the rewards for taking Canada, the provincial governments had to contend with the fearsome and complicated bureaucracy of an eighteenth-century mercantile government—a tangled maze best illustrated by the preparation for the 1709 Quebec expedition. On July 29, 1708, Samuel Vetch, that ambitious and somewhat unscrupulous Boston merchant,[32] presented a lengthy and detailed proposal for the reduction of Canada before the Board of Trade. Entitled "Canada Surveyed," Vetch's proposal enumerated the advantages to be gained, including the end of a considerable financial drain caused by the war (Vetch said a half of one year's loss would pay for the reduction), and the wealth of furs, fish, grain, and naval stores to be found. To realize this tremendous financial opportunity, the British government needed only to provide two battalions of regulars and six men-of-war. New England would provide a thousand soldiers with transport while the middle colonies launched a force of 1,500 against Montreal in the classic two-pronged assault.[33] The Board of Trade sent the proposal to Secretary of State Henry Boyle on August 4, and a week later Boyle wrote back urging the plan be given every consideration.[34]

Throughout the remainder of the summer and that fall the plan underwent study and analysis. In early November the Board of Trade asked Vetch to clarify certain points in his plan and he obliged on the 17th. Vetch stated that the New England colonies would have one thousand men with the best officers, three months' provisions, transports, and pilots ready by the end of April. London would dispatch a frigate to escort these transports to the rendezvous with the British warships off the New Hampshire coast. Vetch also suggested that the government send muskets, flints, and ammunition for the provincials, and he asked that the problem of command—land versus sea, provincial versus regular—be settled before sailing.[35] On November 29, Vetch provided further information on the condition of Canada, including population figures, Indian allies, and the number and location of French forts.[36]

With all their questions answered, the Board of Trade finally placed Vetch's proposal before the Queen on December 1, emphasizing that the West Indies depended on trade from New England and that this trade was disrupted by the war, and so elimination of the French colony would end the disruption.[37] Three months later, on March 1, Her Majesty's instructions were issued to Samuel Vetch to prepare for his expedition to Canada. Vetch sailed for the colonies, arriving in Boston on April 28 where he immediately set out to assemble the provincial contribution.[38] On June 28 Vetch wrote to Secretary Boyle, indicating that there appeared to be "nothing (human speaking) which can disappoint this noble design."[39]

Vetch was wrong, of course. The following day, June 29, the London government learned that the French and Spanish had captured the Bahamas the previous April. On July 1, Charles Spencer, Lord Sunderland, Secretary of State, recorded in his journal that the Canadian expedition had been laid aside and all forces were diverted to retaking the Bahamas.[40]

As the spring changed into summer, and the summer grew old, the provincial forces waited patiently for their English allies. While Samuel Vetch watched his grand dream and ambitions fade into the mists of time, he bombarded the London government with letters to remind them of their commitment to the colonies. In August he pointed out that the provincial forces had been under arms since May 20, "well clothed and exercised every day from that time."[41] In fact, the idle soldiers had been drilled so much Vetch could say "without the least boast . . . that they both do the manuall exercise and fire in platoons and battalion equal to most regiments in the service."[42] But drilling soldiers accomplish very little except to improve their drill, and all the while they continued to eat and to draw their pay and bounty money, "so that it is a vast expense to the Governments here; but what they chearfully pay in hopes of being freed hereafter." The obviously frustrated Samuel Vetch had a warning for the Earl of Sunderland as well. "The too late arrivall of the fleet," he wrote, "would be the last dissappoyntment to all H.M. Colonies who have so heartily and at so vast an expense complyed with Her Royall orders, and would render them much more miserable then if such a thing had never been projected or undertaken."[43]

The British fleet never did arrive that summer. The ship carrying the message announcing the cancellation of the expedition, which left England at the end of July, did not anchor in Boston harbor until early October. The summer of 1709 would not be the last time the provincials would wait in vain for British support, they would do so in 1746 and 1747,[44] but the experience of 1709 proved to be especially bitter. When news of the diversion of the British forces arrived in October, Governor Joseph Dudley, Francis Nicholson, and Samuel Vetch informed the Earl of Sunderland that the consequence of the aborted expedition "we fear will be very prejudicial to H.M. in more respects than one; Besides the total loss of the extraordinary charge of the Crown, and of those Governments, in the summer preparations, which will be a very heavy burthen, and a great discouragement to H.M. good subjects that have with all alacrity expressed their readiness and laid out themselves to do service for H.M., and their country, and to give check to the insolence of their enemies."[45]

In 1690 the provincial governments learned the bitter lesson that the financial costs of war were the same in victory or defeat, and now in 1709 they learned that even cancellation carried a price. The government of Massachusetts estimated they had expended almost £31,000 in support of the abrogated 1709 expedition, in addition to the loss of trade and production through idle ships and workmen.[46] Little New Hampshire had contributed £3,500 it could ill-afford.[47] In this instance the British government soothed the angered and disappointed colonists by reimbursing them for their cost. In fact, paying for expeditions, whether realized or not, became an important English contribution to the partnership.[48] While the British continued this financial support throughout the remainder of the early French wars, payment often encountered the usual bureaucratic procrastination.[49]

In addition to financial backing, the London government contributed in other vital areas to the Anglo-American partnership. They provided much of the ammunition and occasionally muskets for the provincial forces. Although the New England colonies accumulated gunpowder through the imposition of powder duties on shipping tonnage, the amount barely covered their needs for defense of the frontier line. The extraordinary demands of major expeditions on powder and shot proved to be beyond the capabilities of the provincial suppliers. For example, the shortage of powder had severely handicapped the 1690 Quebec expedition. Thomas Savage wrote his brother in England that the soldiers in the landing force each had around three-quarters of a pound of powder and fifteen to eighteen shot, which was soon used up in skirmishing with the French. "We sent aboard for Ammunition and Provision," related Savage, "but they sent us half a Barrel of Powder, which what that was you may judge, amongst near 1200 Men."[50]

Besides the large number of soldiers' muskets involved, the use of artillery greatly increased the consumption of powder on expeditions, especially at Louisbourg where Pepperrell's army consumed great quantities. The forty-two-pounder cannons captured from the French in the Grand Battery each used sixteen pounds of powder per charge.[51] On June 2 Pepperrell reported to Governor William Shirley that he was short of ammunition, and on June 7 he wrote that the army was "quite out of powder."[52] The capture of the French ship *Vigilant* alleviated that particular shortage, but in most instances, the British government provided the extra powder and shot required for major expeditions.[53] As for muskets, Vetch requested British muskets in 1709 to ease supply problems by issuing provincials with standard calibers, but their use as an incentive for recruiting motivated the London government principally.[54]

The third major contribution by the English was the warships of the British navy.[55] The provincial governments did possess, or acquired, small vessels of war. Phips used a forty-four-gun West Indiaman as his flagship in 1690,[56] and for Louisbourg in 1745, the colonies assembled around a dozen ships, the largest of which mounted twenty-four guns. However, these were no match for the large ships-of-the-line available to the French, and they could not protect the transports.[57] The sixty-four-gun *Vigilant* sent to supply Louisbourg could have easily destroyed the fragile provincial fleet if Peter Warren's squadron had not been present. Only the British navy had ships strong enough to keep the French away and support the land forces with firepower.

British regulars constituted another portion of the partnership, but not necessarily in a combat role. In the Anglo-American formula for the reduction of Canada the provincial soldiers would provide the assault forces, and the redcoats would garrison the conquered land after the victory. Another weakness of the New England military system was a lack of soldiers willing to garrison forts. When William Phips captured Port Royal in 1690, his inability to leave a garrison nullified the victory. The French simply reoccupied the post. Provincial soldiers were more than willing to risk their lives in attacking French territory, but they firmly believed "reducing and garrisoning, be . . . two things, quite different, and Distinct from each other."[58] In fact, the concept of enforced garrison duty at an isolated post was so abhorrent to New Englanders, recruiting proclamations for expeditions habitually included guarantees that no provincial soldiers would be required to remain behind against their will.[59]

In his original proposal for the 1709 Canadian expedition, Samuel Vetch simply requested two battalions of regulars be provided, but in his later clarification he left no doubt as to their purpose—to garrison New France after the victory.[60] The Royal Marines who accompanied the provincial forces against Port Royal in 1710 did so not for their fighting ability, but to become the main garrison force for the captured fort. Provincial soldiers participated in expeditions "for Reducing, & not for garrisoning,"[61] and so the English partner had to provide redcoats for that ignoble and endless task.

Another important English contribution to the Anglo-American partnership was the military specialists who conducted the sieges. In Europe the risky nature of battle had led to an emphasis on slow and methodical siege warfare.[62] As a result, engineers and artillery experts became essential to military operations. The specialized knowledge needed to construct fortresses along prescribed and mathematically precise lines was also required by an attacking army to survey the terrain, pick the best artillery positions, and direct the digging of a system of parallels connected by zigzag trenches in order to bring the guns within effective range from which they could breach the walls of the fortification. Therefore, while the generals decided which target to invest, once the siege began, the engineers and technicians took over.[63]

While colonial defenses rarely reached the intricacies of European fortifications, the inclusion of artillery demanded the employment of gunners and the recommendation of engineers as to their placement. Laying an artillery piece required adjustments to the height of the muzzle for the range and "training" left or right for the bearing, as well as the precise calculation of powder charge and knowledge of fuses used in exploding shells. Men with such mastery were rare in the colonies and usually were only found on the few small warships employed in colonial trade. Blacksmiths, through their association with small arms repair, were often expected to become, by some miracle, instant expert gunners.[64]

The number of guns in use at Louisbourg in particular underscored the acute shortage of gunners in the New England military system. As Samuel Waldo, commanding the Grand Battery, indicated to William Pepperrell, "we cant have too many of these usefull men."[65] Too many guns and not enough gunners led to dangerous experiments by amateurs, resulting in exploding barrels and the wounding or killing of precious gunners standing nearby. "I had the misfortune yesterday to be dangerously wounded," wrote one gunner to William Pepperrell, " . . . by the carelessness of one of my assistants who took upon him in my absence to load a gun when I was doing my duty at another bastion, who through ignorance gave that gun a double charge. I hope Your Honor will not impute the above to my fault."[66] One week later, on May 13, Samuel Waldo reported another gunner mortally wounded. Eventually he would order the loading of all cannons with cartridges, rather than ladles, so the charges could be prepared ahead of time by the experts, instead of having amateurs dump in loose powder.[67] But he would also lament that "We are in great want of good gunners."[68] As a result of these shortages, the British furnished colonial expeditions with gunners from the Royal Artillery or, more commonly as Peter Warren did at Louisbourg, sent them ashore from the supporting Royal Navy ships.[69]

As the American colonies also provided little atmosphere for the development and training of military engineers, the British government usually assigned an officer to fulfill that need.[70] Responsible mainly for the building and maintenance of forts, the English engineers also provided assistance and advice concerning any offensive campaigns proposed by the provincial governments. Many engineers came from the middle classes of Europe so their advancement was based on their specific knowledge rather than on political or financial influence. An assignment to the New World away from the main battlegrounds of Europe must have been a veritable exile and a blow to ambition. Therefore, when the professional soldiers or engineers attempted to work with the civilian military system of the New England, the cooperation was often tenuous and the relationship tempestuous. Learning that his replacement had been dispatched in early 1705, Colonel Wolfgang Romer expressed both his joy and relief in a letter to the Board of Trade.[71] "Return thanks for leave to come home," he wrote. "My pen is not able to expres the calamityes and contempts I have suffered and still do suffer."[72] But Joseph Dudley, the Massachusetts governor, also expressed his joy at the replacement. "Colonel Romer is a skilful officer, and served very well here," Dudley informed the Board of Trade, "but his temper is harsh and superior, and very disagreable to the people."[73]

Dudley found the personality of Romer's replacement, Captain John Redknap, more agreeable, but, like Romer, Redknap displayed caution when involved in provincial projects. During the debacle before Port Royal in 1707, when provincial forces twice attempted to take the French fort, the usual British-American prejudices and animosities contributed to the failure. In Redknap's report to London on the expedition he cited ground that was too marshy for proper artillery placement and reports of a French deserter that the fort held five hundred soldiers and a year's provisions as causes for the defeat. But he also expressed discontent with the provincial soldiers, saying that "we have no regular Companys in these parts (but Militia only) and are very difficulty governed especially in any action that is hazardous."[74] Colonial impressions indicate Redknap was negative throughout the campaign, that he recommended ground not even be broken for trench works because their force was insufficient and disobedient, and that he felt that the provincial soldiers in general were "nott ... persons proper for him to venture his reputation on."[75] Historians have generally laid the blame of the botched expedition squarely on the shoulders of the provincials. John Ferling concluded that "despite a manpower superiority of three to one, the New Englanders landed, looked about, concluded that the tumbledown fort at Port Royal was too heavily garrisoned to attack or besiege, and departed seven days later."[76] But the provincials had to rely on the expertise of the English officer Redknap for the conduct of the siege, and he refused to participate. This greatly limited their options.

Such friction became a common by-product of the Anglo-American partnership. In *Roots of Conflict*, Douglas Leach has chronicled the disputes and animosity arising from the uneasy alliance between British regular officers and the provincial military establishment. The nonprofessional colonials in almost all cases had to conform to the methods and command of the regulars, and even then no amount of conformity could ever win the respect of the English professionals.[77] Redknap, as practically the sole regular in the 1707 Port Royal expedition, and certainly as supervising engineer, examined the undisciplined provincial soldiers and convinced himself the expedition was doomed to failure and his career along with it.[78]

Most British officers agreed with Redknap, viewing the independence and ill discipline of the provincials with a kind of horror. Commodore Charles Knowles reported to London after arriving at Louisbourg in 1746 that the provincials "were of so Obstinate and licentious a disposition that not being properly under Military Discipline there was no keeping them in any Order, and . . . I rejoyce at getting rid of them."[79] Peter Warren found the Americans had "the highest notions of the Rights, and Libertys, of Englishmen, and indeed are almost Levellers, they must know when, where, how, and what service they are going upon, and be Treated in a manner that few Military Bred Gentlemen would condecend to."[80] Warren was actually fairly liberal in his attitude toward the provincials, believing that as long as they did their job, "every other Ceremony should in my opinion be winked at," and he let William Pepperrell run the land operation against Louisbourg. But in most Anglo-American expeditions, the British military took firm control. Certainly, for example, there was no question in 1711 that General Hill and Admiral Walker were in command of that joint venture. Even Warren asserted his authority after the fall of Louisbourg and began running the operation. Warren, like Redknap, had probably been protecting himself and his career by letting Pepperrell run the land operation. First, with the land forces provincial, his taking command would have been bad politics, but more importantly, if the operation failed, he could blame Pepperrell and the colonial soldiers. Once the fortress fell, he could take over without damaging his career, and he could even enhance it. Certainly as the years progressed, Warren's recollection of the events placed more and more emphasis on his own contributions and that of the Royal Navy in the success of that operation.[81]

For the individual provincial soldiers the problems and various contributions of the partners made little impression; they embarked on a great and exciting adventure to end the French menace once and for all and to pocket a little plunder along the way. Colonel John Storer of Wells caught the excitement when he left for Louisbourg in 1745: "Casting my care and burden, with my company, into the hand, care and protection of Almighty God, in the great important affair against the enemies of our sovereign Lord the King." As the provincial fleet left Boston Harbor, the captain of Storer's ship fired a salute, and while the men "gave three huzzas" the salute was answered by the guns of the town.[82]

Although begun with excitement and ceremony, the voyage taking provincial soldiers to their target often created problems of its own, principally an epidemic of seasickness. The voyage to Quebec in 1690 took a month, during which time the soldiers, confined on their transports, succumbed to seasickness, smallpox, and other ailments, so many in fact that one-third of the force was rendered unfit for duty by the time Phips dropped anchor in the St. Lawrence.[83] In 1745 Benjamin Stearns found the sea voyage to Louisbourg a harrowing existence. "The seas run mountains high," he recorded in his journal, "a terrible storm we had so bad that I thought that Every minut would be the last and in the mean while our men was exceeding [sick] and did vomit & as if they would dy."[84] Another soldier, describing the same storm, related that everyone on board was sick and crowded together in the hold, while the captain of the vessel got drunk and passed out on the quarterdeck. Fortunately, one of the volunteers was an "old fisherman," who seized the helm and brought the ship safely through the storm.[85]

Having survived the sea voyage, much of the initial enthusiasm remained as the soldiers disembarked at their destination. Storer described men building a blockhouse at Canso as "cheerfully working and leveling the ground."[86] The soldiers at Canso were frequently entertained by the arrival and departure of Royal Navy ships, and even the sound of far-off naval engagements.[87] Others found diversion in music, as the sounds of drums, trumpets, fifes, and fiddles filled the camp.[88] Religious services and sermons inspired those with less frivolous concerns.[89]

When not actually on duty, much of the soldiers' time was taken up with gawking and sightseeing. One anonymous journalist at the siege of Louisbourg reported that during the first few days "many of the Army went Up towards the Grand Battry to Plunder (for as Yet, wee had no Particular Orders,—But Everyone Did what was Right in his own Eyes)."[90] Much of this activity involved foraging for food. Soldiers hunted, picked berries, and plundered local farms. Such forays could be hazardous. During the 1707 Port Royal expedition, Captain Simon Wainwright reported that nine men "were led away by one Mansfield, a mad fellow, to the next plantation to get cabbages in a garden, without the leave and against the will of his officer. They were no sooner at their plunder, but they were surrounded by at least one hundred French and Indians, who in a few minutes killed every one of them."[91]

Soldiers also indulged in the popular vices of smoking and drinking.[92] After the fall of Louisbourg, William Pepperrell established eight "houses of public entertainment" for use by the soldiers, and later that fall prices for various drinks were set by the British command.[93] The presence of spirituous beverages, and the tensions and disparate personalities, also led to fights and brawls. John Storer described one particularly lively bout at Canso in which "Capt. Monteque, with Capt. Bush, Capt ____ and others, held a drunken dangerous campaign—naked swords—and one pistol fired in the fray. Some pricked and some beat, &c."[94]

After listening to Louisbourg veterans describe their adventures in 1745, Jeremy Belknap wrote that "those who were on the spot, have frequently in my hearing, laughed at the recital of their own irregularities, and expressed their admiration when they reflected on the almost miraculous preservation of the army from destruction. They indeed presented a formidable front to the enemy; but the rear was a scene of confusion and frolic. While some were on duty at the trenches, others were racing, wrestling, pitching quoits, firing at marks or at birds, or running after shot from the enemy's guns, for which they received a bounty, and the shot were sent back to the city."[95]

Of course, the frolic and enthusiasm of expeditions soon vanished in the reality of hard work, fear, sickness, and death. Even mundane activities were colored by the grim atmosphere of their existence. The men at Port Royal who had been massacred while foraging for cabbages were described by Simon Wainwright as "being mangled in a frightful manner,"[96] and a soldier at Louisbourg was interrupted while washing his shirt "when he saw a dead man carried by who had had his skull crushed by a shell fragment."[97] Gruesome as these sights might be, the number of actual engagements involving provincial soldiers during expeditions was relatively small. At Port Royal in 1690, Sir William Phips forced the surrender of the position by overwhelming forces, but the landing force at Quebec that autumn had to drive away the French sent to oppose the landing, resulting in a short, lively fight that left four killed and sixty wounded on the English side.[98] At Port Royal in 1707 the provincial soldiers mainly fought off harassing ambushes and attacks by the French and Indian defenders, although one fight during the second siege resulted in sixteen killed and a like number wounded.[99] Francis Nicholson's attack on Port Royal in 1710 employed standard siege operations with the

French surrender forced by artillery fire. At Louisbourg there was some skirmishing by scouts operating on the perimeter of the camp, but otherwise the disastrous assault on the Island Battery was the only action to involve an infantry attack.

Until the breach in the wall was opened by the artillery and the assault began, if any, soldiers participating in sieges served mainly as ditch diggers and pack mules. At Louisbourg they dragged the artillery by hand from the landing beach to the battery positions. "[The New Hampshire soldiers] were employed for fourteen nights successively," wrote Jeremy Belknap, "in drawing cannon from the landing place to the camp, through a morass; and their lieutenant-colonel Meserve, being a ship carpenter, constructed sledges, on which the cannon were drawn, when it was found that their wheels were buried in the mire. The men, with straps over their shoulders, and sinking to their knees in mud, performed labor beyond the power of oxen; which labor could only be done in the night or in a foggy day; the place being within plain view and random shot of the enemy's walls."[100] They also hauled powder and shot to the batteries, as well as provisions to the camp. One journalist described how the high surf impeded the efforts to unload the boats. "[Men] had to wade out to the boats and carry supplies to shore; . . . then had to sleep in wet clothes."[101]

Such labor contributed to the wear and tear on provincial clothing, and it increased appetites for dwindling provisions. Sleeping arrangements often exacerbated the discomfort. Initially, landing forces slept where they could find shelter. At Quebec in 1690, the Reverend John Wise described sleeping on straw in the farm buildings of local *habitants*, until the commander, John Walley, ordered them to the beach for embarkation, afraid, according to Wise, that the French might set the straw on fire. So they left their warm straw, marched about fifty rods, and lay down on wet sand.[102] At Louisbourg some soldiers cut boughs to sleep on until tentage could be landed from the transports.[103] Even when tents were provided, they often proved inadequate both in number and in quality. Simon Wainwright ordered his men to cut thatch to cover their tents at Port Royal in 1707, and at Louisbourg wounded soldiers apparently lay on straw exposed to the weather due to a shortage of tents.[104] The historian Fairfax Downey condemned the inefficiency of the provincial forces in not providing adequate tentage, unlike the British in 1758 who did care for the comfort and health of their soldiers. Of course, the production and procurement of military tents was easier in England where artisans catered to the needs of the army than in the colonies where the use of military tents was minimal.

The sea voyage and the lack of adequate provisions, clothing, and tentage, plus exposure to unusual conditions and numbers of people, resulted in a high proportion of sickness and death from disease on expeditions. Smallpox crippled both the Montreal force and Phips's Quebec army in 1690. In 1707, Simon Wainwright, reporting on the condition of his men, wrote that "there is a considerable number of them visited with violent fluxes, and although we have things proper to give them, yet dare not do it; others taken with mighty swellings in their throats; others filled with terror at the consideration of a fatal event of the expedition, concluding that, in a short time, there will not be well enough to carry off the sick."[105] Disease also devastated the ranks of the provincial soldiers at Louisbourg, especially after the fall of the fortress and during the following winter.[106]

While the final victory over New France would be reserved by the London government for Jeffrey Amherst, James Wolfe, and the British army, the two-pronged assault they employed had been forged by the provincial governments in the previous French wars. And although never achieving their ultimate goal, the Anglo-American partnership did produce victory at Port Royal in 1710 and Louisbourg in 1745. Through all the frustrations of Quebec in 1690 and 1711, Port Royal in 1707, and the operations aborted by the British in 1709 and during King George's War, the provincial governments of New England learned about their strengths and weaknesses and found that their offensive projects were sound, even if the execution of their plans was somewhat sloppy.

The initiation of a major expedition was not undertaken lightly. It put a strain on all segments of society by stripping communities of provisions and manpower and by disrupting the economy. Additionally, in an age of poor communication, the coordination of military forces on two sides of the Atlantic proved difficult at best. If anything, the Anglo-American partnership proved more adept at this coordination than the French. Most French expeditions contemplated against New England targets never passed the planning stages. In 1697 a French plan to capture Boston and then devastate the coastal towns between Salem and Portsmouth came to nothing when the French naval squadron arrived too late, but the French and their Indian allies in Canada, like the New Englanders in 1709, had been idle all summer waiting for their fleet.[107] During the summer of 1746, a French fleet set sail to recapture Louisbourg and then attack the coast of New England. The admiral in command died, his successor committed suicide a few days later, and 2,400 French soldiers and seamen succumbed to disease all without ever firing a shot in anger. A similar attempt the following year was stopped by the British Navy.[108]

Beyond the issue of success, or lack of it, the expeditions provided provincial soldiers with their only exposure to European-style warfare. Of course, fortifications were not as strong nor were the armies involved as large or complicated as in Europe. There were no major battles to force the issue, no Malplaquet to lift the sieges, only the gnat stings of French and Indian war parties fighting a style of war known only too well by the New Englanders. But expeditions, no matter how brief, provided a glimpse at a world rarely seen by provincial soldiers. The drill, the vast fleets, the voyage itself, the uniforms of the regular and the naval officers, and the roar of artillery were never experienced, or for that matter needed, while patrolling "on the backs of towns" or lounging in frontier garrison houses.

Although this brief exposure proved exciting, New Englanders were rarely lured into permanent lives as soldiers. Expeditions served one purpose—the reduction of Canada and the elimination of the French threat to their families, communities, and province. Provincials appreciated the assistance of Great Britain; the gift of weapons, powder, and shot; the loan of warships and garrison soldiers; and the financial support, but they resented the contempt of the regulars who, as Douglas Leach has observed, "tended to look down on the provincials as something of an inferior breed—crude, uncultured, undisciplined, and largely untrained in the science of civilized warfare."[109] The New Englanders knew the only answer to the devastation of their frontiers was the reduction of Canada, and as they could not accomplish this on their own, the Anglo-American partnership created a potentially successful ultimate solution to the French and Indian problem, but in so many ways it became a necessary evil.

6

Stores of War

The Logistical Nightmare

In order to wage war effectively, to fight battles and conduct sieges, soldiers not only require the basic human needs of food, shelter, and clothing, but they must also be provided with weapons and ammunition, the tools that define their profession and announce their intention. Throughout history the difficulties associated with keeping soldiers supplied ("logistics") have increased as the technology of war has become more complicated. By 1700, miles of supply wagons carrying the basics of food, shelter, clothing, weapons, and munitions followed European armies in order for them to fulfill their ultimate purpose.[1] In provincial New England many of the basic human needs of clothing, food, and shelter were supplied by the soldiers themselves or by the inhabitants of the frontier, with the governments of Massachusetts and New Hampshire making up any shortages and providing replacements. Although expeditions and major raids, as we have seen, demanded special measures, the basic needs of food and clothing were still met by the resources available in New England. However, the procurement of weapons and munitions proved to be a greater problem because the New England colonies had no industrial base of their own. Indeed, for the provincial governments of northern New England, supplying their soldiers throughout the early French wars with muskets, powder, ball, and flint was nothing less than a logistical nightmare.

In one respect this difficulty is surprising, because, of all the western societies, conditions in the English colonies had encouraged the most widespread use of firearms. In Europe, weapon ownership was a privilege and a sign of independence and wealth.[2] In France only the nobility had the right to bear arms, the English linked a property qualification with owning a weapon, and in both countries only the privileged classes had the right to hunt.[3] Furthermore, before the refinement and increased production of firearms in the seventeenth century only the wealthy could afford them. However, the American colonies were planted at a time when firearms were becoming more efficient and cheaper to produce, bringing the costs of weapons within reach of individuals of more modest means. The English transplants found that the environment of the New World encouraged the use of firearms. Instead of being a privilege, missile weapons were necessary for survival as the natives would not stand still for the "push of pike."[4]

Consequently, the ownership of firearms by all adult males was mandated by law.[5] In 1693, section five of "An Act for Regulating of the Militia" in Massachusetts stipulated "that every listed souldier and other householder . . . shall be alwayes provided with a well fixt firelock musket of musket or bastard musket bore. . . . or other good firearms to the satisfaction of the commission officers of the company."[6] Even those excused from militia training were required to "be provided with Arms and Ammunition compleat, upon the same Penalty as those that are obliged to train."[7] The militia acts of Massachusetts and New Hampshire made weapon ownership a prerequisite for the status of "freeman" for every young man who turned sixteen, and once a servant was freed he then had three months to equip himself with a musket and ammunition.[8] More than a privilege or a convenience, the ownership of a firearm was a social and a civic responsibility.[9]

The administrative duties of militia officers included the supervision of firearms in their communities. Twice yearly they were required to inspect the condition and suitability of weapons and to check the munitions supply of both the soldiers and the town. The care taken with such inspections, and compliance by the inhabitants, depended a great deal on the quality of the officers themselves and their nearness to areas exposed to the enemy. Much removed from the danger of immediate attack in 1744, John Chandler inspected his Worcester county militia regiment and reported that of nineteen infantry companies and two troops of horse only four could be considered "mostly equipped." Seven were "entirely deficient" or missing arms and twelve were missing all or part of their ammunition.[10] The incentive for maintaining adequate arms and munitions, as well as the responsibility of militia officers and committees, obviously increased with the proximity of the frontier. As William Shirley cautioned Major John Storer of Wells, the town officers had to ensure that their communities were well provided with military stores, otherwise "if an enemy should come upon any place, and the people should be destroyed for want of arms and ammunition, I think their blood would be upon the officers' hands."[11]

Inevitably, however, even under the most diligent of officers, shortages of weapons persisted. Reasons varied, of course. Although the laws stated that boys who turned sixteen were required to provide themselves with weapons, the ultimate responsibility for obtaining the firearms rested with their fathers. But providing firearms for themselves, for servants who performed active military duty, and for all sons over the age of sixteen was expensive, so deficiencies were common.[12] For many, the cost of owning even one weapon was prohibitive. The militia acts attempted to compensate for such cases by ordering those unable to procure a weapon to provide corn or other "vendible goods" equal to one-fifth greater value than the average price of a firearm, this amount to be determined by the officers of the company. These goods were then sold and a suitable weapon purchased, with any excess money returned to the soldier along with the weapon. Those too poor even to provide the necessary goods had to be armed out of the town stock of firearms. If single, men were assigned work by the town constable to pay off the debt, while married men in such circumstances were expected to provide a weapon for themselves and to return the town musket as soon as possible.[13] For some men, at least early in the French war period, the lack of a weapon could become the means of escaping military service. When William Phips assembled his troops for his Quebec expedition in 1690, a large number appeared without weapons and Doctor Benjamin Bullivant described how eighty of them deserted en masse and "with hurra's, haveing beene told they must find theyr own armes."[14]

In addition to cost, the natural attrition common to all mechanical devices contributed to weapon shortages. The historian J. A. Houlding found that the average life expectancy of muskets used in the British army was eight to ten years, at which time they were supposed to be reconditioned and repaired. But rarely were they returned to army ordnance until the muskets had become dangerous to load.[15] After reconditioning, the Crown often shipped these old weapons to the colonies. Therefore the life expectancy of weapons in the colonies depended on age and source, as well as the quality of original manufacture and the responsibility of the owner. Many soldiers appeared at musters with unusable muskets because they had not been, or could not be, repaired. As Governor Joseph Dudley reported to the Board of Trade in 1703, "I am in great want of small Armes, those that we have have been so often repared ... they ... are of Little Service."[16]

Military service on the frontier could be hard on fragile stocks and lock mechanisms, not to mention because of the losses of muskets due to enemy fire or capture. A colonial agent, George Vaughn, reported to the Board of Trade in 1709 that weapons "are dayly lost in the woods in pursuit of the enemy."[17] According to the militia laws, when a soldier had a weapon lost or ruined "not through his own neglect or default, such loss shall be borne by the publick."[18] The records of provincial Massachusetts and New Hampshire overflow with requests to pay for firearms ruined in the service, with some undoubtedly stretching the truth to cover their negligence.[19] With so many soldiers killed or captured, the disastrous attack on the Island Battery at Louisbourg produced a great number of appeals for the compensation of lost weapons and equipment.[20] Firearms were also ruined through carelessness and were destroyed or captured in enemy raids on frontier communities.

In addition to destruction, attrition, and expense, shortages usually occurred simply because the population exceeded the available supply of weapons. "As the people grow more, the Armes grow fewer," wrote Joseph Dudley, and thus simple arithmetic aggravated the problem of arming provincial soldiers.[21] Colonial assemblies continued to reissue militia acts that demanded that all adult males own a weapon, but there never were enough firearms in the colonies to make this ideal a reality. Recent studies have tried to establish gun ownership rates through probate inventories, a process that is inexact but suggestive. Although many probate inventories were outside New England, they reveal gun ownership generally between 60–78 percent.[22]

The statutes required towns to keep a few spare firearms on hand for use by the local militia during drills, but when soldiers were raised for active duty, the provincial governments had to cover any weapon shortages. A soldier without a weapon was not a soldier, and experiences like that described by Doctor Bullivant in 1690 convinced the government that soldiers could not be relied on to secure their own firearms. But economic realities aggravated the problem of procuring suitable weapons. All of the necessary elements for a strong manufacturing base, including cheap labor, investment capital, specific manufacturing knowledge, and a large market were lacking in the colonies. Without these, the creation of a broad-based industry was extremely difficult if not impossible.[23] In addition, according to British mercantile interests, the colonies provided raw materials and in return purchased manufactured goods. While the colonial monopoly on the production of these raw materials was protected, the similar protection of the production of finished goods in the mother country led to laws discouraging manufacturing in its colonies.[24] Because of this, and despite some limited iron foundries such as those at Saugus, Massachusetts, the New England provinces lacked a suitable means of iron and steel production, and without iron and steel, firearms could not be manufactured.[25] Throughout the colonial period, New England depended on European sources, particularly England, for new firearms or metal parts for repair and replacement. Indeed, this demand from the New

World would help accelerate, in true mercantile fashion, the growth of the iron and gun-making industries in England.[26] Appeals for the shipment of arms from the London government, "whereby We shall be able . . . to Defend our selves," remained a constant theme in provincial correspondence to the Board of Trade.[27]

Normally, British weapons were shipped to the governments of New England where they became provincial arms. In 1704 the Board of Trade informed the Queen that five hundred small arms had been sent to Massachusetts, and the assembly would pay for them or "such persons to whom the said arms shall be delivered."[28] However, on other occasions the English military authorities bypassed provincial governments and directly furnished provincial soldiers with muskets as an enlistment incentive for colonial expeditions. For the proposed Quebec expedition in 1709 each volunteer was issued "a good Firelock, Cartouch-box, Flints, Ammunition, a Coat, Hat and Shirt; with an assurance of her Majesty's Princely Favour unto all such as should distinguish themselves," and for Port Royal in 1710 volunteers would "bear the Queen's armes and enjoy them as their own for ever."[29] Similar provisions were made for Cartagena and during King George's War as well.[30]

As the British government often used such opportunities to clear their storehouses of outmoded and inferior weapons, they did not particularly care what ultimately became of the muskets.[31] However, the governments of Massachusetts and New Hampshire generally looked in horror at this practice no matter what the condition of the firearms. They habitually kept close watch on all government arms and the parceling out of free muskets to volunteers by British authorities removed any control the colonial governments might have on their use.[32] The 1709 expedition in particular caused a great deal of concern because the muskets were issued to the volunteers but the expedition never materialized. Massachusetts authorities collected the muskets from the soldiers and put them in storage for "the defence of the Province in any future Expedition." As Governor Dudley explained to the Board of Trade, "if otherwise Absolutely given to the Souldiers, as by Some is Expected, [the muskets] will be soon lost or disposed, beyond any power of the Government to bring them into service again."[33] This action would set a precedent, and soldiers given weapons for other aborted expeditions, such as in 1711 and 1747, would find their muskets reclaimed by their officers before disbanding.[34]

Beyond the direct shipment of new arms from England, provincial authorities made up weapons shortages from town stocks or by pressing (forced borrowing) firearms from individuals not in active service. Indeed, beyond the obvious need for the actual defense of their communities, the reason those men exempt from militia training had to own weapons was to provide a surplus that could be accessed when needed. Those individuals who had their weapons confiscated for government use received compensation. The constant search for miscellaneous firearms by provincial governments could lead to legal problems if the rightful owners were not compensated, as in the dramatic example that follows here.

The saga of Captain Prescott's muskets began during the Cartagena expedition. As an incentive for enlistment, the British government provided volunteers a musket that they were allowed to keep at the conclusion of the expedition. The British military authorities gave the muskets to company commanders, who in turn distributed them to their men. By using this procedure the London government felt it could cut down on administrative red tape by confining their involvement to company commanders rather than with individual soldiers. Apparently, Prescott and his men perished in that ill-fated siege, as did most of the provincial soldiers who took part. Somehow, whether they had never been issued to the company or were returned after the expedition, the muskets belonging to Captain Prescott and his company found their way to New Hampshire, where, in the spring of 1744, Governor Benning Wentworth had them pressed and locked in Fort William and Mary for safekeeping.

A short time later the New Hampshire Assembly informed the governor that Captain Prescott's legal heir had surfaced and had claimed ownership of the muskets. Recalling the precedent of the aborted 1709 expedition, Wentworth believed the fifty muskets still belonged to the British government and advised that until ownership was proven he would hold on to the weapons. Prescott's family sought an ally in their cause by appealing to Governor William Shirley of Massachusetts,[35] and Shirley wrote Wentworth on September 25, "at the request of the administrators of poor Captain Prescot and for the sake of his family." According to the royal proclamation, wrote Shirley, the arms provided to the soldiers would belong to them "or their representatives, if they are since dead," and therefore they have the right to demand their muskets from the representatives of Captain Prescott, "for as to the King the arms are sunk upon the distribution of them and the captains are accountable to the Crown only during the keeping up of the companies, and not after they are disbanded." In effect, as far as the British government was concerned, the fifty muskets were given to Prescott and their responsibility ended there. "I really can't see," concluded Shirley, "upon what just grounds your government can take the arms from the administrators without paying for them."[36]

Prescott's family kept up the pressure on Wentworth throughout the fall of 1744, and the governor was finally forced to admit the weapons did indeed belong to the Prescott family but he was still reluctant to part with fifty British muskets (and these included matching bayonets). On December 19 Wentworth informed the assembly that he had promised the Prescott family he would pay for the muskets or deliver them, and he left it for the representatives to resolve the dilemma. The issue hung there until a dramatic confrontation at the end of January 1745. About sunset on January 31, a "Mr. Prescot who is the owner of the arms . . . sent a carriage for the said arms" and demanded that the assembly pay for them or release the muskets immediately.

However, the situation concerning the muskets had changed considerably since the previous fall. Governor Shirley had just proposed the reduction of Louisbourg, and if New Hampshire was going to support such an enterprise then fifty British muskets would prove very useful. The assembly appointed Colonel Peter Gilman and Eleazer Russell as a committee to negotiate the purchase of the Prescott arms, and Governor Wentworth sent word that if the committee would take immediate action he would wait and settle the matter that evening. The committee met with Prescott's agent, Mark H. Wentworth, who, recognizing a seller's market, informed them he wanted twelve pounds per musket, a premium price. When the committee gave its report, the apparently shocked and indignant House promptly voted unanimously to reject the offer, and then adjourned for the night. Two days later the fifty muskets were delivered to the Prescott family and that seemed to end the matter as far as the government of New Hampshire was concerned. However, there would be a postscript. A year later, one of the participants in the ill-fated attack on the Island Battery at Louisbourg petitioned the assembly to replace his lost weapon and equipment. Joseph Ham described the musket he lost as "one of Prescuts Arms Commonly So Calld" and requested slightly more than £4. The assembly paid him 14 shillings, 9 pence as compensation. So it seems the New Hampshire Assembly purchased one of the Prescott muskets after all—at their own price.[37]

Each soldier issued a weapon by the government had four pence a week deducted from his pay for its use.[38] This money enabled the government to pay the English for the muskets or to compensate the owners of pressed weapons.[39] Provincial officers were required to keep strict account of which of their men had been issued a provincial arm and to collect them when the company mustered out. At Louisbourg, William Pepperrell ordered that company commanders collect all provincial weapons before their men embarked for home and to provide a list of apprentices and servants so their weapons could be collected or pressed as well.[40]

In addition to procuring arms for those soldiers without, provincial governments were responsible for the maintenance or replacement of all weapons, private or government-owned, used for active service. Naturally, being far removed from the major population centers, the maintenance of weapons on the frontier or on expeditions caused great concern. The disarray of the northern frontier after the Glorious Revolution created an acute problem with the repair of arms. Sylvanus Davis reported in August 1689 that the only gunsmith at Falmouth had deserted to a pirate ship that appeared in the bay, taking with him three muskets and all his tools. Therefore, his garrison was in need of spare arms as "sevrell of our Arems Are ought of Kilter and noe Smith to Repaire them."[41] Jeremiah Swain reported the following October that the forces under his command needed an armorer "for we are exposed to send almost 20 miles to have our guns mended."[42] Two years later, John March and Daniel King were obliged to leave a considerable portion of their raiding force at Greenland, New Hampshire, due to illness and because the "badness of their Armes makes them very Insffitient for the Service."[43]

Sergeants sometimes carried mainspring vises and spare springs for quick repairs, but more involved maintenance demanded the work of experts, and there were very few gunsmiths on the frontier.[44] Blacksmiths performed simple gun repairs, and some did specialize enough to become known as gunsmiths. Sir William Phips's father was a blacksmith who settled in Pemaquid and soon became known as a gunsmith.[45] Charles Trafton was captured as a boy of twelve during the 1692 raid on York and was taken into the household of a blacksmith in Quebec where he learned gunsmithing. He continued the trades of blacksmith and gunsmith on his return to York in 1710.[46]

Because of the paucity of resident specialists, most of the gunsmiths who maintained the weapons of the provincial forces were themselves soldiers sent to the frontier. Wounded during the Great Swamp Fight in King Philip's War, Mark Rounds became a soldier-gunsmith on the Maine frontier, serving at Scarborough and Newcastle in the 1680s. He was at Fort William Henry in Pemaquid when the fort fell to the French in 1696. After the war, Rounds was stationed at Fort Mary in Saco, and later he apparently worked out of the new fort at Casco, because he was listed in the company that dismantled that fort in 1715. He subsequently settled in Falmouth.[47] Similarly, Ebenezer Nutting was a blacksmith from Medford who enlisted in Captain Joseph Heath's company during Dummer's War. When Colonel Thomas Westbrook ordered Heath to dismiss his company, the provincial commander arranged for Nutting to return to Falmouth as a "resident in the King's service."[48] Later he allowed Nutting to sail for Boston to get more tools, but Westbrook wrote

Stores of War | 117

William Dummer that "I think it of absolute necessity that he be sent down again as soon as possible, sundry of our Arms being out of Repair."[49] The Eastern Indians also needed access to a gunsmith and often made this a demand in treaty negotiations. In fact, the removal of a gunsmith from Falmouth became one of the stated causes of Dummer's War.[50]

When gunsmiths were unavailable on the frontier, other arrangements had to be made. The Bay government usually hired gunsmiths in the Boston area to maintain commissary stores and the weapons kept at the Castle. In May 1703 the Massachusetts Council reported paying Timothy Wadsworth £53 for repairing and "cleansing" the public store of arms during the previous year.[51] The following August, after the devastating attack on Maine communities, which opened Queen Anne's War, the Bay government ordered that fifty weapons be sent to Kittery and fifty sent to Casco Bay "to be changed with the souldiers by order of the officers, taking in the defective arms and markeing them with the souldier's names, that they may be forthwith amended at their charge respectively, and to be restored to them."[52] Due to the distance and inconvenience involved in shipping weapons home for repair, provincial regiments on expeditions made sure they had blacksmiths along to serve as gunsmiths.[53]

The difficulty in maintaining weapons on the northern frontier was amplified by the bewildering variety of firearms carried by provincial soldiers. There was little standardization of military weapons anywhere during most of the seventeenth century. Calibers and lock mechanisms would be regulated in the British army during the reign of William and Mary, but the English would not establish an issue weapon for all its infantry until the 1720s.[54] Even if it had been financially feasible, and it was not, without an established gun-making industry standardization of weapons was impossible for the New England colonies.

However, provincial governments did attempt to regulate the privately owned weapons used by provincial soldiers. For example, militia acts after 1690 generally required "a well fixt firelock musket of musket or bastard musket bore" and a barrel not less than three and a half feet long. The barrel length was important because infantry drills of the period called for three ranks to fire volleys together. The muskets of the third rank, therefore, had to clear the heads of the front rank. As will be discussed in chapter 9, such formations were rarely used in provincial service, but the firearm regulations came under the jurisdiction of the militia as part of their administrative function, and the militia did use British manuals to train on their muster days, thus the length of barrel was specified. Whether or not shorter barrels, such as the carbines used by mounted troops of militia, were accepted for provincial service is unknown. Most of the weapons served as hunting guns when not in military use and hunting fowlers of the period had extremely long barrels, some over sixty inches in length, so the problem probably rarely came up. With weapon procurement so difficult, and shortages so chronic, the acts always included the loophole "or other good firearms to the satisfaction of the commission officers of the company."[55]

In one respect, the English colonies were somewhat ahead of their European contemporaries in recognizing the superiority of the flintlock, or "firelock," system. As early as 1646, the Plymouth General Court allowed only flint or wheellocks for town property. In 1677 Massachusetts placed an order for five hundred "new snaphaunces of firelock muskets,"[56] and at the start of King William's War requested one thousand "fuzies" from England. The "fusee" or "fusil" was a light musket primarily given to troops who guarded supply trains, troops who soon became known as "fusileers." Because of the ever-present danger of surprise attack, train guards could not rely on lighting their matches; therefore, the fusee always employed the flintlock system. By the 1690s provincial laws insisted that soldiers provide themselves with "firelock" (i.e., flintlock) weapons.[57]

Proven to be more efficient and reliable than its predecessors, the matchlock and wheellock, the smoothbore, flintlock musket had been adopted in western countries by the last decade of the seventeenth century, and it would remain the principal military arm until the 1840s.[58] The most commonly used type of flintlock in the late seventeenth century was the "doglock," so called because it had an external safety catch, or "dog," which hooked on to the back of the cock. After 1700 the doglock would gradually be replaced by the "true" flintlock, whose internal design made the extra safety catch superfluous.[59] Although some specimens of muzzle rifling exist, the types of rifles often associated with colonial America were extremely rare in New England. Their weapons, like all European military muskets, were smoothbores.

Loading procedures changed throughout the early French war period as ignition systems were simplified, and new techniques were developed in the numerous dynastic and colonial wars. During the seventeenth century the main charge was carried in wooden tubes or "bottles" hung from a shoulder belt, called "bandeleroes" or bandoleers: the top was pulled out with the teeth and the charge poured down the barrel. Both top and tube were attached to the bandoleer by cords and were simply left to hang open. A ball was then removed from a leather pouch, which was also attached to the shoulder belt, dropped in the muzzle with some cloth or other wadding on top to prevent the ball from rolling out again, and then both were pushed down the barrel with a rammer. To speed loading, several lead balls could be placed in the mouth for easier access (the dangers of lead poisoning obviously being unknown at the time).

Eventually the use of paper cartridges would simplify the process and eliminate the need for wooden bottles and bullet pouches. Both the ball and main charge were rolled together in a paper tube, the tube torn with the teeth, powder poured down the barrel, and ball and paper (which now served as the wadding) rammed down on the powder. Although the use of paper cartridges was not reflected in military manuals until the 1730s, it appears they were already becoming popular during King William's War. Sylvanus Davis listed "cartridge boxes" taken by some soldiers who deserted Fort Loyal in 1689, and the Militia Act of 1693 required "badeleers or cartouch-box."[60] Archaeological evidence from a ship sunk during the 1690 Quebec expedition revealed both bandoleers and cartridge boxes as well as actual paper cartridges.[61]

Once the main charge had been rammed home, priming powder was poured into the pan and then the "hammer," or frizzen, closed over it. Until the 1730s, priming was usually carried in a separate container, either a bottle-shaped flask or, more commonly in the case of provincial soldiers, a powder horn. Although the printed manuals do not reflect it until much later, by 1745 provincial soldiers were beginning to prime from the cartridge, a practice that increased loading speed considerably.[62] Soldiers on the Louisbourg campaign were ordered to "allow as much powder in each cartridge as will be sufficient to prime too."[63] When priming from cartridge the procedure had to be reversed, with the pan primed and the hammer closed, then the rest of the charge poured down the barrel.

A piece of flint, wrapped in sheet lead or a square of leather and held tightly in the jaws of the cock, ignited the weapon when it struck the face of the hammer and pushed it forward. As the flint hit the hammer, or frizzen, it scraped off tiny pieces of metal. Red-hot from the friction, these "sparks" fell on the priming powder in the pan, ignited it, and the resulting flame found the main charge in the barrel through the flash hole. In order to produce these sparks the metal in the hammer had to be hardened (rehardening was a common repair for gunsmiths) and the flint had to be sharp. Most flints averaged around thirty strikes before they had to be re-sharpened, or "re-knapped." This could be accomplished by gently tapping the striking face with a metal object to carefully flake the flint away or by turning the flint over to allow the action of striking the hammer to chip the flint away. Every flint was different, however. Some bore fifty, sixty, or seventy strikes without the need for re-knapping while others shattered after a few blows. In combat situations there was no time to fool around with re-knapping and flints were replaced as soon as they began to fail.[64]

A soldier also needed cleaning equipment to maintain his firearm, and the Militia Acts generally required him to have a "worm and priming-wire fit for his gun."[65] Without cleaning, the powder fouling in the barrel would eventually render the weapon useless by preventing the ball from being rammed home. The "worm," which screwed on the end of the rammer, gripped a bunch of tow fibers (flax or hemp) and enabled the barrel to be wiped out. The priming-wire kept the flash hole clear; otherwise, flame from the priming powder would not ignite the main charge—a "flash in the pan." In addition to cleaning equipment, provincial soldiers often had lock covers (a piece of leather molded to shape and tied around the lock) and a tompion, or wooden plug, for the muzzle to keep rain or snow from wetting the powder charge.[66]

The calibers of provincial firearms varied as much as the weapons themselves. Nonmilitary firearms generally were sold with a ball mold specifically made for the bore size of the weapon.[67] The English bore system was based on the number of balls that could be cast from a pound of lead, thus a "16 bore" meant sixteen shots to the pound. The bore size could refer to either the diameter of the ball or the measurement inside of the barrel. For ease of loading and to compensate for powder fouling, firearms generally employed a ball that was actually much smaller than the bore of the barrel, the difference being called "windage." Thus a musket with a 10-bore barrel, like the standard British infantry musket, generally loaded a 12-bore ball. Obviously, a great deal of confusion can result if references are not specific. The alternate method of determining caliber was to measure the bore in hundredths of an inch, with a 10-bore barrel measuring out to be about .78.[68]

The militia acts of New England required members of the militia to procure a weapon of "musket or bastard musket bore." With the ascension of William and Mary to the throne, the British military adopted the Dutch bore system for their military weapons, and so musket bore referred to the Dutch 10-bore barrel, which fired a 12-bore ball. The exact meaning of "bastard musket bore" has eluded modern scholars, but apparently it meant a smaller caliber, probably the Dutch carbine caliber (16-bore barrel), which the British would later adopt for its own carbines and fusils.[69] The French, who measured their bores rather than using the English system of lead weight, used a .69-caliber musket and many New England hunting guns or fowling pieces also used this caliber, which by English standards meant a 13 – or 14-bore barrel. Weapons made for the Indian trade catered to the native's preference for a dual-purpose weapon that would serve for both hunting and war with an even smaller caliber to reduce consumption of powder and lead. Gradually reduced in size throughout the colonial period, Indian trade guns eventually would employ a 24-bore ball, enabling the Indians to get twice as many shots out of a pound of lead than the typical British soldier.[70]

Like the Indian, some New England men owned a weapon used both for hunting and military service, and preferred a lighter caliber that consumed less powder and lead. Military fusils with 16-bore barrels, such as those requested by Massachusetts in 1690, were popular as were 13-bore fowling pieces and 20- or 24-bore trade guns.[71] Mixed with 10-bore military muskets and odd-size miscellaneous weapons, this hodgepodge of calibers created logistical problems greater than the supply of the weapons themselves.

The militia acts of Massachusetts and New Hampshire required each company member to provide "one pound of good powder, twenty bullits fit for his gun, and twelve flints," and both governments ordered individual communities to keep a common stock of powder and shot—usually a barrel of powder, two hundred pounds of balls, and three hundred flints for every sixty soldiers on their rolls.[72] This supply of powder, lead, and flints had to come from outside sources because, as in the case of weapons, there were no domestic supplies. In 1642 Massachusetts had attempted to produce its own source of saltpeter, and it established powder mills in 1666, and later more successfully in 1675, but demand far exceeded the supply.[73] The most important source of powder in the English colonies was a duty on shipping tonnage to be paid in gunpowder.[74] The duty was assessed on all ships not owned by residents of the colony, and without it, according to Governor Joseph Dudley, "the Province would be undone for want of powder, being no waies able to supply themselves." The duty was usually one pound of "good new powder for every tun such ship or vessel is in burthen." In periods of peace, captains could substitute a payment of twelve pence per ton, but during war the New England governments insisted that the duty be paid in powder.[75] However, the powder duty did not produce lead and flints, and the powder received from it only covered normal levels of activity. In the end supplies of munitions, like the firearms, had to come directly from England.

As it had in so many instances, the Glorious Revolution inhibited the ability of the New England governments to provide their soldiers with the munitions necessary to wage war. On March 14, 1690, taxes levied to pay for the war effort included payment for a "Dispatch for England to their Majesties providing of Amunition."[76] In addition to the one thousand fusees previously mentioned, the request dispatched in early May asked for "200 Barrells pistoll powder 50 Barrells Common Powder 20 tunn Lead."[77] The wait for these requested supplies caused the fatal delay in sailing for Quebec later that summer. On June 12, the Board of Trade approved a shipment of five hundred fusees, two hundred barrels of powder, and twelve tons of lead, but it could not be shipped in time.[78]

The repeated requests by the government of Massachusetts for powder and shot during the early years of King William's War seriously hampered the negotiations for a new charter. Increase Mather wrote from London that the constant call for aid "was, in effect, to pray for a [Royal] Governor. They could not be so weak as to think the King would send one without the other."[79] Increase Mather's analysis of the situation was apparently astute. According to the historian Richard Johnson, the entreaties for powder, lead, flints, and other war materials throughout the early French wars led to much closer ties with the government in London.[80] As Lieutenant Governor William Stoughton wrote in 1701, the colonies depended "on his Majesties Princely care of us in affording us such Supplies of Warlike Stores and provision" for without ammunition supplies from England the war against the French and Indian enemy could not be waged.[81]

The British government was not always enamored of this dependence. With a heavy commitment to the second war King William was waging against Louis XIV in the 1690s, the constant appeals from Massachusetts caused irritation. In 1695 the Board of Trade, in approving yet another request from the Bay colony, wrote "as to stores of war, it has not hitherto been usual that Massachusetts (being the most considerable Colony on the Continent) should demand or that the King should grant them, and we think it very reasonable that the people should rather be pressed themselves to use their utmost efforts in their defense, Nevertheless we think that ten pieces of cannon and 100 barrels of powder should be sent out with Lord Bellomont."[82] The dependency was not cheap either. The British government estimated that the stores of war needed for the New England colonies in 1703 would cost over £3,213.[83]

Shortages of powder and lead limited the scope and number of scouts, raids, and expeditions, and this scarcity caused unforeseen problems in strategic and tactical plans. The delay of Phips's expedition in 1690 is only the more famous incident. Provincial artillery fire at Louisbourg was curtailed due to powder shortages, and Fort Massachusetts fell in 1746 when the defenders were down to four pounds of powder.[84] Of course, the problems of munitions supply were not confined to the English colonies. The Eastern Indians had similar, if not greater, difficulties in maintaining an adequate supply of powder and lead, especially when the French were not directly involved in a campaign. During the destruction of York, Maine, in 1692 the Indians ripped the lead glazing from windows and stole pewter plates for molding into musket balls.[85] Any battle or skirmish with the Eastern Indians such as Church's raids or Lovewell's fight, even if not a tactical success, could be a strategic victory by forcing the Indians to use up precious supplies of ammunition, resulting in at least a truce while the Indians replenished their stock from the French, or even their former enemies.[86]

Receiving stores of war from the Crown involved much more than making a simple request. Like the proposals for expeditions, colonial appeals for powder, shot, and weapons had to negotiate the bureaucratic labyrinth known as the British government. In October 1707, the government of New Hampshire penned a request for stores of war, because "At present wee labor under a great want of good small armes and ammunition, which are daily waisted and lost in the Wildernesse, in persuite of the Enemy. And by reason of our poverty cannot be supplied."[87] This appeal was not formally presented to the Board of Trade until the following July, when the colonial agent George Vaughn specified types and amounts of stores needed. Vaughn emphasized the need for quick action because "the circumstances of that Province are such as do require a speedy supply, and therefore we desire your Lordship would receive H. M. pleasure upon the said Addresses as soon as conveniently may be."[88]

The Board of Trade passed the request along to the Secretary of State on July 19 who returned it ten days later. With the Secretary's approval, the Board of Trade launched its usual fact-finding investigation to determine the actual needs of New Hampshire. On August 17 they wrote the Board of Ordnance for a list of what stores had previously been sent to the province, and they also asked the former colonial military engineer, Colonel Wolfgang Romer, for his assessment of New Hampshire's request.[89] One week later the Board of Ordnance informed the Board of Trade that stores of war had been last sent specifically to New Hampshire in July 1692, but that frequent shipments had been sent to Massachusetts which "might have been sent to New Hampshire."[90]

Romer's reply took two weeks and he seems to have misunderstood the needs of New Hampshire in making their appeal. Apparently Romer thought the requested supplies were meant for Fort William and Mary exclusively. He described the installation in great detail as well as its defensive status when he left the colonies. As for the provincial request, "the powder demanded seems to me extraordinary and surprising, unless they intend to merchandize therewith, because I am certain the powder-house will not contain that quantity, and I cannot imagine what use they can make of so much powder, when I consider what quantity they receive yearly from the shipping which comes to the province."[91]

On November 8, 1708, the Board of Trade recommended that New Hampshire be sent the stores of war, including small arms and powder, shot, and lead, adding that New Hampshire had not received a shipment since 1692.[92] On November 25 the Queen in Council asked the Board of Ordnance to make "an estimate of the charge of the ordnance stores proposed for New Hampshire."[93] Now the Board of Ordnance had to conduct its own investigation, some of which repeated ground already covered. For example, on January 18, 1709, Ordnance asked the Board of Trade for copies of the Romer report they had received the previous summer, and the Board of Trade complied the following day.[94]

On January 27, 1709, the Queen in Council finally ordered the stores of war be sent to New Hampshire.[95] Two weeks later the Board of Trade admonished Governor Joseph Dudley to send the stores to his northern province only when absolutely necessary and requested that he submit regular accounts.[96] Apparently Romer's remarks about the possible intention to "merchandize" the powder had had its effect. But while the approval had been given, the stores themselves had to be gathered and loaded on ships, and those ships provided armed escort against the prowling French navy. On October 25, 1709, Governor Joseph Dudley wrote to the Board of Trade acknowledging the arrival, "a few dayes since," of the ship *Supply* "bringing H. M. stores for Piscataqua."[97] Almost two years to the day after the government of New Hampshire made its original request, the stores of war arrived in port.

It comes as no surprise to learn that provincial governments were touchy about the waste of powder. Lieutenant Governor John Usher of New Hampshire, never popular to begin with, found himself attacked for wasting powder in useless salutes to his person, especially the powder sent from England in 1692. The fact that Usher lived outside the colony, which irritated the inhabitants, meant that he was constantly sailing in and out of Portsmouth Harbor and so the fort was constantly firing a salute to his ship. In 1703 William Vaughn wrote to the Board of Trade to state that only thirty barrels of the original one hundred remained at William and Mary. Usher refuted this charge, claiming that "some few guns were fired two or three times a year by the Captain of the Fort as a piece of respect to him, but without his order." The British government backed up their lieutenant governor in this instance, but the charges of powder wastage continued to haunt Usher. In 1710 the New Hampshire Council complained to Governor Dudley that Usher, among numerous indiscretions, had wasted nine to eleven barrels of powder in salutes fired to his person. Dudley, who had had a falling out with Usher, agreed with the New Hampshire Council.[98]

The arrival of supplies from England did not end the logistical problems connected with munitions, for distribution caused as many headaches as acquisition. Stored in barrels generally containing about one hundred pounds, powder had to be transported from the coast to individual towns or sent along with military forces where eventually it would be used to fill powder horns, bandoleers, or cartridges. Although blocks of flint were used as ballast in ships coming from England, such flint was useless unless broken down and shaped for use in firearms. Gun flints used in the colonies were shaped and knapped in England and packed in half-kegs for shipment. The flints would be sized for pistols, carbines, or muskets and would need a wrapping of lead or leather to hold the flint in the jaws of the cock. British army flints were prewrapped in lead for easy changing in the field; otherwise, one strip of leather or lead would have to serve many flints.

Lead came to the colonies in the form of bars or sheets; lead could also be cast into balls, which were separated into small kegs according to caliber. The variety of calibers used by provincial soldiers made the distribution of lead most difficult. Kegs of precast balls were broached and the men chose bullets closest to their calibers; if not, the balls had to be melted down again and recast with individual molds. Cartridge papers had to be cut to shape, powder charges measured, and then the ball and powder rolled together.[99] The discovery in the heat of action that the kegs of musket balls were of the wrong caliber could invite disaster, as Benjamin Church found to his regret one frantic day in 1689. During the Battle of Brackett's Woods (in present-day Portland, Maine), word reached Church that the casks of bullets brought on shore were all musket caliber and thus too large for most of the firearms carried by his men. Rushing back to the town, he ordered all casks brought ashore and immediately opened. The lead balls were turned out on the ground and the inhabitants began hammering them into slugs (reducing their diameter by flattening or elongating them). Later, when the enemy had finally been driven off, Church ordered a pursuit but found that most of his men were out of usable ammunition, and in fact most had been forced to hammer their own slugs in the heat of battle.[100]

In 1704, after many years in provincial service, Church made some recommendations to the government on the handling and proper outfitting of soldiers in the field. Among the many suggestions, the old warrior wrote that each soldier should have a bag or "wallet" for shot "of such a size as will fit his gun [and] that every man's bag be so marked that he may not change it. For if so, it will make a great confusion in action." Each soldier should also try his powder and gun before action, and each company should have a reserve barrel of powder with an identification mark "that men may know beforehand, and may not be cheated out of their lives by having bad powder, or not knowing how to use it."[101] It is unknown if Church's recommendations were adopted, although from the continued problems experienced by provincial soldiers with munitions after 1704 it is doubtful, but he at least recognized the difficulties and tried to address them.

The problems of logistics in the early French wars are often ignored for the more glamorous and tangible expeditions and major raids. "It is the dramatic and momentous events at the sharp end of war that jostle for our attention," wrote John Keegan and Richard Holmes," . . . [but] it is no exaggeration to say that tactics—the art of winning battles—is really no more than the art of the logistically possible."[102] The New England colonies often had tactical and strategic plans impeded by the difficulties connected with the procurement of weapons and ammunition. Although the logistical support of armies in the eighteenth century was difficult at best, the economic realities that denied the colonies an industrial base necessary for the support of warfare in the age of gunpowder handicapped New England in its military operations. Restricted in the production of iron and steel, and lacking sufficient powder mills and a domestic supply of lead and flints, Massachusetts and New Hampshire were forced to rely on the English for their war supplies, a reliance that would in turn promote closer ties with the government in London.

But the logistical nightmare did not end with the procurement of weapons and munitions. The inability of the New England colonies to standardize the weapons used by provincial soldiers multiplied the difficulties in the distribution of ammunition tenfold, and at the very least it caused delays in operations while ammunition was sorted or recast, and at its very worst left soldiers hammering their musket balls while in the heat of battle. A solution to the problems of weapons procurement and the allocation of ammunition was beyond the capabilities of the colonial governments. They had neither the industrial base nor the financial ability to issue uniform weapons to all their soldiers. Unlike his redcoated counterpart, the New England provincial soldier would have to contend with shortages of firearms and ammunition throughout the early French war period, and these unavoidable logistical handicaps often contributed to the military setbacks that blackened his reputation.

PART II

The Provincial Soldier

7

Recruiting

Gone for a Soldier

As in almost all military systems throughout history, the provincial governments of Massachusetts and New Hampshire employed both a carrot and a stick in their efforts to find soldiers for active duty. They attempted to encourage or entice volunteers with wages and special incentives tied to the type of service involved, such as scalp money for scouting and plunder for expeditions. Underscored by a foundation of propaganda appealing to various tastes and inclinations, these "encouragements" did produce numerous volunteers, but not always in the numbers needed to get the job done. The colonial governments prepared for such shortages by providing the legal means to press reluctant recruits for service. Thus by use of both the carrot (reward) and the stick (compulsion), the provincial governments found the soldiers to fight their wars.

According to Kyle F. Zelner, in King Philip's War, Massachusetts impressed the majority of its soldiers. Facing a catastrophic war with a suspect militia system, Massachusetts forced men to serve through laws that granted committees of militia broad powers. Operating on their own without direct help from England and with a small population, Massachusetts had little means and little time for experimentation.[1] Although the press remained, the imperial wars brought change. England's increasing ability to support war efforts within the empire, the stabilization of government in Massachusetts, with a growing economy and population, enabled Massachusetts to do what Harold E. Selesky found in Connecticut, to base "military service on economic self-interest."[2] Economic incentives would provide the primary means for finding more volunteers.

Although varying in amount according to both time and place, almost all soldiers employed in "His Majesty's service" received wages. (The only exceptions were the scalp hunters who received no regular wages, performing their services on speculation.) The standard wage during the early French wars in both New Hampshire and Massachusetts graduated between forty shillings per month for privates to £7 per month for captains, to be paid from the time of "detachment" (from the militia, or civilian life) until an orderly discharge, including a "reasonable time allowed them to repair to their usual place of abode."[3] While this may be considered a standard, the provincial governments exhibited a great degree of flexibility in wages offered for services rendered. Soldiers performing short-term service, such as patrols, and garrison duty in coastal forts, especially in peacetime, often received considerably less. For example, soldiers stationed at the Castle in Boston Harbor during King William's and Queen Anne's Wars received five shillings per week for their efforts, exactly half the normal pay.[4] The captain or officer commanding the individual companies received the money and had to provide a receipt to the government. He in turn paid the men.[5] Soldiers performing long-term duty often were paid a month's wages in advance, but scouting parties had to wait until the completion of their task.[6] Officers of scouts submitted their journals and accounts to the assemblies, generally in person, then received the money and returned to distribute it.

Occasionally deductions were made, such as the four pence per week for the use of a provincial weapon,[7] but the practice never approached the level of the English army where the meager pay of the redcoats was consumed by deductions. Of the eight pence sterling paid to British soldiers per day, two were subtracted as "off-reckonings" and basically went to pay for the soldier's clothing and to profit the colonel of the regiment. The rest, known as "subsistence," paid for his provisions and other necessaries. Any money left over could be pocketed by the soldier.[8] Colonial soldiers rarely, if ever, paid for their provisions. During the summer of 1709, provincial soldiers waiting in vain for British support to attack Quebec had eight pence per day "punctually payd him for his victuals" over and above the nine shillings per week provided as wages.[9] Similarly, soldiers involved in the aborted Montreal campaign of 1747 were paid off at a rate of six pence sterling per day "clear of stoppages for provisions or billeting money."[10]

Unfortunately, provincial governments were not always able to pay their soldiers "punctually." Payment for scouting duty depended on how quickly the officer in command could get his accounts together and present them to the assembly, and also on how expeditiously that body could accept the accounts and supply the funds.[11] Soldiers stationed in frontier forts or involved in expeditions also experienced delays in receiving their pay. One of the reasons for the mutinous behavior of the provincial soldiers at Louisbourg in the summer of 1745 was "their not being paid any part of their wages due."[12] Even soldiers posted nearer to home did not always get paid promptly, such as those garrisoning Fort William and Mary in Portsmouth, New Hampshire, during Queen Anne's War, "which is very intolerable to the poorer sort, to do service and not be payed, while the family starves at home."[13]

Bureaucratic red tape often caused delays. War was an extraordinary circumstance that demanded only temporary solutions. Ad hoc committees of war were quickly established at the commencement of hostilities and were dismissed just as quickly at their conclusion, and although government officials probably drew on past experience no standard procedures or permanent bureaucratic department existed to handle the logistical and financial support of military forces. In addition, the colonial assemblies rarely surrendered their tight hold on the purse strings, even to an ad hoc committee of their own members; therefore, all final payments had to be approved by the assemblies. The best example of this situation was the absurd practice of requiring commanders of scouts, no matter how short in duration or few in number, to leave the frontier and report directly, in person, to the provincial assembly. The result was chaos and delays.

The governments of Massachusetts and New Hampshire were also dilatory in their payments to soldiers simply because they did not have the money. It is well known that colonial governments experienced cash-flow problems as the importation of manufactured goods drained the hard currency out of the New World and into the coffers of the mother country, not to mention British laws that restricted flow of coin to the colonies.[14] The solution involved the issuance of bills of credit based on future tax revenue. The financially disastrous Quebec expedition of 1690 forced the first issuance of paper currency and one of the principal debts resulting from that expedition were the wages owed the participating soldiers.[15] The Bay government, confidently expecting victory to provide the wages for their soldiers, had not planned for defeat. Therefore, the promised rewards were written on a piece of paper and distributed to the disgruntled men. "We are stopping the mouths of the soldiers with a new mint of paper money," wrote a Boston merchant, Francis Brinley. "Not many will take it and those that will scarce know what to do with it."[16] Despite the depreciation of the currency during the remainder of the early French wars, the provincial soldiers learned to accept the bills of credit. It was, after all, the only money they were going to receive.[17]

In addition to the promptness of their wages, New England soldiers carefully monitored their rate of pay compared to the soldiers from other colonies and loudly complained if they found themselves on the short end.[18] Massachusetts and New Hampshire soldiers who enlisted for Louisbourg were allowed twenty-five shillings per month for pay, far below the usual forty shillings, but they also were "entitled to all the plunder."[19] However, when denied the plunder after the fall of the fortress, the Massachusetts and New Hampshire soldiers looked askance at their "very low pay," especially when compared to the forty shillings given to Connecticut troops and the fifty shillings going to Rhode Island volunteers. By the fall of 1745, the governments of northern New England had to increase their soldiers' pay to the more usual forty shillings per month if they expected any to garrison the French fort over the winter.[20]

Such vigilance over their wages is understandable considering that the pay of provincial soldiers, even at the normal forty shillings per month, hovered near the bottom of the colonial wage scale. Gary Nash found soldiers' pay in New England to be below that of laborers and common seamen, and far below that of artisans in Boston who averaged five shillings per day when fully employed.[21] Therefore, as an incentive by itself, the wages offered provincial soldiers by themselves probably only attracted the unemployed and disadvantaged.

Provincial governments could also appeal to their citizens' hearts, minds, and souls in calling them to military service. By promoting war as both a patriotic obligation and a religious crusade, or reminding them of their responsibility to protect their communities and families from the savage horde, colonial leaders hoped to enlist volunteers who could ignore the meager pay and serve out of a sense of duty. In newspapers, proclamations, and from the pulpit, New England men were exhorted to strike back at the enemy and to stop the death and destruction on the frontier and the devastation of fishing and trade on the sea.[22]

In his sermon, published in 1700, *Good Souldiers a Great Blessing*, Benjamin Wadsworth identified the just causes for war as defense or self-preservation, the recovery of great damages, and the revenging of injuries, all of which naturally struck at the heart of the New England experience of war. "Would you have your Country spoiled," he asked, "your Houses rifled and burnt, your Goods and Riches taken away, your Children dashed against the stones, your Wives and Daughters ravished before your faces, your Women with Child ript open, your Aged Fathers and Mothers barbarously dragged about the Streets, your Churches overthrown?" Such appeals could and did move men to enlist.[23]

Other men, especially those living on the frontier line, needed no reminders or exhortation to call them to duty. In 1689, Benjamin Church found the people of Casco (Falmouth), Maine, eager to support any military action against the French and Indian enemy, and "willing to venture their lives and fortunes, in the said enterprise, wherein they might serve God, their King, and country, and enjoy quiet and peaceable habitation."[24] Similar sentiments would inspire many on the frontier to participate in patrols and raids, as well as enlist in expeditions. Men such as Johnson Harmon, Jeremiah Moulton, and John Goffe did not participate in military endeavors in search of wealth from the meager wages, but in search of peace and safety for their families, communities, and province. For some, military service became an exciting change from everyday existence, leading to repeated enlistment. Johnson Harmon, a joint commander of the attack on Norridgewock in 1724, was still volunteering for service in 1745. When asking William Pepperrell for some position on the Louisbourg expedition, the old soldier wrote, "I am persuaded their [sic] is something yet for me to do their [sic] before I leave the world."[25]

Harold E. Selesky did not find such spirit in Connecticut, a colony sheltered from the imperial wars by Massachusetts. Selesky found in King William's War that Connecticut had trouble finding soldiers "because no disaster galvanized the population." Selesky concluded that "a military system based on popular consent and participation could be mobilized only when the threat animated and energized the entire colony."[26] Exposed to constant threat of attack, Massachusetts and New Hampshire found some men animated and energized for service.

The provincial governments needed encouragements beyond poor wages and appeals to the conscience and emotion to attract volunteers, so they introduced special incentives that varied according to the type of service. Garrisoning the frontier forts was the least attractive military duty, especially in peacetime, because besides the interminable boredom, it usually paid less than normal service. But under some circumstances there existed a possibility that the soldier could carve out a new home in the community surrounding his post, or at least "moonlight" at odd jobs for extra money. To encourage enlistment for the garrison of the new Fort George at Brunswick, Maine, the Pejepscot Proprietors offered the usual wages and subsistence but indicated that the "Military Service expected from them at present [1715] is like to be so small as to permit them, besides their Wages, to earn money by Labour." The Proprietors promised to pay them as laborers to finish the fort at two shillings per day, and after to find them work in the community splitting staves, shingles or clapboards. After six months they could settle in the community with a grant of one hundred acres, having first obtained a suitable replacement.[27] Such opportunities were rare, however, and on the whole, garrison duty, whether in a fortified house on the frontier or in a provincial fort, was a boring, thankless job and was usually given to the least desirable soldiers, the pressed and hired men who served with the greatest reluctance.

The principal incentive for scouting was scalp money, and here was the opportunity to make some real profit. During King William's War small cash awards had been offered for all adult Indian males, dead or alive. The volunteers from Newbury who pursued the Indians that attacked the town of Dover in 1689 were offered £8 for every fighting man taken or killed, and the following year £12 were offered, "in leiu of Wages," for every Indian male captured or killed.[28] Rates fluctuated throughout that war as the government set rewards for specific missions and withdrew them afterward.

But early in Queen Anne's War, the Bay government set a standard policy and offered substantial rewards for the scalps of adult male Indians, with the greatest amount awarded to those who served without regular pay.[29] Those volunteers who "maintain themselves free from the Province charge" would receive £40, volunteers in service £20, regular forces (pressed men) £10, and pursuit forces £30.[30] Within a few years the reward for volunteers without wages from the province was increased to £100 (£60 for those with pay) and would remain at that level at least through the end of Dummer's War.[31] The rewards were quite impressive when compared to a Boston artisan's annual income of £40 or to the salary of Increase Mather as the president of Harvard at £50.[32] The thought of volunteering did prove quite popular among the more adventurous sort, who balanced the risk, commitment of time, and no guarantees with the possible return, and considered the gamble worthwhile.[33]

In raising soldiers for expeditions the governments of Massachusetts and New Hampshire, as well as London, became most inventive and generous, although the generosity often proved to be illusory. For their participation in major expeditions the men of New England were offered three kinds of incentives. The first category included bounties and gifts of equipment. Although the provincial governments could not hope to match the munificence of British authorities, they did contribute whatever they could. For the Port Royal expedition of 1707 the soldiers were given coats of a uniform color, creating a "red" regiment and a "blue" regiment to "add life to the service."[34] The provincial government repeated the contribution of red and blue coats for the Quebec expedition of 1709 and the Port Royal assault the following year. In 1709 they also paid the volunteers a bounty of £12.[35] It was also during the aborted expedition of 1709 that the British government sent muskets and ammunition to be distributed to the soldiers as further incentive for enlistment.[36]

The firm commitment of British forces in the Quebec expedition of 1711 prompted the London government to go all out in providing "encouragements" for provincial recruits, so much so that the New England governments had to contribute very little that year. The Crown provided, in addition to a musket, "a coat, breeches, stockings, shoes with buckles, two coloured shirts, coloured neckcloths, and hat, gratis." And for those soldiers who "distinguished themselves," land grants would be provided from the conquered territory.[37]

Of course, the promise of land grants vanished on the shoals of the St Lawrence River, and the uniforms provided apparently left much to be desired. The clothing had been packaged in bundles and shipped over with the fleet, enough for both the land forces going to Quebec, and those attacking Montreal from Albany. When the expedition ended, the muskets were collected from the returning soldiers and added to the provincial stores.[38] The Crown ordered Colonel Francis Nicholson to dispose of the uniforms as best he could. He sold some at auction and sent the rest to the garrison at Annapolis Royal.[39] Complaints from the garrison concerning these uniforms poured into Whitehall. They were "the worst that ever was seen in these parts ... unfit for so cold a climate, being only a sort of frock without any lining and no waistcoats ... [and] are extreamly damaged and withall so slight and thinn, etc., several of the men must perish, if care is not taken to send a compleat clothing fitt for so cold and uncomfortable a climate."[40]

The individual who supplied the uniforms expressed shock at the complaints. "[The] Sergeants surtout coates were made of the best Glocestershire cloaths," he wrote, "and 1396 of the centinell's coates, the rest of the centinells with whole thick kerseys, which are as dear as cloath, but allowed by everybody to wear much longer, and is what all the foreigners cloath withall. As to their not being lined H. M. saved largely thereby in what was given the militia." Here is illustrated the normal ignorance of Englishmen for conditions in the New World. Because the provincials were only "militia" they could suffer through a Canadian winter with the comforting, and perhaps warming, thought that they had saved the government some money by going without linings, and waistcoats for that matter.[41]

In 1740 the British also supplied provincials enlisting for Cartagena weapons and uniforms, but perhaps remembering the previous experience, they sent examples of both for display purposes. They also gave the provincials tents and agreed to provide transport home after the expedition for those who desired. As most of the colonials who participated died during that disease-infested siege, there were few complaints.[42] The provincial governments aided the British in their recruiting by adding a few incentives of their own. For example, New Hampshire offered three months' pay in advance, instead of the usual one, a £5 bounty, and a "good new blanket." Massachusetts paid "five pounds in bills of old tenor or one pound thirteen shillings and four pence in bills of new tenor" plus a "good and convenient blanket."[43]

The recruiting incentives offered for Louisbourg were quite meager in comparison to the previous expeditions. Like Port Royal in 1707, Louisbourg was conceived and initiated by the provincial governments and so they could not draw on the British for equipment. Recruits for the great expedition were offered a £4 bounty, £1 for billeting money to get them to the various mustering areas, and a blanket.[44] Due to the great disappointments arising from Louisbourg, the governments of New England had to substantially increase their incentives to find recruits for the Canada expedition the following year—offering their highest bounty ever (£30) and, of course, a blanket.[45]

Exemption from any military press for three years constituted a second form of incentive offered by New England authorities, included in the encouragements for both the Port Royal expedition of 1710 and for Cartagena thirty years later.[46] But by far the most controversial form of incentive for expeditions was the promise of a share of any plunder captured from the enemy—a promise that had little chance of becoming a reality but may have been the most influential encouragement of all.

From the very beginning of the French wars the provincial governments dangled the lure of plunder and booty before their potential recruits. Soldiers accompanying Sir William Phips to Port Royal in 1690 were told that "If the French shall not surrender Upon the Articles Offered them; but shall necessitate our Forces to Expose themselves in the Assault . . . Then besides their stated Pay, the just Half of all Plunder taken from the Enemy shall be shared among the Officers and Souldiers."[47] This offer is quite restrained and specific, following the European custom that fortresses or towns taken by assault could be plundered by the soldiers. Port Royal did surrender to Phips and he and his army proceeded to remove everything that was not nailed down, leaving the empty shell to be reoccupied by the French at their leisure. However, though the soldiers shared in the plunder, they had not taken the fort by assault as stipulated in the recruiting proclamation. The French commander had recognized the inevitable and capitulated after a token defense. Phips's plundering of the fort was seen by many as a violation of the surrender agreement, including the French commander who sued Phips for his personal belongings.[48]

But Phips had proved that victory was possible and plunder a reality, which explains the anticipation for the attack on Quebec that fall and the bitter disappointment experienced when they failed, especially by government leaders who expected to pay their soldiers with the riches of New France. Despite this setback, the prospect of plunder would be offered to all future volunteers but without the qualifications expressed in 1690. Soldiers sailing for Quebec in 1711 were simply promised that the plunder would be "apportioned the same, justly and equally," and those volunteering for the British expedition against Cartagena "shall . . . have their just share and proportion of all plunder or Booty."[49]

With the exception of Port Royal in 1690, none of the colonial expeditions before 1745 produced plunder because all but one failed. Only at Port Royal in 1710 did they manage to capture the French stronghold, but as the colonial and British leaders decided to keep the fort this time, the soldiers were not allowed to strip it. Despite this poor return, prospects for plunder at Louisbourg seemed plausible to many. Louisbourg was not a small, isolated fort, but a rich port city, and the recruiting proclamations had been blunt and to the point concerning any spoils—the volunteers shall be "entitled to all the plunder."[50] It may have been the very real prospects for plunder that encouraged Massachusetts and New Hampshire soldiers to initially accept less than normal wages.

However, when the fortress fell, the terms of the surrender protected the property of the residents and thus denied plunder to the provincial soldiers. The disappointment was deep and profound. There was "a great Noys and hubbub a mungst the Soldiers a bout the Plonder," reported one soldier, and William Pepperrell wrote to Governor William Shirley about the "spirit of discontent" because the soldiers "have been disappointed of the chief part of the plunder to which they were entitled by his Excellency's proclamations."[51] Adding to the discontent was the fact that Peter Warren's British squadron daily snatched fat French ships that in ignorance sailed toward the captured port. According to custom, all sailors shared prize money from captured ships, but the land forces received nothing. "Could I persuade myself the land forces would have a share in the immense riches that have fallen into [our] hands," wrote one soldier, "I think some considerable part is due to them in Equity but am much afraid they will never receive any."[52]

He was right, of course, and the attraction of plunder as a recruiting incentive evaporated, which is why the governments of Massachusetts and New Hampshire had to offer such a high bounty the following year to raise troops for an attack on Quebec. As the Reverend Thomas Smith of Falmouth,

Maine, reported in his journal, "[Recruiting for] the expedition to Canada goes on in this Province, but slowly; our people being dispirited on account of the sickness and their unfair treatment at Cape Breton."[53]

Disillusionment and resistance to military service was not uncommon in the early French wars. Similar to the aftermath of Louisbourg, the disappointment of the aborted 1709 Quebec expedition created difficulties for those recruiting for the Port Royal campaign the following summer,[54] and the New England authorities often had trouble finding sufficient men to garrison their forts and serve on the exposed frontier. Despite all the incentives offered and all the propaganda underscoring the necessity and responsibility to defend the provinces and attack the enemy, the provincial governments still could not produce enough volunteers for their military requirements, and thus they had to press or draft soldiers to fill their quotas.

Although a "method to be made use of in cases of great necessity only,"[55] the press was used quite frequently throughout the early French wars to flesh out provincial companies, especially those bound for service on the frontier where the government had to defend the garrison houses and forts, maintain patrols, and dispatch raiding parties. "For the more speedy levying of souldiers for their majesties service," the governments of Massachusetts and New Hampshire passed numerous acts for "Levying Souldiers" during the French wars, which provided the legal right to force men into military service.[56] When it became necessary to press soldiers, the government would employ the administrative branch of its military system to perform that duty—the local militia.

In *Arms for Empire: A Military History of the British Colonies in North America, 1607–1763*, Douglas Leach provided an excellent description of the procedures used in pressing soldiers. When raising troops for the frontier, or even expeditions, towns often had quotas assigned and were expected to maintain that number by furnishing replacements whenever necessary. Following the record book of a captain of militia from Salisbury, Massachusetts, Leach found that the local militia officers would assemble their men, call for volunteers to fill the town's quota, then, when the number of volunteers proved inadequate, impress the balance.[57]

For those who declined to serve when pressed there were two options, one of which was legal. The Levying Acts provided exemption through the payment of a fine within a limited time. In 1693 a £5 fine paid within two hours of being pressed bought exemption, and there was no dishonor attached to this procedure as "all persons so paying the said fine of five pounds shall be esteemed to have served."[58] The fine was increased to £10 in 1699 and stayed at that level through 1748, with the time limit eventually expanded to twenty-four hours in 1746.[59] The fine enabled militia officers to hire someone to serve in the pressed man's place.

Militia officers could be quite inventive in pressing individuals, and they used their knowledge of local conditions and inhabitants to advantage. For example, the captain of the Salisbury company pressed three men when one was needed, and the three pooled their resources to hire a substitute, thus filling the town's quota.[60] However, militia officers who refused to press were subject to penalties themselves, and any who accepted a bribe to keep someone from the press could be fined up to ten times the original bribe.[61]

This system of fines and substitutes resulted in three recognized levels of provincial soldier: the volunteers, pressed men, and hired soldiers. In the opinion of government officials and many officers, the hired soldier came definitely last on the list. Not only had hired soldiers refused to volunteer, but, being passed over in the press, they were also less than desirable in the eyes of their town officers. When Timothy Dwight was ordered to reduce his garrison at Fort Dummer at the conclusion of Dummer's War in 1725, he was instructed to "act without the least Partiality [in deciding who would stay] Having a regard to length of time they have been in the service, if their Volunteers or pressed (not hired) men."[62] It seems that the hired men were last on the list.

The second method of refusing a press was simply to hide or run away. During the Glorious Revolution men pressed for service did not report because "the Government [was] not Settled," but with the "settlement" of a new government and the passage of new acts, the failure to report after being pressed resulted in three months of imprisonment.[63] Occasionally men who refused the press were victims of economic or personal problems. Despite the inventiveness and sympathy of local militia officers, not everyone could produce £5 or £10 with two hours' notice. During Dummer's War, two men pressed for service on the frontier neither paid their fine nor reported at the rendezvous. "One of them no body pities or is concerned for," but the other was considered by his fellow soldiers as a victim of circumstances.[64]

However, the provincial governments cared not if individuals were to be pitied or censured; contempt for the press resulted in unfilled quotas and handicapped the war effort. New England authorities found that as King William's War progressed, the number of men escaping from the press increased, most of them fleeing south to other colonies. The Bay government expressed the problem succinctly in 1702 in the preamble of "An Act in Addition to the Act for Levying Souldiers":

> Whereas it has been found by often experience, that when warrants have been issued for the detaching or impressing of souldiers for the defence of the country, the ablest and fittest for service have absconded and hid themselves from the impress, by means whereof the officers have been necessitated to send persons less capeable, to the great dishonour and disadvantage of the service, and discouragement of the officers appointed to conduct and lead them forth.

To remedy the situation the government ordered officers of all militia companies to keep a list of their most able men, up to one quarter of their company, who would be ready at a moment's notice to go into service. Any detachment or press could "speedily be supplied out of the men so enlisted."[65] Although in the summer of 1703 Governor Joseph Dudley would report to London that he had dispatched "200 men of the best quarter part of the Militia [to the frontier], who have been ten months detached by vertue of an Act of the Assembly,"[66] this legislation would not stop the flow of "draft dodgers" out of the province. By April 1704, Dudley would be complaining that the "young fellowes the fittest for service" were running to Rhode Island and he could not get them back.[67] The only other solution seemed to be to stiffen the penalties for avoiding the press, especially for those who left the province. By 1746 those caught leaving Massachusetts to escape military service could be sentenced to twelve months in prison and a fine of £20.[68] However, this solution was no cure, and the problem of men not "attending" the press would remain throughout the French war period.

To support the prevalent argument, as expressed by James Kirby Martin and Mark Edward Lender, that provincial soldiers were "not militia, but rather out casts from middle class society, unfortunates who had been lured or legally pressed into service," historians have placed considerable emphasis on the numerous statutes allowing for the pressing of soldiers. Lawrence Delbert Cress wrote that the exemption fee freeing pressed men from duty "allowed propertied persons to avoid service with little difficulty and left the burden of military service on those unable to purchase exemptions." However, throughout all the French wars the bulk of provincial soldiers were volunteers who enlisted under no compulsion from the government. Only a small proportion of soldiers raised in northern New England were pressed or hired men, but while the proportion was small, perhaps 10 to 30 percent of any given force, those men still had to be found in order to complete provincial companies. Provincial governments passed a great many laws and regulations to find a relatively small number of men, and thus too much reliance on the levying acts to determine who did active service has caused distortions.[69]

In addition to quotas assigned to the militia, provincial officers recruited directly to fill their companies. First, the government laid a foundation of propaganda, usually in the form of proclamations outlining the purpose of the service and the rewards or incentives available to volunteers, which were posted in public buildings throughout the colony.[70] Then the officer chosen by the committees of war or the overall commander, and approved by the government, were "authorized and impowered" to "beat his drum within the Regiments of Militia," or to "beat up for Voluntiers throughout this Province" for "His Majesty's Service."[71]

In theory this referred to the actual beating of a drum in a public place, such as a town square or at a fair or market, in order to draw a crowd. In Europe a recruiting party traditionally consisted of a junior officer, a sergeant, and a drummer. The drummer would attract the crowd, and then the officer seated himself behind the drum while the sergeant gave a memorized, and hopefully inspiring, recruiting speech. The potential recruit, if any, would approach the officer and sign or make his mark using the drumhead as a desk. The officer would hand him his bounty and the sergeant would take charge of the new soldier.[72]

This was the origin and literal meaning of the beating order, but in reality the phrase "beat his drums" was synonymous with "recruit and enlist," and the recruiting officer proceeded by himself from town to town looking for men to fill his company. The easiest approach in this situation was to contact the local militia officers and have them assemble their men.[73] The provincial officers could then make a speech about duty, God, and province. All officers of the militia and town officials were ordered by the government to offer no "Obstruction or Molestation herein, but on the Contrary to Afford him all the necessary encouragement and Assistance."[74] Benjamin Church provided the best example of this process:

> Colonel Church no sooner received his commission, but proceeded to the raising of men, volunteers, by going into every town within the three counties, which were formerly Plymouth government; advising with the chief officer of each company, to call his company together, that so he might have the better opportunity to discourse and encourage them to serve their Queen and country. Treating them with drink convenient, told them [that] he did not doubt but with God's blessing to bring them all home again. All which with many other arguments, animated their hearts to do service. So, that Colonel Church enlisted, out of some companies, near twenty men, and others fifteen.[75]

The historian John K. Mahon indicated that officers given beating orders were recruiting outside the militia system, as opposed to the quota system, and thus attracted the "lowest social stratum."[76] But beating orders specifically mentioned the regiments of militia, and provincial officers recruiting for active service used the administrative function of the militia, which was to keep track of eligible men. If those outside the militia system joined, it was because they were attracted by the drums of the assembly, had read or heard about the proclamations, and had taken the opportunity to join.

Outside of the militia system, provincial officers could find men reduced to inactivity and availability by economic crisis or by the war itself.[77] When the frontier towns of Maine were abandoned during King William's War, communities along the North Shore found "many of the Easterne men In towne prompt and Ready for the service."[78] At the beginning of Dummer's War, John Penhallow wrote to Governor Samuel Shute from the Maine frontier that "there are here several smart lusty young men that have been robbed of all they had by the Indians, who would be glad to be in the service if your Excellency would be pleased to admit of it, they cannot possibly subsist here without."[79] Similarly, two years later Colonel Thomas Westbrook informed the government that "I believe I can enlist the number of thirty men & more generally young men and such as must leave the county if not enlisted."[80]

A popular and well-respected provincial officer like Church would have little difficulty enlisting soldiers, but if he was unknown, or the intended service suspect or unpopular, such as the Cartagena expedition of 1740, recruiting could be a discouraging process. Given "beating orders and articles of encouragement for enlisting a company of volunteers" from New Hampshire for the Cartagena expedition, John Eyre reported that he "did beat up in the several towns in the province where there was any prospect of success, and made several journeys forth and back and was indefatigable therein the better to effect the proposed enlistment." Unfortunately, Eyre found no success in raising his company but "was put to as great expence as if the design had been effected." In fact, he "spent seventy days viz. from August the 8th: to October:16th: and the sum of forty-five pounds fifteen shillings and nine pence to procure and encourage the enlistment of soldiers, for which, . . . your petitioner [had] no compensation over and above the allowance granted to a common soldier."[81]

Even a successful officer found recruiting a time-consuming and expensive occupation. To raise the forces necessary for his 1696 raid, Benjamin Church traveled twice throughout eastern Connecticut and Plymouth colony, "dureing which Time your Petitioner is well assured That he Spent in horse hire, Travelling the aforesaid journeys, passing Ferrys, upon Companyes, and in Necessary Treating of divers persons for an Accomodation in the premises, above Six and thirty pounds money, whereof he only received Twenty Seven pounds out of the Publick Treasury."[82]

Provincial recruiting officers also had to contend with indecision and antipathy from potential recruits and even communities as a whole. As Thomas Westbrook discovered in 1724 when trying to find recruits in Maine, "one day they say they will Enlist, another they don't know."[83] Samuel Waldo, recruiting men for Louisbourg in 1745, encountered considerable resistance in Falmouth, Maine. "I have given the utmost attention to the raising levys," he wrote to William Pepperrell, "which has met with some obstruction from persons who I had not suspected, nor would you I think. One a Justice of Peace near Stroudwater I am well asured has told some that if they went they would dye there, & be damned to, others who are concerned largely in the fishing trade imaging the Embargo will be taken off on the Departure of the fleet." In addition to the prospect of a return to normal economic pursuits, Waldo found the Indian threat also discouraging others from enlisting, with the principal minister of the town against "drawing" men out of the town for that reason.[84]

Community, familial, and economic responsibilities often clouded the personal decision to perform provincial service. The prospect of an expedition or major reinforcement for the frontier produced discussions and meetings throughout northern New England, but particularly so in towns along the frontier. Gatherings were held at public houses or the homes of prominent men for discussions concerning the merits and consequences of participation, discussions that often ran late into the night.[85]

Military service meant a reduction in manpower for a community and lessened their ability to maintain their economy and even defend themselves. Writing to the Bay government in the summer of 1690, the Reverend John Emerson described the distress of Gloucester caused by the absence of men in provincial service. "There is forty seaven of our souldiers under a presse, the case so stands with us that if they be not released . . . wee must all be forced to leave the towne . . . We shall not have the men left to keepe up a watch, nor in any wise much lesse to withstand an enemy, which we are every day & night in expectation to breake in upon us, by reason that we are a front towne upon the sea . . . besides, there will be nothing neare enough left to get in hay & harvest, so that wee must of necessity be forced to kill our cattall, and [are] in great danger of being famished."[86]

Such considerations could produce a "backwardness in some of [the] men to leave their towns," and even an outright refusal to serve.[87] In March 1725, the town of Lancaster, Massachusetts, which had been rotating men on patrol and garrison duty, was suddenly ordered to have "all the scout and standing soldiers to appear . . . with 50 days provisions at Dunstable." The men of the town "utterly refused to go."[88] In their petition to the governor, town leaders explained that "the men that are sent for from among us, are most of them inhabitants, employed in scouting, those that are inhabitants are frequently changed by leave from your honour, so that some that are employed are heads of familys." They pointed out that the town would be weakened and exposed if men were removed, and some had just returned home. "If all the men that are sent for, must go," they concluded, "the familys there will be in a manner wholly destitute of men."[89] Two months later when he learned of Lovewell's disastrous fight with the Pequawket Indians, Colonel Eleazer Tyng marched north with a quickly assembled force. However, the men he raised refused to proceed until Tyng had written the governor to defend their towns because their departure had left the communities "very destitute and naked."[90]

For men with families the decision to perform active duty often went beyond economic support and defense but hinged on very personal considerations as well. Major Samuel Appleton, who commanded the men from Newbury sent north to Dover in 1689, found that military service could not have come at a worse time. "Besides Afflicting providence of God upon my family before I came from home in bereaving me of 2 children, I have just now advize of the death of a third together with the indisposition of my wife and the extraordinary illness of another of my children all which necessitates my hasting home, however I am so Disposed to the Defence of the Countrey and the preservation of this place in order to it that am very unwilling to give the people of this place any discouragement by my removal till I have your Honors Answer."[91] Many provincial soldiers with wives and families must have felt as William Pepperrell did when he wrote to his wife from Louisbourg in 1745 that "although it is the earnest desire of my soul to be with you and my dear family, but I desire to be made willing to submit to him that rules and governs all things well; as to leave this place without liberty I don't think I can on any account."[92]

In addition to communities and families, the economies of the northern New England provinces as a whole suffered as well, for almost all of the soldiers contributed to the economy in some way if only as laborers.[93] In 1710 Governor Joseph Dudley informed the Board of Trade that men are "necessarily taken off from their labour into the service of the war, to guard the frontiers, and this year especially to that degree that every fifth man in the Province was obliged to serve, there being 2,000 of this Province in armes, and our lists of the whole in ordinary make but 10,000."⁹⁴ Reduction in the production of naval stores for the British navy in particular had repercussions in the highest levels of the English government. In reply to the concerns over naval stores expressed by Whitehall during Queen Anne's War, Governor Dudley could only indicate that among his soldiers in service "are all my loose people that should be employed in those manufactoryes."⁹⁵

The common thread tying all these concerns together, and perhaps the principal consideration for enlistment, was length of service. Most duties were short term as patrols and scouts, for example, and troops raised for general duty on the frontier rarely served for more than a year.⁹⁶ Recruitment proclamations for expeditions habitually included the assurance, "to satisfie the countrie troops," that provincial soldiers would not be made to remain as a garrison against their will.⁹⁷ More than any other consideration, the time spent away from community, family, and employment concerned New England men the most, and any attempt to hold them in service caused deep resentment.

The issue of enforced absence came to a head at Louisbourg. Governor William Shirley and William Pepperrell found themselves embarrassed by success. Having captured the French fortress they now had to hold on to it. Shirley had expected the British to assume responsibility for the fort and provide a garrison, but Whitehall was focused on the Jacobite Rebellion of Charles Stuart and was not about to dispatch redcoats across the Atlantic until the threat to the Hanover dynasty was stopped. Even if Bonnie Prince Charlie had not made his bid to place his father on the throne it would have taken some months for the British to send a garrison to Louisbourg. Unfortunately for Shirley, his men had expected to go home after Louisbourg fell, preferably with their pockets lined with plunder. Now they would have to remain for an indeterminate time.

Shirley did allow a few soldiers to return home. Nine days after the surrender he suggested to Pepperrell that the lame and sick and "any persons who are under contracts for masts" be allowed to leave.⁹⁸ But in early July he had a letter read to the army in which he congratulated the men on their "glorious acquisition" and charged them to "preserve it from falling again into the enemy's hands." Shirley also hoped they would not "sully the honour of their arms by any murmurs or discontent or strife."⁹⁹ The murmurs and discontent grew throughout the summer despite Shirley's admonitions. At the end of July the governor advised his general to keep all the men except those belonging to "exposed Eastern parts."¹⁰⁰

The murmurs and discontent grew to a threatened mutiny by mid-September. Added to the poor pay and lack of plunder, the forced extension of their service had angered the provincial soldiers to the point of rebellion.[101] Ragged, lousy, sick, disappointed, and homesick, the New England soldiers wanted to go home. Only an appearance and speech by Shirley himself averted disaster. Still the discontent continued, the soldiers "uneasy at their prospect of being detained here from their families till Spring, and some of them for want of cloaths."[102] The Assembly of Massachusetts became concerned that the extended service had reduced "due confidence in the promises of the government."[103]

In early October one man from each company was allowed to return to New England to gather clothing and supplies for their comrades.[104] By the end of October and into early November, soldiers raised as reinforcements and replacements began to arrive, and some of the original volunteers were allowed to go home.[105] But the damage had been done, and many a disillusioned soldier left Louisbourg vowing never to serve on an expedition again. As one anonymous soldier expressed the feeling:

> Faire Well Cape: Britton
> faire well all you fases
> That Bread Such Disgreases
> a gainst Solders that are True to their King
> for I boldely Do Say
> If they once git away
> Your will Be hard Poot to it to Catch them again[106]

With the various incentives, the press, the commitment to community, family, and occupation, and the complications of occasional extended service, who did serve in the provincial forces of New England? And why did they? Many historians probing this question have tended to agree with the assessment suggested by John Shy in 1963. Discussing the "changing character of recruitment in the eighteenth century," Shy theorized that "a growing number of those who did the actual fighting were not the men who bore a military obligation as part of their freedom . . . with more social pariahs filling the ranks, and military objectives less clearly connected to parochial interests, respectable men felt not so impelled by a sense of duty or guilt to take up arms." Shy concluded that "fighting had ceased to be a function of the community as such."[107] James Kirby Martin and Mark Edward Lender concurred with this theory, believing that "those who were expendable in society—the down and outers—were deemed to be the appropriate persons to be sent off to engage in full-scale combat at some distant point on the map."[108] As colonial society detached itself from military obligation, and its soldiers became more mercenary, they would be, according to Martin and Lender, the "field substitutes for more favored, property-holding militiamen."[109] Once again, contemporary British observations seem to support this theory. Lord Loudon, the British commander in the last French and Indian war, complained that the New England soldiers "are not the men they use[d] to send out, but fellows hired by other men who should have gone themselves."[110]

However, some recent studies have contradicted this impression. Fred Anderson examined Massachusetts soldiers who served in the last French war and disagreed with the conclusion they were desperate volunteers seeking relief from their lowly status, or hired men substituting for disinterested militiamen. On the contrary, 88 percent of the provincial soldiers were volunteers and only 2 percent were pressed and 10 percent hired.[111] "The soldier's patterns of occupation, residence and movement before enlistment give little indication that these were men driven by necessity into military service." Anderson found that Massachusetts soldiers were not "second-class, hireling manpower," but for the most part young men who sought to increase their prospects for independence from parental control through military service.[112]

Similarly, Myron O. Stachiw studied Massachusetts soldiers in Dummer's War and the Cartagena campaign and recognized three distinct types of recruits. First were young, unmarried sons of locally prominent families who had not received their inheritance and had enlisted for adventure and booty. The second category was middle sons of less wealthy families who were not expected to inherit a great deal of land. Enlistment meant a better, or quicker, start in life, or, for older men, a chance for land grants or booty to provide for their own sons. The families of these soldiers often had a long record of military service. Finally, there were men of little property, the "loose people," whose service is emphasized by John Shy and the others.[113]

An inquiry into the men who performed active military service from Dover, New Hampshire, in 1745 reinforces the theory that provincials were not drawn principally from the disadvantaged in New England society. Fifty-one men have been identified as enlisting for the Louisbourg campaign from the New Hampshire community, and, while they were away, forty more spent a week in August patrolling the woods north of Rochester.[114] Although the type of service was quite different—with the former being an expedition involving a sea voyage and a minimum of three to four months away from home and the latter a short, local patrol—the profile of the men who served in both was exactly the same.[115] Of the ninety-one soldiers from Dover, seventeen are obscure, simply names on the roll. No records exist and their family names are not recognized as prominent in the town records, and indeed, they probably represent the down and outers of Dover society. Of the fifty-one whose ages are known, only one was under twenty. Twenty-six fell between twenty to twenty-nine years of age; six were thirty to thirty-nine; and eighteen were forty or over, including two men who were fifty-nine when they went to Louisbourg.

Of the twenty-seven men whose marital status could be discovered, eight were single, and with one exception, those who were married had either been married less than eight years, or more than seventeen. With one exception the middle range of years married, eight to seventeen, was missing from *both* companies. The one exception to the missing middle marriage range was Sergeant Benjamin Libby who had been married eleven years when he went to Louisbourg. He was also fifty-two and was the only married man from Dover to remain at Louisbourg over the winter. A marriage at forty-one suggests a second wife, but no record exists of a first marriage. Why he remained in Louisbourg although married will probably never be known.[116]

Coupled with the low number of men in their thirties this figure of middle marriage range is suggestive, but only suggestive. The sampling is too small to be conclusive of anything. But as a randomly chosen test the men from Dover seem to resemble more the soldiers described by Anderson and Stachiw. Many of the men who served came from prominent families in the town with the same last names appearing in both the Louisbourg company and the patrol. For example, the Hayes family had three men in provincial service in 1745. Elihu Hayes, a twenty-seven-year-old cordwainer, left his wife of six years with a two-month-old infant when he went to Louisbourg, and he took his apprentice, Stephen Evans, along with him. Elihu's brother, John Hayes, thirty-four and single, went on patrol that summer, along with their first cousin, Ichabod Hayes, who would later achieve some social standing as town moderator in 1766.[117] Actually, Stephen Evans, the cordwainer's apprentice, would accomplish even more. He later gained considerable wealth from trade and shipbuilding, served as moderator and selectman, was chosen representative to New Hampshire's Revolutionary Assembly in 1775 and 1776, and commanded a regiment at Saratoga, becoming New Hampshire's highest-ranking soldier.[118]

Answering the question of who performed active service and why they did so is not an easy task. The conclusions are so often diluted through generalization and a glut of exceptions. As in all human endeavors, the reasons men go to war are almost as varied as the number of participants involved. The decision is a personal one, and it can result from mere impulse or a careful consideration of all potential rewards and consequences. According to Myron Stachiw, war signified several things to provincial soldiers, including escape, self-improvement, adventure, and a show of patriotism, and to this list can be added the motives of revenge and religious fervor.[119]

Recruits escaped from debt, family conflict, unemployment, or servitude. Bounties, plunder, and even wages attracted those seeking self-improvement—including independence from parental control or the ability to provide independence for children. Expeditions and major raids attracted those seeking adventure, whether the young sowing wild oats before marriage and commitment, or the old wanting a last fling before the end of life itself. New Englanders also served out of a sense of duty and patriotism to their community, province, and king, as well as an obligation to their church and God. Ann M. Little, in *Abraham in Arms: War and Gender in Colonial New England*, indicates that masculinity pushed men to enlist. Little wrote that "war was key to the performance of manhood."[120] Finally, for those living on the frontier, military service offered an opportunity for revenge, a chance to strike back for the loss of property and loved ones. For individual New Englanders pondering their future, any combination of these reasons could influence their decision to "go for a soldier."

The answer to the question of who served and, equally important, who did not is only slightly less complex but perhaps placed on a firmer foundation. The recent research of Fred Anderson, Myron Stachiw, and others points away from the theory that between 1689 and 1763 the provincial soldiers of New England were drawn increasingly from the outcasts and downtrodden in society, forced to serve by economic pressures or by the government through the press. The evidence seems to indicate that provincial service attracted the same soldiers throughout the French wars. First, they were volunteers, with only a relatively small percentage of pressed or hired men. Second, they came from one of four major groups. The first group were single men of established families, including young men serving with their fathers or on their own, or older men, bachelors, or widowers, all usually seeking some adventure or a change of pace. The second group were those young men recently married or about to be, seeking independence from parents, or simply a better start for their new families. The third group were older men with children approaching the age of independence who needed to be provided for, and lastly, the fourth group were the downtrodden and destitute who had nowhere else to turn. Absent from these groups are middle-aged men with large families on whom the economic pressures of maintaining the farm or trade descended the hardest.

The one exception to this picture is involvement in extended service. Here the contrast with regular service is quite startling, and the image of the New England soldier closely resembles that portrayed by Shy, Martin and Lender, and the others. When performing patrols, raids, expeditions, and even garrison duty at frontier forts in time of war, the four groups enumerated above composed the forces involved. But the lonely vigils at garrison houses, at provincial forts between conflicts, at Port Royal after 1710, and at Louisbourg after October 1745 were left to the outcasts and downtrodden, to the pressed and hired men.

Anathema to New England men, extended military service was avoided if at all possible. Provincial commanders on the frontier put their pressed and hired men in the garrison houses, keeping their more reliable volunteers for patrols and raiding, and only a desperate or a pressed man would garrison a fort during peacetime. A survey of company rolls taken in September and November at Louisbourg reveals that, with the exception of officers, it was overwhelmingly the single men and those names without records that remained behind. During the period of the mutiny, in anticipation of sending men home, company rolls were drawn up indicating which men were married and how many children they had, as well as their physical condition at that time. The September rolls were compared with those taken in November. For example, Ephraim Baker's company from Boston, Hopkinton, and Framingham had four married privates in September, but only one remained in November, but of ten single men, nine remained. Peter Staple's company from a "frontier town" in Maine had eleven married men in September and four of them remained, but sixteen of eighteen single men stayed. John Storer's Company from Wells had twelve married men of whom six were listed in November; eleven of the original thirteen single men were also listed. And in Thomas Perkins's company, all five married privates went home, while only five of eleven single men were allowed to leave. Incidentally, only nine of Dover's fifty-one men stayed at Louisbourg; in addition to the aforementioned Sergeant Libby, five were single and three were obscure.[121]

With the exception of the small number of pressed and hired men, the typical provincial soldier did not separate "military service from the responsibilities of citizenship,"[122] but undoubtedly he weighed the obligation to community and province along with the economic advantages when deciding to enlist. Only extended tours made men balk, because these tours revealed the weakness of the New England military system and thrust those "expendable" members of society into the forefront of provincial service.

8

Officers

Chosen to Lead

The ability of the provincial governments of northern New England to recruit soldiers and undertake military operations depended mainly on their officers. Despite the incentives, the propaganda, and the press, the soldier's decision to serve often centered on who the soldier would serve under, and, once constituted, the probability of any provincial force accomplishing the objectives set forth by the government rested on the competency and skill of the officers involved. Therefore, the historical impression of inconsistency and ineptitude of New England soldiers has been frequently connected with a lack of experience and proficiency on the part of provincial military leaders at all levels. Provincial soldiers chose to enlist and serve under particular individuals. As few New England men were eager to entrust their lives to strangers, a certain familiarity with any potential officer became a common prerequisite, but on the whole provincial soldiers chose their officers on the basis of experience and reputation and not on their inclination to be compliant and indulgent. The ability to lead patrols and raids, to direct firefights, to care for the well-being of his men, and achieve a modicum of success marked the long-serving provincial officer. On the other hand, incompetence on a level suggested by most historical interpretations resulted in social disgrace.

The New England governments gave commissions to their officers based on several criteria, including recommendations from military, provincial, and local leaders; prior service; or special circumstances. The soldiers approved of the choice by their willingness to volunteer to be led by the officers.[1] When quotas were sent to the local militia, the companies were assembled and the intended service described, including who would be commanding both the company and the overall operation. In most cases the company commander would be from that town or a neighboring community and thus well known to the potential recruits. Provincial officers given "beating orders" who presented themselves before militia assemblies or other gatherings had to promote not only the intended operation but themselves as well.² Dr. Alexander Bulman found the men of York enthusiastic over the prospects of attacking Louisbourg in 1745, but even with general approval of the design, "some decline enlisting till they know who shall be the general officers as also who shall be their particular Captain."³ As Fred Anderson found during the last French war, the decision to enlist meant choosing a leader.⁴ This selection was important. Once made, only death, desertion, or discharge could release a provincial soldier from the control of his company officer.

The level of rank affected who served. Field rank officers—those who commanded districts on the frontier, larger raids, and expeditions—tended to be drawn from the upper ranks of society. Winthrop Hilton, who initiated winter raids during Queen Anne's War and commanded one of the two regiments at Port Royal in 1707, descended from John Winthrop and Samuel Dudley, and he was prominent in the mast trade. He would be nominated for membership on the New Hampshire Council before his death in 1710.⁵ Thomas Westbrook, the commander of the Maine frontier during Dummer's War, was the son of a member of the New Hampshire Council and a prominent merchant and land speculator in his own right.⁶ William Pepperrell had been a leading citizen of Kittery, Maine, and colonel of the York county militia regiment before being appointed to command the Louisbourg expedition.⁷

In an unpublished study of New Hampshire officers serving in the French wars, Ranz Esbenshade found that of twenty field grade officers studied, eighteen had held political office prior to their command, either in the assembly or on the council. Only one of the twenty was commissioned without any previous military exposure, although only eight had been provincial officers at the company level, the remainder having held high rank in the militia regiments.⁸

The fact that the provincial government chose its commanders from the upper class is not surprising. It would be hard to find any government in the history of warfare that placed the conduct of a military operation in the hands of an unknown individual drawn from the lowest ranks of society. It was essential for recruitment that the soldiers have confidence in both their company officer and their overall commander. The former could recruit successfully with a local reputation, but the latter needed a status that extended over a wider geographic area.

For company-level command, however, the provincial governments could draw from a greater reservoir of candidates, and here, perhaps because the criteria were less restrictive, they achieved far greater results. One source of names came from recommendations provided by politicians, local political and militia leaders, and other provincial officers. Throughout the French war period, especially in preparation for expeditions and major raids, the governors, lieutenant governors, members of the assembly and council, and field commanders were approached by individuals, by letter or in person, requesting a provincial commission for their son, nephew, or neighbor.[9] William Pepperrell was bombarded with recommendations for young men after his victory at Louisbourg,[10] although in one instance there was a change of heart. Nathaniel Sparhawk withdrew an earlier recommendation, saying "as to young Royall I am very sorry I was prevailed on the say a word on his behalf. His uncle imposed on me. After I wrote I found him to be the most worthless wretch; so I hope you will have taken no notice of him, at least to the disadvantage of any person living."[11]

Some recommendations, especially those from provincial officers, concerned men who had distinguished themselves through their service as privates and noncommissioned officers.[12] Many provincial officers came up from the ranks, learning from practical experience and the tutorage of other officers. Finding military life appealing, these individuals often achieved fame and further advancement through repeated service. John Goffe, who would lead numerous scouts during King George's War and rise to the provincial rank of lieutenant colonel during the last French war, began his military career as a private under John Lovewell in 1725. Eleazer Melvin, another private serving with Lovewell on his last raid, achieved some fame as an officer of scouts based at Fort Dummer and at Number Four in the 1740s. Jeremiah Moulton, of York, Maine, began Dummer's War as a sergeant, quickly rose to lieutenant, then captain, and eventually became colonel of a regiment sent to Louisbourg in 1745.[13] Even the most famous provincial officer in all the French wars, Robert Rogers, initiated his illustrious career as a teenage private under Captain Daniel Ladd by patrolling the New Hampshire frontier in 1746.[14]

Former Indian captives with special knowledge of language and terrain provided another source of company officers. In this instance the terrifying episode of captivity altered the direction of their lives, thrusting them through fate into a military career. When John Gyles was captured at Pemaquid in 1689, he probably had no concept of a future life beyond that of a farmer like his father. But kept among the Eastern Indian tribes for the remainder of King William's War, he became a prominent interpreter for the Bay government and eventually rose to serve as a fort commander on the Maine frontier.[15]

Other officers, especially those involved in raids, probes, and scalp hunting, found military service an extension of their peacetime occupations of hunter and woodsmen. While most hunters became guides or pilots, a few managed to achieve status as leaders of men. The most obvious example is John Lovewell, who was known as a successful woodsman, but John Goffe's father had been a prominent hunter as well, and Goffe undoubtedly passed his experience on to his son.[16]

In rising from the ranks, company-level provincial officers contrasted starkly with their counterparts in the British army. Fred Anderson found in the last French war that "when soldier's occupations are analyzed with respect to rank, the most striking characteristic to emerge is the absence of any clear-cut division between officers and enlisted men with respect to civilian livelihoods . . . In the Massachusetts regiments . . . over half of the company-grade officers had manual occupations and, indeed, followed the same ones as privates."[17] Provincial commanders and their governments were not above ignoring social standing and even military protocol in advancing experienced and talented men in rank. As the Bay government told Colonel Thomas Westbrook during Dummer's War, though he should give preference to officers according to seniority, Westbrook could advance younger officers who were "more than Ordinary Useful."[18]

In the British army a commission did not depend on experience or ability as much as it did on wealth and social status.[19] Most British officers held their commission through the purchase system, which placed a monetary value on military rank so high it would exclude all those outside at least the gentry class. Those few who achieved a commission from the ranks or outside the gentry class did so only after long service or under the extraordinary demands and vacancies created by major wars. Since they could not possibly purchase a higher rank, such individuals were generally doomed to remain at the levels of their original commissions.

Because the backgrounds of provincial officers differed so much from their own, British officers viewed them with a combination of horror and disgust. In British soldiers' eyes, provincial officers were "Blacksmith's, Taylors, Barbers, Shoemakers and all the Banditry them Colonies afford."[20] Samuel Vetch's British second-in-command at Annapolis Royal referred to the provincial officers as "a parcell of mercenary fools and pedlars."[21] To the English aristocrats who controlled the British army, provincial officers could never be knowledgeable or professional concerning military matters. Their colonial counterparts were, in the words of Douglas Leach, "uncultured, undisciplined . . . amateurs at war."[22]

In the provincial service both the experience of officers and the similarity with their men regarding occupation and social status encouraged recruiting. While overall commanders were often chosen for their familiarity, even, in some cases, their notoriety, among the general population,[23] company-grade officers had to draw on their reputations as successful and experienced military leaders, as well as their personal standing in their communities in order to encourage men to enlist in their companies.

Fred Anderson discovered that officers drew on family relationships and close friends in recruiting, and thus "the provincial regiments [in the French and Indian War] were in some measure bound by kinship ties."[24] Anderson believed the "operation of the provincial forces depended on personal contacts between officers and enlisted" and that "rather than a uniform hierarchy of officers and men, a provincial army was in fact a confederation of tiny war bands bound together by an organic network of kinship and personal loyalties."[25] Such close ties between officers and enlisted men were "incomprehensible to regular soldiers like the redcoats, who understood that a virtually unbridgeable chasm separated officers from other ranks."[26]

Anderson's conclusions can be extended throughout the early French wars as well, where company rolls also reveal close familial relationships between soldiers and their officers.[27] In addition to a network of family and friends, company-level officers relied on their reputations to bring in recruits. John Storer of Wells, a man whose family had long been military leaders in the community, raised sixty-one soldiers in one day for Louisbourg.[28] Men such as Johnson Harmon, Benjamin Church, John Lovewell, or John Goffe rarely had difficulty finding men for their scouting companies because they had reputations as effective military leaders.

Officers commissioned by the provincial governments without such a reputation could encounter great difficulty in finding recruits. Commissioned to raise and command a company in William Pepperrell's regiment for Louisbourg, Moses Butler of Berwick, Maine, informed his colonel on February 20, 1745, that he had been "very much obstructed in the afair by Sum of your Noble Officers of Berwick." The next day he wrote Pepperrell that "Jehabod Goodwin the last night had with him a considerable number of the Enlisted men at his House and . . . Discouraged them from going in this Expedition with such a Sorry fellow as I am which Causes the men not to appear this day to sign the Enlistments." In fact, Butler had no success with recruiting until he found an acceptable lieutenant. On February 23, he indicated Peter Grant had volunteered to be lieutenant "which is more to the Exceptance of the People . . . Mr. Grant seems to be Very Harty in the Expedition/ by this Night we shall have forty men if not more."²⁹ The history of Butler's company at Louisbourg leaves the impression that the suspicions about the captain being a "sorry fellow" were correct. The company roll in September lists Lieutenant Peter Grant in command and Captain Moses Butler as "gone home."³⁰

Having recruited their forces, provincial officers found their military duties listed in the commissions and instructions provided by the government. Officers were instructed to "take care that the worship of God be duly and constantly maintained and kept amongst you; and to suffer no swearing, cursing, or other profanation of the holy name of God; and, as much as in you lies, to deter and hinder all other vices amongst your soldiers."³¹ They were to maintain watches and wards, and scouting parties and to try to destroy the enemy without themselves being surprised "or otherwise betrayed by their Treachery."³² Officers had to keep the government apprised of developments through reports and journals. During Dummer's War, officers were expected to submit copies of their journals every two weeks.³³ Finally, provincial officers were ordered to "take effectual care that the Soldiers under your conduct, be kept under good order and discipline."³⁴

The maintenance of the worship of God was generally left to the ministers who accompanied the soldiers. Paid by the government, these martial men of God administered to the souls of soldiers on expeditions and on the frontier, including those garrisoning the forts and conducting the raids.³⁵ But while ministers disciplined the spirit, the officers disciplined the soldiers. Disciplinary problems among provincial soldiers involved such infractions as "shooting a gun on the parade," getting drunk, sleeping on watch, carelessness leading to damage or injury, and refusing to perform duties.³⁶ For such transgressions, a soldier could "be punished at the discretion of the Commission officers of the Garrison Company or Troop whereto he belongs by putting into the Bilboes [stocks], laying Neck & Heels, riding the wooden horse or running the Gantlet."³⁷

For example, Benjamin Stearns recorded in his Louisbourg journal that "Corporal Lakin orders Stephen Barron to gard the armes at which said Barron told Corporal to kiss his ass! for which abusive afrunt he ordered him to ride the pickets one [hour]."³⁸ John Burk related in his journal that two soldiers rode the horse at Number Four, both for sleeping on watch. The horse or picket was a beam suspended five or six feet above the ground on which the soldier sat. It was common for weights, such as cannonballs or muskets, to be dangled from the feet, further straining the muscles of the legs and the hip joints.³⁹

To lay a man "neck and heels," the prisoner sat on the ground with his knees drawn up before him. His ankles were tied and the rope passed up between his legs and around his neck, tied off short to draw his head down toward his knees. A stick was placed under his knees, long enough to project out on each side, and his arms brought under the stick with his wrists tied together before his shins. Usually he was gagged as well by having a stick, or even a bayonet, secured in his mouth.[40] A soldier running the gauntlet ran between two lines of fellow soldiers who hit him on the back with sticks or ramrods. Sometimes the guilty party was forced to carry a heavy weight to slow him down. Such a punishment could be quite severe, depending on how many men were in the line and how many times the soldier had to go through it.[41]

Provincial officers did not use flogging on a regular basis. One soldier at Louisbourg after the surrender received thirty-nine lashes for stealing a winding sheet off a corpse, but this is a rare occurrence in extant records.[42] Riding the horse and laying neck and heels were more common punishments, especially on the frontier line, and they were accepted by provincial soldiers as reasonable penalties for minor infractions.

If exposed to harsher punishments, colonial soldiers could be quite vocal in their complaints. When Governor Edmund Andros raised provincial soldiers for the Maine frontier in the autumn of 1688, he placed them under the command of English officers drawn from the detachment of redcoats stationed in Boston at that time. As Douglas Leach indicated in *Roots of Conflict: British Armed Forces and Colonial Americans, 1677–1763*, "the regular officers found the New Englanders stubbornly averse to any command they thought discriminatory or unreasonable; when the officers tried to overcome the problem with harsh discipline, the provincials quickly marked it down as bestial cruelty."[43] The soldiers later described frequent beating with canes and half-pikes. One Captain Lockhart beat a soldier "with his Cane, and kicked and abused him in such a wise the blood ran out of his mouth. The souldier did say upon his death, which was quickly after, that The abuse he received . . . was the imediate cause of his death."[44]

Another soldier, accused of breaking into a store house, was tortured by a Lieutenant John Jordan for his confession. Jordan tied him up by "One hand lifted fully stretched out above his head binding the other hand behind him to One of his legs." The soldier was suspended over a sharp stake "so that if he indeavored to rest his Arm that Bore the whole weight of his body then was his Naked foot forced to rest (without Rest) upon the aforesaid stake for two hours together."[45] As Douglas Leach concluded, "Regular officers required instant, unquestioning obedience from their own men, and presumably expected the same from the colonial troops. The latter, however, were accustomed to the much looser discipline of the militia, maintained by officers with whom they were personally acquainted."[46]

Provincial officers rarely, if ever, resorted to the kind of physical abuse that was common in European armies. Putting a man on the wooden horse or laying him neck and heels for an hour was one thing, but inflicting severe injuries was quite another. In fact, colonial officers rarely punished capital offenses without the consent of the government who would order the formation of a court-martial or even try the accused in a civil court. Both the government and the provincial officers were quite sensitive to the negative impact on recruiting that a summary execution would produce. In 1692, Benjamin Church's instructions from the governor ordered him to form his own court-martial among his officers if any soldier committed an offense and that he should "inflict such punishment as the merit of the offence requires, death only excepted, which if any shall deserve, you are to secure the person, and signify the crime unto me by the first opportunity."[47] During a scout in 1723, commanded by Johnson Harmon, a soldier fired at a tree just as another man named Stockbridge passed near it. "The bullet struck a tree and Glancing Straingley did unhappily kill the said Stockbridge," reported Harmon. Although he was convinced it was an accident, Harmon had "confined" the man and awaited instruction from the government.[48] Lieutenant Governor Dummer replied that "the Man Slayer must be tried by a Court Martial, and I shall in a Short time give out a Commission for that Purpose. In the meantime though you are to keep him under Restraint, You need not be very rigorous and severe to him, seeing you are fully convinced as you say that the Mischief was purely accidental."[49]

This sensitivity to the administration of severe or capital punishment was reflected in the response to the most common offense committed by provincial soldiers—desertion. Laws passed at the close of the seventeenth century stipulated that deserters shall be "proceeded against as a felon, and shall suffer the pains of death, or some other grievous punishment." But the responsibility of administering this justice was removed from the commanders in the field. Deserters were to be tried by the county courts "or at a court of oyer and terminer by commissioners to be specially appointed and impowred for that purpose."[50]

Provincial soldiers deserted either in large groups by consensus or as individuals. As a conscious decision expressed by a majority, or a large minority, collective desertion resulted in far less prosecution or popular indignation.[51] The group decision to desert occasionally had the tacit approval of the officers. After the first attempt to capture Port Royal in 1707, Governor Joseph

Dudley ordered the force held together for a second attack. However, the New Hampshire soldiers deserted in droves while waiting for the decision to renew the assault. William Dudley, the governor's son and "Secretary of War" for the expedition, reported to his father that the New Hampshire officers "do encourage or at Least wink at the Desertion of their men."[52]

As in the case of Port Royal, collective desertion usually resulted from a feeling of disappointment and futility. When the men of Theodore Atkinson's regiment found themselves posted at a fort on Lake Winnipesaukee rather than assaulting Quebec in 1746, 170 of them deserted. They had enlisted to defend New Hampshire from a French attack, and to perhaps assault Quebec, not to garrison a fort on the frontier. Discouragement, frustration, and boredom drove them to desert and little was done to stop them. After all, the officers themselves were not immune to such feelings.[53]

Unlike collective action, desertion on an individual level rarely received understanding or approval. The act of individual desertion carried with it the risk of infamy and social disgrace, not only from fellow soldiers, many of whom were friends or relatives, but from the deserter's community as well. Perhaps the most famous incident of desertion, in this case in the face of the enemy, was that of Benjamin Hassell. A member of John Lovewell's company during that last fateful raid (and Lovewell's cousin), Hassell believed the company to be destroyed by the first fire of the Indians. He quickly fled the field, ostensibly to get reinforcements from the men left at the makeshift fort they had built. However, Hassell's description of the fight convinced the others that reinforcements would be too late, and all agreed to a hasty withdrawal to the settlements. Back in Dunstable, Hassell and the others reported to Eleazer Tyng, who then passed the word of Lovewell's fight on to Lieutenant Governor William Dummer.

Hassell's actions resulted in instant infamy. The day following Tyng's report, Dummer informed Lieutenant Governor John Wentworth of New Hampshire that "One of Cpt. Lovewells Men is run from him and left him engaged with the Indians at Pigwacket last Lords Day and pretends that they were overpowered by Numbers and that he saw Cpt Lovewell fall and heard him Groan, and that he him self was cutt off from the Company by the Indians Pressing between them though Hee Cant Deny but our people were charging the Enemy briskly when he left."[54] In his instructions to Tyng, Dummer wrote that he had "not Time at present to make any Observations on the ill Management of Hazzel & the ten Men at the Fort who have so cowardly deserted their Commander and fellow Soldiers in their Danger." Tyng was ordered to lead a company to the site of the fight and to take Hassell with him as a pilot.⁵⁵ However, Hassell pleaded illness and refused to accompany Tyng to the battle site.⁵⁶

The men who had fled from the fort were not censured by public opinion because it was understood that their decision had been based on the description provided by Benjamin Hassell, but Hassell soon became *persona non grata* in the communities along the Massachusetts frontier (although the condemnation was subdued to a certain extent because he was a cousin of John Lovewell, thus an attack on his conduct was an insult to the hero's family). Because the threat of public disgrace was very real, affecting not only the soldier but his family as well, individual desertions rarely involved volunteers. It was the pressed men, those with few ties to the communities they left, or the faceless "have-nots" assigned to garrisons and forts on the frontier who deserted.⁵⁷ Collective desertion where a soldier made a statement by leaving with his friends and neighbors was acceptable, but the abandonment of those friends, neighbors, and relatives was not undertaken lightly by established freemen of New England communities.

And in the case of desertion, as in so many aspects of the provincial military system, the influence of officers—their personalities, abilities, and standings in their communities and province—often proved to be a crucial element. Incompetent officers had little control over their men, which in turn led to desertion and discipline problems. Even competent officers could not maintain control if separated from their commands. In particular, the necessity to post men at frontier garrison houses scattered an officer's company over a wide geographic area. As pressed soldiers were often assigned to these garrisons, the lack of direct supervision could lead to desertion.⁵⁸

During the upheaval of the Glorious Revolution the ability of provincial officers to control their men was impaired and so their competency to command was questioned. Joseph Prout reported to the Bay government in 1689 that the soldiers left to protect Falmouth, Maine, "are most of them of Ill behavior and take little notice of their Commander, Espeshally Since their Captain went hence . . . I would not reflect upon any man, but I am fully persuaded that if thay are not Speedily under a prudend Commander thier Cariage here will be dishonorable to God and to the Country, and Unsafe for this Town for many of them do often Swear that they will march away home."⁵⁹

For men who volunteered to serve under a particular officer, the removal of that officer led to the threat of collective desertion. The volunteers whom Samuel Appleton led north from Newbury after the Destruction of Dover in 1689 fully expected to return with their commander. After briefly pursuing the Indians, they remained in garrison until the threat died down. Local leaders asked the Bay government for Appleton to remain because his company would not stay without him. Appleton assumed the pressed men would remain and the volunteers would leave with him, but the number of pressed men was small compared to the volunteers and thus they were vulnerable if attacked. Appleton needed orders to keep the pressed men on the frontier, for apparently even they expected to leave when he did, and he suggested more soldiers be raised to replace his Newbury volunteers.[60]

Two years later, after the disastrous raid led by John March and Daniel King ended and the survivors posted on the frontier, New Hampshire community leaders reported that "we heare that there is great [murmuring] among the soldiers in the Garrisons for that both the Captains are going away, and many of them we are informed will not stay when their Chief Commanders are gone."[61] John March reported the soldiers and "likewis the wounded also very desirous of our staying there, and also Major Vahn and the Rest of the Gentelmen att the Esterne Parts." Daniel King had been persuaded to remain a few days longer, but the government needed to send "Some fitting person to take care of the Whole."[62]

The attachment between provincial officers and their men grew from a mutual respect that extended beyond the time spent in military service. Good officers inspired trust and affection and, in turn, unlike their European counterparts, they exhibited genuine respect and concern for their men. Of course, some company-level officers had been privates themselves at some point, and their commands were likely to contain many relatives and neighbors, but even field-grade provincial commanders never forgot that their soldiers were fellow citizens, not, as one British officer said of his men, "a parcel of mercenary, fawning, lewd dissapated creatures, the dregs and scum of mankind."[63]

James Converse supported former soldiers in their attempts to get aid from the provincial governments.[64] His concern for the plight of soldiers and his willingness to assist them are reflected in a letter written in 1700 to the Speaker of the House of Representatives on behalf of John Baker. "I cannot get off from the Old theam," wrote Converse. "Hear is A poor Wounded Soldier, who had A trade and hous and land, and wherewith to live Comfortabley but hath spent all, and more, by Reason of A wound he Received in his Majesties' Service ... I know you love a soldier too well to see him Wronged, where it is in Your power to help."[65]

The respect and affection between soldiers and officers also revealed itself in the reaction of men to the death of their commanders. When Winthrop Hilton's masting party was ambushed in 1710, one hundred men immediately volunteered to attempt a rescue and pursue the enemy. Hilton's body was found and returned to Exeter for burial with "the several Troops in great Solemnity attending his Corps."⁶⁶ Benjamin Hassell's flight from Lovewell's final battle was obviously caused by the shock of seeing his commander fall. Hassell saw Lovewell hit on the first volley, and the death of his officer triggered his panic. Although he would indicate the company had been outnumbered and he cut off by the press of the Indians, Hassell's most vivid memory was "that he saw Captain Lovewell fall and heard him Groan."⁶⁷

The ability of provincial officers to inspire their men received its severest test while under fire. John Keegan and Richard Holmes observed that for military leaders the normal fear of death and of being a coward is "heightened by the knowledge that they have a status to maintain, and the realization that the lives of their subordinates hang upon their decisions."⁶⁸ The ability to survive such pressures depends upon an individual's personality and moral stamina. For some men the excitement and fear of combat enhances their martial qualities, while others break under the emotional weight. James Converse showed courage and strength under fire during the siege of Storer's garrison, where he threatened to shoot anyone who suggested surrender, and he personally directed the fire of the soldiers and inhabitants.⁶⁹ When John Lovewell and his lieutenant fell at the first volley during the fight at Pequawket, the command fell on Ensign Seth Wyman, who, in the words of Samuel Penhallow, "behaved himself with great Prudence and Courage, by animating the Men and telling them, 'That the Day would yet be their own, if their Spirits did not flag'; which enlivened them anew."⁷⁰ Wyman continued to direct the fight, which lasted for several hours.

For provincial officers, especially those on the company level or commanding raiding parties and patrols, leadership involved a physical presence as well as spiritual control. They were expected to be in the forefront of any action—physically leading their men in the fight. John Lovewell's wounding by the Indian at the pond and his subsequent mortal wounding on the first volley fired by the main Indian party resulted from his presence at the head of his company. When the force commanded by John March and Daniel King ended their fruitless raid and embarked at Maquoit during the summer of 1691, the Indians fired on the remnants of the company that remained ashore. Captain Samuel Sherbourne was among the slain as he and several of the company officers felt their men should embark first.⁷¹

Benjamin Church emphasized the need for his physical presence at the head of his men. During his last raid in 1704, according to his recollections, the "ancient and unwieldy" sixty-five-year-old colonel had a Sergeant Edee boosting him over fallen trees. Church would "lay his breast against the tree, the said Edee turning him over, generally had catluck, falling on his feet, by which means [he] kept in the front" during a pursuit of some Indians.[72] Later in Nova Scotia, Church divided his command into three sections, sending two around the flanks of the enemy force, while he drew the attention and the fire of the French on himself by standing in full view.[73]

The need to physically lead his men involved Church in an amusing episode during his 1692 raid into Maine, although it is probably only amusing in hindsight. During a rest in Casco Bay, Church allowed his Plymouth Indians to camp on shore where they were ambushed just before dawn by a large force of French Indians. Hugging the bank along the shore, the Plymouth Indians held off the enemy until Church could land his provincial soldiers. Church, assisted by James Converse, passed the word that he would give three shouts as a signal for an attack, and then, having shouted three times, he and Converse launched themselves up the bank and toward the enemy. However, Church's valiant charge ended abruptly when Converse frantically yelled that no one else had followed them! The two officers hastily retreated back to the bank under heavy fire where they organized another assault and, this time followed by their men, drove the enemy away.[74]

Inspiring trust in their men and animating them to perform their duties often proved easier for provincial officers than maintaining a cordial working relationship with each other. The Louisbourg expedition proved to be especially straining in this regard. A Colonel Richmond seemed particularly adept at rubbing people the wrong way. On May 18, he placed Captain Daniel Ladd and his whole company under arrest because Ladd apparently marched by Richmond as he left the trenches without informing the colonel how many men he had. Ladd was so disgusted with Richmond that he refused to "order his men any more nor have anything to do with them."[75] On June 5, Samuel Rhodes complained to William Pepperrell that after his company had returned from a fatiguing scout, he was placed under the command of Richmond. "I have not the least inclination to be put under Coll. Richmond. A difference has happened between us . . . which I resent and reflect upon with a just indignation, since I am a volunteer and a gentlemen." Rhodes asked Pepperrell to reconsider his assignment, indicating that "in case you don't ease me in this point I don't care one farthing if the next minute I am shot through the head." If placed under Richmond's command, Rhodes fully expected to see blunders and end up in trouble.[76]

Animosity and dissension also occurred occasionally between provincial officers and governors. After ordering Colonel Thomas Westbrook to conduct a raid along the Maine coast in August 1724, Lieutenant Governor William Dummer fired off angry letters when Westbrook offered alternative plans and requested more soldiers. "Collo. Westbrooks Packet is enough to make one Sick," wrote Dummer to Secretary Willard. "What Hee has done allready as well as what Hee further insists on seems to tend directly to Confound our hopefull designes . . . It was Impossible to express in more Strong termes My orders above all things that Hee should make no delay and yett Hee seems to have no Idea of it."[77] Westbrook soothed Dummer's temper by pointing out that his communication had been sent before he received Dummer's instructions and that he had every intention of conducting the raid as soon as possible.[78]

Difficulties between provincial officers and their English counterparts have been well documented. As Douglas Leach observed in *Roots of Conflict*, when provincial units were joined with the regular army, the provincials had to play by the regulars' rules.[79] English officers holding a royal commission believed the lowliest English ensign outranked any provincial officer, and, as Leach indicates, "the contempt and disgust so frequently expressed by the British officers inevitably were detected and resented by the provincials, especially those officers who had some regard for their own ability, experience, and worth."[80] In proposing his assault on Quebec in 1709, Samuel Vetch insisted that all problems of command—land versus sea, provincial versus regular—be settled before the expedition sailed.[81] Later as commander of Annapolis Royal with a combined garrison of provincials and Royal Marines, Vetch found that "what creates me a great deall of uneasiness is the multitude of officers of different Companys, whose jarrs about command and rank create me . . . endles trouble, which the setlement of the garrison upon a regular footing would wholly prevent."[82]

Personality clashes and professional jealousies between officers became particularly debilitating when military enterprises were conducted by committee. Councils of war involving senior officers were common in eighteenth-century armies: Phips held them in 1690 and Peter Warren and William Pepperrell met regularly during the siege of Louisbourg in 1745. But when one officer was unwilling, or unable, to take the final responsibility for a decision, chaos and usually defeat resulted. Benjamin Church's instructions for his 1690 raid included the order "to consult your council, the commanders or commission officers of your several companies, when it may be obtained, the greater part of whom to determine." When he later called a council of officers according to these orders, Church's plan to extend the raid was voted down because the other captains wanted to go home.[83] In 1704 Church used an officers' council vote to supersede orders from the Bay government.[84]

However, it was the Port Royal expedition of 1707 that best illustrates the disastrous consequences of councils of war. Two regiments were raised under the command of Francis Wainwright and Winthrop Hilton, and John March commanded over all. In addition, John Redknap, the British military engineer for the colonies, accompanied the forces, as did Governor Joseph Dudley's son, William, in the capacity of Secretary of War.[85] The antagonism between the provincial officers and Redknap, backed by the Royal naval officers present, not to mention clashes between the provincial officers themselves, proved to be the undoing of the expedition. According to Samuel Penhallow, "A Council of War being called, it was resolv'd that the Artillery should be landed, and their lines forces: But thro' the Unfaithfulness of some, and cowardly Pretentions of others, little was done in annoying the Enemy . . . if the Officers on board her Majesty's Ship had been true and faithful, matters had succeeded to good advantage. But instead of pressing on, they did rather clog and hinder the Affair: For by crafty Insinuations they afterward obtained a second Council, which the General not so well weighing as he ought, proved the overthrow of the whole Design."[86]

March apparently was reluctant to proceed without the backing of the professional English officers because he did not overrule the decision of the second "fatal council of war."[87] Governor Dudley was furious when he heard March had withdrawn the army, as were the citizens of Boston who taunted John Redknap and the other two officers sent to report the failure. Dudley decided that a second attempt should be made, and he then compounded March's command problems by sending three civilian commissioners along with authority to overrule him. During the second siege John March broke down under the strain and turned the command over to Francis Wainwright. As the situation at Port Royal had changed very little, and in fact had worsened because the French had strengthened their position, Wainwright eventually withdrew his army.[88]

Despite a long and valued service against the French and Indians, which included the dogged defense of Falmouth during the massive Indian attack in August 1703, John March would never again hold a provincial command.[89] His fate illustrates the consequences of failure for provincial officers—oblivion. The governments of northern New England and their citizens were willing to punish any perceived incompetence, cowardice, or neglect on the part of their officers. While courts-martial were always a possibility, public censure proved to be the most common punishment.[90]

In addition to the Port Royal expedition of 1707, the defeat at Quebec in 1690 and the loss of Fort William Henry in 1696 created the greatest outcry against the officers in command. While some blamed William Phips for the failure to capture the French capital in 1690, the commander of the land forces, John Walley, garnered his share of complaints. Walley seemed to lose his nerve once he and his soldiers were ashore. When the New Englanders pushed back the French forces sent to oppose or harass the landing, many expected Walley to order an immediate assault on the town. But time passed with no command, and the adrenaline of the provincial soldiers began to dissipate.

The Reverend John Wise searched for Walley throughout the army and finally found him in an obviously depressed state. Wise asked him what he was doing and Walley replied, "I cannot rule them. To Whom I replyed sir you must not expect when men are let loose upon an Enemie that they should attend all the Ceremonies martail and that are in fashion in a field of Peace But Sir said I what do you intend to doe he replyed I think they intend to lodge here all Night." Wise urged an immediate attack because the men were "Warme by to Morrow they will Stiffen and Coole." The attack never occurred, and Wise later found Walley wandering about "swallowed up with thoughts which I can deem from first to last to be only the Invincible Arrest of fear."[91] Others noticed Walley's paralysis as well. As one anonymous participant concluded, "but what is an army of Lyons when they must not go on Except a frighted Hart shall lead them?"[92] Although Walley would hold important political and militia posts, he never served in the field again.

However, no officer had more contempt heaped upon him than the man who surrendered Fort William Henry to the French in 1696—Pasco Chubb. A citizen of Andover, Massachusetts, Chubb had served on the Maine frontier for several years by leading patrol and raiding parties before he was ordered to relieve John March as commander of the provincial fort at Pemaquid.[93] In February 1696, several prominent Indian chiefs approached the fort to parley for the exchange of prisoners. According to Cotton Mather, during the meeting outside the fort "Chub found an Opportunity, in a pretty Chubbed manner, to kill the famous Edgeremett, and Abenquid, a couple of Principal Sagamores, with one or Two other Indians."[94] Later that summer Fort William Henry was invested by several hundred French and Indians with naval support and artillery. Chubb initially put up a brave front, but with a crumbling fort, overwhelming enemy forces, and the fear of what the Indians would do to him and his command because of the incident in February, "Chub," as Mather observed, "with an unaccountable Baseness, did Surrender the Brave Fort at Pemmaquid into their Hands."[95]

On his return to Boston, Chubb was thrown in jail to await a court-martial. On November 18, he petitioned the Bay government to be either tried or given bail "whereby he may be inabled to take Some care of his poore family." Chubb described himself as "avery poore man, haveing a wife and children to Looke after which by reason of his confinement and poverty are reduced to a meane and necessitous Condition, haveing not wherewithall either to defray his prison necessary charges or to releive his Indigent family."[96] However, Chubb was not released and sat in jail throughout the winter. In March a vote was taken in the House of Representatives "that Capt. Chub, who hath Long Laid in prison may be Brought to his Tryall: the negglect whereof is agreivance."[97] Never brought to trial, Chubb was released that spring to live quietly in Andover. Less than a year later, in February 1698, Indians killed both Chubb and his wife, apparently in revenge for his treachery two years before.[98]

The military theorist Carl von Clausewitz wrote that "there have been many instances of men who have shown the greatest resolution in an inferior rank, and have lost it in a higher position. While, on the one hand, they are obliged to resolve, on the other they see the dangers of a wrong decision, and as they are surrounded with things new to them, their understanding loses its original force, and they become only the more timid the more they become aware of the danger of the irresolution into which they have fallen, and the more they have formerly been in the habit of acting on the spur of the moment."[99] Such was certainly the situations of John March and John Walley. Placed in positions beyond their capabilities, these men let their insecurity and indecision lead to defeat. As Samuel Penhallow said of March, "he was a Man of good Courage, and a true lover of his Country. But the Business that he undertook was too weighty for his Shoulders to bear."[100] The consequence of their personal failure was an ignominious end to a public career. While Pasco Chubb may have been handed more than he could handle at Fort William Henry (more likely the task was impossible), the loss of such an expensive fort led inevitably to severe public censure.

While quick to condemn incompetence, New Englanders were just as eager to reward success. Military advancement, high militia rank, and positions in government came to many officers who proved their competence in the field. Ranz Esbenshade found that while only 10 percent of New Hampshire's company-level officers held political office before their service, 65 percent attained it after.[101] For taking command after Lovewell's death and leading the company in their day-long battle, Ensign

Seth Wyman was made a captain and given a silver sword.[102] Commodore Charles Knowles presented Phineas Stevens with a sword for his defense of the fort at Number Four in 1747.[103]

Benjamin Church rose to the rank of lieutenant colonel of militia, and for his 1704 raid the Assembly of Massachusetts "voted him Thanks for the good Services he did both to the Queen and Country."[104] And after his service in King William's War, James Converse also became lieutenant colonel of his militia, and in March 1703 he was selected as Speaker of the House of Representatives. Later that summer Converse would be placed in command of all forces in the field.[105]

This is in contrast to service in Connecticut far removed from the war. In *War and Society in Colonial Connecticut*, Harold E. Selesky indicated that for company-level officers "military service did not translate easily into political prominence."[106] Selesky concluded that "martial glory was not a path to political power in Connecticut."[107] However, societies bearing the brunt of war look differently on their military commanders. On the northern frontier, such service could lead to higher social and political positions.

However, one negative aspect of military success was the potentially deadly attention of the Eastern Indians who knew the English commanders and where they lived. A Frenchman captured after the attack on Salmon Falls in 1689 confessed that "their design was not against this place . . . but principly against Monsuir Tyng and the place where he lived."[108] Major Charles Frost of Kittery, Maine, the commander of all of the provincial soldiers on the eastern frontier after January 1695, was ambushed in 1697 as he walked home from church. According to local legend. the Indians opened Frost's grave the night after his burial, carried his body to the top of Frost's Hill, and tied it to a stake.[109] Jeremy Belknap wrote that Winthrop Hilton "was so brave and active an officer that the enemy had marked him for destruction; and for this purpose a party of them kept lurking about his house." In 1706 the Indians attacked a party going to mow a field because they believed Hilton was among them.[110] When Hilton was eventually killed while masting in the summer of 1710, the Indians "with utmost revenge struck their Hatchets in his Brains, leaving a Lance in his Heart."[111]

Provincial officers were not "subservient to the wishes of their men," and they did not rely on "coaxing and wheedling" to command.[112] Provincial soldiers entrusted their lives to an officer, and his ability and reputation were very much a factor in their decision to enlist. In his study of New Hampshire officers, Esbenshade concluded that "instead of *commanding* platoons of well-drilled riff-raff, the provincial officers *led* groups of fellow citizens."

Those fellow citizens had little patience with incompetence. In describing the qualities of a military leader, Clausewitz wrote that "if we take a general view of the four elements composing the atmosphere in which War moves, of *danger, physical effort, uncertainty,* and *chance,* it is easy to conceive that a great force of mind and understanding is requisite to be able to make way with safety and success amongst such opposing elements, a force which . . . we find termed by military writers and annalists as *energy, firmness, staunchness, strength of mind and character.*"[113] In most cases provincial soldiers tried to follow men with such qualities. Those possessing them had little need for strict discipline to control their men.

9

Battle Drill and Fighting Spirit

The military historian Richard Holmes wrote that military training "has two clearly identifiable functions. Its most obvious task is to instill exactly what its name suggests: an adequate level of training in such things as weapon handling and minor tactics. Its second, though by no means less important, function is to inculcate the military ethos in recruits."[1] The soldier must undergo training to learn the tactics and techniques that will enable him to function under fire, to use his weapons properly, and to understand and obey orders, often referred to as "battle drill." The soldier must also learn to overcome the instinctive urge for self-preservation and subordinate his individualism to the needs of his tactical unit, as well as prepare himself for the stress of combat. Constant repetition, the emphasis on "spit and polish," and the use of close order drills in modern basic training are only a few of the techniques used to build morale and make recruits "feel like soldiers."[2] From the Spartan phalanx to the modern rifle company, training has been the forge that welded a single tactical unit from its disparate individual members.

Ostensibly, it is a deficiency in such training that has contributed so much to the tarnished image of the New England provincial soldier. "Haphazardly trained and poorly disciplined" during infrequent frolics called "training day," provincial soldiers, unlike their professional European counterparts, could not hope to cope with the increasing complexities of eighteenth-century warfare.[3] However, the battle drill, the first function of military training, must prepare the soldier for the type of combat he will encounter or it serves no purpose, and it could even be counterproductive. The Spartan would have found twentieth-century training techniques, beyond the physical fitness benefits, of little use in learning how to handle his shield and spear, and obviously, the employment of Spartan tactics on the modern battlefield would be suicidal. Similarly, the type of training and discipline usually indicated as deficient in provincial soldiers prepared them for a kind of combat they never experienced, and an increase in such training would have been superfluous, even dangerous.

In addition, while the second function of intense training is to forge the fighting spirit that carries a soldier through the stress of battle, it can exist without such discipline. As Carl von Clausewitz observed, "a certain plodding earnestness and strict discipline may keep up military virtue for a long time, but can never create it; these things therefore have a certain value, but must not be overrated . . . Beware then of confusing the *spirit* of an Army with its temper."[4]

The primary source of formal military training for provincial soldiers, and the one most often used to illustrate the inadequacy of the provincial military system, were the periodic militia training days. By the beginning of the French wars, militia officers in northern New England were mandated by law to muster their companies "four dayes annually, and no more, to exercise them in motions, the use of arms, and shooting at marks, or other military exercises," with regimental musters to be held once every three years.[5] The infrequency of training recognized the endless occupational and familial demands on citizen soldiers, as when the Royal Government, concerned with the economic livelihood of its colony of New Hampshire, admonished the governor that "neither frequency nor unreasonableness of remote Marches, Musters and Traynings be an unnecessary Impediment to the affairs of the planters."[6]

While recognizing the militia training day as an important social node for early American communities, historians have concluded that any actual military value was negated both by their sporadic nature and the tendency for them to rapidly disintegrate from military drill to holiday frolic. Despite the obvious presence of danger during the Indian wars of the seventeenth and eighteenth centuries, New Englanders had to be constantly reminded of the serious purpose behind the training days. Cotton Mather warned members of the militia that they should not look on training day as a time of diversion and recreation, or for sitting around smoking, and in 1679 laws were passed to prevent the sale and use of strong drink because the militiamen "committ many disorders of drunkeness, fighting, neglect of duty, &c."[7] In addition to the extracurricular activities just listed, militia members looked forward to concluding training day with a mock battle whenever powder supplies permitted. According to the historian Morrison Sharp, militia officers loved the "pageantry of roar and shout and gay color of a regimental muster," especially the sham fight.[8] Near the end of King Philip's War, Richard Waldron of Dover, New Hampshire, captured two hundred Indians by involving them in such a simulated battle "after the English fashion," except that Waldron's men were not shamming, and this "treachery" made him a target for Indian vengeance in 1689.[9]

However, in spite of the holiday atmosphere, or perhaps in some cases because of it, attendance at militia training days could be dismal. "I can't spare the time to train" and "There are enough to train without me" were familiar excuses offered by truant members of the militia according to Cotton Mather.[10] Colonial assemblies attempted to force attendance at training day through the imposition of fines. Applied toward the purchase of much-needed equipment for their company, the busy, indifferent, or wealthy militiaman could actually make a contribution to his company by skipping training and paying such a fine.[11] If the fine was not paid, however, the individual could be laid neck and heels or made to ride the wooden horse for up to an hour at the next muster he attended.[12] Although fines were increased throughout the period, absenteeism at militia training would remain chronic.

Like the militia organization itself, training day served mainly as an administrative purpose. Four times each year, according to statutes, the clerks of individual militia companies were to "take an exact list of all persons living within the precincts" who qualified for the militia, and it was probably not coincidental that these same companies were ordered to train four times a year, thus providing the clerks a convenient opportunity to make out their lists.[13] In addition, officers were instructed to biannually "give order for a diligent enquiry into the state of [their] company . . . of the defects of arms or otherwise."[14] They were then ordered by law to drill their men in "motions, the use of arms . . . or other military exercises." However, allowing time for the men to arrive in the morning, calling the roll and correcting the muster list, inspecting arms and equipment, eating, and performing the all-important mock battle left precious little opportunity for actual drill and training, training that would in theory have made them better equipped for their military duties.

Yet for most types of service the militia training day served as all the formal military preparation that provincial soldiers received. Garrison duty left them too scattered to drill effectively, and soldiers stationed in forts spent most of their time on sentry duty, scouting, supplying, and repairing the structure. Patrols and raids were initiated as soon as the forces were assembled, both to increase the opportunity for surprise and decrease the cost to the province. Only expeditions granted the opportunity for advanced training in the military discipline before soldiers entered combat, but such training often proved unnecessary or less an instrument of education than a cure for idleness.

The troops assembled for the aborted attack on Quebec in 1709 drilled all summer, until they could, in Samuel Vetch's opinion, "do the manuell exercise and fire in platoons and battalion equall to most regiments in the service."[15] But colonial leaders had fully expected to embark their soldiers the minute they were assembled, so any subsequent training was simply a by-product of the British failure to arrive. Thirty-six years later the provincials involved in the Louisbourg expedition spent a month at Canso drilling in preparation for the assault on the French fortress, but the delay was caused not by the need to train the troops but by the presence of ice around the island of Cape Breton. William Pepperrell reported that he kept the men drilling for their "health and spirits" as much as for any improvements in their discipline.[16]

The infrequency of training, the holiday atmosphere, and the chronic absenteeism created the impression that provincial soldiers were unprepared for war, that they were wanting in discipline and drill—discipline, which in the eyes of British officials and many subsequent historians, would have brought the provincials closer to the European ideal. A sampling of historical interpretation underscores the opinion that provincial soldiers were inferior to their European counterparts because they lacked proper training. American units "generally suffered from low morale and slack discipline"; therefore, the most "important fighting [was] done by European troops . . . [because] American troops in general lacked discipline and training in European tactics."[17] Indeed, the "superiority of regulars was repeatedly demonstrated."[18] Guy Chet recently observed that "the absence of a military tradition and a standing army in New England lent itself to military incompetence."[19] But what kind of training were they lacking? Was the European ideal necessary for the provincial soldier? Or was it even wise? Would increased training have made them better equipped for war?

As indicated earlier, the purpose of military training is to prepare the soldier for combat, and so it is necessary to understand the nature of that combat and what the common soldier needed to know to function properly in order to evaluate the efficiency of any training program. There were three main categories of land warfare in the early eighteenth century—the linear tactic battle, the siege, and *la petite guerre*. The linear tactics of the eighteenth century developed initially during the religious wars of the sixteenth and seventeenth centuries when pikemen and musketeers were welded together in mutually supporting roles on the battlefield, the muskets providing long-range missile combat and the pike close-range shock and defensive capabilities. But by the close of the seventeenth century, improvements in firearms and the introduction of the bayonet merged the two roles of pikeman and musketeer.[20] The increased reliability of the flintlock musket gradually shifted emphasis from close combat (the "push of pike") to fire combat so that, even with the flexibility offered by the bayonet, it became increasingly rare for armies to close within the range of cold steel.[21]

Tacticians found that the most effective way to employ the firepower of the smoothbore muskets was to lay down volleys against the enemy. The term "volley" means firing muskets simultaneously. It could mean mass firing by whole battalions, but European armies usually employed smaller volleys by smaller tactical units rather than unloading all muskets at the same time. For example, in the early eighteenth century the British used a system called "platoon fire." The battalion was divided into eighteen platoons and six of these, distributed evenly along the line, would fire together. By the time the third group of platoons had fired, the first would have reloaded, thus providing, theoretically at least, a continuous fire. In such a system firing had to be very controlled and by command only.[22] In addition to loading and firing on command, the soldier had to master the marching maneuvers that enabled the battalion to cross the battlefield to an effective killing range, or 75 to 100 yards.[23] The battalion would be required to change from column to line, move around obstacles and compensate for casualties, plus be prepared to assume special formations designed to repel an attack by cavalry or other threats, all the while maintaining the close formation required for effective firing.

In contrast, siege warfare, as has been noted in chapter 5, was the warfare of the engineer and required very little technical knowledge on the part of the common soldier. For him, siege warfare was a war of shovel, pick, and axe. Drafted to help the sappers move the artillery closer to the wall, soldiers dug protecting trenches or made wicker baskets called "gabions," which, when filled with dirt, lined the top of the trenches. In addition, they tied brush into bundles called "fascines," which could be used by attacking forces to fill any holes or ditches close to the wall. When the artillery was close enough, they attempted to batter a hole in the main wall of the fortress called a "breech," the debris from the hole falling into the ditch in front to form a rough ramp for the attacking infantry. Normally the fortress would seek terms of surrender at this point, but if an assault became necessary it was generally made at night where the darkness and the rough climb over the debris ramp precluded any attempt at formation. "Into the breech" meant a wild scramble over broken stone and masonry in darkness under heavy fire. Under such circumstances, victory for the assaulting troops traditionally included the privilege of sacking the town or fortress for three days.[24] Obviously, sieges did not involve linear tactics. Only when an enemy force attempted to lift the siege from the outside might a besieging army actually fight a linear tactic battle, unless, of course, the enemy employed the third form of combat in its attempt to lift the siege—*la petite guerre*.

La petite guerre, or "the little war," as it developed in the New World, involved combat that was, as Cotton Mather wrote, "what your Artists at Fighting do call, *A la disbanded* (Spanish for 'separately, not in company formation')."[25] Soldiers fought with wide spaces between them, what contemporary military theorists called "extended order." Although on occasion firing was by volley (especially when a surprise attack was attempted),[26] once a battle developed, soldiers found cover and fired when they saw a target. The scope of the battlefield and the combatants in *la petite guerre* were small and the tactics simple.

Of the three types of combat, linear tactics required the most extensive training. It demanded soldiers act as one and act only on command. "Constant repetition of the basic drill movements," observed John Keegan and Richard Holmes, "was designed to ensure that the soldier could load and fire his weapon and master a number of tactical formations. Proficiency in drill gave soldiers a real advantage on the battlefield: they could fire faster and move more efficiently than their opponents . . . many drill movements would have been repeated till they had become conditioned reflexes."[27] In his study of the training of the British army in the eighteenth century, J. A. Houlding identified five phases in the instruction of the redcoat. Phase one involved the "manual exercise"—the long, slow sequence in which a recruit learned to load and fire his musket, carry it on the march, and perform ceremonial movements. Once he had mastered loading his musket, he moved on to phase two, or the "platoon exercises," which featured the firing of volleys. "Evolutions" covered very basic marching commands, including rank and file movements, facing, open and closing ranks, and so on.

From these first three phases the soldier learned "the use of his weapons, the ability to move in regulated way, and a docile obedience,"[28] and the soldier put them to use in the last two phases of his training: "firings" (platoon firing, firing advancing, retreating, and on the spot) and "maneuvers" (the linear movements of the battlefield on a battalion level). Both of these involved officers more than the men as they were required to give the commands to fire at the correct time or to order their platoon or subdivision to perform some maneuver that would accomplish the grand maneuver of the battalion. Linear tactics demanded coordination and absolute, unquestioning obedience, and Houlding, echoing Keegan and Holmes, found that the life of the British soldier consisted of "endless drill—to the end that the skills acquired [as a recruit] should through constant mechanical repetition be honed to a level of perfection verging on the conditioned reflex."[29] However, a high influx of recruits, or the common dispersal of the battalion in peacetime, could reduce the efficiency of a British regiment to the point where it would take years to make it fit for service again.[30]

In addition to drill and combat experience, British officers relied on printed manuals to understand the complicated commands associated with linear tactics, and the manuals used by provincial or militia officers throughout the early French wars were either reprints or compilations of these British military instructions. Published in 1690, *An Abridgement of the English Military Discipline* contains little more than the manual exercise for loading and firing the musket, as well as the coordination of pikes and musketeers and the exercise for grenadiers. Twenty-six commands and motions were required for the soldier to load his musket, and the use of matchlocks and bandoleers with wooden chargers are indicated by such commands as "Blow off your loose corns," "Handle your chargers," and "Open them with your teeth."[31] Such elaborate commands can be confusing to the modern historian who imagines that soldiers went through such long procedures at all times, but this exercise was designed to teach ignorant English farm boys who had never handled a weapon how to load and fire. The eighteenth-century British military writer Bennett Cuthbertson recommended that "as soon as a Recruit is master of all the motions in the Manual and Platoon-Exercise, he must be trained to the use of Powder, to which most of them have at first that aversion, which may reasonably be expected in ignorant unexperienced peasants, whose heads are filled with the most dreadful apprehensions of its effects, from the stories told them out of fun, by the old Soldiers: it requires some practice to get the better of this dislike, and to prevail on them to load with coolness."[32] The very specific commands not only left nothing to chance in the instruction but instilled a rhythm in the loading and firing consistent with the principle of controlled volley fire. During battle when speed was essential, the number of commands was reduced drastically and the soldier performed many of the tasks automatically but with a rate consistent with the rest of his platoon.

One quote from the Louisbourg campaign has been frequently misinterpreted as proof of the general ignorance of New Englanders in military matters. John Ferling employed the quote when he observed that provincial soldiers "were often even less prepared for war than their leaders. Enroute to Canada in 1745, ill-prepared New Hampshire soldiers 'were Ordered Ashore . . . and Taught How to Use the firelock.'"[33] Ferling reiterated this interpretation in his *Struggle for Continent: The Wars of Early America* when he observed that provincial officers "were compelled to teach their callow troops such rudimentary arts as how to fire their muskets."[34] However the term "firelock" is significant. It was used as the command of execution for the manual of arms. What the observer was referring to was this long-loading sequence featured in all the military manuals of the period and nothing more. Certainly it is not evidence that provincial soldiers did not know the basics of loading a firearm. The New Hampshire troops were brought on shore and drilled primarily to give them something to do.[35]

The loading commands in *An Abridgement* were reproduced exactly, even in the same typeface, in Nicholas Boone's *Military Discipline: The Compleat Souldier or Expert Artillery-Man*. Published in Boston in 1701 (a second, slightly upgraded edition was published in 1706), the *Military Discipline* was another compilation of military instruction taken from various sources. In addition to the manual exercise, Boone included an extensive section on marching. Soldiers were to be drawn up in four or six ranks one and a half feet apart. The distance between files varied from close order (one and a half feet) through order (three feet), open order (six feet), and double distance (twelve feet). The majority of marching commands of the period involved one of three basic maneuvers—doubling, wheeling, and countermarching. Doubling (or undoubling) simply meant turning six ranks into three, four ranks into two, or vice versa. In "doubling to the front" the men in the second, fourth, and sixth ranks moved forward diagonally into the space to the right or left of the man in front of them, thus turning six ranks into three. The variations on this maneuver were numerous to cover any tactical situation and could be quite complex, as in the jaw-breaking command "Half files double your front to the right and left inward."

Wheeling was performed at close order and changed the front of the unit 90 or 180 degrees by swinging the ranks like a door, the men near the pivot taking smaller steps than those near the outer flank, maintenance of the rank formation during the maneuver being of prime importance. In countermarching, the head of each file turned and marched back through the gaps with the rest of the files following, similar to the techniques used by modern marching bands. Countermarching was sometimes combined with volley firing. When the front rank fired, the men turned and passed through the other ranks to the rear while the next rank stepped up to take their place. This form of firing was rapidly losing fashion, however. The method had originally accommodated the heavy matchlock muskets, which required rests and a protracted time to reload. As each rank moved into position it planted its rests and blew on the match in preparation to fire. The lighter, more efficient flintlock decreased loading time and enabled soldiers to dispense with the rest, so a new method of volley fire was developed in which the front rank kneeled, the second rank stooped, and the rear stood upright and all fired and reloaded together.

The latter method would eclipse the former as the eighteenth century progressed, and the British experience in the War of the Spanish Succession would introduce new techniques, which are reflected in William Breton's *Militia Discipline: The Words of Command and Directions for Exercising the Musket, Bayonet, & Carthridge* published in 1733.[36] Breton's manual indicates the general acceptance of both paper cartridges in loading as well as the close order form of volley firing, including a new "locking" technique. Introduced to the British army in the 1720s, locking eliminated the need for the middle rank to "stoop" when firing, which was uncomfortable, unsteady, and hazardous to the collarbone. The front rank still kneeled but the second rank stepped to the right slightly to fire over the shoulders of the front rank. The third rank stepped over even further so their muskets fell in the interval between the files.[37] Marching maneuvers continued to emphasize doubling, wheeling, and countermarching, with the following modification in the method of doubling. Instead of the even-number ranks doubling the odd to their front, the fourth, fifth, and sixth ranks marched forward so the fourth rank doubled the first rank.[38]

In the 1740s American publishers turned away from compilations and simply reprinted British military authors *in toto*. With editions published in 1743, 1744, and 1747, Humphrey Bland's *An Abstract of Military Discipline* in particular soon became the standard manual used in New England.[39] The loading sequence in Bland was reduced somewhat from previous manuals, reflecting the widespread use of paper cartridges, and marching maneuvers still involved doubling and countermarching (the British would not abandon doubling until the Seven Years' War when they adopted the close-order marching style of the Prussian army).[40]

I have elaborated on these maneuvers to demonstrate that the manuals available to provincial officers provided instruction for one type of warfare only—the linear tactic battle. The nature and complexities of linear tactics demanded constant drill and constant attention to detail to maintain an adequate level of efficiency. It was the enormous amount of time and energy required to keep their own regiments "fit for service" that convinced British officers that provincials, with their infrequent militia frolics, could never be equal to the challenge of war. Linear tactics required that the soldiers act as one, so even those rare training days accomplished little because the militia company that trained was not the provincial company that took the field. When the volunteers and pressed men from several towns assembled, the rhythms of loading and volley fire would be lost and the marching a potential disaster.[41]

However, this European style of training served no purpose in the context of war on the New England frontier. According to John Keegan and Richard Holmes, "linear formations and methodical volleys—even if they worked as well in battle as they did on parade—were suitable only on certain sorts of terrain."[42] In fact, the wooded terrain of North America so influenced the tactics of war that the first true linear battle did not occur until the Plains of Abraham in 1759.[43] Until that battle, and especially in the early French wars, all combat involved, or at least was influenced by, the tactics of *la petite guerre*. Even sieges were colored by *la petite guerre* as the relieving forces consisted largely of Indians.[44]

The close order, linear formations presented in the manuals ran counter to the tactics of *la petite guerre*. Linear tactics required action without thought. "The tactics of the period," observed J. A. Houlding, "sought to exclude chance in favor of control, rather than attempting to take advantage of uncertainty by encouraging in the men a spirit of initiative or individualism. A complete and docile obedience and automaton-like reflex responses to command were the touchstone of the other ranks; endless repetition of a few basic skills, together with an iron discipline, seemed to ensure both." In contrast, *la petite guerre* required some independence of action. In the wooded terrain beyond the frontier line soldiers operated in dispersed formations, often separated from their commander or the main party. Once action was joined, the use of cover was the discretion of the individual, it required independent thought, and, unlike their British counterpart, provincial soldiers took careful aim at their targets. Even the French regulars had to learn this lesson. W. J. Eccles pointed out that the Troupes de la Marine stationed in Canada were useless until they had several years of experience in forest campaigning, "fighting as individuals rather than as drilled mass units."[45]

Perhaps the issue of aiming best illustrates the difference between linear tactics and *la petite guerre*. Cotton Mather said, "The Best Marks-man will ... be the best Souldier. The Benjamites that can shoot to an Hairs Breadth will probably carry the day," and he recommended prizes be given for the best shooting at training day.[46] Provincial training actually placed a great deal of emphasis on "shooting at a mark." Early in the seventeenth century, Plymouth colony ordered that, in order to conserve powder, all shooting at training day be at a mark, and in 1679 Massachusetts ordered that militia officers "not onely traine theire souldiers in theire postures and motions but alsoe at shooting att Markes."[47] J. A. Houlding found that British authorities, despite the fact their manuals did stress the importance of shooting at a target, issued only two ball cartridges per man *per year* in peacetime. "Since controlled volley fire was considered more important than individually aimed fire—and the peacetime issue of ball is a clear measure of just how much importance was attached to volley fire, over aimed fire—it was upon volley fire in platoon that peacetime training was concentrated. Squibs [blanks] provided a sufficient degree of realism for this purpose."[48] The British would not encourage marksmanship until being involved in war in America in the last French war after they had extensive experience with fighting in the New World. As J. A. Houlding wrote, "Target practice was given pride of place in the training carried on in North America by 1758–9, this being one of the fruits of experience in the campaigns against New France."[49]

Not only did the techniques differ between *la petite guerre* and linear combat, but it was actually dangerous to instill close-order drill on men whose principal fighting involved ambush and the effective use of terrain. At the Battle of Brackett's Woods in 1689, Benjamin Church "bid his Indian soldiers scatter, [and] run very thin, to preserve themselves and be better able to make a discovery of the enemy."[50] Church always ordered the men under his command to "run very thin" because he knew close formations provided too much of a target. During his fifth raid into Maine in 1704 he was infuriated during one action to find "so many of the army in a crowd together, acting so contrary to my command and direction, exposing themselves and the whole army to utter ruin, by their so disorderly crowding thick together. Had an enemy come upon them in that interim, and fired a volley amongst them, they could not have missed a shot."[51]

The inadequacy of the infrequent and riotous militia training should not be used to gauge the provincial soldiers' preparation for war. Muster-day training involved linear formations and linear tactics, and thus taught a way of war foreign to them. The absenteeism and the fact that the militia company that trained was not the group that saw active service together indicates that, beyond the administrative function, militia training served no purpose. Provincial soldiers could not be automatons; they had to think and react to situations, at the very least find cover and choose their own targets. As Benjamin Church ordered his company when confronted by a potential enemy, they had to "clap down and cock their guns."[52] Recognizing the essential elements for frontier fighting, Church recommended that soldiers in service should be inspected by "men of known judgement" to "see if their arms be good and they know how to use them in shooting right, at a mark, and that they be men of good reason and sense to know how to manage themselves in so difficult a piece of service as this Indian hunting is."[53] This training was not written in manuals: provincial soldiers and officers learned it in the field and passed it on verbally and in practice.

Actually, Church's comment provides a key to understanding how New England soldiers trained for war, because essentially what they were learning were hunting techniques. The tracking, concealment, and marksmanship required in hunting game had been adapted by the Indians to warfare with gunpowder weapons, and thus hunting techniques served provincials far better than doubling, wheeling, and volley fire. Not surprisingly, New England's best military leaders and scouts were often described as great hunters, as when Samuel Penhallow characterized John Lovewell as a man "endowed with a generous Spirit and Resolution of serving his Country, and well acquainted with hunting the Woods."[54] Richard Slotkin, in his *Regeneration Through Violence: The Mythology of the American Frontier, 1600–1860*, recognized that "hunting" was a recurring theme in the literature of New England during the French War period. "The exorcism of the Indians is likened to the hunting down and slaying of rapid beasts embodying all qualities of evil."[55]

British officials, and some historians, would continue to disparage the provincial soldier because he lacked European-style training, yet, as Keegan and Holmes have indicated, such training could also "submerge initiative and rational thought . . . The Prussian army lost the battle of Jena in 1806 despite the excellence of its drill, and the Israeli army, one of the most consistently successful forces of this century, is not noted for its zeal for presenting arms."[56] The provincial soldiers knew that the want of formal education in linear tactics was not a handicap in their experience; they proved their ability in the woods of New England, although British military and government officials were slow to recognize it. When Governor Jonathan Belcher addressed the New Hampshire legislature in February 1740, he noted that the "officers of the militia tell me the two regiments of the province are well furnished with arms and ammunition and that they are exercised according to law. But that the appearances are thin on Muster days the fine for non-appearance not being equal to twelve pence stirling." Belcher reminded the assembly he had repeatedly requested that the fines be raised, and he urged them once again to vote for an increase so "the private companies in their musters and also the regiments at their general musters may be full and so the whole militia better disciplined and fitted for the service whenever there may be occasion for them. Such a law as I now mention passed about two years ago in the Mass Bay and the fine appearance of the militia of that Province is hardly to be equalled in any of his Majesty's dominions."[57] The House weighed very carefully his words and replied the following day that "With respect to what you mention of the fine appearance of the militia of the neighboring Province . . . though ours may never equal them in show we shall be glad to do everything in our power that they may be capable of doing as much real service when called to it."[58]

Doubling, wheeling, countermarching, and volley fire were fundamental to battle drills for European soldiers preparing for linear tactic combat, but these tactics had little relation to warfare on the northern frontier of New England. Proficiency in such tactics requires a commitment to long and consistent hours of training, a commitment only possible for the professional soldier, or at least extended terms of enlistment. The provincial soldiers of New England would not and could not devote themselves to mastering a form of combat they had little use for. Although European-style linear formations provided a "fine appearance" on muster day, and gave the sham battle a sense of choreography, an increase in this training would not have prepared provincials for the combat of *la petite guerre* and would actually have been detrimental, if not suicidal.

But while the European training proved useless as a battle drill, such preparation is only half the purpose of military discipline. It also prepared soldiers for the stress of combat by instilling a fighting spirit and unit cohesion. "Battle is a harrowing business," wrote John Keegan and Richard Holmes:

> In addition to the physical risks of death or injury, the soldier is subjected to the intense psychological pressures generated by exhaustion, privation, noise, worries about family and friends, and the sight of comrades being killed and wounded. Yet, as Field-Marshal Haig admitted: "Men are not brave by nature." The fighting spirit that enables the soldier to meet the stress of battle must be built and sustained: training, comradeship, leadership and discipline all play their parts in its creation.[59]

In *Acts of War: The Behavior of Men in Battle*, Richard Holmes specified that the "prime purpose of military training is to produce effectiveness on the battlefield. Much of it is devoted, either directly or indirectly, to enabling the soldier to cope with the stress-filled environment of combat."[60] Military discipline, training, traditions, and ceremony all serve to submerge an individual within a larger entity, which will, hopefully, overpower the primal urge for self-preservation. Alan Moorehead, a World War II war correspondent, noted that "the drill, the saluting, the uniform, the very badges on your arm all tend to identify you with a solid machine and build up a feeling of security and order. In the moment of danger the soldier turns to his mechanical habits and draws strength from them." John Keegan and Richard Holmes found Moorehead's observation "brilliantly perceptive. The process of military training is designed as much to inculcate the group cohesion and solidarity upon which fighting spirit depends as it is to produce an adequate level of technical or tactical expertise."[61]

Such was the purpose of European military traditions and training in the eighteenth century. The colorful uniforms, the flags, and the ceremonies of the regimental system instilled in recruits and soldiers a belief that they belonged to something greater and more important than their individualism. The creation of automatons through repetitious and harsh drilling also attempted to aid soldiers in coping with battlefield stress; it provided what Richard Holmes called "a raft of familiarity in an uncertain environment."[62] Less charitably perhaps, but with the certain conviction of the European officer class, Frederick the Great put it another way. "If my soldiers began to think," he said, "not one would remain in the ranks."

Carl von Clausewitz referred to the fighting spirit created by such military training and discipline as the "military virtue." He believed that military virtue is "distinguished from mere bravery, and still more from enthusiasm for the business of War." These attributes are individual gifts not possessed by most men. Military virtue is a corporate spirit.[63] Military training and discipline instilled this corporate spirit and also created a bonding or comradeship among the disparate individuals gathered into European armies. As one eighteenth-century French military theorist wrote,

> Personal bravery of a single individual does not decide on the day of battle, but the bravery of the unit, and the latter rests on the good opinion and the confidence that each individual places in the unit to which he belongs. The exterior splendour, the regularity of movements, the adroitness and at the same time firmness of the mass—all this gives the individual soldier the safe and calming conviction that nothing can withstand his particular regiment or battalion.[64]

It is the absence of European discipline and traditions that has led so many historians and other observers to the conclusion that provincial soldiers lacked fighting spirit or the military virtue. Provincial units served only a short time together, never more than a year and usually only for a few weeks or months, then they disbanded and other units were created. Thus they could never equal European units in fighting spirit. In describing the disastrous Quebec expedition of 1690, the historian James Truslow Adams concluded that "the self-flattering belief . . . that training of any sort is a waste of time, and that, in military affairs, competent commanders and disciplined troops can be found at any moment in a crisis, had again proved a costly fallacy."[65] Francis Parkman agreed with this assessment, finding that "Massachusetts had made her usual mistake. She had confidently believed that ignorance and inexperience could match the skill of a tried veteran, and that the rude courage of her fishermen and farmers could triumph without discipline or leadership."[66]

European battle was normally very deliberate in nature. It often took literally hours to set up artillery and maneuver regiments into position before commencing the action. This provided soldiers with considerable time for reflection and anticipation, and for most soldiers the ordeal of anticipation is harder on the emotions than the fighting itself. "It is hard to exaggerate the degree of stress imposed by this feeling of pre-contact apprehension," wrote Richard Holmes, "which usually occurs, with varying intensity, before every battle in which a soldier participates . . . The tension that builds up, especially before a setpiece action, can almost become unbearable."[67]

During the awful tension before the battle, tension created by the fear of death, wounds, and cowardice, European soldiers drew strength from the military virtue. In watching the enemy move their battalions into position, or listening to the roar of cannon and musket fire, the soldier could remember the traditions of his own regiment, see the war-torn colors bravely flying over his head, and trust in the unit spirit to carry them through the coming ordeal.

But provincial soldiers rarely experienced this kind of anticipation. Only in a handful of actions, usually associated with expeditions, did New Englanders share the prebattle trial of their European counterparts. The landing at Quebec in 1690 was such an occasion, as was the attack on Cartagena in which the provincials actively supported the redcoat assault. The most famous action that allowed New Englanders the chance of reflection before combat was the attack on the Island Battery at Louisbourg in 1745.

It was decided that the Island Battery, which prevented the British ships from entering the harbor, should be taken by storm in a night action. Loaded into boats, the provincials began their nerve-racking row to the island. There was plenty of time for anticipation and reflection as the boats made their agonizing approach. As the story is frequently told, it was a drunken soldier who ruined the plan by raising three cheers when he landed. This shout alerted the French, who opened up on the loaded boats still floundering in the water. However, the tension of the approach may have had more to do with the soldier's indiscretion than alcohol. Soldiers experiencing such prebattle tension find release when the fighting begins.[68] After approaching an enemy held island in the dark, expecting any minute to be fired on with grapeshot and canister, the physical act of landing must have felt like a relief, expressed by this one soldier, whether under the influence or not, as an untimely cheer.

For most provincial soldiers the surprise and ambush of warfare on the frontier thrust them directly into action, providing little time for reflection or anticipation. If springing an ambush, prebattle contact with the enemy was brief, and if on the receiving end of a surprise attack it was nonexistent. Rather than a gradual buildup of adrenaline and emotional acceptance, provincial soldiers had to react in seconds to an instant and dangerous change in their circumstances. They had no time to reflect on military traditions, uniforms, flags, or ceremonies.

La petite guerre produced unique pressures and anxieties of its own, especially for soldiers involved in patrols and raids. Provincial soldiers did not reflect only on what might happen, but when. The enemy was unseen and unknown, delineated only by the limits of the imagination. Indeed, many provincial scouting parties, far removed from assistance, found their worst enemy to be the imagination. Seth Wyman's scout toward Monadnock Mountain in 1707, which resulted in a court-martial "for their returne home in a mutinous disorderly manner," underscores the special fears promoted by the wilderness.[69] Early in the morning, Wyman dispatched two scouting parties—one to the right, and one to the left—to search for signs of the enemy. According to the deposition provided by Samuel Scripture, the left scout found the tracks of Indian dogs or wolves and followed them for about a quarter of a mile. Suddenly, they met the right scout "who called us away and told us they believed there was a thousand Indians upon which we hastened away but [the other] scout ran so fast that I could not come up with them to understand what their discovery was." The excited men crowded around Wyman and his officers until Wyman, fearing that they made too good a target, "ordered his men to stand farther off and give room that he might discourse his officers, upon which many of them ran away."

Jonathan Butterfield confirmed Scripture's account and added that Wyman "talked of marching immediately to the Place of discovery but many of our men moved off disorderly." Wyman's deposition confirms that he "incouraged his men by telling them that they had a brave advantage of the Enemy, in that they had discovered them and were not themselves discovered." Some of the officers, believing the account of a thousand Indians, disagreed and recommended caution, "upon which Sergeant Tarbol threw down his Cap, and offered himself to go if but four men would go with him." The officers pointed out that most of the men had already left, and so Wyman found himself "too weak to attaque them and accordingly made the best of my way home."

Richard Holmes indicated that "once a panic gets under way it develops a frenetic momentum of its own," and such was the case in the Wyman scout.[70] Despite the encouragements of Seth Wyman, who would years later be cited for bravery for his actions in Lovewell's last battle, and of Wyman's sergeant, the original panic caused by the overactive imagination of the right-hand scout could not be contained. A similar occurrence happened to a company of New Hampshire men sent by Lieutenant Governor John Wentworth to the scene of Lovewell's fight in 1725. The company, with orders to meet with a Massachusetts company being sent on the same errand, arrived at Lovewell's temporary fort and went no further. Apparently the image of what had happened to Lovewell and his men loomed large in their minds. Wentworth wrote to Lieutenant Governor William Dummer that he was concerned over the mismanagement of the affair. "We all accounted them stout men," but they had been discouraged by not meeting the other company. "Its a strange thing our people should be so dispirited," concluded Wentworth, "there was in the 53 I sent out 40, as likely lusty Middle aged men as can be found in our hole Province but so it was."[71]

Later that fall, Dummer cautioned Colonel Thomas Westbrook not to let the reports of a force of five hundred Indians descending from Canada spark the imaginations of his men. "I observe the soldiers make a handle of it for Cowardice by every small party they meet with afterwards."[72] Westbrook replied that he "always caution every body to make less rather than more of what they hear or see, relating the Enemy notwithstanding some make the most of everything."[73]

The constant threat of the unseen enemy in the wilderness haunted soldiers in the New World, and some succumbed to the threat before it actually materialized. Richard Slotkin, in *Regeneration Through Violence*, indicated that "the Puritan who lost his self-restraint in the terrors of an Indian fight knew that he had been overthrown by the powers of his own inner darkness, allied with the darkness of the woods."[74] However, some New Englanders did not fear the wilderness or the woods. Benjamin Church never allowed his imagination to run away from him; neither did John Lovewell, Johnson Harmon, nor James Converse. In addition, the fears of the unseen enemy, like the fears before a linear tactic battle, often left when action was joined. For the European soldier, the military virtue, the fighting spirit raised through training and ceremony, brought him through the carnage, while the repetitious drill guided his hands with little thought. But without this training and discipline, the provincial soldier had to draw on other strengths to carry him through the horror of combat.

The reasons that men fight in battle are different from the reasons that they enlist. Provincial soldiers volunteered mainly for financial gain, but also for a chance at adventure, and for their province and king. However, when the fear and adrenaline surge accompanying combat began, New Englanders did not think of the financial security their service might bring, nor did they think of the benefits to their country. Other motives drove them to fight and possibly die.

Hatred of the enemy, especially the Eastern Indians, was intense. As John Keegan and Richard Holmes indicated, armies in Europe in the eighteenth century tended "to slip into peaceful co-existence between battles" and exhibited a reluctance to kill his other outside the confines of battle. But on the New England frontier, there was no such peaceful coexistence. Unlike the French "enemy," the Eastern Indians were "rebels" known for their treachery and cruelty.[75] Indians were rarely shown quarter in battle, and the Indian male who found himself a prisoner was often abused and tormented, even killed. This hatred also found expression in the words of mortally wounded men who wanted to "kill one more" before they died.[76]

Stimulus for this hatred was widespread. Provincial soldiers and local pursuit forces often came on unbelievably gruesome scenes. When Captain Johnson Harmon and his scouting company surprised and killed some fifteen Indians in 1722, they found the hand of an Englishman near the camp. A quick search discovered the body of Moses Eaton of Salisbury laid on the stump of a tree, "having his Tongue, Nose and private parts cut off."[77] Besides such descriptions of dismemberment, stories of people roasted and partially eaten, such as Robert Rogers of Salmon Falls in 1690 and William Moody of Exeter in 1709, made lasting impressions as well.[78]

But the killing of pregnant women seemed to provoke the greatest indignation. In this respect, the death of Goody Webber in 1703 proved particularly prominent.[79] A resident of Perpooduck, Webber was one of the victims of the massive attack on Maine communities on August 10, 1703. A letter describing the results of the assault reported that the Indians "ript up one Goody Webber that was big with child and laid her child to her breast and so left her. At Spurwink river they knockt one Jordans sucking Childs brains out against a Tree."[80] Samuel Penhallow vividly described the incident twenty-two years later in his history of Queen Anne's and Dummer's Wars,[81] and Benjamin Church, in explaining the purpose of his 1704 raid and providing justification for both the enthusiasm of recruits and the events that transpired, referred to the fate of Goody Webber and other victims of Indian brutality.

> To see a woman that those barbarous savages had taken and killed, exposed in a most brutish manner (as can be expressed) with a young child seized fast with strings to her breast. [The] infant had no apparent wound, which doubtless was left alive to suck its dead mother's breast, and so miserably to perish and die ... Another instance was, of a straggling soldier, who was found at Casco, exposed in a shameful and barbarous manner. His body being staked up, his head cut off, and a hog's head set in the room; his body ripped up, and heart and inwards taken out, and private members cut off, and hung with belts of their own, the inwards at one side of his body, and his privates at another, in scorn and derision of the English soldiers.[82]

When Church and Penhallow published such descriptions in their histories, when ministers like Cotton Mather and Benjamin Wadsworth preached in their sermons how the Indians have "horribly Murdered some Scores of your dear Country-men, whoose Blood cries in your Ears," and how inhabitants of the frontier have witnessed "Children dasht against the stones" and "Women with Child ript open," they were following a common practice in the history of war that is called dehumanizing the enemy.[83] Richard Holmes observed that the dehumanization of the enemy enables soldiers to distinguish killing in battle from murder, and that "racial and cultural differences accelerate this process."[84] Numerous studies have shown that the English settlers in the New World were racists, that they viewed the natives as lower beings than themselves. The savagery of the Indian was likened to wild beasts, and the tactics of *la petite guerre*, which employed hunting techniques, reinforced this view of inferiority.[85]

In addition to the basic racism evident, the labeling of the Eastern Indians as "rebels" and "traitors" increased the animosity, because in warfare an "enemy" often earned respect, clemency, and fair treatment according to "civilized" codes of honor, but "traitors" and "rebels" deserved no such consideration. The treatment of Scottish Highlanders by the British army in

1746 provides one contemporary example of this view. While New England captured and garrisoned the French fortress of Louisbourg, the English army fought against the last Stuart pretender to the throne, Charles Edward Stuart. Bonnie Prince Charlie's army consisted mainly of Gaelic-speaking clansmen from the Highlands of Scotland who represented a culture as alien to the English as their colonists found in the Native Americans. After the bloody defeat of Bonnie Prince Charlie's army at the Battle of Culloden in April 1746, wounded Highlanders were systematically slaughtered on the field of battle, and the English army spent the next few months "pacifying" the Highlands with sword, musket, and hangman's rope. There was no thought given to mercy because these strange wild men were traitors and rebels to the crown. As one English volunteer expressed it, "This rebel host had been most deeply in debt to the publick for all the rapine, murder and cruelty; and since the time was now come to pay off the score, our people were all glad to clear the reckoning, and heartily determined to give them receipt in full."[86] This sentiment could easily have been expressed by a New England provincial soldier.

As New Englanders employed Indian allies, the British army employed Highland units in their army, so the cultural differences by themselves were not enough to pinpoint the target of retribution. Neither was the designation as traitor or rebel only. The rebels in the thirteen colonies were treated with tremendous civility and tolerance by the British army when compared to the treatment of the Highland rebels. Rebels they may have been, but they were also kinsmen: they were racially equal. No, it was the designation as traitors and rebels coupled with the racism that intensified the bitter enmity. It indicated the level of chastisement to be meted out to these animals.

The policy concerning Indian tribes in colonial New England is strewn with contradictions. They were viewed as a separate political unit requiring formal declarations of war and peace treaties, yet they were also considered subjects of the King.[87] When Samuel Shute declared war on the Eastern Indian tribes in 1722, he declared "the said Eastern Indians, with their Confederates, to be Robbers, Traitors and Enemies to his Majesty King George." They were traitors by virtue of their "repeated Submissions to his Majesty's Crown and Government."[88] Rebels and traitors are political equals who have turned against the community; therefore, the wars with the Eastern Abenaki were in effect civil wars. Added to the racial differences, this only increased the level of animosity. As traitors to the Crown, and as savage beasts, the Eastern Indians deserved no mercy or consideration.[89] Thus, a broadside ballad published on August 24, 1724, describing the slaughter of Sebastian Rale and the Norridgewocks was entitled "The Rebels Reward."[90]

Battle Drill and Fighting Spirit | 191

One manifestation of this hatred can be seen in the killing of Indian prisoners. Richard Holmes and John Keegan have pointed out the tricky business of surrendering in battle. As Holmes wrote, it is "more difficult to train soldiers in the exercise of deliberate restraint than it is to imbue them with combative zeal."[91] During the initial fight between the provincial soldiers and the French at Quebec in 1690, the Reverend John Wise remembered that a French officer tried to surrender to John March as the New Englanders chased the fleeing enemy. "Capt. March perceiving it beat back his Men and did what he could . . . but could not be obeyed [as] Things were in such an hurry [the Frenchman] was shot dead."[92] During an attack on a village in 1704, Benjamin Church saw a group of soldiers standing around a hut. When his men told him there were people in the house who would not come out, "I hastily bid them pull it down, and *knock them on the head*, never asking whether they were French or Indians; they being all enemies to me."[93] Such occurrences are common in all battles where successful surrender depends so much on timing.

However, provincial soldiers never bothered to take Indian prisoners in action, and they rarely kept male Indian captives found alive after an engagement. It was beyond the heat of battle where the intense hatred that New Englanders felt then manifested itself in the almost routine killing of male prisoners. Such executions, as well as the disregard of Indian flags of truce, often brought the censure of contemporary civilians and subsequent historians, but it continued nonetheless, with apparently little remorse. In 1690, Benjamin Church captured a small Indian fort near Pejepscot, releasing five white captives and taking about eleven Indian prisoners. In questioning one of the male prisoners, "the soldiers being very rude, would hardly spare the Indian's life," and obviously intended to kill him. The white captives pleaded for the Indian because he had helped them during their captivity. Church burned the village and crops and then ordered the killing of the prisoners except two females and the helpful male. However, during the march back, his soldiers, apparently both white and red, continued to harass and threaten the lone male Indian prisoner until he finally escaped.[94]

In 1694, John March seized three prominent chiefs who approached Fort William Henry under a flag of truce and sent them to prison in Boston. To March, the Indians abrogated their right to the normal customs of due to their status as traitors and beasts. A year and a half later Pasco Chubb also ignored a truce flag and killed four Indians, two of them chiefs. In October 1710, a scouting party under Shadrach Walton caught an Indian party clamming on the Maine coast. One of the captives proved to be a chief from Norridgewock. When questioned about the whereabouts of other clamming parties, the chief "made no Reply, and when they threatened him with Death, he laughed at it with contempt." Walton turned the chief over to his friendly Indians who promptly killed him, and this action loosened the tongue of the dead chief's wife.[95]

Once instilled, the killing habit is often difficult to break, and the difficulty increases where race and culture divide two enemies. Even when a war stops, enmity may not disappear. Normally at the conclusion of a war, the combatants withdraw behind established national borders and therefore further contact is limited. Such was the case in New England where the English colonists, outside those directly involved in trade, had little contact with their French counterparts to the north. Richard Holmes found that the "concept of a hateful and inhuman enemy rarely survives contact with him as an individual."[96] This enlightenment can occur during wars where formal and informal truces between battles allowed curiosity to blossom into peaceful encounters with the foe, or it can happen some time after the conclusion of peace settlements.[97]

However, even Richard Holmes had to admit that this forgiveness and understanding could be blocked in situations where race or culture was involved. For New Englanders, especially those living on the frontier, separation with the Eastern Indians between wars was rarely possible. The Eastern Indians frequently visited the English frontier communities. As they came to trade, or passed through on their travels, Indians asked for food and shelter from the English colonists. It was during such interaction that red and white men came to know each other personally, but this familiarity did not breed understanding. As the historian Charles Clark indicated, "The only certainty was a permanent and deeply felt hostility between the two races, nurtured since the time of King Philip's War by treachery and savagery on both sides, which could not be ended by a peace treaty."[98]

If the soldiers ever had the occasion to forget their hatred, the Puritan ministers of New England were present to remind them, although such reminders came before any action, not during. When Cotton Mather said the Indians "have horribly Murdered some Scores of your dear Country-men, whoose Blood cries in your Ears, while you are going to Fight, Vengeance, Dear Country-men! Vengeance upon our Murderers!" he did so to encourage volunteers and to animate men who had already enlisted.[99] These religious reminders of duty and Indian cruelty tended to proceed from political rather than spiritual motives.[100]

However, ministers did accompany soldiers, serving with them in forts and on expeditions and scouts. Some ministers even participated in combat. Their presence was encouraged by both the soldiers and the provincial governments.[101] Such ministers often found themselves in the thick of the fight. The minister of Casco participated in the Battle of Brackett's Woods in 1689, the Reverend John Wise was active during the landing at Quebec the following year, and the young graduate of Harvard and student of theology, Jonathan Frye, shouldered a musket and fell mortally wounded with Lovewell in 1725.[102]

However, there is little evidence to indicate that religion, despite the presence of ministers in battle, provided the fighting spirit to carry soldiers through combat. Christian soldiers they may have been on the whole, but when the musket balls flew it was not their obligation to God that motivated their action. Even the ministers did not necessarily call upon religious images in the heat of battle. When Reverend Wise found soldiers chasing the French instead of attacking the city during the landing at Quebec in 1690, he told one group that they were "out of your Witts we did not come hither to drive a parcel of Cowardly Frenchmen from Swamp to Swamp but to attack Kebeque thither Gentlemen is our business, Why Dont we march away for the Towne of Kebeque." The following day when John Walley had ordered the landing troops back to the beach, Wise perceived that the men had lost spirit, but he did not preach: "I challenge them to get up and run for a Dram of the bottle a Temptacon fit for Souldiers."[103]

To understand where provincial soldiers got their fighting spirit it is necessary to reiterate the most important purpose of military training—the bonding of men into a cohesive group, what Clausewitz called the "corporate spirit." As Richard Holmes wrote, "For the key to what makes men fight—not enlist, not cope but fight—we must look hard at military groups and the bonds that link men within them."[104] By fostering a sympathy and affection, as well as respect, between men in a military unit, the fear of dishonor and cowardice motivates them to fight.

What the European training and discipline attempted to create artificially among the strangers constituting their armies, provincial soldiers brought with them into service naturally. Volunteers knew each other, or knew each other's towns and families, and they knew the officers they chose to serve under. An Englishmen joining a line regiment in the British army surrendered his ties to the outside world. His enlistment was for life, and the regiment became his new home. But provincial volunteers serving only for a short time maintained a connection to community and family, and their failure to serve honorably would bring shame on those communities and families as well as on themselves. The emphasis here is on the volunteers who tended to have ties to communities. The have-nots of society who were pressed or hired did not always have such ties, and thus they could not be relied on in battle. This is why frontier commanders placed have-nots in garrisons and took volunteers on their raids.

Other soldiers have performed remarkably well without the need of formal military discipline. The Swiss soldiers of the fifteenth century served in companies and units drawn from the same valley, village, or guild. The soldiers knew each other and knew their reputations would be judged on the battlefield. They carried the bonds of the village with them to the army, and their reputation for ferocity and giving no quarter became legendary.[105] The original Swedish army of King Gustavas Adolphus also carried this community spirit with them, as all regiments were recruited from their own districts. The British government in the eighteenth century rarely had reason to complain of the performance of Scottish Highland troops on the battlefield. These men also retained a strong connection to their home communities, which became a pledge of their good behavior. Misbehavior or cowardice meant shame and even the punishment of eviction for families at home. With such a natural fighting spirit, the British government usually allowed Highland regiments little time for training and would send them to war zones as soon as they were raised.[106] Numerous examples exist throughout military history where soldiers drew on other resources beyond training, where, as one British war correspondent described the Boer army in the late nineteenth century, the "wonderful intelligence in the individual . . . plays the part of cultivated discipline."[107]

The bonds of the community taken into military service gave the provincial soldier fighting spirit. The connections of familial and neighborly ties were recognized and fostered by allowing soldiers to choose the officers under whom they would serve, and by stipulating in levying acts that volunteers "will not be compelled to . . . change companies without their consent."[108] Samuel Waldo believed one of the reasons for the failure of the attack on the Island Battery at Louisbourg was the breaking of these communal bonds. Whole companies were not involved in the attack but rather individual volunteers taken from all companies, most under new officers chosen for the assignment. Waldo wrote to William Pepperrell that the men involved in the attack should be under their own officers and that "severall men were detatched against their will." He wondered "whether stragling fellows, some 2, others 3, 4, and 7 out of a company, should go on this design. I am firmly of opinion that such without any officers belonging to them will be a disservice."[109]

The threat of dishonor and shame among men bonded in a military unit, whether through training or communal ties, can be a powerful force. Richard Holmes wrote that "there are occasions when this desire to preserve status is quite literally stronger than the fear of death."[110] Ann M. Little observed that for natives and provincials alike, "war was a key performance of manhood."[111] Such was the case of Richard Jacques. Jacques was Johnson Harmon's son-in-law and Jacques supposedly killed Father Sebastian Rale during the Norridgewock raid in 1724. Jacques continued to serve in the provincial military and later went to Louisbourg. According to family legend, Jacques was with a scout near Penobscot Bay sometime after returning from Louisbourg when his commander ordered him to take his men across an open field. Jacques argued that it was a perfect spot for an ambush, but his commander insisted, calling Jacques a coward. Stung by the accusation, Richard Jacques's honor and pride led him out into that open field where, as he had predicted, he fell mortally wounded from an ambush.[112]

Richard Holmes has also indicated that group spirit does not necessarily produce positive results. Soldiers who refuse to advance or become involved in a mass panic are also acting within the spirits of a group. In the provincial service, collective action involved less shame and dishonor. Scouting companies who broke and scattered when attacked by overwhelming forces were considered to have shown prudence rather than cowardice. The mutinous spirit at Louisbourg was also condoned by the general approbation within the ranks of the New England regiments. But, as previously mentioned, the kinship and communal ties brought to provincial military service allowed few individual acts of dishonor or cowardice.

The Reverend Thomas Symmes recognized this spirit when he wrote about Lovewell's last fight. According to Symmes, Lovewell's men discussed their options before leaving their packs to investigate the Indian sighting. Although an enemy ambush was a very real possibility, and the reduction of their numbers through sickness had increased their vulnerability, Lovewell's men decided to continue. "We came out to meet the Enemy; we have all along Pray'd God we might find 'em; and we had rather trust Providence with our Lives, yea Dy for our Country, than try to Return without seeing them, if we may, and be called Cowards for our Pains."[113]

Warfare on the New England frontier was fought by different rules and under different conditions than warfare in Europe, and so it is unreasonable to judge provincial soldiers by a European standard. *La petite guerre* demanded instant individual decisions and judgments, and linear warfare demanded automatic conditioning. Frontier warfare focused on surprise and ambush, while European warfare operated with the deliberate, set-piece battle. "Regulations designed to keep dull-witted conscripts together on the shoulder-to-shoulder battlefields of the blackpowder era," wrote Keegan and Holmes, "are inappropriate in an age when weapons and tactics demand dispersion on the battlefield, and when initiative may be more important than blind obedience. In the last analysis, fighting spirit centres upon the morale of the individual soldier and the small group of comrades with whom he fights."[114]

Provincial volunteers took with them into combat the bonding of community and kinship, and they had no use for the kind of discipline and training required of European soldiers. As Benjamin Church remarked, provincial soldiers had to "be men of good reason and sense," not machines.[115] When musket shot and war cries announced an Indian ambush, officers did not want automatons dulled by repetitious drills, they needed men who would react instantly and follow them in a charge, or "clap down" and take careful aim at an elusive enemy. Such men were produced through experience with the wilderness environment, not on the drill fields of Europe.

10

Battle Experience

Facing the Enemy

It has almost become a cliché to say that battle is the ultimate objective of soldiers.[1] Soldiers exist in order to fight: combat defines their function. Despite the fact that battle is infrequent, so infrequent that many soldiers never experience enemy fire, its impact looms large. During battle, the adrenaline flow produces a wide range of behavior from apparent calm to wild exhilaration. As John Keegan and Richard Holmes wrote, "Many soldiers experience battle as a half-remembered blur, a mosaic somehow fragmented and haphazardly reassembled."[2] The prevailing feeling before battle is fear—fear of death and fear of cowardice, but beyond the fear, according to Keegan and Holmes, "A single question looms large, dwarfing every fear of death and wounds. 'What will battle really be like?' "[3]

The combat experienced by provincial soldiers differed greatly from the war experiences that their contemporary European counterparts had. European battles were distinguished by the roar of artillery and musketry, and a choking, blinding blanket of powder smoke as armies numbering tens of thousands battered and clawed at each other. All maneuvering was deliberate and slow on the battlefield for fear that confusion or untimely enthusiasm might destroy tactical designs. Combat lasted most of the day, ending with the retreat of one army or darkness. European siege warfare created a similar environment—the constant roar of cannon and a deliberate, almost leisurely pace.[4]

Provincial soldiers rarely participated in this form of combat. At Quebec in 1690 they listened to the firing of Sir William Phips's naval guns bombarding the town. The sieges of Port Royal in 1710, Cartagena in 1741, and Louisbourg in 1745 also exposed provincials to European-style battle conditions. Louisbourg in particular impressed provincial soldiers because the roar of cannon fire was so unusual. One anonymous diarist recorded on May 13 that "Eighty Cannons have been Discharged in a Quarter of an hour," and four days later he wrote, "now while I am writing none but those that hear (or that have been in Some such an Engagement) Can Think how much firing there is here, Cannons Constantly A going, and Bombs, etc. and Altho I'm Two Miles from them they Don't Seem to be above Sixty rods they are so powerful."[5]

But Louisbourg and Cartagena were the exceptions, not the rule. Governed by the tactics of *la petite guerre*, a battle on the northern frontier, if we can use that grand term for such an action, tended to be short and sharp, often not lasting more than thirty minutes. The roar of artillery did not disturb the combatants, and the numbers involved rarely exceeded more than a few hundred, frequently much fewer. More commonly, frontier combat pitted a handful of desperate men in a swift, savage test of wills in the forested wilderness that delineated the colonies of New France and New England.

Examples of such combat are numerous. In January 1707 Colonel Winthrop Hilton surprised eighteen Indians at dawn and killed all but one while they were asleep. Once the firing began, the action probably lasted no longer than five minutes.[6] Similarly, Johnson Harmon and a company of thirty-four soldiers investigated some campfires they detected as they rowed up the Kennebec River one night in July 1722. They found eleven canoes pulled up on shore and then stumbled over some sleeping Indians in the dark. The provincials opened fire and killed fifteen Indians without sustaining any casualties. The whole affair lasted ten minutes.[7] In September 1725, as a scout of six men were resting on their return to Fort Dummer, they heard a noise like running, looked up, and saw fourteen Indians charging their camp. The white men opened fire but the surprise was complete and two of the soldiers were killed, three captured, and one managed to slip away. The actual fight lasted only two or three minutes.[8]

The attack on Norridgewock in 1725, New England's most successful engagement with the Eastern Indians, probably lasted only twenty minutes. While Johnson Harmon took half of the force to sweep through the cornfields, Jeremiah Moulton attacked the village. Dividing his men into three sections, he posted one-third on the north side of the village, another third to the south, and advanced toward the east gate with the remainder. As Johnson Harmon later related the events,

> There was not an Indian to be seen, being all in their wigwams. Our men were ordered to advance softly, and to keep a profound silence. At length an Indian came out of one of the wigwams . . . and discovered the English close upon him. He immediately gave the war whoop and ran in for his gun . . . the warriors ran to meet the English, the rest fled to save their

lives. Moulton, instead of suffering his men to fire at random through the wigwams, charged every man not to fire, upon pain of death, until the Indians had discharged their guns. It happened as he expected; in their surprise they overshot the English, and not a man was hurt. The English then discharged in their turn, and made great slaughter, but every man still kept his rank. The Indians then fired a second volley, and immediately fled towards the river . . . they made the best of their way to the River, where they had about 40 Canoes; we followed them so close that they put off, without their Paddles, not having time to take them; we then presently beat them out of their Canoes, Killing the greatest part of them; the River being about 60 Yards over and Shallow, our Men followed them over . . . with such fury, that but one of their Canoes arrived upon the other side, but others Waded and Swam over, so that we judge about 50 Men, Women and Children got over . . .

We then returned to the Town, where we found Monsieur Ralle the Jesuit, their chief Commander, in one of the Indians houses, who had been continually firing upon a Party of our Men, that were still in the Town: the said Ralle having Wounded one of our people, Lieut. Jaques soon Stove open the door of said house, and found him loading his Gun, who upon Jaques's coming in, Declared Voluntarily, That he would give no quarter, nor take any; Jaques hearing that, and seeing him loading, shot him thro' the head.[9]

Harmon reported that the Indians initially "Stood their ground 4 or 5 minutes" before they broke for the river.[10] The resulting pursuit across the river probably did not last longer than fifteen or twenty minutes.

However, if both sides survived the opening attack, physically and psychologically, it was not uncommon for firefights of several hours to develop. In fact, combat on the northern frontier either resolved itself very quickly or persisted for several hours. In 1688, the initial confrontation between soldiers and Indians at North Yarmouth over prisoners resulted in a firefight that ended only by darkness.[11] In July 1690 a scouting party tracking an Indian raiding party caught them near Wheelwright Pond in present-day Lee, New Hampshire. The fight lasted most of the day and resulted in the death of one of the captains and fourteen other provincial soldiers.[12] When John March's and Daniel King's men were ambushed on the beach at Maquoit Bay the following year, resulting in the death of Captain Samuel Sherbourne, the survivors retreated to their sloops, which were grounded by low tide. The Indians then kept up a firefight with the sloops most of the night.[13]

Lovewell's last battle turned into another extended engagement. Early on the morning of May 8, 1725, John Lovewell and his men heard a gunshot nearby, and upon investigating, they found a lone Indian hunting. In an exchange of fire the Indian was killed and Lovewell and another man wounded. On returning to their packs sometime around ten o'clock, they walked into an ambush. Lovewell, Lieutenants Josiah Farwell and Jonathan Robbins, and several others fell mortally wounded on the first fire, but the provincial soldiers maintained their composure, returned the fire, and, under the leadership of Ensign Seth Wyman, regrouped along the shore of a pond. The battle settled down into a firefight that continued for ten hours until the Indians finally withdrew, leaving the survivors of Lovewell's command to make their best way home.[14]

The length of such encounters and the frequency of firing were limited by ammunition supplies and loading procedures. The militia requirement of "one pound of powder, twenty bullits fit for his gun, and twelve flints" would be considered a minimum amount and probably reflects the ammunition carried by members of the militia engaged in pursuits.[15] But provincial soldiers involved in scouting and expeditions carried anywhere from thirty to sixty ball, either loose or wrapped with the powder in cartridges. Larger amounts than this presented problems in transportation. If the ball was carried loose, then the powder was carried in a separate container, usually a powder horn. A large ox horn could carry a pound of powder. It is impossible to know the loads used. British military cartridges from the American Revolution period contained six drams, or roughly 164 grains of powder.[16] Some of this was used to fill the pan; the rest went down the barrel as the main charge. A pound of powder contains 7,000 grains of gunpowder, so, using the British cartridge as a measurement, a pound of powder could supply the means to fire roughly forty-two 12-bore balls from a 10-bore musket. This would represent four and a half pounds of weight. A British-style shoulder cartridge box of the period was made to carry eighteen cartridges, which was frequently augmented by a waistbelt box that contained another eighteen cartridges for a total of thirty-six rounds. If made for a 10-bore British musket, the thirty-six cartridges would weigh approximately four pounds, not including the weight of the cartridge box itself. Added to the weight of the musket, a knapsack filled with spare clothes and blanket, a hatchet or hunting sword, and food, thirty-six cartridges represented a reasonable limit for traveling through the woods. The number of rounds could be increased without adding to the weight by reducing the bore size of the muskets. Thus a soldier using a 16-bore ball could carry twelve more cartridges than a soldier using a 12-bore ball with no increase in weight, which is why smaller caliber fusils and hunting arms were preferred by provincial soldiers and Native Americans.[17]

Soldiers with fewer than thirty rounds soon depleted their ammunition in any sustained action. At Quebec in 1690 the New Englanders drove off the French soldiers who opposed their landing and chased them for several miles. "Our Men had spent the greatest part of our Ammunition in this skirmish," Thomas Savage reported, "having taken ashore with them about three quarters of a Pound of Powder a Man, and about fifteen or eighteen Shot."[18] Benjamin Church had experienced similar problems a year earlier when the men under his command were thrust into the Battle of Brackett's Woods at Falmouth, Maine, with no chance to fill their cartridge boxes or pouches. When Church "ordered that all his army should pursue the enemy . . . they told him that most of them had spent their ammunition; that if the enemy had engaged them a little longer, they might have come and knocked them on the head."[19]

In addition to ammunition supplies, loading procedures limited the length and intensity of engagements. It is often pointed out that British officers expected their soldiers to load and fire their muskets every fifteen to twenty seconds on the drill field. Actually, British soldiers could not achieve a loading rate of four shots per minute until both the priming flask was eliminated (priming from a cartridge became common in the 1730s) and the wooden ramrod was replaced by a metal one. This rate refers to drill as well, commonly done with blanks, and not combat conditions. Under the stress of combat and loading with ball, two shots per minute were considered good.[20] Provincials were not introduced to priming from a cartridge until the 1740s; even then, the use of powder horns for priming remained widespread.[21] In addition, extended firing increased the accumulation of powder fouling in the barrels, which would eventually interfere with ramming and slow the whole procedure.[22]

Thus, a loading speed of two shots per minute under combat conditions would be considered very good, even unusual. Such a rate of fire impressed Captain Eleazer Melvin enough for him to make a note of it in his scouting report. In May 1748, Melvin led a scout from Fort Dummer to the area around the French fort at Crown Point. While they watched Lake Champlain, a canoe containing twelve Indians came within view. "Apprehending we might make some spoil upon them, and fearing we should have no better opportunity, we agreed to fire upon them, and accordingly fired six times each in about 3 or 4 minutes."[23]

Short cuts in the procedure could produce quicker loading times. One method was to seat the ball on the powder by thumping the butt of the musket on the ground rather than using a ramrod.[24] The thumping also forced powder through the flash hole into the pan, thus eliminating the need for priming.[25] The legendary story concerning the death of the Pequawket chief Paugus during Lovewell's fight illustrates the advantages of this method. During the course of the firefight, John Chamberlain's weapon became fouled with powder residue and he withdrew to the pond to clean it. While there, he saw Paugus performing the same duty nearby. Apparently Chamberlain knew Paugus personally and issued a challenge to him, which was accepted. Both men began to reload but Chamberlain, "trusting to the priming of his gun by a thump on the ground," finished first and took careful aim while Paugus was priming from his horn. Chamberlain's ball killed Paugus as he was in the act of aiming.[26] The story may be apocryphal, but this method is recorded throughout the flintlock period.

However, despite these incidents, firing during an extended fight tended to be slow and deliberate, both to conserve precious supplies of ammunition and to make every ball count if possible. Samuel Penhallow reported that after the fall of Lovewell, "Ensign Wyman took upon him the command of the shattered Company, who behaved himself with great Prudence and Courage, by animating the Men and telling them, 'that the Day would yet be their own, if their Spirits did not flag'; which enlivened them anew, and caused them to fire so briskly, that several discharged between twenty and thirty times apiece."[27] Over the course of a ten-hour battle, this means an average firing rate of one shot every twenty minutes.

Of course this is an average rate. Evidence seems to indicate that the intensity of battle fluctuated with periods of furious firing interspersed with lulls.[28] One reason for the lulls beyond the need to catch a breath or clean a weapon was to let the gun smoke dissipate so the enemy could be seen. Black powder produces a white cloud of sulphurous-smelling smoke that reduced visibility if not blown away by a breeze. The volume of smoke produced on European battlefields was known to envelop armies and even obliterate the sun. But even in the relative small engagements on the northern frontier, powder smoke hampered aim and reduced the rate of fire. During a running fight between a fishing shallop and several canoes filled with Indians, the English, according to Samuel Penhallow, "spent five pounds of Powder, and when the Enemy ceased their chase, they had not one quarter of a pound left . . . The number of [Indians] that fell was then unknown, because of a continued Cloud of Smoke."[29]

In addition to musket fire and smoke, combat was punctuated by the sounds of shouting and yelling. Soldiers shouted encouragement and information to each other throughout the heat of battle. Like Seth Wyman at Lovewell's fight, officers in particular yelled encouragements to keep up the spirits of their men. The story related by Cotton Mather about the inhabitants of Gloucester and some French and Indian raiders gives a feeling for this type of communication in combat. On July 14, 1692, six of the enemy were seen by the residents of one garrison and the men, including one Ebenezer Bapson, sallied out to fight them.

> Bapson presently overtook two of them, which run out of the Bushes, and coming close to them, he presented his Gun at them, and his Gun missing fire, the two men Returned into the Bushes. Bapson then called unto the other persons, which were on the other side of the Swamp, and upon his call, they made Answer, "Here they are! Here they are!" Bapson then running to meet them, Saw Three men walk softly out of the Swamp by each other's Side; the middlemost having on a white Waistcoat. So being within Two or Three Rod of them, he Shot, and as soon as his Gun was off, they all fell down. Bapson then running to his supposed prey, cried out unto his Companions, whom he hear on the other side of the Swamp, and said, he had kill'd Three! But coming almost unto them, they all rose up, and one of them Shot at him, and hearing the Bullet whis by him, he ran behind a Tree, and loaded his Gun, and seeing them lye behind a Log, he crept toward them again, telling his Companions, they were here! So, his Companions came up to him, and they all Ran directly to the Log, with all speed; but before they got thither, they saw them start up, and run every man his way.[30]

Soldiers also shouted, yelled, and screamed inarticulate war cries during the heat of battle. As Richard Holmes observed, "War cries are a time-honoured means of boosting one's own fighting spirit and attempting to diminish the enemy's."[31] When the French ambushed the provincial soldiers landing below Quebec in 1690, the New Englanders "Shouting and rushing upon the Enemy at once they run away as fast as [their] legs could carry them."[32] During fights on the frontier, both Indians and provincials added their cries to the din of battle. In 1722, the Eastern Indians captured a few fishing vessels at Canso, Nova Scotia. According to Samuel Penhallow, one captain sent to recapture the ships kept most of his men below decks as he approached a prize ship filled with

Indians. "The Indians being flushed with Success, and having thirty nine on board one of the Vessels which they had took, and seeing no more Men on board the English then what was usual, commanded them to strike for that they were their Prize. Unto whom Captain Eliot reply'd that he was hastening to them; and in an instant called his Men on Deck, who fired on them with a loud Huzza, and clapt them on board; which was so surprising a Salutation, that they made a most dreadful yelling."[33] The Reverend Thomas Symmes captured the essence of this yelling and screaming in his description of Lovewell's fight. "The Fight continu'd very Furious and Obstinate, All towards Night," he wrote. "The Indians Roaring and Yelling and Howling like Wolves, Barking like Dogs, and making all Sorts of Hideous Noises: The English Frequently Shouting and Huzza'ing, as they did after the first Round."[34]

Soldiers on both sides also taunted and shouted insults at each other, usually in an attempt to draw the enemy out into the open. Francis Parkman wrote that when they had trouble coming to grips with the French forces outside Quebec in 1690, "the New England men taunted them as cowards who never fight except under cover."[35] Although some historians have interpreted this as an indication the provincials still clung to European-style warfare, it was no more than goading the French to reveal themselves, as Ann M. Little observed, by questioning their manhood.[36] According to Cotton Mather's stimulating account of the siege of Storer's garrison in 1692, the Indians used the same taunts. "The Indian replied unto Captain Converse, Being you are so Stout, why don't you come and Fight in the open Field, like a Man, and not Fight in a Garrison, like a Squaw?"[37] Familiarity between New Englanders and the Eastern Indians through trade and other contacts promoted the exchange of insults during battle. According to the legend, John Chamberlain and Paugus knew each other quite well and hurled personal affronts before their duel on the shore.[38]

In almost all circumstances, the Indian method of warfare—the hit-and-run raid, ambush, and surprise—governed combat on the northern frontier. "They are extremely skilful in the art of surprizing, and watching the motions of an enemy," according to one description published in 1757. "They disperse themselves thro' a country singly, or in very small parties, and lie on the lurch, to pick up stragglers, or procure intelligence: in which they act with an astonishing patience and indefatigableness . . . remaining in one place, and often in one posture, for whole days and weeks together, till they find an opportunity to strike their stroke, or compass their design, whatever it may be."[39]

One of the few firsthand English observations of Indians preparing and executing an ambush is contained in the report of Caleb Lyman.[40] Acting on intelligence from Albany that the Indians had established a fort on the Connecticut River, Lyman led a scout of five friendly Indians to investigate sometime in May 1704. Approaching the supposed site of the fort, they halted "to consult what Methods to take; and soon concluded to send out a Spy, with Green Leaves for a Cap and Veste, to prevent his own Discovery, and to find out the Enemy." The scout had no sooner left, however, when they saw two Indians in a canoe and heard the firing of a gun. Lyman recalled the scout and "concluded to keep close till Sunset."

At Sunset, Lyman and his five Indians moved down to the river where they saw smoke from a campfire. With "utmost Care and Diligence" they worked their way to within twelve rods of the enemy's wigwam.

> But here we met with a new Difficulty, which we feared would have ruined the whole Design: For the Ground was so covered over with dry Sticks and Brush, for the space of five Rods, that we could not pass, without making such a *Crackling*, as we thought would alarm the Enemy, and give them Time to escape. But while we were contriving to compass our Design, God in his good Providence so ordered, that a very *small* Cloud arose, which gave a smart *Clap of Thunder*, and a sudden Shower of Rain. And this Opportunity we embraced, to run thorow the Thicket; and so come undiscovered within sight of the *Wigwam*; and perceived by their Noise, that the Enemy were awake. But however, being unwilling to lose any Time, we crept on our Hands and Knees till we were within three or four Rods of them. Then we arose, and ran to the side of the *Wigwam*, and *fired* in upon them: And flinging down our Guns, we surrounded them with our *Clubs* and *Hatchets*, and knockt down several we met with.

Although accounts of the preparation are rare, the impact of the surprise attacks is well known. According to John Gyles's clear description of the attack on Pemaquid in August 1689, the men had worked in the fields all morning, stopped to eat, then went back to work, dividing into groups among the various fields. The fort fired the signal cannon and Gyles's father said he hoped the news was good. "But to our great surprise, about thirty or forty Indians at that moment discharged a volley of shot at us from behind a rising ground near our barn. The yelling of the Indians, the whistling of their shot, and the voice of my father, whom I heard cry out, 'What now! What now!' so terrified me (though he seem to be handing a gun) that I endeavored to make my escape. My brother ran one way, and I another, and looking over my shoulder I saw a stout fellow, all painted, pursuing me, with a gun in one hand and a cutlass glittering in the other, which I expected in my brains every moment."[41] When Gyles tripped, the Indian tied him up and led him to where the other prisoners were being gathered before being taken into a long captivity.[42]

The Indians relied on this scattering effect, and the psychological paralysis induced by sudden shock, to give them a quick and easy victory. Flushed like so many quail, the enemy, isolated and terrified, would be dispatched with a tomahawk or knife because the Indian muskets had been discharged in the initial attack. However, despite the romantic descriptions provided by Hollywood, novelists, and even historians, hand-to-hand combat between two equally prepared opponents during the French and Indian wars was an extremely rare occurrence. The Eastern Indian involved in or even confronted with such an encounter usually withdrew from the action.[43] It should be emphasized that the sources describing Indian war combat are all white accounts, many of which have undoubtedly been exaggerated or altered by time. However, the conclusions presented here are based on an overall impression covering sixty years of warfare, not on any particular incident. Eastern Indians avoided close combat whenever the odds were not overwhelming in their favor.[44]

This aversion to hand-to-hand combat was noticed and misinterpreted as cowardice. Cotton Mather exhorted communities on the frontier to maintain their watching and warding, because they faced a "Mischievous Enemy; but a cowardly one. The Cowards never durst Assault you, but when they can surprize you. Though they have come Three or Four Hundred miles to molest you, yet if they find you Awake when they come, away they Go again."[45] In the nineteenth century, Jeremy Belknap observed that the Indians "appeared not in the open field, nor gave proofs of a truly masculine courage."[46]

Indian behavior in battle, as well as the interpretation of that behavior as cowardice, illustrates the differences between European and Native American cultures. John Keegan and Richard Holmes wrote that "fighting in primitive warfare takes a form quite other than that known in 'advanced' societies. Much of it is of a low-level endemic quality—ambush and raiding . . . Since there is no intention to win, however, the fighting is conducted at long distances, usually with missiles, and casualties few . . . A death, even a serious wounding, is normally the signal for the battle to be brought to an end and overtures of peace to be initiated."[47] Francis Jennings agreed with this assessment. He found that Indian warfare produced far fewer casualties than "civilized" warfare, and that, on the whole, European society was far more violent than its Native American counterpart.[48]

In *Primitive War: Its Practice and Concepts*, Harry Turney-High wrote that the prime motive of the American Indian was individual glory: honor went to the individual, not the village or the tribe.[49] Thus, opportunities for martial glory would be gauged by the individual, and his judgment in the moment, whether to refrain or proceed, would be respected by his peers. Europeans, on the other hand, traditionally view war in a more communal sense. The purpose for war is communal (be it town, country, or kingdom), and the fear of cowardice, of letting down community or comrades, often surpasses the logic of the combat situation, even the prospect of death.[50]

The Eastern Indian also took with him the handicaps and burdens of wilderness living. Because he lived in a hunting society whose numbers were relatively small, every male played an important role in the support of families and the village. Death or a debilitating wound diminished the ability of the family and the tribe to provide food, and unlike their white adversaries, the Indians had no governments to petition for pensions or relief to compensate for death or disability. Thus, the Eastern Indian and the New England provincial soldier entered battle with different social pressures. Finally, religious beliefs contributed to the native psyche. To Native Americans, all living things possessed certain power, but this power ebbed and flowed. As James Axtell wrote, this personal power "could be acquired and lost. Since a person's current power was always uncertain, the Indians avoided competition, fostered respect for other persons, and approached all encounters as if potentially dangerous."[51] These thoughts probably produced a good dose of caution.

Perhaps this caution explains the repeated instances where Indians refused to approach provincials who appeared prepared and ready to fire on them. As shown in chapter 2, on numerous occasions, individuals in garrison houses saved their lives by giving the appearance of preparedness and strength by shouting commands to imaginary defenders or thrusting unloaded and useless weapons out the loopholes.[52] In April 1747 three boys uncovered a party of Indians who had laid an ambush for some men working in a nearby field. The Indians fired prematurely and one of the boys returned the fire, wounding an Indian. The other boy aimed his weapon but did not fire it, which kept the Indians at bay until the men arrived to drive them off.[53]

The most famous example of Indian prudence involved the family of Hannah Dustan. The story of how Hannah Dustan was taken captive from her home in Haverhill, Massachusetts, and how she then killed and scalped her captors, is legendary, but the adventures of her husband, Thomas, are less well known. At the first sign of the attack on March 15, 1697, Dustan rode to his cabin from the fields and told his eight children to run for the nearest garrison. His wife had just given birth and was sick in bed, so Dustan made the hard decision to abandon his wife in order to save the children. Mounting his horse, he galloped after them.

The Indians easily caught up with the fleeing Dustan family, whose speed was inhibited by the short legs of the younger children. "Dustan well knew that the savages would not venture within gun-shot until they had first drawn his fire," wrote the nineteenth-century historian Samuel Adams Drake. "Urging his little flock to quicken their pace, he wheeled his horse and levelled his gun at the nearest pursuers, who instantly halted expecting a shot. Dustan, however, knew better than to throw his only chance away. He kept the Indians covered with his gun until the children had widen the distance between them, then cooly rode back to rejoin them."[54] Dustan continued to point his loaded weapon at the Indians who halted and dove for cover until his family made it safely to a garrison. The Indians tried firing random shots at the horseman, but eventually gave up the chase.

It is conceivable that a party of Europeans in a similar situation would have simply rushed Dustan in the belief that he could only shoot one of them, and to not do so would be to play the coward. Certainly Lovewell and his men showed no hesitation in approaching the lone Indian just before their fateful battle, a confrontation that resulted in the death of the Indian and the wounding of Lovewell and another man. However, the Eastern Indian calculated the odds of survival differently than the European. They tried to gauge the effects of their surprise on the enemy and withdrew when the advantage disappeared. Believing in the axiom it is better to "run away and live to fight another day," they preferred long-distance firefights to close hand-to-hand combat because it was easier to disengage from the former if the tide turned against them. Therefore, Francis Jennings's observation that "there were no innate differences between Indians and Europeans in their capacity for war or their mode of conducting it" is not strictly true.[55] Their capacity for war may have been similar, but the tactical conduct of battle revealed subtle cultural distinctions.

In the late 1950s, John K. Mahon wrote an article analyzing Anglo-American methods of Indian warfare.[56] Covering the period from King Philip's War to Anthony Wayne's expedition against the Indians in the Ohio Valley in 1794, Mahon emphasized the Indian tactic of surprise achieved by means of ambush, and he recalled the British general Henry Bouquet's description of the Indian in battle. According to Bouquet, the Indians fought in scattered formation during a firefight, trying to surround their enemy, giving ground when pressed, and returning when the pressure ceased. Mahon concluded that the secrets to fighting Indians were coordinated movement and the use of the bayonet. "American militiamen, many of whom were practiced marksmen and few of whom knew how to handle a bayonet, naturally preferred to rely on marksmanship."[57] This involved provincials in inconclusive firefights that often produced as many white casualties as Indian deaths. Provincial weapons—fowlers, rifles, and trade guns—could not mount a bayonet, and thus they were "disqualified for effective use in the type of Indian fighting that depended upon shock action rather than weapons-fire to inflict destructive defeats."

Henry Bouquet used coordinated movement and the bayonet to defeat the Indians at the Battle of Bushy Run during Pontiac's Rebellion in 1763, and at the end of the century Anthony Wayne ordered his men to "Rouse" the Indians with the bayonet, fire at their backs, and charge again to prevent them from reloading. Therefore, the bayonet "became a decisive weapon in organized Indian fighting," and, as "only disciplined bodies of soldiers could make effective use of them," the true hero of the Indian wars was the "trained regular soldiery, first the redcoats and then their American counterparts, were more important than unorganized frontiersmen in breaking the power of the Indians."[58] Unfortunately, Mahon's thesis is flawed because he has misinterpreted the evidence. It was not the bayonet that was so effective, but the tactic of charging itself.

Provincial soldiers adopted many Indian tactics during the course of their long wars, especially the surprise and ambush. Scouting companies were ordered to "be silent in their Marches, and patient and vigilant in their waiting for the Enemy, that if it be possible they make a Discovery of themselves by their [musket] Fires, but to be sure not by Shooting or other Noises."[59] At Norridgewock in 1724, Jeremiah Moulton ordered his men to "advance softly, and to keep a profound silence" as they approached the Indian village.[60] The following year, a scout commanded by John Lovewell discovered a party of ten Indians camped near a pond in present-day Wakefield, New Hampshire.[61] Lovewell prepared his ambush with care. He divided his men into firing teams of five each, then drawing near the sleeping Indians after midnight, he fired his own gun as a signal. Each five-man team fired in succession, catching the Indians in various stages of reaction and destroying the whole party.[62]

Such surprise tactics were used successfully on numerous other occasions, and in their practice they differed little from Indian usage.[63] Provincial soldiers also adopted the Indian custom of using cover and fighting in scattered or extended formation. But the battlefield tactics of the New Englanders and the Eastern Indians differed in one important respect. When on the receiving end of an ambush, provincial soldiers, if they survived the initial effects of surprise both physically and psychologically, often rushed at their enemy. In fact, for veterans of frontier warfare, the charge became an automatic response to an ambush and produced three possible results. Either the Indians broke and fled, the provincials were stopped by superior forces (in which case they scattered themselves and headed for home), or both sides settled down into a long firefight.[64]

Provincial soldiers used the charge because of the Indians' aversion to hand-to-hand combat. In *Souldiers Conselled and Comforted*, Cotton Mather encouraged soldiers to attack boldly when confronted with Indians. "Your Enemies have made themselves notorious for this quality [of running away] . . . it is easier to kill them then to find them; so they can rarely Take any but a shaking Trembling Aim at one that boldly faces them . . . [so] at the first Appearance of the Tawney Pagans, then Courage! brave Hearts; Fall on!"[65] Benjamin Church frequently ordered a charge when confronted by an enemy force. He had his men charge across a bridge during the Battle of Brackett's Woods in 1689.[66] The following year, he and his company chased a force of Indians through their village, and later in the raid would put to flight an enemy party that had ambushed his Plymouth Indians.[67] Church would command similar assaults during his last raid in 1704.[68]

Of course, the tactic did not always work. At Casco Bay in 1690, thirty men sallied out from Fort Loyal to investigate some musket shots. Perceiving that their cattle were staring at a fence that lined the woods, the company charged the fence with a cheer and was met with a withering volley that killed the lieutenant in command and thirteen others. The survivors ran to a nearby garrison-house and held off the enemy until dark when they slipped back into the fort.[69] Lovewell's men also apparently charged after the first shock of the ambush, but meeting obviously superior numbers they retreated to the edge of the pond and began their long firefight. Francis Parkman emphasized the "unusual" behavior of the Indians during Lovewell's fight "in rushing forward instead of firing from their ambush,"[70] and others, such as John Mahon, have agreed with this interpretation.[71] Mahon wrote that the "Indians deviated from the usual pattern by breaking cover and rushing in mass toward the whites. Then, after volleying at one another in the open, both sides closed in and grappled hand-to-hand."[72] However, Indians often rushed forward after their initial volley to increase the psychological impact of the surprise attack.[73] The Indians attacking Lovewell followed their usual pattern of firing and rushing forward. If they found the enemy had not scattered or fallen apart, Indians quickly terminated their rush and took cover to continue firing. There is no indication that any hand-to-hand fighting took place during the battle. When Lovewell's men did not scatter at the first volley, the Indians were content to use firepower to beat the English. There was no wild melee, no swinging hatchet and musket butt, just a firefight.[74]

Lovewell's men apparently charged forward themselves after the initial volley, meeting the Indians at close range. The best evidence for this comes from the account of Benjamin Hassell, the man who panicked and left the action to report the premature destruction of the company. When Lieutenant Governor William Dummer related Hassell's story of Lovewell's wounding and his flight to Colonel Thomas Westbrook, he added that Hassell "Cant Deny but our people were charging the Enemy briskly when he left."[75] There is no reason to suggest Hassell lied in this observation, because it only worsened his own position. Seth Wyman's account, published in the *Boston Newsletter* a couple of weeks after the battle, also confirms this.

> Returning to the Place where they left their Packs, before they could reach it, one of the English discovered an Indian, and calling out to the rest, the Indians rose up from their Ambush, Shouted and fired, as did the English at the same Instant . . . After the first Fire, the Indians advanc'd with great Fury towards the English, with their Hatchets in their Hands, the English likewise running up to them, till they came within 4 or 5 Yards of the Enemy, and were even mix'd among them, when the Dispute growing too warm for the Indians, they gave back, and endeavour'd to encompass the English, who then retreated to the Pond, in order to have their Rear cover'd, where they continu'd the Fight till Night.[76]

Apparently both sides advanced after the first fire, the Indians as part of their ambush tactic, the whites as the automatic response to Indian attack. As they came "within twice the length of their Guns," the Indians realized the whites had not scattered and remained a cohesive fighting force.[77] Lovewell's men found that the Indians were not retreating and obviously outnumbered their small band, especially in light of the casualties they had just suffered. Therefore, they both withdrew and began their firefight. It is perhaps the fact that the Indians had not fled when the whites charged that left the impression that the Indian behavior in that engagement was unusual, but it was only a matter of timing. The English charged before the Indians had completed the surprise phase of their attack.

This automatic impulse to charge the enemy is illustrated in perhaps the most vivid account of combat on the frontier: Eleazer Melvin's journal of his 1748 scout to Crown Point. After Melvin and his men fired on the Indians in the canoe (see above), they heard signal guns at the French fort and so, knowing a pursuit force would soon be sent, started their journey back to Fort Dummer. The next day they crossed the trail of 150–200 tracks obviously belonging to the enemy and assumed they represented the pursuit force. Melvin and his men followed the banks of Otter Creek, crossed over a mountain range, and came upon a branch of the West River.

> Our provision being very short, we began our march before sunrise, and travelled till about half after 9 o'clock; being by the side of the river several of the company desired to stop to refresh themselves, being faint and weary, whereupon we halted and began to take off our packs, and some were set down, and in about a half a minute after our halting, the enemy rose from behind a log and several trees, about 20 feet or 30 at farthest distant, and fired about 12 guns at us, but do not know whether any men received any hurt, tho' so near;—whereupon I called to the men to face the enemy and run up the bank, which I did my self, and several others attempted, but the enemy were so thick, they could not. I was no sooner jumpt up the bank but the enemy were just upon me. I discharged my gun at one of them, about eight feet from the muzzel of my gun, who I see fall,—and about the same time that I discharged my gun, the enemy fired about 20 guns at us, and killed 4 men . . . The men which were left alive most of them fired immediately on the enemy, several of which shots did execution, as can be witnessed by several who see the enemy fall;—but seeing the enemy numerous and their guns discharged, they retreated. Several ran across the river, where they had some of them opportunity to fire again at the enemy. Some ran up the river, and some down, and some into a thicket on the same side of the river. For my own part, after I saw my men retreat, and being beset by the enemy with guns, hatchets and knives. Several of them attempted to strike at me with their hatchets. Some threw their hatchets, one of which, or a bullet, I cannot certainly tell which, carried away my belt, and with it my bullets, all except one I had loose in my pocket. I ran down the river, and two Indians followed me, and ran almost side by side with me, calling to me, "Come Captain," "Now Captain," but upon my presenting my gun towards them (though not charged) they fell a little back, and I ran across the river, charged my gun, moved a few steps, and one of them fired at me, which was the last gun fired.[78]

Most of the elements of frontier combat are contained in this action. The Indians fired on the provincial soldiers from ambush in a classic surprise attack. Eleazer Melvin, who was a veteran of Lovewell's last battle, instantly ordered and led a charge up the bank. Melvin encountered an Indian at close range and fired at him with his musket. His men attempted to follow but a second volley, and the obviously superior size of the enemy force, halted their forward motion. The provincial soldiers returned the fire, inflicting casualties on the uncovered Indians, and then with muskets empty, they dispersed to make their escape.

Although momentarily checked by the attempted charge and return fire of the whites, the Indians recognized the odds changing in their favor when they perceived the soldiers scattering. At this point Melvin, who had advanced the farthest, became exposed and vulnerable, and the Indians closed in, throwing knives and hatchets at him because most of their guns had been discharged. Melvin ran down the riverbank with two Indians paralleling his course and taunting him in the hope he would stop his flight. But Melvin kept them at bay by pointing his empty, and useless, musket at them until he crossed the river. The Indians stopped their pursuit at that point, sending a parting shot to speed him on his way. The whole action lasted only a few minutes, and the number of shots fired were very few. Most of the participants fired their weapons only once, with only a few of the whites who crossed the river, and the Indian who fired the last shot at Melvin, getting off a second round.

Melvin's account illustrates the difference in attitude between the Eastern Indians and provincial soldiers. This culturally based difference is subtle, but existed nonetheless. The Indians entered battle with considerable caution and a belief that death brought little glory. Discretion was indeed the better part of valor to the Eastern Indian, and no cultural dishonor resulted from its use. Thus Eleazer Melvin, like Thomas Dustan, was able to fend off his pursuers with a useless gun. In contrast to this, the white cultural approach to battle encouraged provincial soldiers to exploit the caution of the Indian. Therefore, charging the enemy, if physically possible, became an almost automatic response. Certainly, Melvin ordered his charge with little reflection or thought.

Mahon's erroneous conclusion that regular soldiers using the bayonet were the most effective Indian fighters in the colonial period is based on a misconception. It was not the bayonet the Indians fled from at Bushy Run and Fallen Timbers, but the charge itself. It was the charge, and the prospect of hand-to-hand combat, that "roused" the Indians and enabled Anthony Wayne's men to shoot them in the back. This tactic had not been developed by regular troops, British or otherwise, but by provincial soldiers. Indeed, Mahon's thesis is further weakened by the fact that British regulars, and their American counterparts, never received any training in the use of the bayonet. In his study of British army training, J. A. Houlding found that "bayonet drill was, curiously, rather neglected in the eighteenth century . . . [but] from Marlborough's campaigns onwards it was the touch-stone of British Tactical thinking that heavy fire power was all-important; and so it was doctrine perhaps, as much as indifference, that dictated the army's approach." In fact, the only time the British redcoat received specific training in the use of the bayonet was during the Scottish Highland rebellion in 1745, when they faced a foe who charged with sword and shield, preferring hand-to-hand combat over missile combat. This was a style of fighting the redcoats found unfamiliar and very disconcerting.[79]

There is no right or wrong involved in cultural attitudes; they are just different. Combat is a test of wills between two opponents, and in reacting to this test the opposing forces draw on instincts honed by their individual societies and traditions. In the French, New Englanders faced an enemy who may have differed in temperament, politics, and religion, but whose basic cultural background was the same. Both were Europeans, and their battles, like Port Royal and Louisbourg, came closest to the European model.

However, in opposing the Eastern Indians provincial soldiers not only had to face a foe with deep cultural differences, but they had to fight that foe on their own terms. Indian warfare dictated the style of combat on the northern frontier. The strategy was simple—attempt to gain a superior psychological edge through the use of surprise attack. Tactically, the Eastern Indians maximized the effects of surprise by firing, then rushing the foe with hideous yelling. Ideally the enemy would scatter and could be destroyed piecemeal. If they did not scatter, the Indians were content to use overwhelming firepower to wear down their foe in long firefights. New Englanders adapted to this warfare by employing the surprise attack themselves and were more than willing to match the Indians musket for musket in a firefight if they could. But they also used the charge whenever practical to break up enemy formations and possibly drive off Indian raiding parties. Such a tactic could backfire, but the success rate made the charge an almost automatic response for many veteran soldiers.

While combat on the northern frontier did not approach the vastness and grandeur of European battles, it was just as intense and just as deadly. Wreathed in powder smoke and their ears ringing with musket shots, screams, and shouted instructions, provincial soldiers tried to remain tuned to the rhythm of battle. Instantaneous individual decisions had to be made concerning cover, targets, and the functioning of weapons, while maintaining a group identity for the tactical options of scattering, charging, or holding ground. It was a type of combat that became quite familiar to twentieth-century soldiers—small-unit action in thick cover depending on individual actions and individual consequences. For provincial soldiers, it was a form of battle they knew well.

11

The Wounds of War

Beyond all considerations of higher taxes, food shortages, economic disruption, and political upheaval, the final cost of war is measured in the pain of wounds and the finality of death. As in all human conflict, provincial soldiers found that the immediate consequences of combat were dead and wounded comrades, but military service in the seventeenth and eighteenth centuries also promoted the spread of deadly disease, which, in an age of relatively primitive medical knowledge, led to more deaths than bullets. Understandably, the need for doctors on the frontier and for expeditions was acute, but their numbers were few and in administering to wounded and sick soldiers, New England doctors, finding their supplies and personal stamina exhausted, often succumbed to the very diseases they fought and their deaths only exacerbated the problem of medical care. In addition, while the dead could be quickly buried, the wounded had to be cared for, sometimes for extended lengths of time. The medical bills and relief paid to the wounded, as well as compensation for widows and families of the slain, further complicated the war effort and added to the financial burden of provincial governments. While faith in God helped New Englanders accept these sorrows, war, as always, brought pain and suffering beyond the power of faith to alleviate, especially the psychological wounds of war.

With hand-to-hand combat rare, the physical wounds suffered in battle by provincial soldiers usually resulted from gunshots.[1] As wounds in the trunk—in the stomach, bowels, or chest—were normally mortal, leg and arm wounds, followed by head wounds, were the most prevalent among survivors. For example, Richard Hunniwell, the Maine woodsman and pilot, reported that he had "been wounded Severall Times in his Arme by divers Shott."[2] John Ellenwood, a Beverly, Massachusetts, resident pressed for service on the Maine frontier in 1696, "was sorely wounded in my right hand my fore finger being shott away and the rest of my hand So grevously Shattered and Torn and bones broaken that it hath been thereby rendred almost altogether useless Ever Since."[3] Such descriptions would remain consistent throughout the early French wars.[4]

Some extremely fortunate men survived wounds that were normally mortal. Eleazer Davis was wounded in the stomach and had part of a thumb shot off during Lovewell's fight. He somehow managed to remain alive and staggered into Berwick nineteen days later.[5] Cotton Mather related the amazing story of Simon Stone, who was part of the relief force sent to aid Hilton's garrison in Exeter, New Hampshire, during the summer of 1690. In the ensuing battle Stone received nine gunshot wounds and two cuts with hatchets and was presumed dead. However, when his comrades came to bury him they found him still alive. According to Mather, an "Irishman" in the company suggested they put Stone out of his misery. Rejecting the Irishman's advice, the provincials gave Stone a drink of "fair water" and then a drink of "strong water." Stone opened his eyes and began his long road to recovery.[6]

Edged weapon cuts, like those received by Stone, usually occurred after a soldier was wounded. Delivered as a *coup de grâce*, the Indians used their hatchets to dispatch the wounded and helpless whom they could not take as prisoners. Usually referred to as being "knocked in the head," this was the treatment recommended for Simon Stone by that dispassionate Irishman. The survival rate after this treatment was obviously very low. That Simon Stone recovered from two hatchet blows, in addition to his other wounds, was a tribute to his strength and constitution.

Although small arms and handheld weapons caused the vast majority of battle wounds suffered by provincials, soldiers were also exposed to cannon fire at Louisbourg. From the few descriptions in the extant journals, it appears that most of the traumas produced by artillery shells and round shot were of a decidedly lethal nature. One anonymous chronicler saw a dead man carried back from the trenches with "his skull crushed by a shell fragment." One gunner had his "head split in two" by a shell fragment. The journalist also reported that one soldier had his "leg shot off by a cannon ball; another shot in the elbow, had to be amputated; another shot in the knee, not expected to live."[7]

Enemy musket fire and artillery shells obviously constituted a hazard to soldiers engaged in military operations, but another source of serious injury and even death were accidents and simple carelessness. On October 25, 1704, a minister in the town of Gardiner volunteered to stand night guard in a garrison as the inhabitants had been out on pursuit all day. According to Samuel Penhallow, the minister "being cold ... was coming down to warm himself; when one between Sleeping and Waking, or surpriz'd thro' excess of Fear, fir'd upon him as he was coming out of the watch tower." The minister staggered to the door of the garrison and collapsed inside. He forgave the man who had shot him and died within an hour.⁸ In chapter 8 an incident was mentioned that occurred during a scout in February 1723 commanded by Johnson Harmon, when a soldier fired his musket at a tree and the bullet "Glancing Straingley" killed another man. In replying to Johnson Harmon's report on the death from the ricochet, Lieutenant Governor William Dummer wrote, "I hope the Soldiers will be warned for the Time to come of such Carelessness & Folly, You must give strict Orders that no Guns be fired but at the Enemy, Unless by the Leave and in the Presence of an Officer."⁹

Combatants on the northern frontier, on both sides, not only shot each other by accident, but shot themselves as well. This was usually accomplished by carelessly holding the muzzle while they pulled their weapons toward them. The cock would be caught on something and pulled back, releasing the sear from the tumbler inside the lock and allowing the cock to fly forward when cleared from the obstruction. Cotton Mather related, with unrestrained satisfaction, that the Irishman who so cold-bloodedly suggested that Simon Stone be put out of his misery was crippled a few minutes later when he used the cock of his gun to pull a canoe to shore while holding the muzzle. The gun went off and broke his arm.¹⁰ On two other occasions, according to Mather, French Indians were killed in the same manner. One was a "a famous kind of a Giant among the Indians; a Fellow Reputed Seven Foot High . . . this famous and bloody Fellow accidently Shot himself to Death, by his Gun going off, when he was foolishly pulling a Canoe to the Shore with it."¹¹ In a similar occurrence, a provincial soldier on a scout in 1725 "took hold of his Gun that stood among some Bushes drew it towards him with the muzzle towards him some twigg caught hold of the cock, the Gun went of, and shott him through, he died Imediately."¹²

Freak accidents also took their toll on provincial soldiers. Joseph Bane told government authorities that while he was stationed at Fort Mary in Saco, his captain ordered him to fire his gun to set the watch. The gun exploded and "his hand Broke into peeces: his thumb and three fingers shoot off by splitting of [the] Gun."¹³ At Louisbourg the exploding of improperly loaded cannons also caused considerable death and injury.¹⁴ The force of an exploding cannon barrel is tremendous. One observer at Louisbourg reported that one section of a burst gun "landed on a house and crashed down through it into the cellar."¹⁵

Soldiers also accidentally cut themselves with axes and hatchets. John Lovewell recorded that on his second raid in February 1725, one of his men cut himself badly with an ax and had to be carried home by six others.¹⁶ During the following fall, Simon Willard reported that one of his men had also cut himself with a hatchet and had to be carried home.[17] In 1748 Lieutenant John Burk indicated one of the soldiers at Number Four also had an accident with an ax.[18] Other bizarre incidents injured soldiers as well. Willard reported that another soldier on his scout cut his foot on a rock, and Burk related that while they were building a new privy or "little house," a soldier named Cory "tore his ass" sliding off the roof.[19]

While wounds in battle, accidents, and carelessness caused their share of suffering and death, illness and disease accounted for far more. It is a well-known fact that in the early modern period, and actually up until the twentieth century, disease killed more soldiers than bullets, and the early French wars in New England proved to be no exception.[20] The various expeditions, with their greater numbers of participants, were particularly deadly in this regard. During Phips's expedition to Quebec in 1690, smallpox helped defeat the two-pronged assault by halting the attack on Montreal while seasickness and fever laid low a substantial portion of Phips's army before he even arrived. Even more would die on the return voyage from smallpox and camp fever.[21] Simon Wainwright reported from Port Royal in 1707 that "there is a considerable number of [soldiers] visited with violent fluxes, and although we have things proper to give them, yet dare not do it; others taken with mighty swellings in their throats; others filled with terror at the consideration of a fatal event of the expedition, concluding that, in a short time, there will not be well enough to carry off the sick."[22]

The deadly consequences of Cartagena and Louisbourg are also well known. Of the 3,600 Americans, from all colonies, enlisted for Cartagena, only 500 returned: the rest were victims of disease.[23] The sickness at Louisbourg began to take hold after the fortress had fallen, and it multiplied throughout the fall and winter. At the end of January 1746, William Pepperrell wrote to Governor William Shirley that they had buried 561 men, and 1,100 were sick and dying at a rate of three, four, or five daily. Pepperrell indicated that the daily death rate had been as high as fourteen or fifteen.[24] In the end, more than 2,000 provincial soldiers would die from disease at Louisbourg.[25]

While the illness associated with expeditions is familiar, sickness struck provincial forces posted on the frontier as well. Throughout the early French war period, illnesses swept through the garrisons at forts, crippled scouting forces and hampering planning and operations. In 1690 James Converse reported to the Bay government from Portsmouth that "our Soldiers are sick some of the small pox and others of A feaver, I have borrowed bread for the Hospetall, and the sick in severall places . . . I beseech your Honors to Consider what difficulty I meet with to provide Oatmeal, butter, Candle &c, for the sick with my own money."[26] His lament would be echoed by other frontier commanders. In 1712 Samuel Moody reported a fever in the garrison at Casco where ten soldiers were in bed, and during King George's War a sickness called "black tongue" swept through the fort at Gorham, Maine.[27] Thomas Westbrook, a commander on the Maine frontier in Dummer's War, found that so many men had died or had been discharged due to illness that he had trouble forming raiding parties, and those that did go out often were aborted due to sickness.[28]

Benjamin Church related one amusing incident concerning sickness among frontier soldiers. On returning to Portsmouth after his 1690 raid, rumors spread through his company that Church was being ordered to take them out again. When some of the men feigned symptoms of smallpox in order to be excused from further duty, Church arranged for them to be placed in a house where the people already had the disease. He said that they all would have to stay in the building until the disease ran its course: "Whereupon they all presently began to grow better, and to make excuses." Church told officials the best cure was to let them go home.[29]

British military leaders blamed a lack of discipline and cleanliness for the prevalence of illness in colonial troops. Commodore Charles Knowles comments on conditions at Louisbourg when he arrived to relieve Peter Warren seem to be explicit regarding the lack of elementary precautions to prevent illness. "The confused, dirty beastly Condition I found this Place in is not to be expressed . . . these New England Folks were so lazy, that they not only pulled one End of the House down to burn which they lived in, but even buried their dead under the Floors and did their Filth in the other corners of the House rather than go out of Doors in the Cold."[30] There is no question that provincial inexperience dealing with such large numbers of soldiers played a part here, although by the time Knowles arrived the provincial soldiers stationed at Louisbourg were mostly pressed and hired men. British officers did impose clean habits on their soldiers, such as the regular changing and cleaning of uniforms, as part of the system of discipline. However, in general the provincial experience with disease reflects only the general inadequacies of the age concerning medical knowledge. Certainly the redcoats decimated at Cartagena or the thousands of British seamen struck down by scurvy and other illnesses did not die any differently than provincial soldiers. John Keegan and Richard Holmes reported that 135,000 of the 185,000 sailors recruited by the Royal Navy during the Seven Years' War died of disease. Terrible losses due to disease would continue in war until the twentieth century.[31]

For soldiers involved in raids and probes, the problems of wounds, accidents, and sickness were increased fourfold by their being stuck in the middle of the wilderness miles from the nearest settlement. Although such problems existed in all the wars, Dummer's War provides the best examples of this added complexity. In the fall of 1724 Samuel Wheelwright led a company of fifty men toward Pequawket and this turned into a march of misery. On November 25 they marched eight miles and repeated the same the next day. Travel was difficult due to early snow. On the 26th, three men went home sick.

> 27th marched 15 miles, 4 more went back sick. 28th sent back 12 more sick: 30th Lay still, —fould weather, and men sick; —within 10 miles of 'Osaby Pond.' —Dec. 1. When I came to muster the men in order to march some were sick some Lame and Some Dead tired Could not get above 18 or 20 that was fitt to march forward upon which I called the officers together for Advice and soe Concluded to Return again which was Contrary to my Enclination.[32]

The following summer a scout of men led by Seth Wyman and John White encountered similar results. After they staggered into Dover, Richard Waldron described the scout to Lieutenant Governor John Wentworth as told to him by the captains.

> last night came in here Capts Wyman and White and say that before they got to Penny Cook their men began to be taken sick, with a bloody flux, soe that they were forc'd to Send Sundry back before they got to Penny Cook and that the distemper Increased daily till they had not men enough to carry their own and Sick mens packs, and at last hardly 20 men in a company were the Successive rains were very hurtfull and very much retarded their march by raising the brooks and rivers, and by that time they got to the upper end of Winnipicisauky pond they found their further March as was designed Impracticable so were forced to return bringing in one of their Sick men upon their Shoulders.[33]

Both Seth Wyman, hero of Lovewell's Fight, and John White were among the sick, and both men would die soon after their return.[34]

Lovewell's last raid provides perhaps the most poignant examples of the difficulties associated with wounds and sickness in the wilderness. Almost immediately after leaving Dunstable, three men turned back when an old wound disabled one of the soldiers. By the time the company reached

Ossipee Pond, another soldier, Benjamin Kidder, fell ill. Lovewell and his men constructed a crude fort and left Kidder in the care of their doctor, William Ayer, along with eight men to guard them. Lovewell then pushed on to his fateful battle.

After the fight the shattered company pulled itself together and began their retreat to the crude fort. Four of the wounded—Lieutenant Josiah Farwell, the young chaplain Jonathan Frye, Josiah Jones, and Eleazer Davis—seemed to be too hurt to travel, and were left behind with the promise that help would be sent. The remainder, many of whom were also wounded, split into three parties and made their way home. When they arrived at their fort, they found it abandoned with a note left saying all of Lovewell's company had been killed. Some food had been left and while they refreshed themselves, another wounded man, Solomon Keyes, arrived. Keyes had been wounded three times and had crawled away during the fight after calling out that he was a dead man. However, Keyes found a canoe, crawled into it, and floated to safety.

Meanwhile, the other four men, realizing that help would be a long time coming, struggled on as best they could. After his return and partial recovery, Eleazer Davis described his adventure to Samuel Penhallow. "The report he gave me was," wrote Penhallow,

> that Lieut. Farewell, with Mr. Fry their Chaplain, Josiah Jones, and himself, who were all wounded, march'd towards the Fort; but Jones steer'd another way, and after a long fategue and hardship got safe into Saco. Mr. Frye three days after, thro' the extremity of his Wounds, began to faint and languish, and died . . . Mr. Farewell held out in his return till the eleventh day; during which time he had nothing to eat but Water and a few Roots which he chewed; and by this time the Wounds thro' his Body were so mortified, that the Worms made a thorow Passage. The same day this Davis caught a Fish which he broil'd, and was greatly refresh'd there with; but the Lieut. was so much spent, that he could not taste a bit. Davis being now alone in a melancholy desolate state, still made toward the Fort, and the next day came to it, where he found some Pork and Bread, by which he was enabled to return as before mentioned.[35]

The possibility of wounds, accidents, and sickness, especially when these misfortunes happened far removed from home or settlements, made medical care and doctors of prime importance to provincial soldiers. Doctors participated in all expeditions; they served on the frontier and even accompanied all but the smallest of scouting parties. In fact, some raids were delayed because the soldiers refused to go out without a doctor. Whether pressed for service or volunteers, New England doctors tended the sick, patched up the wounded, and provided care for long-term recovery. In many instances doctors also caught the illnesses of their patients and died themselves. In this respect Louisbourg proved particularly deadly to provincial physicians.

At the beginning of King William's War, there were very few surgeons on the northern frontier. Field commanders consistently applied to the Bay government to provide surgeons for the eastern frontier. Jeremiah Swain wrote in October 1689 that his command was "under great disadvantage by reason of the sickness of many the want of a chyrurgeon," and that November, Captain Simon Willard, the commander of Massachusetts forces in Maine, indicated that he "should be glad if Doctor Hardin [Arden] had some Encouragement and that your Honors would send him to Casco: We may loose men of sicknes or wounds without a Doctor."[36]

The situation had not improved by the summer of 1691 when John March and Daniel King began their raid along the Maine coast. This trouble-plagued scouting party found themselves further hampered by a lack of a doctor willing to accompany them. In the march from Haverhill to Exeter they lost fourteen men through lameness or illness, and by the time they reached Portsmouth half their men were unfit for anything but garrison duty. March and King requested reinforcements and permission to press men locally to fill their companies, as well as a surgeon. "Wee cannot gett a Doctor here So that wee can prossecute not anything to the purpose with out one."[37] The local leaders William Vaughn and Charles Frost amplified the problem for Massachusetts authorities. "A Surgeon must be also Sent . . . for wee have but 3 in these parts and two of them are wholly uncapable of travail and the 3d has the York wounded men under his care they all say they have already done more for the Country Service, than all the Surgeons in the Country Soe that none can be had here."[38] The government pointed out to Vaughn and Frost that as "a Chyrurgion cannot be timely fitted out hence for that Service, its of necessity that one of yours do attend it." They had assumed one of the local doctors would accompany March and King, "otherwise we should have done . . . but shall hold our Selves concerned to see him paid as if he had been sent from hence."[39]

On July 17, March reported the failure to secure a surgeon, despite the efforts of William Vaughn and Charles Frost and their "perswasive Arguments and profittable promises." Vaughn "offered that if any one of them would goe he (with the rest of the Gentlemen) would collect or contribute a considerable Sum of mony to Satisfaction," but the doctors were not moved. They had worked in the country's service and "have not been paid any thing for all their disbursments." March and King warned that their plans were "frustrated, for our men will not goe with out a Chirurgion."[40] Vaughn and Frost confirmed their failure in this respect. They had no difficulty finding volunteer soldiers, as the raid fell "between hilling their Corne, and their Hay and English harvest, we found them Soe Spirited to it that noe thinge would have Diverted the Design, But . . . the want of A Surgeon (with out which men would not goe) and none to be Obtained here, on Any termes."[41]

The Bay government was "very unhappy" that this raid could be ruined by the refusal of the local doctors. "It seems strange and very absurd that notwithstanding the proposals and Encouragements offered they should decline their Majesties Service." The government could also not understand why March and King had not simply "constrained one of them to have gone upon this Emergency." In the end they were forced to send a doctor with the reinforcements.[42] However, the Massachusetts authorities seemed to have been correct about being unable to "fitt out" a surgeon in a hurry, because March and King later reported after their encounter with the Indians on the beach that "our doctor [was] Not provided with things convenient for our wounded men."[43] The shortages of doctors would continue to be a problem on the frontier. In 1695 Charles Frost indicated that the "souldiers are discoridg for want of a Curirgent there is non in our Country if we should have wounded men as we may Expect I know not what to doe with them."[44]

As a precious commodity, surgeons were carefully protected from harm. Before attacking an Indian village during his 1690 raid, Benjamin Church ordered his "captains to draw out of their several companies sixty of their meanest men, to be a guard to the Doctor and knapsacks."[45] John Lovewell built his crude fort and left behind eight soldiers to protect the doctor and the sick Benjamin Kidder. But provincial officers could not protect their doctors from the diseases they fought, and often the shortage of surgeons was aggravated by their succumbing to illness and exhaustion. With all the sickness on the Maine frontier during Dummer's War, Colonel Thomas Westbrook had difficulty finding enough doctors and keeping them alive. Westbrook's original instructions when he became commander of the Massachusetts forces in the fall of 1723 had been explicit concerning surgeons. "You are allowed three Surgeons only for the Forces, one to be posted at Brunswick Fort, an other at Falmouth, and the other to be posted at York, but either of them may be ordered to march with the companies when you shall thought necessary. The said Surgeons will be allowed Five Pounds per Month, each."[46] But by the following spring the situation had become desperate. Sickness gripped most of the provincial forts, and the care of the wounded became difficult at best. Repeatedly, Westbrook asked the government for more doctors. On March 23 a Sergeant Samuel Smith was shot during an ambush near Arundel, Maine. Six days later, Westbrook reported that

> they . . . have taken a great deal of pains to get a doctor for the wounded man, they went to Portsmouth and brought one as far as York, and there he was taken sick, so they returned and went as far as Greenland but could get none from thence, they came to Falmouth for Doctor Negus, who was taken sick the 27th Instant and died the 29th between eight and nine in the morning. We have had an Instance of the like sudden death in the past week, a stout man about twenty five years of age was taken sick and died in about forty hours—we stand in Absolute necessity of two doctors to visit the sundry sick amoung us and likewise to dress the wounded man Doctor Bulman having his hands full at Richmond and Arrowsick. I doubt not but your Honor will take speedy care to send them.[47]

On April 1, Westbrook wrote that he hoped Doctor Bulman might be spared to visit the sick at Falmouth, but several men were very ill at Arrowsick, and two had died.[48] The next day he wrote that offensive operations were questionable due to widespread illness, and he added in a postscript that "the wounded man died the 1st Instant. I am afraid for want of a doctor."[49]

The Doctor Bulman mentioned by Westbrook refers to Dr. Alexander Bulman of York, Maine, a man who comes closest to being a true military doctor. Bulman was born in 1702 as the son of a Boston baker.[50] He came to Maine as a surgeon to the provincial forces under Westbrook in 1722, and obviously from Westbrook's descriptions, he performed above and beyond the call of duty in administering the sick at Fort Richmond and Arrowsick. In fact, during the spring and summer of 1724, Bulman was by all indications the only doctor available on the frontier. Westbrook advised Lieutenant Governor Dummer in August that Bulman was the only doctor available to accompany the raiding force, and "he being very much fatigued I must entreat your Honour to send another Doctor down to march that he may have some respite."[51]

Bulman apparently impressed the inhabitants enough for the town of York to vote £100 to have him settle in the town for the rest of his life. Bulman purchased a home near the meeting house in the center of town and continued his practice in York.[52] He and his wife, Mary, became close friends of William and Mary Pepperrell of Kittery. When the Louisbourg expedition was proposed in early 1745, Bulman showed keen interest and support, but he tied his own participation to the actions of his friend, William Pepperrell. On February 4, Bulman wrote to Pepperrell to inform him of the response to recruiting efforts in York. As for his own participation, Bulman wrote that "I have some reason to conclude from what I have heard that your Honor has declined, so that I look upon my [self] free from any special obligation to attend the present service."[53] However, Pepperrell did accept the commission as overall commander, and Alexander Bulman was named as surgeon to Pepperrell's regiment and as personal surgeon to the commander-in-chief.

After the fall of the fortress, Bulman apparently wrote his wife, like so many others on that expedition, that he would soon be coming home. Mary Bulman replied that she was "Glad to hear of your Speedy return home and allso of your health I pray God continue and confirm it to you and give . . . occasion to rejoice in his goodness while apart."[54] But Bulman was not to return. As the weeks went by, his time and talents were increasingly in demand to tend the growing number of sick men. Finally, in early September, Bulman himself became ill. On September 5, the Reverend Stephen Williams "found him in a sweet frame of mind," but on his return the next day, the minister found Bulman "very low."[55] On the 11th, Pepperrell wrote to his wife, saying,

> And now my dear, I must tell you something of the distress and anguish of my soul. My prudent and valiant Doctor Bulman, although has had his health finely until about six days past, was taken with a nervous fever and given over. I expected the day past he would not have lived, but blessed be God there is some hopes this morning. The lord in great mercy continue him to us if it is his holy and blessed will.[56]

Pepperrell's prayer would not be answered. On the same day that he wrote those lines, Alexander Bulman died.[57]

The treatments that doctors like Bulman and the others gave their patients, or themselves received, were obviously primitive and rudimentary compared to modern medical practices. The documentation on actual treatment is sparse and can only hint at the medicines and remedies employed, but records do paint a small picture of military medical methods. One soldier at Louisbourg, George Mygate from Springfield, Massachusetts, left an account of his illness and treatment. As a member of the force who arrived after the fortress had fallen, he spent part of the summer picking berries and hunting, but he eventually began to feel ill. Mygate recorded that he "had not been well for a while, went to bed woke up in the middle of the night with a fever and a pain in the chest." His illness worsened and he was taken to the hospital and given "ipecec and salt vitriol." Mygate seemed to improve for a while, and then suffered a relapse. The doctors advised several cures, he was "bled to be cured of a cough, which caused him to vomit; next day took a physic." His journal entries were taken over by Caleb Lamb at that point, and eventually Lamb would record the death of his friend George Mygate.[58]

Wounds, illness, and the remedies had to be endured or administered without any means of easing the pain. Because of the advance of medical science, and the development of pain-reducing drugs and anesthesia, twenty-first-century men and women shrink from any thoughts of unnecessary suffering, and they marvel at the strength, and bad fortune perhaps, of those in the past who experienced such pain. People in the past did not feel any less pain than we do, and they were not stronger or more stoic in their view of pain. The only difference is that we often have the choice of feeling pain or not; they knew no alternative. It is the choice that makes our acceptance so difficult. At Louisbourg, according to the historian Fairfax Downey, "the wounded lay ranged in double rows on piles of loose straw. Some moaned steadily, others, to stifle their agony, chewed leather straps or blocks of soft pine."[59] At Number Four, Lieutenant John Burk recorded how the soldier named Cory who "tore his ass sliding off the House" had his wound dressed the next day. "O'h he grieved," observed Burk. The following day was much the same. "Corys ass drest," wrote Burk. "O how he squirms."[60]

For many soldiers, especially those with serious wounds, the agony of pain and treatment could continue for years. Thomas Footman, wounded in the fight at Wheelwright Pond in 1690, was under a doctor's care for more than seven months, during which time he was "not able to put on his Cloathes."[61] Jonathan Stanhope had "Very often Served his Majesty in the Wars Against the French and Indian Enemy," but on June 19, 1746, near Number Four, he "Received a very grievous Wound in his Arm, . . . Your poor petitioner has Suffered Extreme pain, and after the best Means to Obtain healing, Still remains under much pain, and is rendered utterly uncapable to labour." Stanhope wrote this petition four years after his wounding.[62]

These few stories represent only a fraction of the incidents involving long-term care of wounded soldiers. All of them involved a financial burden far beyond the capabilities of the individual soldiers, including doctors' bills, support of the soldier and his family during convalescence, and the continued maintenance of those crippled and unemployable. Recognizing the need to compensate soldiers wounded in battle, if for no other reason than to aid recruiting, the governments of Northern New England passed laws mandating this support. As early as 1635, Plymouth provided that any soldier who should "returne maymed and hurt he shall be mayntayned competently by the colony duringe his life."[63] Massachusetts and New Hampshire added similar provisions, assisting "maimed or otherwise disabled" soldiers to all their levying acts.[64]

At the start of each conflict the provincial legislatures established ad hoc committees to hear petitions and recommend appropriate compensation if any.[65] To prevent fraud, petitions generally had to be presented in person, and applicants frequently had to provide corroborating depositions from former commanders, fellow soldiers, or doctors. Petitions included such information as military service performed, the circumstances and extent of injuries, and an accounting of expenses incurred. Soldiers sought a payment to cover the cost of medical treatment, and they requested personal compensation for the suffering and loss of work. The latter could be in the form of a cash payment, land grant, or an annual pension.[66]

The cost of medical care could be quite extensive when treatment became prolonged. Thomas Footman wrote to the Bay government in March 1692 that his wounds had not healed, and he could not "Exspect to be ever Able to work to get a Competent Living, your peticioner being Reduced to so weake and Low Estate nothing to help himself for present nor for futuer no wages Reseved, nor non to pitte a pore wounded soulder, Charritye also grone Cold the doctors they demand mony."[67] In 1747 Samuel Drown petitioned the New Hampshire Assembly for "Some provision for me to prevent my Soffering and for my comfortable support," and his female relations petitioned the government "for Nursing of Samuel Drown" during his three-month convalescence, expecting "the Common wags that Is allowed for nurssing."[68]

The saga of John Baker illustrates the difficulties associated with the petition process. According to his petitions, Baker was born in Cambridge and brought up in Woburn—both in the state of Massachusetts. He was pressed into service during King Philip's War and wounded in the Swamp Fight at Narragansett when a musket ball broke his arm and passed through his body below the shoulder. Sent to Rhode Island to be cured, he recovered and learned the weaver's trade, worked hard, saved his money, bought some land, and built a house in Woburn. However, every so often his wounded arm would "break out." Baker sold his holdings in Woburn and moved to Swansea where he was again pressed for service during King William's War and sent to the Maine frontier.

According to Baker, the severe cold of the northern climate caused his wounded arm to swell up, and "It broak out with many holes through my arme." In March 1700, one doctor wrote that Baker's arm was "Hollow from the shoulder to the Elboe the Boane foul the arm had five holes in it above and under his Armpit Alwayes Runing now it is Almost fild up with flesh and there are now but three holes in it."[69] By 1700, Baker had been under the care of several doctors for years, and between the doctors' bills and his inability to work, he was "never like to be my own man, and I have spent all I have in the world, my father dead, my mother a poore widow, I have nothing to help my selfe."[70]

Baker submitted a petition to the Bay government, but when he came to Boston to present it in person, "his Lordship was so bad with the gout that I could not Come to spake with him: which Jurney was greatly to my Damige in respect of my wound."[71] A later attempt to present his petition got nowhere because he could not appear in person. The government also apparently insisted he get depositions, "sworn by a magerstreat," from other soldiers who participated in the Swamp Fight to prove he was wounded in the provincial service. He appealed to James Converse to intervene on his behalf, and Converse wrote to the government that Baker was a "poore Wounded soldier" who had spent all he had and was now not "worth A Groat." Converse pointed out that Baker had sent in a petition the previous year but because his wound had prevented him from coming to court nothing had been done.[72]

As he was "lyable to be thrown into Gaol by the doctors," Baker wanted the doctors' bills paid and, "being disabled to work at my trade, and . . . a great famaly to maintaine," he requested a yearly pension. In the case that the assembly balked at the pension, Baker pointed out that "many skilfull do think this wound will be my death at last,—and what I pray for is not like to continue long." Baker was allowed £10 to pay his bills and an annual pension of £4.[73]

A pension or some kind of continued support was the goal of many wounded soldiers. The amounts involved, generally £3 to £5 a year, could not provide full support, especially if the soldier had a family, but it kept them from starving until they recovered and augmented any later wages. For example, Charles Makarty lost his hand early in King William's War, and he spent ten weeks under the care of a doctor. He requested a payment for the doctor's bills, "such Annual pay for the future as is generally allowed by the King to maimed and disabled souldiers," and a license to "keepe a house of publick Entertainment."[74] Some soldiers were willing to be posted in garrisons or provincial forts in return for continued government support. In September 1695, Abraham Cook was in a party of soldiers gathering wood for Fort William Henry at Pemaquid that was ambushed by an enemy war party. Cook "received a Shott in his left arme, which by reason thereof was Cutt of from his body." Despite the loss of his arm, Cook served at the Castle in Boston Harbor after his recovery.[75] In 1748, Ebenezer Eastman petitioned the government of New Hampshire to let Joseph Pudney, "a soldier formerly wounded in the service," be "posted at some garrison in Pennecook."[76]

On the whole, the governments of Massachusetts and New Hampshire phased out the granting of pensions and substituted cash payments for wounded soldiers. The early Plymouth law had only mentioned pensions as compensation, but the levying act of 1693 said only that pensions formerly granted would be continued and that wounded soldiers in the future would be compensated "as this great and general court shall order." Massachusetts would continue to grant pensions in special cases through Queen Anne's War at least, but by 1744 the levying act contained no reference to pensions, stipulating that relief was at the discretion of the government.[77] The elimination of pensions was obviously a cost-saving move and an attempt to simplify provincial bookkeeping and finances. A soldier in his early twenties given an annual pension of £5 could realize £150 to £200 if he lived another thirty to forty years. Therefore, a single payment of £20 to £30 saved the government a considerable amount of money.

Instead of the requested pension, soldiers were given a lump payment "and have no future allowance." For the loss of his hand when his gun exploded, Joseph Bane received £4 and 10s.[78] Eleazer Rogers was paid £20 for the loss of an eye.[79] Gradually specific values seemed to be attached to specific types of wounds. The loss or incapacitation of an arm netted the petitioner £20, while a leg wound produced £30 to £40.[80] Other injuries were evaluated on a case-by-case basis. For example, Joshua Jackson, a blacksmith from Portsmouth, New Hampshire, "receivd a blow on the Small of his Back from a Cannon shot while in the Trenches" at Louisbourg and could not continue his trade. Jackson was paid £30 for his troubles.[81]

Provincial governments also paid cash settlements to the nearest relatives of the dead. Amounting to considerably less than the compensation paid to the wounded, survivor benefits were really no more than a token acknowledgment of service provided and loss incurred. As deaths from disease and battle far outnumbered the wounded and maimed, the governments of New Hampshire and Massachusetts could never hope to compensate widows and parents on the same level: there were simply too many of them. In *Urban*

Crucible, Gary Nash has shown that the losses suffered at Cartagena and Louisbourg struck Massachusetts families hard. In Boston alone a census taken the year after the Cartagena campaign revealed 1,200 widows, of which a thousand were in "low circumstances."[82] Louisbourg would later add hundreds to that figure. The attack on the Island Battery alone, in which over a hundred men lost their lives, probably left dozens of women without husbands and hundreds of children without fathers.

Therefore, death compensation was meager at best. Enlistment proclamations for Louisbourg promised that "widows or nearest relatives of any officer or soldier that is slain or shall otherwise loose his life in the service, shall be entitled to four months pay."[83] As the monthly pay for private soldiers was 25 shillings, this amounted to a compensation of £5 for relatives of private soldiers. If any more was desired, they would have to petition the government. One list of petitioners compensated by the New Hampshire Assembly after Louisbourg reveals that widows were paid anywhere from £2 to £7, and a review of other petitions indicates that £3 was the most common sum allotted to the wife of a slain soldier.[84]

But beyond these figures and statistics were families who had their emotional loss compounded by sudden economic hardship. Tabitha Cass of Kensington, New Hampshire, "Widow and Relict of Jonathan Cass," wrote that the "Hardships and Difficulties" her husband experienced at Louisbourg "so Destroyed his Health that when he Returned the Last of August past he was obliged to be Carryed from the Vessell to his House being unable to walk himself and so Remained Sick and under the Doctors hands till the 13th of September when he Died." Tabitha indicated the doctor's bills and other "Necessarys for him" had amounted to a great deal, so "That Your Petitioner is in Low Circumstances and has a Large Family of Children to maintain." The New Hampshire Assembly paid her doctor bills and gave her £5 in compensation.[85]

Even harder hit was Sarah Trefethen of New Castle. Her husband volunteered for Louisbourg, and soon after his return "he was taken sick, of which sickness he died in about ten days. That he left your Petitioner with a number of Small Children, That after the death of your Petitioners husband, the whole Family, one excepted, was taken Sick whereby your Petitioner was put to great Straits and difficultys, that she has not wherewith to pay the Funeral charges and Doctors Bills." The assembly paid her funeral and doctor bills and also awarded Sarah £3.[86]

The pain of loss is graphically depicted in the petition of Hugh Montgomery. Hugh was a joiner, "advanced in years and almost past his Labour," who had a "son brought up to his Trade and was Master of it, who went in the

Late Expedition against Louisbourg Who was Killed in the attempt upon the Island Battery where he lost his Arms and all that he had with him, and afterwards all that he had in his Tent was taken away by unknown hands." Hugh's son had been using a provincial musket, so when Hugh received the four months' pay as compensation, the cost of the musket was deducted from it. "That the Death of his said Son is a very heavy and Grievous loss to your Petitioner," wrote the old man,

> not only with Respect to his Relation to him and the strong ties of Natural Affection (which in this Case were Increased by a Constant dutiful behavior) but in Special, with Regard to the profit of his Labour in the Prime time of his Service, being about Nineteen Years of Age when he listed and Particular Circumstances of your Petitioner, his said Son being his Chief Support the staff of his Age, and the main Stay of his Family, by the Remarkable Diligence and application of the Youth in his Business, and his thorough Mastery of it.
>
> That Your Petitioner humbly Conceives it not only agreeable to Natural Justice to make such as hazarded their lives for the Service of their Country in so Eminent and Extraordinary a manner, or the Relations of those who died in the Service, a Generous Reward proportioned to the Hazzrds and Benefits of the Event, but also Agreeable to the Practice of all other Places in this and like Cases, Especially where families are Reduced to a State of Indigence by the Loss of their Relatives—-and therefore it Seems a Singular Instance of Severity and unkind usage to make those who lost their Arms in that desparate attempt on the Battery aforesaid to pay for them which in Effect Punishing instead of Rewarding those who laid down their lives for their Country (and what Effect this may have on others may be worthy Consideration) nor are those who died so, in this Particular Instance the less to be Considered, because they did not Succeed in the Enterprize since they shew their good Will and Courage for the Public service and thereby Intimidated the Enemy.

This petition captures all the consequences of a soldier's death for those he left behind. It indicates the level of the personal tragedy as well as the economic blow to the family. In this case the joiner expected his son would be his support in his old age and carry on his trade. The petition even addresses the inequities of the compensation system, hinting that future recruitment could be hurt if the government continued to be parsimonious. This emotional, sagacious, and eloquent appeal netted Hugh Montgomery £15.[87]

The treatment and support of wounded soldiers further complicated the war effort for the governments of New Hampshire and New England. Doctors were essential to military operations yet were difficult to find and very vulnerable, and beyond the immediate needs of the service medical care was always costly, especially when protracted. However, provincial governments willingly provided for wounded soldiers and compensated the families of those slain in the service. To fail in this duty would have undermined the whole structure of provincial recruiting. Many provincial soldiers were the economic as well as the emotional support of their families, and some sort of guarantee of financial compensation in case of disaster, no matter how feeble, figured in the decision to volunteer. Doctors' bills were paid in full, yearly pensions granted to the disabled, or cash paid as compensation for injury and loss. And if the pensions and cash payments amounted to very little, a token acknowledgment in many cases, it was better than nothing.

For the majority of New England men and women, religion eased some of the emotional stress of war. The knowledge of God's guiding hand and his predetermined plan for man provided both comfort and understanding. In *Providence and Patriotism in Early America*, the historian John F. Berens wrote that to New Englanders of the seventeenth and early eighteenth centuries, God controlled all the natural and human occurrences in the universe. "Political and military developments occupied the colonial mind," observed Berens, "but behind them the hand of God was always discerned." The Indian wars were a chastisement but limited in nature by God. Their ultimate end was not destruction but reformation.[88]

Each victory came as God's divine blessing, and New Englanders never doubted their ultimate triumph. According to Cotton Mather, the reluctance of the Indians to engage in hand-to-hand combat and their tendency to run away from provincial charges was divine providence—God made the Indians afraid.[89] Mather also believed that although the provincial soldiers could not find the Indian enemy in King William's War, "it is Reported by Returned Captives, That the Hand of God reach'd them, when the Hand of Man could not find them, and a Mortal Sickness did at a Strange Rate carry off multitudes if them."[90]

The victory at Norridgewock also indicated God's goodness toward his chosen people. The Reverend Benjamin Colman wrote in his preface to Samuel Penhallow's history of the Indian wars that "In a special manner, the wonderful Victory obtained August 12, 1724, over the bold and Bloody Tribe at Narridgwalk, and their sudden Destruction that Memorable day, was the singular Work of God; And the Officers and Soldiers piously put far from themselves the Honour of it." God sent them the information on where the guards were, and God brought them to the village at just the right time. As for the death of the Jesuit, Sebastian Rale, "he who was the Father of the War, the Ghostly Father of those perfidious Salvages, like Balaam the Son of Beor, was slain among the Enemy, after his vain Endeavors to Curse us."[91]

Such praise for the providence of God was common among all the inhabitants of New England, not just their ministers. After rescuing two boys from their captives in the summer of 1698, one Deerfield man was heard to exclaim, "Tis God, and not we, that have wrought this deliverance!"[92] In 1745, Mary Bulman wrote her husband at Louisbourg of the "joyful news of your Safe Victorious Entrence into the City of Cape Briton. Glory to God in the Highest who has brought his people in the Strong Holds of our Enemys with so Little affusion of Blood—the right hand of the Lord and all mighty arm Hath Done Great things for us where we are blest."[93]

But even more than an explanation of victory, God's direct guidance of all events mitigated somewhat the despair of defeat and the pain of death, injury, sickness, and destruction. Military disasters and personal loss were not viewed as senseless or meaningless; they were part of God's predetermined plan. Cotton Mather believed that with all the careful preparation, energy, and prayers put into the Quebec expedition of 1690, "nothing but an Evident Hand of Heaven was likely to have given such a Defeat unto it."[94] An anonymous member of that expedition was more explicit in citing the reasons for the failure. God gave the Iroquois smallpox, which stopped the attack on Montreal. God sent contrary winds to delay Phips's fleet. God brought Frontenac into the city with 3,000 men just before the English arrived, the report of which so terrified the faint-hearted John Walley. God sent diseases into the provincial army. However, the author of this interpretation pointed out that God expects the righteous to suffer before he gives them final victory.[95]

Even bizarre and strange occurrences were explained as occurring because of God's personal intervention. A gunner frustrated with his shooting at Louisbourg exclaimed, "God damn me if I don't strike the gate this time!" and was killed almost immediately when a shell fragment split his skull in two. Most interpreted this as a judgment for his blasphemous language. When Eleazer Young's musket exploded in his face while on a scout near Lake Winnipesaukee, "Providence so ordered that the Gun split all in Pieces." It was fortunate for Young that Providence caused the explosion, because the government did not pay compensation for guns lost through the owner's neglect, such as improper cleaning or loading.[96]

The destruction of frontier communities provided further evidence of God's wrath. After the attack on York, Maine, in January 1692, the inhabitants of Wells told the Bay government that "God is still manifesting his displeasure against this Land, he who formerly hath set to his hand to help us, doth even write bitter things against us. The course of God's most sweet and rich promises, and gracious providences may justly be interrupted by the sins of his People."[97] The death of York's minister in that attack was perceived as a particular sign of God's "dreadfull displeasure agaynst us."[98]

New Englanders also turned to thoughts of God's judgment to console the loss of family and friends. When Joseph Storer of Wells heard of the death of Charles Frost, the popular community and military leader from Kittery ambushed while returning from church in 1697, he exclaimed, "The good Lord keep us in these perilous times! The good Lord sanctify it to us all!"[99] In late September 1745 the Reverend Benjamin Colman and his wife wrote to William Pepperrell at Louisbourg and acknowledged the death of Alexander Bulman. The Colmans, like Pepperrell, knew the Bulmans and they indicated that Mary Bulman's faith would sustain her in this loss. "His dear and lovely spouse spent a day with us this week," they wrote, "and is returned home. Our hearts bleed for her when the evil tydings reach her. But her heart is fortified by Grace."[100]

But the belief in both predestination and God's active participation in the affairs of man only went so far in easing the psychological wounds of war. Despite the fact that Cotton Mather said "The Almighty God is to be acknowledg'd as the Author of whatsoever Military Skill or Strength any children of men do excel in," Providence provided no excuses for individual failure.[101] John Walley, Pasco Chubb, and Benjamin Hassell could not blame God as the author of their actions. No one doubted that the New England Puritans were God's chosen people, as such would emerge triumphant, but, as Robert Pike observed in 1689, "we may be a peopl saved of the Lord though a peopl that distroy ourselves."[102] Therefore, the actions of cowards worked in opposition to God's ultimate triumph. Men like Walley, Chubb, and Hassell were part of God's affliction on his chosen people.

The Indians were another manifestation of God's displeasure. In 1691 the inhabitants of Wells believed that God "let loose the heathen upon us by holden us off from our improvements, keeping us close in garrison."[103] Benjamin Colman observed that God had planted his people in the New World, "Yet to humbly and prove us, and for our Sins to punish us, the Righteous God hath left a sufficient Number of the fierce and barbarous Salvages on our borders, to be pricks in our Eyes, and thorns in our sides, and they have been and are like the Boar of the Woods to waste us, and the Wild Beasts of the field to devour us."[104] Samuel Penhallow believed the English had no one to blame for the Indian attacks but themselves. "God has made them a terrible Scourge for the punishment of our Sins," wrote Penhallow. "And probably that very Sin of ours in neglecting the welfare of their Souls."[105]

War inevitably inflicts psychological wounds on those exposed to it, despite the consolation, even the bulwark, of religion; the early French wars were no different. At this great distance and with the few existing records we can only speculate on the extent of this, however, an incident which took place in Maine at the end of King George's War suggests that abhorrence of the Eastern tribes was the principal psychological wound suffered by both provincial soldiers and the inhabitants of the frontier. In October 1748, the Treaty of Aix-la-Chapelle ended the conflict between the English and French; however, the provincial governments of New England would not formally conclude their war with the Eastern tribes for another year. After a preliminary peace conference held in Boston in June 1749, the delegates of both sides met at Falmouth, Maine in October to sign the peace treaty. Among the provisions of the treaty was the stipulation that private quarrels and grievances would be settled through the courts in order to prevent the gradual escalation of violence that had always led to war.[106]

On December 2, six white men attacked a small party of Indians near Wiscasset, Maine, resulting in the death of one Indian and the wounding of two others. Four days later, two Indian women, including the widow of the slain man, arrived at the home of Sheriff Samuel Denny in Georgetown to report the attack. Soon after, a deputy sheriff, Samuel Harnden, and two others arrived to report the same incident. Denny issued warrants for the arrest of the accused men but fearing that "the matter might [not] be properly managed," he went himself to supervise the arrests. He also sent someone to help the wounded Indians "in order to quiet them and for their support and . . . if posable to keep them from informing the other Indians." The situation was obviously explosive.

Two of the accused turned themselves in to Denny, and two others were arrested by Harnden, but the deputy sheriff told Denny that "a mob was ris to rescu them. I went with him to the plase and on our landing was met by a number of armed men with their fases disgise by being blacked. I declared who I was and went a shore on which a fray arose in which I was knocked down and had sum slite wounds but we subdued them." Denny arrested five of the six men involved in the murder and detained those who had attempted to prevent their capture. All men apparently came off a small vessel anchored nearby. The sixth man accused of killing the Indian, Obediah Albee Jr., made his escape and was believed to be on his way home to Massachusetts. Denny informed the Bay government that fourteen Indians, "young and old," were destitute because of this "axadente."[107]

On December 13, an ad hoc committee of the Massachusetts House of Representatives established to study Denny's report recommended that the accused be brought to Cambridge for trial as the court in York was not scheduled to meet until June and this might allow the prisoners time to escape. They also recommended that a proclamation be issued for the arrest of Obediah Albee, that a surgeon be sent to aid the Indians, and that relief be provided for those relatives in need. The House concurred in all recommendations except they voted to hold the trial in Maine, ordering that the prisoners be transferred to the jail in York.[108]

Meanwhile, Samuel Denny released the men who had attempted the rescue and determined that of the six involved in the original incident, Benjamin Ledite and Samuel Ball, along with the missing Albee, were actually at fault. Denny started Ball and Ledite on their journey to York and retained the other three men as witnesses.[109] On December 22, Sheriff Joseph Blany of Marblehead reported that he had captured Obediah Albee. An informant told Blany where Albee was, and Blany encouraged the informant to apprehend Albee so he could claim the reward, but "they Declined to do so saying they Desired to have nothing to do in affair." Blany had one of his deputies arrest Albee and lodged him in the Salem jail.[110]

The following day, however, the best-laid plans of the Bay government fell apart as the other five men—Samuel Ball, Benjamin Ledite, and the three witnesses—all escaped. The sheriffs of Suffolk, Middlesex, Worcester, and Bristol counties were alerted to search for and apprehend the five men. A reward of £50 was offered for them and £25 for anyone known to have aided in their escape. The government believed that in the case of Ball and Ledite, who escaped while staying in Falmouth, the deputy sheriff transporting the prisoners was either negligent or sympathetic to the prisoners, and they instructed the Justice of the Peace in Falmouth, Jabez Fox, to issue a warrant for the sheriff's arrest.[111]

On January 1, Fox reported the details of the prisoners' escape at Falmouth. On the snowy night of December 15, at about eleven o'clock in the evening, Ball and Ledite were released "by Sundry persons that appeared in a Mobbish manner" at the house about two miles outside of town where the prisoners were spending the night. The mob took the men into the woods where pursuit was impossible due to the snowstorm. Fox issued warrants for their arrest and blanketed the region with handbills describing the prisoners.[112] Fox attempted to discover who had been in the mob that released the men but had little success. On December 30, Fox learned that the men had been seen at Gorham and so ordered an officer "with a strong guard all armed . . . to Search every House in said Town." Fox was told the men had arrived in Gorham on the 16th and had been sheltered there until the 27th.[113]

On January 11, Jeremiah Moulton, a commander at Norridgewock in 1724, a colonel at Louisbourg in 1745, and now the sheriff of York County, reported that he had the two men safely incarcerated in the York jail. Moulton had strengthened the jail and hired nine armed guards to watch over them.[114] On January 16 the House of Representatives announced that Samuel Ball, Benjamin Ledite, and Obediah Albee were being held for trial, and a few days later the governor proclaimed that a special court would meet in York on February 22 to hear the case.[115] However, due to illness, only two judges were able to travel to York so the trial had to be postponed until the regular session in June.[116]

The delays caused by the rescues and the illness of the judges began to create considerable apprehension among provincial officers at Fort St. George, the most exposed fort on the Maine frontier. The Indians had been told that such transgressions would be punished but there was little evidence of this. In January the widow of the slain Indian was given two blankets, one for herself and one to bury her husband in "as . . . it was their custom." She was also given other supplies as well.[117] In April, Lieutenant Jabez Bradbury wrote from Fort St. George asking why there had been no trial, and he expressed the opinion that "if there is not speedy satisfaction Given to the Indians on that account it may be attended with ill Consequences."[118] The Indian chiefs concerned also wrote the government to express their disappointment at the delay, reminding the Bay government of the promises made in the treaty signed the previous October. Asserremo, the chief of the Worranock Indians, indicated that his young men "would have you be Quick in putting thos murderers to Death within a months time to cover the blood that now lyes on the ground which we are Desirous may be covered or else all will not be well."[119] The government could only instruct their officers to explain the intricacies of the English court system to the Indians as best they could and to wait for June.

Obediah Albee, considered the main instigator in the attack, came to trial first. Albee was transferred from Salem to York in mid-June, where a jury, "chosen by the Towns in that County," acquitted him of all charges.[120] The government now found itself in a quandary, trapped between appeasing the Indians to prevent a war and the obvious feelings of their own people. They knew the other two men would be acquitted as well, and they also knew the Indians would never understand why. As a result, they delayed the inevitable. Ball and Ledite were transferred to a jail in Middlesex County, but the vote in the House transferring the trial from York to Suffolk County was defeated on the third reading. The prisoners were later transferred back to York but the records have not revealed if their trial was ever held, and their ultimate fate is unknown. The Indians harbored the injury until the outbreak of the next war.[121]

This incident denotes the depth of feeling instilled by the long wars with the Indians. Despite the fact that war had brought nothing but death, captivity, and destruction to the frontier, most of the inhabitants were willing to risk a new outbreak in order to prevent the punishment of three men for killing an Indian. The mob that freed Samuel Ball and Benjamin Ledite at Falmouth, the residents of Gorham who sheltered them for eleven days, and the jury that acquitted Obediah Albee clearly indicated where their sentiments lay. Jabez Fox could not understand the actions of the people living in Gorham, a town that had experienced the fury of the enemy just a few years earlier. As he told the authorities in Boston, "I must say I am exceedingly surprised to find such a spirit almost universally prevailing amongst those that live the most Exposed to the Indian Enemy in Warr time, as there seems to be at present to secure murderes from the hands of Justice."[122]

Even more interesting perhaps is that both Benjamin Ledite and Samuel Ball had been provincial soldiers, and the stories they told Jeremiah Moulton hint at the psychological wounds of war. Moulton apparently questioned the two men extensively after they surrendered themselves in early January. Both naturally pleaded innocent to the charge of murdering the Indian at Wiscasset, and they appeared to have been just as startled at their rescue in Falmouth as the officers they were taken from. Moulton reported the two men "were unexpectedly surprized out of their sleep there and carried off in the night and bid to go about their business by a Number of Persons all unknown to them." Benjamin Ledite told the sheriff that he was originally from Seekonk, Massachusetts, and had "been out sometime in the Province Service in this country as a Soldier in the late Indian Warr." Samuel Ball, who Moulton referred to as a "Transient Person," declared that "his father was killed by the Indians the first of the war and himself for the most part been improved as a Soldier ever since." Moulton indicated Ball had served in Nova Scotia and gave the impression he had spent most of King George's War in provincial service.[123]

In the *Northern Colonial Frontier, 1607–1763*, Douglas Leach observed that the "daily perils of life on the frontier colored the pattern of pioneer character." Opposing forces learned to despise each other, and while some early historians blamed the Indians for being savages, and later historians have condemned the English as insensitive racists, the problem was not so simple. Leach correctly pointed out that the Indians were indeed victimized, by both New France and New England, but there is no ignoring that peaceful frontier inhabitants were slaughtered in gruesome ways.[124] The intensity of the conflict was increased by ignorance and insensitivity on both sides, an ignorance created primarily by cultural differences.

Much has been written about the level of violence in European society in the seventeenth and eighteenth centuries, some of it to mitigate the stereotype of Indian savagery and cold-bloodedness.[125] Francis Jennings may be correct when he observed that "many of the aspects of so-called savage war were taught to Indians by European example" and that "plenty of sadism was evident in both cultures."[126] However, logical and correct observations concerning the pervasiveness of such practices do not ease the pain of a man viewing the ripped and mutilated body of a pregnant woman. Such a man feels only a blind hatred.

While it is important for us to understand that the gruesome practices of the American Indian probably pale in comparison to the torture methods used in judicial punishments, or the level of violence and cruelty experienced in the Thirty Years' War, it must also be understood that those who experienced the violence, no matter what the source, did not have the same objectivity. André Corvisier wrote that for European society in the sixteenth and seventeenth centuries, because of the high level of violence, "the sight of blood did not bring about the same revulsion that it does today."[127] However, I suspect this is not the case. The frontier communities of northern New England experienced decades of bloody war, and there is no indication they were inured to death. Provincial soldiers and the inhabitants of the frontier experienced loss like they experienced their war, on an individual and personal level. Samuel Ball apparently felt the loss of his father, and men like Benjamin Church detested the sight of hacked and mutilated men, women, and children. Such pain and loss resulted in a desire for retribution, and retribution led to the escalation of bloodshed and atrocities. It is the ultimate psychological wound.

Afterword

After suffering the disastrous defeats of Lexington and Concord and Bunker Hill, General Thomas Gage observed that the New Englanders "in all their Wars against the French, . . . never Showed so much Conduct, Attention, and Perseverance as they do now."[1] Because Gage, like most British officers, had always viewed the provincials with the blinders of prejudice, his surprise is understandable. But historians who have disparaged earlier provincial performance have had to explain the success of Lexington and Concord as well, and in their opinion, the British finally met the true citizen soldier. James Kirby Martin and Mark Edward Lender wrote that "Gage's regulars were not fighting against unfortunates who had been dragooned into service and whose primary goal was to stay alive. They had run into propertied freeholders operating locally, actually defending hearth and home. That was the unique strength of the militia system. Whether it could be equally effective on a broader scale, however, was yet to be seen."[2] To bolster this theory, historians stress the prevalence of the Whig ideology promoting the notion of a citizen soldier and abhorring the thoughts of a standing army. Although Lexington and Concord seemed to provide a confirmation of this belief, "by late 1776, patriot leaders would be consciously reverting to the French and Indian War pattern of seeking out the unpropertied in their quest to defend liberty and implant republicanism in America for the propertied citizens of society."[3]

The ideology of the citizen soldier was certainly important to pamphleteers and political leaders trying to justify their actions to peers at home and abroad, and there can be no doubt that many Massachusetts men were disturbed for ideological reasons by the presence of regulars in Boston, but it is doubtful this idea fostered superior military ability. In reality, the minutemen at Lexington and Concord and the provincial soldiers of the French wars represent no paradox. The men the redcoats faced on the march from Concord to Boston were fundamentally no different from the New England soldiers who served in those earlier conflicts.

Gage, and most of his fellow officers, underestimated the abilities of the New England soldiers due to class and cultural prejudice. And some historians have followed this practice, listening perhaps a little too much to those European professionals. They have compounded this error by only concentrating on the major events of the French war period. The failures of the various expeditions have only confirmed their opinion that the provincial soldiers were ignorant of war and poor soldiers (thus like Thomas Gage they are left with the puzzlement of April 19, 1775).

The story of New England's military effort in the early French wars is far more nuanced than the simple story often depicted. The provincial soldier was not always the incompetent amateur as he is so often portrayed, especially in comparisons with both his French and Indian enemy and redcoated ally. The governments of northern New England and their soldiers operated under the severe handicap of having to fight wars without the immediate logistical, technological, and financial support available to European nations. The lack of industry, military engineers, warships, money, and soldiers willing to serve for long periods of time would always have to be addressed in war, first with an Anglo-American partnership, and then with a Franco-American partnership in the War for Independence. And their ignorance of European warfare, of wheeling, and platoon fire, and unthinking obedience, remained until they had to learn it to fight a linear tactics war.

Like their French adversaries, they had to accommodate their European temperament to the realities of a wilderness environment and the Native American way of war. The Native American way of war affected the New England military efforts both in defense, particularly patrols and garrison houses, and in offense (raiding parties). The men on the New England frontier learned how to move and survive in the woods beyond the line of settlements. However, New Englanders did not abandon European military strategy. They built forts (crude in comparison to European fortifications but forts nonetheless) and they mounted European-style expeditions to attempt to reduce French strongholds and even New France itself. This hybrid approach marks the New England martial efforts in the early French wars as truly American, a mixing of cultures. It is probably adaptability that made the New England soldier unique, or "exceptional." No, they were not perfect. To paraphrase the New Hampshire Assembly, they did not do well at martial show, but when it came to real service in war as it developed in North America, they did fairly well indeed.

Notes

PREFACE AND ACKNOWLEDGMENTS

1. John Shy, "A New Look at the Colonial Militia," in *A People Numerous and Armed: Reflections on the Military Struggle for American Independence* (Oxford: Oxford University Press, 1976).
2. Shy, "A New Look at the Colonial Militia," 29.
3. John Keegan, *The Face of Battle: A Study of Agincourt, Waterloo and the Somme* (New York: Vintage, 1976); Sylvia Frey, *The British Soldier in America: A Social History of Military Life in the Revolutionary Period* (Austin: University of Texas Press, 1981); J. A. Houlding, *Fit For Service: The Training of the British Army, 1715-1795* (Oxford: Oxford University Press, 1981); John Keegan and Richard Holmes, *Soldiers: A History of Men in Battle* (New York: Viking, 1986).
4. Richard H. Kohn, "The Social History of the American Soldier: A Review and Prospectus for Research" *American Historical Review*, 86 (1981), 564.

INTRODUCTION

1. Goffstown was named for John Goffe, the leader of numerous scouts who became a lieutenant colonel in a provincial regiment during the last French and Indian war. Westbrook was named after Thomas Westbrook, who commanded the provincial forces in Maine during Dummer's War. See William Howard Brown, *Colonel John Goffe: Eighteenth Century New Hampshire* (Manchester, NH: Lew A. Cummings, 1950); William Blake Trask, *Letters Of Colonel Thomas Westbrook and Others Relative to Indian Affairs in Maine, 1722-1726* (Boston, 1901), 2.
2. For the full story of the Deerfield raid and its aftermath, see Evan Haefeli and Kevin Sweeney, *Captors and Captives: The 1704 French and Indian Raid on Deerfield* (Boston: University of Massachusetts Press, 2003) and Richard I. Melvoin, *New England Outpost: War and Society in Colonial Deerfield* (New York: Norton, 1989).
3. Quoted in Douglas Edward Leach, *Roots of Conflict: British Armed Forces and Colonial Americans, 1677-1763* (Chapel Hill: University of North Carolina Press, 1986), 130-31.
4. I. K. Steele, *Guerrillas and Grenadiers: The Struggle for Canada, 1689-1760* (Toronto: Ryerson Press, 1969), 13.
5. Richard H. Marcus, "The Connecticut Valley: A Problem in Intercolonial Defense," *Military Affairs*, 1969 33 (1), 230.
6. Jeremy Belknap, *The History of New Hampshire* (Reprint of 1831 edition, New York, 1970) Vol. 1, 296.

7. John Fiske, *New France and New England* (Boston, 1902), 242.
8. Francis Parkman, *Count Frontenac and New France under Louis XIV* (Boston, 1896), 285.
9. John Ferling, *A Wilderness of Miseries: War and Warriors in Early America* (Westport, CT: Greenwood Press, 1980), 16.
10. Edward P. Hamilton, *The French and Indian Wars: The Story of Battles and Forts in the Wilderness* (New York: Doubleday, 1962), 93.
11. Guy Chet, *Conquering the American Wilderness: The Triumph of European Warfare in the Colonial Northeast* (Boston: University of Massachusetts Press, 2003), 62.
12. Ibid., 100.
13. Jeremy Belknap, *The History of New Hampshire*, Vol. 1, 295.
14. Samuel Adams Drake, *The Border Wars of New England, Commonly called King William's and Queen Anne's Wars* (1897, reprint of 1910 edition, Williamstown, MA: Corner House, 1973), 143.
15. Ibid., 55.
16. W. J. Eccles, *The Canadian Frontier, 1534–1760* (Albuquerque: University of New Mexico Press, 1974), 11, 139.
17. Harold L. Peterson, *Arms and Armor in Colonial America, 1526–1783* (New York: Bramhall House, 1956), 155.
18. John K. Mahon, "Anglo-American Methods of Indian Warfare, 1676–1794," *Mississippi Valley Historical Review*, 45 (1958), 254.
19. Ibid., 274.
20. Steele, *Guerrillas and Grenadiers*, 132.
21. For references concerning the Americanization view, see John Morgan Dederer, *War in America to 1775: Before Yankee Doodle* (New York: NYU Press, 1990) and John Grenier, *The First Way of War: American War Making on the Frontier* (New York: Cambridge University Press, 2005).
22. Armstrong Starkey, *European and Native American Warfare, 1675–1815* (Norman: University of Oklahoma Press, 11.
23. Ibid., 44.
24. Chet, *Conquering the American Wilderness*, 3.
25. Ibid., 71.
26. John Ferling, *Struggle for a Continent: The Wars of Early America* (Arlington Heights, IL: Harlan Davidson, 1993), 134.
27. John Shy, "A New Look at the Colonial Militia," in *A People Numerous and Armed: Reflections on the Military Struggle for American Independence* (London: Oxford University Press, 1976), 31.
28. See Lawrence Delbert Cress, *Citizens in Arms: The Army and Militia in American Society to the War of 1812* (Chapel Hill: University of North Carolina Press, 1982), and Ferling, *A Wilderness of Miseries*.
29. Leach, *Roots of Conflict*, 132.
30. Ibid., 164.
31. Louis E. D. Forest, *Louisbourg Journals: 1745* (New York, 1932), 198.
32. Quoted in J. A. Houlding, *Fit for Service: The Training of the British Army, 1715–95* (Oxford: Oxford University Press, 1981), vii. It may be truly said of men like James Wolfe that they actually have no prejudices—they hate everyone.
33. Ferling, *A Wilderness of Miseries*, 19–20.

34. Cress, *Citizens in Arms*, 57.
35. Ferling, *Struggle for a Continent*, 81.
36. Gary B. Nash, *The Urban Crucible: The Northern Seaports and the Origins of the American Revolution*, abridged ed. (Cambridge: Harvard University Press, 1986), 36–39, 71; Douglas Leach, *Arms for Empire: A Military History of the British Colonies in North America, 1607–1763* (New York: Macmillan, 1973), 270–71.
37. See John Brewer, *The Sinews of Power: War, Money, and the English State* (Cambridge: Harvard University Press, 1988).
38. Drake, *The Border Wars of New England*, 143.
39. Hamilton, *The French and Indian Wars*, 39.
40. Chet, *Conquering the American Wilderness*, 100.
41. Carl von Clausewitz, *On War* (1832; New York: Penguin, 1985). The first part of the quote is on page 140, and the second half is on page 227.
42. Like so many accounts, they seem to concentrate on what happened after Phips arrived at Quebec.
43. Clausewitz, *On War*, 227.
44. Richard R. Johnson, *Adjustment to Empire: The New England Colonies, 1675–1715* (New Brunswick: Rutgers University Press, 1981), 378.
45. Cress, *Citizens in Arms*, 8.
46. W. J. Eccles, *Canada Under Louis XIV, 1663–1701* (London: McClelland and Stewart, 1964), 157.
47. Eccles, *The Canadian Frontier*, 139; Parkman, *Count Frontenac*, 251.
48. Eccles, *The Canadian Frontier*, 139.
49. For the purposes of this study, an expedition is defined as involving artillery and naval support.
50. Eccles, *The Canadian Frontier*, 11.
51. Port Royal—1690, Quebec—1690, Port Royal—1707, Quebec—1709, Port Royal—1710, Quebec—1711, Louisbourg—1745, Quebec—1746, Montreal—1747.
52. Frontenac planned an invasion of the English colonies in 1690 but it never left the planning stage. Another such expedition in 1697 was aborted when the French fleet arrived too late. In 1746 and 1747 the French attempted to recapture Louisbourg. See chapter 5 for more detail.
53. See Fred Anderson, *A People's Army: Massachusetts Soldiers and Society in the Seven Years' War* (Chapel Hill: University of North Carolina Press, 1984); Fred Anderson, *Crucible of War: The Seven Years' War and the Fate of Empire in British North America, 1754–1766* (New York: Knopf, 2000); Fred Anderson, *The War That Made America: A Short History of the French and Indian War* (New York: Penguin, 2005); Walter R. Borneman, *The French and Indian War: Deciding the Fate of North America* (New York: HarperCollins, 2001); Warren R. Hofstra, ed., *Cultures in Conflict: The Seven Years' War in North America* (Lanham, MD: Rowman and Littlefield, 2007).
54. For a sampling, see Alden T. Vaughn, *New England Frontier: Puritans and Indians, 1620–1675* (Boston: Little, Brown, 1965); Russell Bourne, *The Red King's Rebellion: Racial Politics in New England, 1675–1678* (New York: Oxford University Press, 1990); Eric Schultz and Michael J. Tougas, *King Philip's War: The History and Legacy of America's Forgotten Conflict* (Woodstock, VT: Countryman Press, 1999); Jill Lepore, *The Name of War: King Philip's War and the Origins of American Identity* (New York: Knopf, 1998).

55. It occurred to me that William Pitt's escalation and the resulting heavy involvement by British regulars may have influenced the way that New Englanders approached that war in comparison to the previous conflicts, although, in comparing my conclusions with Anderson's, this influence appears to have been minimal.

56. Dederer, *War in America*, 18.

CHAPTER 1

1. Joseph Dow, *History of the Town of Hampton, New Hampshire: From Its Settlement in 1638, to the Autumn of 1892* (Salem, MA, 1893 [reprinted, Somersworth, NH, 1970]), 227.

2. "Letter from Henry Dow to Major Pike," in James Phinney Baxter, ed., *Documentary History of the State of Maine* (Portland, ME, 1897), Collections of the Maine Historical Society, 2nd series, Vol. V, 296–98. The attack on Hampton never materialized.

3. "Proposals, June 10, 1698," in Baxter, *Documentary History*, Vol. V, 513.

4. Douglas Edward Leach, *Arms for Empire: A Military History of the British Colonies in North America, 1607–1763* (New York: Macmillan, 1973), 81; Samuel Adams Drake, *The Border Wars of New England, Commonly Called King William's and Queen Anne's Wars* (1897; reprint of 1910 edition, Williamstown, MA: Corner House, 1973), 142.

5. Leach, *Arms for Empire*, 224–25.

6. Cotton Mather, *Decennium Luctuosum* (1699; reprinted in Charles H. Lincoln, ed., *Narratives of the Indian Wars, 1675–1699*, New York, 1913), 191; William Hutchison Rowe, *Ancient North Yarmouth and Yarmouth, Maine, 1636–1936* (Yarmouth, ME, 1937), 43–50.

7. Samuel Penhallow, *The History of the Wars of New England with the Eastern Indians* (Boston, 1726; facsimile reprint, annotated by Edward Wheelock, Williamstown, MA, 1973), 83–90; Jeremy Belknap, *The History of New Hampshire* (reprint of 1831 edition; New York, 1970), Vol. 1, 201.

8. Herbert Milton Sylvester, *Indian Wars of New England* (Boston, 1910), Vol. III, 342.

9. "Wm Vaughn & Richard Martyn to the Gov. & Council, March 17, 1690," in Baxter, *Documentary History*, Vol. V, 57.

10. Penhallow, *History of the Wars*, 15; Sylvester, *Indian Wars of New England*, Vol. III, 380–82; Hugh D. McLellan, *History of Gorham, Maine* (Portland, ME, 1903), 49.

11. Mather, *Decennium Luctuosum*, 219.

12. Belknap, *History of New Hampshire*, 138.

13. "F. Hooke & N. Fryer about attack on York, Jan 25, 1692," in Baxter, *Documentary History*, Vol. V, 310.

14. "Charles Frost to Lieut Gov Stoughton, Sept 7, 1695," in Baxter, *Documentary History*, Vol. V, 429. Three years earlier, reports circulated that Wells had been destroyed due to the volume of smoke seen over the village, but the residents had only been burning brush to prevent ambush. "Letter from Samuel Sewell, Boston, July 11, 1692," *American Antiquarian Society*, Curwen Family Papers, Box #1, folder #4.

15. *Background of Selective Service* (Washington, 1947), Vol. II, Massachusetts Militia Laws, 17, 19; New Hampshire Militia Laws, 15.

16. Drake, *Border Wars of New England*, 30–31.

17. Mather, *Decennium Luctuosum*, 267–68.

18. "Letter from Francis Hooke to the Governor & Council, Aug. 13, 1691," in Baxter, *Documentary History*, Vol. V, 288; Drake, *Border Wars of New England*, 205–6, 242–43.

19. "Wm Vaughn & Richard Martyn to Gov. & Council, March 18, 1690," in Baxter, *Documentary History*, Vol. V, 51. Salmon Falls was part of Dover, New Hampshire, and is now called Rollinsford, New Hampshire.

20. Mather, *Decennium Luctuosum*, 243–47.

21. John Brewer, *The Sinews of Power: War, Money, and the English State* (Cambridge: Harvard University Press, 1988), 8. Brewer indicates that in the last quarter of the seventeenth century the French averaged 120,000 in their land army; the Dutch, 110,000; and the British, only 15,000.

22. Leach, *Arms for Empire*, 8–9; Howard H. Peckham, *The Colonial Wars, 1689–1762* (Chicago: University of Chicago Press, 1964), 26; "An Act for the Regulating of the Militia, May 14, 1718," New Hampshire Laws, *Background of Selective Service*, 53; "An Act for Regulating the Militia, Nov. 22, 1693," Massachusetts Militia Laws, *Background of Selective Service*, 140.

23. Thus by the "last quarter of the seventeenth century," according to Lawrence Delbert Cress, "the militia had ceased to be the principal military arm of the colonies." See Lawrence Delbert Cress, *Citizens in Arms: The Army and Militia in American Society to the War of 1812* (Chapel Hill: University of North Carolina Press, 1982), 5. See also Richard R. Johnson, *Adjustment to Empire: The New England Colonies, 1675–1715* (New Brunswick: Rutgers University Press, 1981), 377; James Kirby Martin and Mark Edward Lender, *A Respectable Army: The Military Origins of the Republic, 1763–1789* (Arlington Heights, IL: Harlan Davidson, 1982), 20; John Shy, "A New Look at the Colonial Militia," in *A People Numerous and Armed: Reflections on the Military Struggle for American Independence* (London: Oxford University Press, 1976), 30–31; John Ferling, *A Wilderness of Miseries: War and Warriors in Early America* (Westport, CT: Greenwood Press, 1980), 16; John Ferling, *Struggle for a Continent: The Wars of Early America* (Arlington Heights, IL: Harlan Davidson, 1993), 118; Leach, *Arms for Empire*, 21.

24. Darrett B. Rutman, *A Militant New World, 1670–40* (New York: Arno Press, 1979), 686; Leach, *Arms for Empire*, 45–46; Alden T. Vaughn, *New England Frontier: Puritans and Indians, 1620–1675* (Boston: Little, Brown, 1965), 71–89.

25. "The Charter of the Province of the Massachusetts-Bay" in Massachusetts Militia Laws, *Background of Selective Service*, 137. The emphasis is mine.

26. *Acts and Resolves of the Province of Massachusetts Bay, 1692–1714* (Boston, 1869).

27. "Instructions for Major Robert Pike, May 30, 1690," in Baxter, *Documentary History*, Vol. V, 117; Mather, *Decennium Luctuosum*, 218.

28. Nathaniel Bouton, ed., *Documents and Records Relating to the Province of New Hampshire* (Manchester, NH, 1869), *New Hampshire Provincial and State Papers* [hereafter NHSP], Vol. II, 124–25.

29. Emerson W. Baker and John Reid, *The New England Knight: Sir William Phips, 1651–1695* (Toronto: University of Toronto Press, 1998), 173.

30. Bouton, *NHSP*, Vol. II, 135.

31. James Phinney Baxter, ed., *Documentary History of the State of Maine* (Portland, ME, 1907), Collections of the Maine Historical Society, 2nd Series, Vol. IX, 2, 13.

32. Bouton, *NHSP*, Vol. II, 127.

33. J. A. Houlding, *Fit for Service: The Training of the British Army, 1715-95* (Oxford: Oxford University Press, 1981), 90-94. When the British adopted alternate fire and abandoned platoon fire by the end of the eighteenth century, the companies were kept intact as firing units, although their officers, especially captains, still commanded subdivisions (in this case, two companies) instead of just their company, and the regiment was still considered a battalion for tactical purposes.

34. Morrison Sharp, "Leadership and Democracy in the Early New England System of Defense," *American Historical Review*, 5 (1945), 245; Drake, *Border Wars of New England*, 144.

35. John R. Galvin, *The Minute Men: A Compact History of the Defenders of the American Colonies, 1645-1775* (New York: Pergamon-Brassey's, 1967), 29.

36. Timothy Breen, "Persistent Localism: English Social Change and the Shaping of New England Institutions," *William and Mary Quarterly*, 3rd Series, 32 (1975), 22-23. Political control through localism apparently worked, according to Breen. "A survey of Massachusetts records reveals no instance in which the colony's rulers attempted to employ the militia as a police force, as a tax collector, or as an instrument of social control."

37. Fred Anderson, *A People's Army: Massachusetts Soldiers and Society in the Seven Years' War* (Chapel Hill: University of North Carolina Press, 1984), 27.

38. Mahon, *History of the Militia*, 5. The standing militia was according to law; volunteer militia volunteered for particular duties; war volunteers volunteered for an extensive period, or for service beyond colonial or state boundaries.

39. Rutman, *A Militant New World*, 405.

40. Penhallow, *History of the Wars*, 39.

41. "Letter from Wm Vaughn & Richard Martyn to the Governor and Council, Sept 26, 1691," in Baxter, *Documentary History*, Vol. V, 292; see chapter 2 for further details.

42. Thomas Church, *The History of the Great Indian War of 1675 and 1676 Commonly Called Philip's War, also, The Old French and Indian Wars, from 1689 to 1704* (1716; Hartford, CT, 1845 edition), 155.

43. Isaac Hammond, ed., *Miscellaneous Provincial and State Papers* (Manchester, NH, 1890), *New Hampshire Provincial and State Papers*, Vol. XVIII, 215.

44. "An Act for the Regulating of the Militia, May 14, 1718," New Hampshire Laws, *Background of Selective Service*, 53; "An Act for Regulating the Militia, Nov. 22, 1693," Massachusetts Militia Laws, *Background of Selective Service*, 140.

45. William Blake Trask, *Letters of Colonel Thomas Westbrook and Others Relative to Indian Affairs in Maine, 1722-1726* (Boston, 1901), 53.

46. Ibid., 55.

47. Ibid., 18.

48. "Col T. Westbrook to Lt Gov W. Dummer, August, 1724," in James Phinney Baxter, ed., *Documentary History of the State of Maine* (Portland, ME, 1907), *Collections of the Maine Historical Society*, 2nd Series, Vol. X, 216.

49. "Act Respecting the Military," Massachusetts Militia Laws, *Background of Selective Service*, 85-86.

50. "Lawes and Liberties, 1647," Massachusetts Militia Laws, *Background of Selective Service*, 52.

51. Martin and Lender, *A Respectable Army*, 18.

52. Baxter, *Documentary History*, Vol. IX, 14.

53. Ibid., 57.

54. Ibid., 76.
55. Ibid., 2; "Letter dated September 1, 1696," *American Antiquarian Society* [hereafter cited as *AAS*], Mass. Collections, 1629-1869; Baxter, *Documentary History*, Vol. V, 51.
56. Baxter, *Documentary History*, 13.
57. Charles Edward Banks, *History of York, Maine* (Boston, 1931-1935), Vol. I, 318.
58. Rowe, *Ancient North Yarmouth*, 98.
59. Belknap, *The History of New Hampshire*, 131-32; Mather, *Decennium Luctuosum*, 269-70; Drake, *Border Wars of New England*, 182-83, 189; Sylvester, *Indian Wars of New England*, Vol. III, 359. Captain James Converse pursued one raiding party for three days without success. See Mather, *Decennium Luctuosum*, 221.
60. Belknap, *The History of New Hampshire*, 207.
61. Baxter, *Documentary History*, Vol. IX, 9; Abijah P. Marvin, *History of the Town of Lancaster* (Lancaster, MA, 1879), 146.
62. Mather, *Decennium Luctuosum*, 260.
63. Penhallow, *The History of the Wars*, 32.
64. Ibid., 44.
65. Ibid., 39.
66. Drake, *Border Wars of New England*, 86.
67. Dow, *History of the Town of Hampton*, 229; Drake, *Border Wars of New England*, 109.
68. See Penhallow, *The History of the Wars*, 15, 36, 102; Baxter, *Documentary History*, Vol. V, 57, Belknap, *The History of New Hampshire*, 294; Sylvester, *Indian Wars of New England*, 342; Mather, *Decennium Luctuosum*, 271-72.

CHAPTER 2

1. Thomas Hutchinson, *The History of the Colony and Province of Massachusetts Bay* (London, 1768; reprint, Cambridge, MA, 1936), 75.
2. Douglas Edward Leach, *The Northern Colonial Frontier, 1607-1763* (New York: Macmillan, 1966), 113. Or to use a more colloquial phrase, "It was a dirty job, but someone had to do it."
3. "The Committee's Report, May 27, 1715," James Phinney Baxter, ed., *Documentary History of the State of Maine* (Portland, ME, 1916), *Collections of the Maine Historical Society*, 2nd Series, Vol. XXIV, 239.
4. Cotton Mather, *Frontiers Well-Defended* (Boston, 1707), 3.
5. Jeremy Belknap, *The History of New Hampshire* (1831; New York, 1970), Vol. 1, 287.
6. Herbert Milton Sylvester, *Indian Wars of New England* (Boston, 1910), Vol. III, 390.
7. "Petition of John Kinsley in Behalf of a Child of Abraham Collins, July 4, 1690," James Phinney Baxter, ed., *Documentary History of the State of Maine*, (Portland, ME, 1897), *Collections of the Maine Historical Society*, 2nd Series, Vol. V, 130-31.
8. Belknap, *The History of New Hampshire*, 291-92.
9. "Petition of Jane Ryly," in Baxter, *Documentary History*, Vol. V, 126-27.
10. Baxter, *Documentary History*, Vol. XXIV. This volume contains extensive examples of these transactions. Gordon E. Kershaw, *The Kennebeck Proprietors, 1749-1775* (Somersworth, NH: New Hampshire Publishing Co., 1975), 18-19. These holdings predated the law, which allowed land to be confiscated by the government if abandoned without official permission.

11. Cotton Mather, *Decennium Luctuosum* (1699; reprinted in Charles H. Lincoln, ed., *Narratives of the Indian Wars, 1675-1699*, New York, 1913), 220; Baxter, *Documentary History*, Vol. IX, 42.

12. "Letter from Francis Littlefield & Others to the Governor and Council, July 21, 1691," in Baxter, *Documentary History*, Vol. V, 274.

13. William Pencak, *War, Politics and Revolution in Provincial Massachusetts* (Boston: Northeastern University Press, 1981), 41; Samuel Adams Drake, *The Border Wars of New England, Commonly Called King William's and Queen Anne's Wars* (1897, reprint of 1910 edition, Williamstown, MA, 1973), 95.

14. Baxter, *Documentary History*, Vol. IX, 39; *Maine Province and Court Records* (Portland, ME, 1947), Vol. III, 300.

15. "Letter Charles Frost & Others to the Govr & Council, March 26, 1690," in Baxter, *Documentary History*, Vol. V, 70; "Letter from Major R. Pike to the Gov & Council, June 23, 1691," in Baxter, *Documentary History*, Vol. V, 260-61; "Letter from Francis Littlefield & Others to the Gov. & Council, July 21, 1691," in Baxter, *Documentary History*, Vol. V, 274-75.

16. "Frontier Towns to Be Strengthened, March 21, 1690," in Baxter, *Documentary History*, Vol. V, 61; "Letter from Francis Littlefield & Others to the Gov. & Council, July 21, 1691," in Baxter, *Documentary History*, Vol. V, 274-75; "Yore and Kittery Petcon, Sept. 1695," in Baxter, *Documentary History*, Vol. V, 427-29; "Mr Wheelwright's Peticon on behalfe of the Town of Wells, Granted Dec. 1696," in Baxter, *Documentary History*, Vol. V, 471-72; "Petiton of the Selectmen of Kittery," in Baxter, *Documentary History*, Vol. V, 482-84; "Kittery Petition presented Sept 1697," in Baxter, *Documentary History*, Vol. V, 490-92; *American Antiquarian Society*, Mass. Col. 1629-1869, Box 3, Folder 11: Militia returns, Officers commissions and Misc. Papers 1696-1762; Everett S. Stackpole, *Old Kittery and Her Families* (Lewiston, ME, 1903), 174.

17. "Proposals, June 10, 1698," in Baxter, *Documentary History*, Vol. V 513.

18. "Journal of the House, June 4, 1747," in Nathaniel Bouton, ed., *Documents and Records Relating to the Province of New Hampshire from 1738-1749* (Nashua, NH, 1871), *New Hampshire State and Provincial Records*, Vol. V, 510.

19. Charles E. Clark, *The Eastern Frontier: The Settlement of Northern New England, 1610-1763* (New York: Knopf, 1970), 192-93.

20. For more about the Isle of Shoals' checkered past, see Clark, *The Eastern Frontier*.

21. "Petition of the Inhabitants of the Isle of Shoals, Jan 26, 1692," in Baxter, *Documentary History*, Vol. V, 312-13.

22. "Address of Some of the Inhabitants of the Isle of Sholes to the Governor and Council, March 12, 1692," in Baxter, *Documentary History*, Vol. V, 363.

23. "Letter to Capt Willey and the Inhabitants of the Isle of Sholes, March 19, 1692," in Baxter, *Documentary History*, Vol. V, 370.

24. "Letter from the Governor & Council to the Inhabitants of the Isles of Sholes, March 19, 1692," in Baxter, *Documentary History*, Vol. V, 372.

25. *Journals of the Rev. Thomas Smith and the Rev. Samuel Deane* (Portland, ME, 1849), 113. The Reverend Thomas Smith of Falmouth wrote in his diary in 1744 that "the soldiers came down here. The Province have raised five hundred, three hundred of them for the eastern country . . . eighty-five of them are posted in this town, and two of them in my garrison."

26. Stackpole, *Old Kittery*, 177; see also Charles Edward Banks, *History of York, Maine* (Boston, 1931–1935), Vol. II, 225.

27. *American Antiquarian Society*, Mass. Col. 1629–1869, Box 3, Folder 11: Militia returns, Officers commissions and Misc. Papers 1696–1762; Baxter, *Documentary History*, Vol. IX, 247.

28. Mather, *Decennium Luctuosum*, 243–44; Chandler E. Potter, *The Military History of New Hampshire from Its Founding until the Present Time (Report of the Adjutant-General of the State of New Hampshire for the Year Ending June 1, 1866)* (Concord, NH, 1866), 20; Baxter, *Documentary History*, Vol. V, 260, 314, 320.

29. Stackpole, *Old Kittery*, 177, 179–80; Banks, *History of York, Maine*, Vol. II, 222–27; *Journal of Rev. Smith*, 113.

30. See Potter, *The Military History of New Hampshire*, 55; Lt. Joseph Storer, owner of a prominent garrison in Wells, had a license for keeping a public house. See *Maine Court Records*, 288. The Gilman family who owned a garrison in Exeter, New Hampshire, were all political leaders in the community, officers in the local militia, and operators of a public house out of their garrison. See Robbins Paxson Gilman, *The Old Logg House by the Bridge* (Portsmouth, NH: Peter E. Randall, 1985).

31. Hutchinson, *History of Massachusetts*, 50.

32. Edward Emerson Bourne, "Garrison Houses, York County," in *Collections of the Maine Historical Society*, 1876, Vol. VII, 112–13.

33. Gilman, *The Old Logg House*, 39–42.

34. William Hutchison Rowe, *Ancient North Yarmouth and Yarmouth, Maine, 1636–1936* (Yarmouth, ME, 1937), 46; Leach, *Northern Frontier*, 81; Hutchinson, *History of Massachusetts*, 50.

35. Bourne, "Garrison Houses," 116.

36. Mather, *Frontiers*, 4.

37. "Letter from Capt John Floyd to the Governor and Council, Jan. 27, 1691," in Baxter, *Documentary History*, Vol. V, 314.

38. Banks, *History of York, Maine*, Vol. II, 225.

39. Stackpole, *Old Kittery*, 177.

40. Clark, *Eastern Frontier*, 70.

41. Potter, *The Military History of New Hampshire*, 107–8; Banks, *History of York, Maine*, Vol. II, 222–27; Stackpole, *Old Kittery*, 177.

42. William Blake Trask, *Letters of Colonel Thomas Westbrook and Others Relative to Indian Affairs in Maine, 1722–1726* (Boston, 1901), 17.

43. "Simon Willard about Visit to Boston, May 9, 1690," in Baxter, *Documentary History*, Vol. V, 95.

44. Mather, *Frontiers*, 20–21.

45. "Elisha Andrews to Gov & Council, Oct 31, 1690," in Baxter, *Documentary History*, Vol. V, 156–57.

46. "Letter to Gov from David Parsons, Leicester, May 31, 1725," in *American Antiquarian Society*, Mass. Col. 1629–1869, Box 3, Folder 11: Militia returns, Officers commissions and Misc. Papers 1696–1762.

47. "Elisha Andrews to Gov & Council, Oct 31, 1690," in Baxter, *Documentary History*, Vol. V, 156–57.

48. "Letter Wm Vaughn & Richd Martyn to the Gov & Council, March 20, 1690," in Baxter, *Documentary History*, Vol. IX, 59–60.

49. Baxter, *Documentary History*, Vol. IX, 216–17.

50. Ibid., 74.

51. "Letter Joseph Prout to Isaac Addington, Esq, Sept 16, 1689," in Baxter, *Documentary History*, Vol. V, 8.

52. "Petition of Abram Prebble, May 25, 1698," in Baxter, *Documentary History*, Vol. V, 500–504.

53. "Commissioners to Impress Provisions, May 30, 1690," in Baxter, *Documentary History*, Vol. V, 124. No restitution was made for impressed cattle belonging to inhabitants who had fled the frontier. See also "Col. T. Westbrook to Lt Gov. Dummer, April 21, 1724," in James Phinney Baxter, ed., *Documentary History of the State of Maine* (Portland, ME, 1907), *Collections of the Maine Historical Society*, 2nd Series, Vol. X, 191.

54. *Maine Court Records*, 300.

55. "Letter from Wm Vaughn to Gov. Bradstreet, Nov. 1691," in Baxter, *Documentary History*, Vol. V, 303.

56. "Joseph Prout to Isaac Addington, Sept 21, 1689," in Baxter, *Documentary History*, Vol. V, 10–11; "Letter Richd Buckley Commr to Isaac Addington Secretary, Oct 26, 1691," in Baxter, *Documentary History*, Vol. V, 299–300.

57. "Letter from Secry Allyn of Cont concerning illness of Magistrates & contribution for families of soldiers at Eastd, Dec 3, 1691," in Baxter, *Documentary History*, Vol. V, 309.

58. "Order to several Majors as to collection of Provisions &c. for Soldiers, Nov, 1691," in Baxter, *Documentary History*, Vol. V, 304.

59. "Instructions for Captain Simon Willard, Nov 28, 1689," in Baxter, *Documentary History*, Vol. V, 12–13.

60. "Letter Joseph Prout to Isaac Addington, Esq, Sept 16, 1689," in Baxter, *Documentary History*, Vol. V, 8.

61. "Letter Joseph Prout to Gov. Bradstreet, Sept 18, 1689," in Baxter, *Documentary History*, Vol. V, 9.

62. "Joseph Prout to Isaac Addington, Sept 21, 1689," in Baxter, *Documentary History*, Vol. V, 11.

63. "Minutes of Massachusetts Council, August 19, 1703," *Calendar of State Papers, Colonial Series, America and West Indies, December 1, 1702–1703* (reprint of 1913 edition; Vaduz, 1964), Vol. 21, No. 1039.

64. "Minutes of Massachusetts Council, August 19, 1703," *Calendar of State Papers*, Vol. 21, No. 1039.

65. "Minutes of Massachusetts Council, August 23, 1703," *Calendar of State Papers*, Vol. 21, No. 1044.

66. "Letter James Converse to Gov. & Council, Nov 3, 1690," in Baxter, *Documentary History*, Vol. V, 157.

67. Hugh D. McLellan, *History of Gorham, Maine* (Portland, ME, 1903), 60.

68. Sylvester, *History of the Indian Wars*, Vol. III, 400.

69. Potter, *The Military History of New Hampshire*, 16.

70. "Letter from John Alen & Others to the Governor & Council, Sept 28, 1691," in Baxter, *Documentary History*, Vol. V, 295.

71. "Letter from Richd Buckley Commr to Isaac Addington Secretary, Oct. 17, 1691," in Baxter, *Documentary History*, Vol. V, 299.

72. "Complaint against Three Soldiers, April 7, 1690," in Baxter, *Documentary History*, Vol. V, 73.

73. Baxter, *Documentary History*, Vol. IX, 13, 73.

74. "Sre from Capt King and Capt March Red July 12, 1691," in Baxter, *Documentary History*, Vol. V, 264.

75. "Letter from Wm Vaughn to Governor & Council, Aug 13, 1691," in Baxter, *Documentary History*, Vol. V, 289.

76. Trask, *Letters of Colonel Thomas Westbrook*, 54.

77. "Joseph Prout to Isaac Addington, Sept 21, 1689," in Baxter, *Documentary History*, Vol. V, 10.

78. Baxter, *Documentary History*, Vol. IX, 42. Unsubstantiated legends called into question the backbone of some provincial soldiers. The nineteenth-century historian Samuel Adams Drake related the story of an attack on the Bradley garrison in Haverhill on February 8, 1703. While the men were at work elsewhere, Bradley's wife was boiling soap, and a soldier, Jonathan Johnson, was "loitering around the house." The Indians burst in, capturing Hannah Bradley, after she gamely threw a ladleful of boiling soap in the face of the first Indian, and they easily killed the loitering soldier named Johnson. Four years later, in the same town, Indians attacked the garrison of the town's minister, Benjamin Rolfe. They fired through the door, shattering the wood and wounding the minister, then bursting through; they killed the minister and his wife and child. "Paralyzed with fear, the cowardly soldiers were slain while begging for mercy." Drake, *The Border Wars of New England*, 244.

79. Baxter, *Documentary History*, Vol. IX, 42.

80. "Letter from Elisha Hutchison to the Governor & Council," in Baxter, *Documentary History*, Vol. V, 336.

81. Samuel Penhallow, *The History of the Wars of New England with the Eastern Indians* (Boston, 1726; facsimile reprint, annotated by Edward Wheelock, Williamstown, MA, 1973), 13.

82. Drake, *The Border Wars of New England*, 218.

83. "Lt-Governor John Usher to Council of Trade and Plantations, February 19, 1704," *Calendar of State Papers, Colonial Series, America and West Indies, 1704–1705* (reprint of 1916 edition, Vaduz, 1964), Vol. 22, No. 120.

84. Belknap, *History of New Hampshire*, 203n.

85. Banks, *History of York, Maine*, Vol. II, 317.

86. Belknap, *History of New Hampshire*, 289.

87. Edward E. Bourne, *The History of Wells and Kennebunk* (Portland, ME, 1875), 202.

88. "Col. T Westbrook to Lt Gov. Dummer, April 21, 1724," in Baxter, *Documentary History*, Vol. X, 192. See chapter 1 for the friction created between provincial commanders and local militia leaders over inadequate defense precautions.

89. Potter, *The Military History of New Hampshire*, 22–23.

90. Drake, *The Border Wars of New England*, 99–100.

91. Ibid., 287.

92. Ibid., 219; Penhallow, *History of the Wars*, 35; Douglas Leach, *Arms for Empire: A Military History of the British Colonies in North America, 1607–1763* (New York: Macmillan, 1973), 130.

93. The behavior is consistent with the Indian approach to tactics and battle. For more about the Indian psychology in war, see chapter 10.

94. Refer to Mather, *Decennium Luctuosum*; Drake, *The Border Wars of New England*; Penhallow, *The History of the Wars*; and Bourne, *The History of Wells*, concerning attacks on garrisons in Exeter, July 1690; York, January 1692; Lancaster, July 1704; Arrowsick, September 1722; and Kennebunk, April 1747.

95. Bourne, "Garrison Houses," 114.

96. A "mantlet" was a movable shield that protected sappers as they began new sections of trenches during a siege (Keegan and Holmes, *Soldiers*, 173).

97. Details on the siege come from Mather, *Decennium Luctuosum*, 232–40; Drake, *The Border Wars of New England*, 76–81; see also Hutchinson, *History of Massachusetts*; Bourne, *History of Wells*.

98. W. J. Eccles, *Canada Under Louis XIV, 1663–1701* (London: McClelland and Stewart, 1964), 157.

CHAPTER 3

1. Hutchison Papers, *Collections of the Massachusetts Historical Society*, 85–87. Andros provided a detailed account of the forts and forces he had left in Maine to defend the frontier and the resulting chaos created by the "subversive" government in Boston. The "subversives" replied to this account by offering their own opinions about these forts and the forces posted there. See James Phinney Baxter, ed., *Documentary History of the State of Maine* (Portland, ME, 1897), *Collections of the Maine Historical Society*, 2nd Series, Vol. V, 120–23.

2. Baxter, *Documentary History*, Vol. V, 120–23.

3. Thornton J. Wingate, "Ancient Pemaquid, An Historical Review" in *Collections of the Maine Historical Society*, Vol. V (Portland, ME 1857), 282; Robert L. Bradley, *Maine's First Buildings: The Architecture of Settlement, 1604–1700* (Maine Historic Preservation Commission, 1978), 11; *Calendar of State Papers, Colonial Series, America and West Indies, January, 1693 to 14 May, 1696* (reprint of 1903 edition, Vaduz, 1964), Vol. 14, No. 454.

4. Bradley, *Maine's First Buildings*, 11. No name has emerged from the records for this fort. It was always referred to as the "fort at Casco" to distinguish it from its predecessor, Fort Loyal. In *Maine Forts*, Henry Dunnack referred to this installation as the "New Casco Fort." See Henry Dunnack, *Maine Forts* (Augusta, ME, 1924), 236.

5. Chandler E. Potter, *The Military History of New Hampshire from Its Founding until the Present Time (Report of the Adjutant-General of the State of New Hampshire for the Year Ending June 1, 1866*, Concord, NH, 1866), 20–21; "Lt-Governor John Usher to Council of Trade and Plantations, March 21, 1705," *Calendar of State Papers, Colonial Series, America and West Indies, 1704–1705* (reprint of 1916 edition, Vaduz, 1964), Vol. 22, No. 966; "Col. Wolfgang Romer's reply to Council of Trade and Plantations, August, 30, 1708," *Calendar of State Papers, Colonial Series, America and West Indies, June, 1708–1709* (reprint of 1922 edition, Vaduz, 1964), Vol. 24, No. 123. Romer claimed that Governor Dudley stopped work on the fort when Romer's replacement, Captain John Redknap, arrived in the colonies.

6. *Calendar of State Papers, Colonial Series, America and West Indies, December 1, 1702–1703* (reprint of 1913 edition, Vaduz, 1964), Vol. 21, No. 302.

7. "Governor Joseph Dudley to Council of Trade and Plantations, October 2, 1706," *Calendar of State Papers, Colonial Series, America and West Indies, 1706–1708* (reprint of 1916 edition, Vaduz, 1964), Vol. 23, No. 511.

8. "Governor Joseph Dudley to Council of Trade and Plantations, March 1, 1709," *Calendar of State Papers*, Vol. 24, No. 391.

9. Gordon E. Kershaw, *The Kennebeck Proprietors, 1749–1775* (Somersworth, NH: New Hampshire Publishing Co., 1975), 16–17.

10. James Phinney Baxter, ed., *Documentary History of the State of Maine* (Portland, ME, 1916), *Collections of the Maine Historical Society*, 2nd Series, Vol. XXIII, 234–50. The structure had originally been called Fort Andros. Fort George was dismantled in 1737. See Dunnack, *Maine Forts*, 232.

11. Kershaw, *The Kennebeck Proprietors*, 19. Fort Richmond was enlarged in 1741 and was dismantled in 1754 after Forts Western and Halifax were built further up the Kennebec. See Dunnack, *Maine Forts*, 240.

12. Dunnack, *Maine Forts*, 108.

13. Michael D. Coe, *The Line of Forts: Historical Archaeology on the Colonial Frontier of Massachusetts* (Hanover, NH: University Press of New England, 2006), 5.

14. They called the fort "Atkinson" after their commander. Potter, *The Military History of New Hampshire*, 83.

15. Ibid., 50–51; Hugh D. McLellan, *History of Gorham, Maine* (Portland, ME, 1903), 44–46.

16. The east wall was twelve feet; the north, ten; and the west wall, eighteen. Variations in the ground, which was mostly ledge, accounted for some of the differences.

17. Cotton Mather, *Decennium Luctuosum* (1699, reprinted in Charles H. Lincoln, ed., *Narratives of the Indian Wars, 1675–1699*, New York, 1913), 240–41: Wingate, "Ancient Pemaquid," *Col Me Hist Soc*, Vol. XXIII, 282. "Eighteen-pounders" refers to the weight of the shot.

18. An excellent reconstruction of Number Four exists in Charleston, New Hampshire.

19. Herbert Milton Sylvester, *Indian Wars of New England* (Boston, 1910), Vol. III, 372.

20. Coe, *The Line of Forts*, 52.

21. McLellan, *History of Gorham, Maine*, 44–46.

22. Richard Melvoin, *New England Outpost: War and Society in Colonial Deerfield* (New York: Norton, 1989), 194, 216–17.

23. Baxter, *Documentary History*, Vol. XXIII, 244.

24. Ibid., 240.

25. Ibid., 249.

26. Ibid.

27. Watts not only provided his "boy" for a cook, but provisions and a sloop. The £30 must have been a bonus of some kind.

28. Baxter, *Documentary History*, Vol. XXIII, 254–58. The records were precise and the cost of the fort was actually £688, 9 shillings and 4 pence.

29. James Phinney Baxter, ed., *Documentary History of the State of Maine* (Portland, ME, 1907), *Collections of the Maine Historical Society*, 2nd Series, Vol. IX, 86; Samuel Adams Drake, *The Border Wars of New England, Commonly Called King William's and Queen Anne's Wars* (1897; reprint of 1910 edition, Williamstown, MA, 1973), 84.

30. Baxter, *Documentary History*, Vol. IX, 113; Dunnack, *Maine Forts*, 232.

31. James Phinney Baxter, ed., *Documentary History of the State of Maine* (Portland, ME, 1907), *Collections of the Maine Historical Society*, 2nd Series, Vol. X, 99.

32. Bradley, *Maine's First Buildings*, 11.

33. "Council of Trade and Plantations to the Queen, November 7, 1704," *Calendar of State Papers*, Vol. 22, No. 645; "Queen in Council to Governor Joseph Dudley, January 11, 1705," *Calendar of State Papers*, Vol. 22, No. 806. In addition to rebuilding the fort at Pemaquid, Whitehall attempted to use these threats to force the Massachusetts Assembly to provide a salary for Governor Dudley, which they had steadfastly refused to do. When Dudley's name was connected to a scandal involving trade with the enemy, he apparently decided he had better drop the issue of a salary for a while, and with it dropped the pressure to rebuild Pemaquid. A small fort was eventually built there.

34. Potter, *The Military History of New Hampshire*, 21.

35. "Minutes of New Hampshire Council in Assembly, December 7, 1703," *Calendar of State Papers*, Vol. 21, No. 1365.

36. "George Vaughn to Council of Trade and Plantations, July 6, 1708," *Calendar of State Papers*, Vol. 24, No. 19. Later in the same report he seems to contradict himself by reporting that "the condition of the Castle is tollerably well at the present so far as is finished but will yearly want repairs."

37. "Col. Wolfgang Romer's reply to Council of Trade and Plantations, August, 30, 1708," *Calendar of State Papers*, Vol. 24, No. 123. By this time Romer was back in England, having been replaced by Redknap.

38. Nathaniel Bouton, *Documents and Records Relating to the Province of New Hampshire from 1738-1749* (Nashua, NH, 1871), *New Hampshire State and Provincial Papers* [hereafter cited as *NHSP*], Vol. V, 11-12.

39. Ibid., 18-20.

40. Ibid., 21-22.

41. Jeremy Belknap, *The History of New Hampshire* (reprint of 1831 edition, New York, 1970), Vol. I, 170; "William Vaughn to Council of Trade and Plantations, January, 1703," *Calendar of State Papers*, Vol. 21, No. 225.

42. Belknap, *The History of New Hampshire*, 286.

43. Sylvester, *Indian Wars of New England*, Vol. III, 302.

44. "Lt-Governor William Dummer to Timothy Dwight at Fort Dummer, Dec. 28, 1725," in Massachusetts *Historical Society*, Misc. Bound.

45. Baxter, *Documentary History*, Vol. IX, 161.

46. Baxter, *Documentary History*, Vol. XXIII, 251-52.

47. "A List of Men Belonging to Fort Mary at Saco, this 13 September, 1704," in *Maine Historical Society, Miscellaneous Papers*, Vol. I.

48. Baxter, *Documentary History*, Vol. XXIII, 251-52.

49. Dwight B. Demeritt Jr., *Maine Made Guns and Their Makers* (Hallowell, ME: Maine State Museum Press, 1973), 6.

50. Demeritt Jr., *Maine Made Guns*, 3-4. For more about gunsmiths, see chapter 6.

51. Baxter, *Documentary History*, Vol. X, 384; John Gyles, *Memoirs of Odd Adventures, Strange Deliverances, &c.* (Boston, 1736, facsimile reprint in *The Garland Library of Narratives of North American Indian Captivities*, New York, 1977), 41-44. Of his experiences building Fort George, Gyles wrote, "My Wages were very small, yet the Gentlemen-Proprietors ordered me only *Five Pounds* for my good service."

52. Baxter, *Documentary History*, Vol. IX, 165–66.
53. John Norton, *The Redeemed Captive* (Boston, 1748, facsimile reprint in *The Garland Library of Narratives of North American Indian Captivities*, New York, 1977), 4.
54. Francis Parkman, *Count Frontenac and New France under Louis XIV* (Boston, 1896), 380.
55. See later in this chapter.
56. See chapter 7.
57. "Journal of Lieutenant Burk," Stevens Family Papers, Special Collections, University of Vermont.
58. Baxter, *Documentary History*, Vol. IX, 43.
59. "Journal of Lieutenant Burk."
60. Coe, *The Line of Forts*, 120–24.
61. Ibid., 153.
62. Ibid., 124.
63. Ibid., 124–28.
64. Baxter, *Documentary History*, Vol. XXIII, 252.
65. Belknap, *History of New Hampshire*, 285.
66. Potter, *The Military History of New Hampshire*, 82.
67. Baxter, *Documentary History*, Vol. IX, 29–33.
68. Ibid., Vol. X, 179.
69. J. A. Houlding, *Fit for Service: The Training of the British Army, 1715-95* (Oxford: Oxford University Press, 1981), 13.
70. Ibid., 13–17.
71. Baxter, *Documentary History*, Vol. IX, 32–33. "Beat to arms" was a long roll on the drums, which was the signal for soldiers to drop everything and fall in or take their assigned positions to prepare for attack.
72. Samuel Penhallow, *The History of the Wars of New England with the Eastern Indians* (Boston, 1726; facsimile reprint, annotated by Edward Wheelock, Williamstown, MA, 1973), 7; "Journal of Lieutenant Burk."
73. Nellis M. Crouse, *Lemoyne d'Iberville: Soldier of New France* (Ithaca, NY: Cornell University Press, 1954), 106.
74. Ibid., 105–11.
75. Crouse, *Lemoyne d'Iberville*, 113; Wingate, "Ancient Pemaquid," *Collections of the Maine Historical Society*, Vol. XXIII, 290.
76. Drake, *The Border Wars of New England*, 111; Crouse, *Lemoyne d'Iberville*, 113.
77. Crouse, *Lemoyne d'Iberville*, 114. Chubb was crucified for his action, but many historians, including Thomas Hutchinson and Francis Parkman, have concluded he could not have held the fort under the circumstances. For more about Pasco Chubb, see chapter 8.
78. Baxter, *Documentary History*, Vol. XXIII, 17.
79. Norton, *The Redeemed Captive*, 4.
80. Ibid., 6–7.
81. Baxter, *Documentary History*, Vol. XXIII, 17.
82. "Westbrook to Lt-Governor Dummer, Sept. 23, 1722," *Maine Historical Society, Miscellaneous Papers*, Vol. I.
83. Sylvester, *Indian Wars of New England*, Vol. III, 380–82.
84. Penhallow, *The History of the Wars*, 8.
85. Ibid., 86.

86. As the Pejepscot Company correctly pointed out (see above), stone forts were less susceptible to this tactic.

87. Drake, *The Border Wars of New England*, 52.

88. Norton, *The Redeemed Captive*, 6.

89. Sylvester, *Indian Wars of New England*, Vol. III, 380–82.

90. Norton, *The Redeemed Captive*, 8; Coe, *The Line of Forts*, 31–34. Norton reported that when they decided to surrender, only four pounds of powder remained in the fort.

91. John K. Mahon, "Anglo-American Methods of Indian Warfare, 1676–1794," *Mississippi Valley Historical Review*, 45 (1958), 261.

CHAPTER 4

1. James Phinney Baxter, ed., *Documentary History of the State of Maine* (Portland, ME, 1897), Collections of the Maine Historical Society, 2nd Series, Vol. V, 337.

2. *The New Webster Encyclopedic Dictionary of the English Language* (Chicago, 1970).

3. Nathaniel Bouton, *Documents and Records Relating to the Province of New Hampshire from 1738–1749* (Nashua, NH, 1871), *New Hampshire State and Provincial Papers* [hereafter cited as *NHSP*], Vol. V, 577; Baxter, *Documentary History*, Vol. V, 89–90, 125.

4. James Phinney Baxter, ed., *Documentary History of the State of Maine* (Portland, ME, 1907), *Collections of the Maine Historical Society*, 2nd Series, Vol. IX, 6; Charles Edward Banks, *History of York, Maine* (Boston, 1931–1935), Vol. I, 319.

5. American Antiquarian Society, Mass. Col. 1629–1869, Box 3, Folder 11: Militia returns, Officers commissions and Misc. Papers 1696–1762, "Instructions to Colonel Tyng"; Bouton, *NHSP*, Vol. V, 247.

6. Baxter, *Documentary History*, Vol. V, 89–90; Samuel Penhallow, *The History of the Wars of New England with the Eastern Indians* (Boston, 1726; facsimile reprint, annotated by Edward Wheelock, Williamstown, MA, 1973), 99–100, Notes 28.

7. William Hutchison Rowe, *Ancient North Yarmouth and Yarmouth, Maine, 1636–1936* (Yarmouth, ME, 1937), 98.

8. James Phinney Baxter, ed., *Documentary History of the State of Maine* (Portland, ME, 1916), *Collections of the Maine Historical Society*, 2nd Series, Vol. XXIII, 150.

9. "Journal of Jeremiah Moulton, May, 1723," *Massachusetts Archives*, Vol. 38A:21. Because of the significance of this entry in depicting patrol duty, I have altered the original spelling and construction considerably. There were few punctuation marks, and even fewer correctly spelled words. Deciphering such writing would have detracted from its impact.

10. "Minutes of Massachusetts Council, August 11, 1703," *Calendar of State Papers, Colonial Series, America and West Indies, December 1, 1702–1703* (reprint of 1913 edition, Vaduz, 1964), Vol. 21, No. 969, 1025.

11. Samuel Adams Drake, *The Border Wars of New England, Commonly called King William's and Queen Anne's Wars* (1897; reprint of 1910 edition, Williamstown, MA, 1973), 238–41; "Governor Joseph Dudley to Council of Trade and Plantations, March 1, 1709," *Calendar of State Papers, Colonial Series, America and West Indies, June, 1708–1709* (reprint of 1922 edition, Vaduz, 1964), Vol. 24, No. 391.

12. For an example, see Isaac Hammond, ed., *Miscellaneous Provincial and State Papers* (Manchester, NH, 1890), *New Hampshire State and Provincial Papers*, Vol. XVIII, 214.

13. "Governor Joseph Dudley to Council of Trade and Plantations, March 10, 1705," *Calendar of State Papers, Colonial Series, America and West Indies, 1704–1705* (reprint of 1916 edition, Vaduz, 1964), Vol. 22, No. 947.

14. *Annals of Lancaster, Massachusetts, 1643–1825* (Clinton, MA, 1884), 226.

15. Francis Jennings, *The Invasion of America: Indians, Colonialism, and the Cant of Conquest* (New York: Norton, 1976), 19. As Jennings pointed out, the strategy of destroying food supplies was common among European commanders.

16. Ibid., 61–67.

17. James Phinney Baxter, ed., *Documentary History of the State of Maine* (Portland, ME, 1907), *Collections of the Maine Historical Society*, 2nd Series, Vol. X, 199, 280; "Governor Joseph Dudley to the Council of Trade and Plantations, April 20 1704," *Calendar of State Papers*, Vol. 22, No. 260.

18. Thomas Church, *The History of the Great Indian War of 1675 and 1676 Commonly Called Philip's War, also, The Old French and Indian Wars, from 1689 to 1704* (1716; Hartford, CT, 1845), 184–85; Cotton Mather, *Decennium Luctuosum* (1699; reprinted in Charles H. Lincoln, ed., *Narratives of the Indian Wars, 1675–1699*, New York, 1913), 225–26; Drake, *The Border Wars of New England*, 67–69. Church ordered the execution of his prisoners.

19. Howard H. Peckham, *The Colonial Wars, 1689–1762* (Chicago: University of Chicago Press, 1964), 42.

20. Penhallow, *The History of the Wars*, 23–24.

21. Baxter, *Documentary History*, Vol. IX, 323–24.

22. "Governor Joseph Dudley to the Council of Trade and Plantations, March 10, 1705," *Calendar of State Papers*, Vol. 22, No. 947.

23. Baxter, *Documentary History*, Vol. X, 280, 199; Baxter, *Documentary History*, Vol. IX, 474.

24. Church, *The History of the Great Indian War*, 158. See the accounts of Benjamin Church, Winthrop Hilton, Shadrach Walton, and John Lovewell later in this chapter.

25. Jeremy Belknap, *The History of New Hampshire* (reprint of 1831 edition, New York, 1970), Vol. 1, 221–22; Mather, *Decennium Luctuosum*, 223–24.

26. Drake, *The Border Wars of New England*, 206–7; Belknap, *The History of New Hampshire*, 295.

27. Baxter, *Documentary History*, Vol. V, 280–81. For more about the March-King raid, see below.

28. Ibid., 426–27.

29. Ibid., Vol. X, 155

30. Ibid., 203–4.

31. This despite the fact that Cotton Mather suspected some of them were passing information to the French. See Mather, *Decennium Luctuosum*, 203.

32. Christian died "with a violent bleeding" during a scout heading up the Merrimack River in 1725. See *Annals of Lancaster*, 225; Baxter, *Documentary History*, Vol. X, 272.

33. "Minutes of Massachusetts Council, August 23, 1703," *Calendar of State Papers*, Vol. 21, No. 1144.

34. Baxter, *Documentary History*, Vol. X, 226.

35. Ibid., 21.

36. *Annals of Lancaster*, 231–33.

37. Penhallow, *The History of the Wars*, 110.

38. Baxter, *Documentary History*, Vol. V, 292–93. See chapter 2.

39. Ibid., Vol. X, 226.

40. Francis Parkman, *Count Frontenac and New France under Louis XIV* (Boston, 1896), 104.

41. Herbert Milton Sylvester, *Indian Wars of New England* (Boston, 1910), Vol. III, 380–82. See chapter 3 for more details on this siege.

42. Baxter, *Documentary History*, Vol. IX, 141; *Annals of Lancaster*, 241.

43. *Annals of Lancaster*, 233. For more about the consequences of sickness, see chapter 11.

44. Baxter, *Documentary History*, Vol. V, 431.

45. William Blake Trask, *Letters of Colonel Thomas Westbrook and Others Relative to Indian Affairs in Maine, 1722–1726* (Boston, 1901), 11–12.

46. Church, *The History of the Great Indian War*, 247. Presumably, these men were only fit for garrison duty.

47. Baxter, *Documentary History*, Vol. IX, 140–43; *Annals of Lancaster*, 224–41; Mather, *Decennium Luctuosum*, 223–24.

48. Church, *The History of the Great Indian War*, 158.

49. Cagon's descriptions of the terrain over which they traveled and of their campsites are so detailed it is almost possible to follow their exact route on a modern map of New Hampshire.

50. "Journal of Captain John Cagon," *Massachusetts Archives*, Vol. 38A, 19, 20.

51. Samuel A. Green, *Groton During the Indian Wars* (Groton, MA, 1883), 98–101. For more about this incident, see chapter 9.

52. Baxter, *Documentary History*, Vol. V, 261–63.

53. Ibid., 264–70; Joseph Dow, *History of the Town of Hampton, New Hampshire: From Its Settlement in 1638, to the Autumn of 1892* (Salem, MA, 1893; reprinted, Somersworth, NH, 1970), 227.

54. Baxter, *Documentary History*, Vol. V, 277.

55. Ibid., 280–83; Dow, *History of Hampton*, 227.

56. Church, *The History of the Great Indian War*, 160–70; Drake, *The Border Wars of New England*, 39.

57. Mather, *Decennium Luctuosum*, 225–26; Church, *The History of the Great Indian War*, 180–93.

58. Church, *The History of the Great Indian War*, 223–40; Drake, *The Border Wars of New England*, 113–14.

59. Church, *The History of the Great Indian War*, 184.

60. "Francis Nicholson and Samuel Vetch to Earl of Sunderland, June 28, 1709," *Calendar of State Papers*, Vol. 24, No. 604.

61. Mather, *Decennium Luctuosum*, 203; Baxter, *Documentary History*, Vol. IX, 70.

62. Penhallow, *The History of the Wars of New England*, 8; "Minutes of Massachusetts Council, October 14, 1703," *Calendar of State Papers*, Vol. 21, No. 1144.

63. Penhallow, *The History of the Wars of New England*, 9; "Address to the Massachusetts Assembly by Governor Joseph Dudley, October 27, 1703," *Calendar of State Papers*, Vol. 21, No. 1201.

64. "Governor Joseph Dudley to the Council of Trade and Plantations, December 19, 1703," *Calendar of State Papers*, Vol. 21, 1398.

65. "Governor Joseph Dudley to the Council of Trade and Plantations, January 1, 1707," *Calendar of State Papers*, Vol. 23, No. 691.

66. "Gentlemen Concerned in Providing Masts to the Council of Trade and Plantations, February 14, 1706," *Calendar of State Papers*, Vol. 23, No. 113.

67. Church, *The History of the Great Indian War*, 245–49. For Church's recommendations concerning firearms, see chapter 8.

68. Penhallow, *The History of the Wars of New England*, 17.

69. Church, *The History of the Great Indian War*, 165–85; Drake, *The Border Wars of New England*, 196–99.

70. "Governor Joseph Dudley to the Council of Trade and Plantations, December 28, 1703," *Calendar of State Papers*, Vol. 21, No. 1398, 1422.

71. "Minutes of New Hampshire Council in Assembly, December 23, 1703," *Calendar of State Papers*, Vol. 21, No. 1409.

72. Baxter, *Documentary History*, Vol. IX, 140–43. Hilton described the Indian town as being circular with about 100 wigwams and storehouses surrounded by a palisade.

73. Ibid., 142.

74. "Governor Joseph Dudley to the Council of Trade and Plantations, March 3, 1704," *Calendar of State Papers*, Vol. 22, No. 159; Baxter, *Documentary History*, Vol. IX, 142.

75. Penhallow, *The History of the Wars of New England*, 11.

76. Baxter, *Documentary History*, Vol. X, 326.

77. Ibid., Vol. IX, 180; "Governor Joseph Dudley to the Council of Trade and Plantations, April 20, 1704," *Calendar of State Papers*, Vol. 22, 260.

78. Belknap, *The History of New Hampshire*, 259.

79. Chandler E. Potter, *The Military History of New Hampshire from Its Founding until the Present Time* (Report of the Adjutant-General of the State of New Hampshire for the Year ending June 1, 1866 (Concord, NH, 1866), 23; "Journal of the Rev. John Pike," *Massachusetts Historical Society Proceedings, 1875–1876*, Vol. XIV, 145; Penhallow, *The History of the Wars of New England*, 40–41. It is now Scarborough, Maine.

80. Penhallow, *The History of the Wars of New England*, 40.

81. Trask, *Letters of Colonel Thomas Westbrook*, 11–12.

82. "Minutes of Massachusetts Council, December 2, 1703," *Calendar of State Papers*, Vol. 21, No. 1344.

83. See chapter 7.

84. "Governor Joseph Dudley to Lt-Governor John Usher, November, 28 1703," *Calendar of State Papers*, Vol. 21, No. 1425f. The term "volunteer" can be confusing here. The new bounty hunters were referred to as volunteers, but there were also volunteer soldiers (as opposed to pressed soldiers and hired soldiers). Dudley was concerned that the volunteer soldiers would imitate the bounty hunters, who went out when they pleased, whereas soldiers, who had a guaranteed income from the government, could be ordered to march anywhere and at any time. To eliminate confusion in the present work, the new kind of volunteer will be always referred to as scalp hunters.

85. "Governor Joseph Dudley to Lt-Governor John Usher, November 28, 1703," *Calendar of State Papers*, Vol. 21, No. 1425 h.

86. *Journals of the Rev. Thomas Smith and the Rev. Samuel Deane* (Portland, ME, 1849), 121.

87. The commission in snowshoe companies was a provincial rank and was considered separate from the local militia rank, even though the men in the company belonged to both. For example, Seth Pomeroy received two commissions from the government: one as an officer in the militia and one as an officer of the local snowshoe company. The first was political, and the second was military. See Louis E. de Forest, ed., *The Journal and Papers of Seth Pomeroy* (New Haven, CT, 1926), 10–11.

88. Baron St. Casteen, and his son after him, maintained a trading post on the Penobscot River. Sebastian Rale came to the New World with Frontenac in 1689 and took over the mission at Norridgewock almost immediately. A raiding party under Thomas Westbrook supposedly found incriminating letters at Norridgewock proving that Rale, with the blessing of the French government, was purposely agitating the Indians against the English. At least that was the story. John Fiske, *New France and New England* (Boston, 1902), 235–43; Penhallow, *The History of the Wars of New England*, 99.

89. Penhallow, *The History of the Wars of New England*, 84.

90. Ibid., 86–87.

91. For more about the specifics of the fight, see chapter 10.

92. "Journal of Johnson Harmon" in Banks, *History of York*, 326–29; Fannie Eckstorm, "The Attack on Norridgewock: 1724," *New England Quarterly* (1934), 541–78; Thomas Hutchinson, *The History of the Colony and Province of Massachusetts Bay* (London, 1768; reprint, Cambridge, MA, 1936), 235–37.

93. Eckstorm, "The Attack on Norridgewock: 1724," *New England Quarterly* (1934), 553–55. Estimates on the number of enemies killed are always subject to a great deal of imagination and guesswork, but Norridgewock represents the greatest number of Indians slain in one action (including both sexes and all ages, of course) since the beginning of the French wars

94. Penhallow, *The History of the Wars of New England*, 106.

95. Fiske, *New France and New England*, 244.

96. Penhallow, *The History of the Wars of New England*, 112–17; Hutchinson, *History of Massachusetts Bay*, 239; George Hill Evans, *Pigwacket* (Somerville, MA, 1939), 62–66. See chapter 10 for more details on the fight.

97. Baxter, *Documentary History*, Vol. XXIII, 151. "16th came upon tracks of Indians, left packs with 16 men and pursued"—Lovewell's Journal of his February scout.

98. In particular, see Thomas Symmes, *Historical Memoirs of the Battle at Piggwacket, or Lovewell Lament'd* (Boston, 1725).

99. See Penhallow, *The History of the Wars of New England*, 113, 116.

100. Charles E. Clark, *The Eastern Frontier: The Settlement of Northern New England, 1610–1763* (New York: Knopf, 1970), 97. "After this fight," wrote Jeremy Belknap, "the Indians moved away from Pequawket until the peace." See Belknap, *The History of New Hampshire*, 210.

101. Hammond, *NHSP*, Vol. XVIII, 223.

102. See William Howard Brown, *Colonel John Goffe: Eighteenth Century New Hampshire* (Manchester, NH: Lew A. Cummings, 1950), 38–40.

103. Brown, *John Goffe*, 48.

104. "Journal of Capt Eleazer Melvin," *New Hampshire Historical Society Collections*, Vol. 5 (1837), 208–11. For more details on this raid, see chapter 10.

105. Melvin Journal, *NHHS*.

106. Brown, *John Goffe*, 48. See chapter 3 for more information on Fort Atkinson.
107. Drake, *The Border Wars of New England*, 165.
108. Ibid., 37.
109. Ibid., 113–14.
110. Ibid., 202.
111. Penhallow, *The History of the Wars of New England*, 19.
112. Ibid., 40; Drake, *The Border Wars of New England*, 220.
113. "Governor Joseph Dudley to Council of Trade and Plantations, September 15, 1703," *Calendar of State Papers*, Vol. 21, No. 1094.
114. Penhallow, *The History of the Wars of New England*, 60–61.
115. Guy Chet, *Conquering the American Wilderness: The Triumph of European Warfare in the Colonial Northeast* (Amherst: University of Massachusetts Press, 2003), 144.
116. Ibid.
117. W. J. Eccles, *Canada under Louis XIV, 1663–1701* (London: McClelland and Stewart, 1964), 173.
118. John Ferling, *Struggle for a Continent: The Wars of Early America* (Arlington Heights, IL: Harlan Davidson, 1993), 87.
119. John Grenier, *The First Way of War: American War Making on the Frontier* (New York: Cambridge University Press, 2005), 37.
120. Ibid., 37–38.
121. Penhallow, *The History of the Wars of New England*, 9.
122. See Eccles, *Canada under Louis XIV*, 171.

CHAPTER 5

1. W. J. Eccles, *The Canadian Frontier, 1534–1760* (Albuquerque: University of New Mexico Press, 1974), 139.
2. Jeremy Belknap, *The History of New Hampshire* (reprint of 1831 edition, New York, 1970) Vol. 1, 295.
3. "Lt-Governor John Usher to Council of Trade and Plantations, June 28, 1708," *Calendar of State Papers, Colonial Series, America and West Indies, 1706–1708* (reprint of 1916 edition, Vaduz, 1964), Vol. 23, No. 1592.
4. "Governor Joseph Dudley to the Council of Trade and Plantations, March, 1709," in James Phinney Baxter, ed., *Documentary History of the State of Maine* (Portland, ME, 1907), *Collections of the Maine Historical Society*, 2nd Series, Vol. IX, 264. Cotton Mather compared the French and Indians to Rooks in a tree. See Cotton Mather, *Decennium Luctuosum* (1699; reprinted in Charles H. Lincoln, ed., *Narratives of the Indian Wars, 1675–1699*, New York, 1913), 214.
5. See "Nicholas Bayard to Francis Nicholson, August 5, 1689," *Calendar of State Papers, Colonial Series, America and West Indies, 1689–1692* (reprint of 1903 edition, Vaduz, 1964), Vol. 13, No. 320. See also "Elisha Hutchison to Elisha Cook, March 31, 1690," *Calendar of State Papers*, Vol. 13, No. 802.
6. Anon, "Phips Expedition to Canada," *Proceedings of the Massachusetts Historical Society*, Vol. XV, Second Series, 318.
7. John Brewer, *The Sinews of Power: War, Money and the English State* (Cambridge: Harvard University Press, 1988), 12.

8. Ibid., xv.
9. Anon, "Phips Expedition to Canada," 318.
10. Belknap, *The History of New Hampshire*, 177.
11. Ibid., 180.
12. Ibid.; "Governor Joseph Dudley to Council of Trade and Plantations, November 15, 1710," *Calendar of State Papers, Colonial Series, America and West Indies, 1710-June, 1711* (reprint of 1924 edition, Vaduz, 1964), Vol. 25, No. 491.
13. "Thomas Savage to his brother in England, 1691" (originally published in London, 1691), *Collections of the Massachusetts Historical Society*, 2nd Ser., Vol. III, 257. Nevertheless, even preserved food was subject to spoiling if held too long. See Nathaniel Bouton, *Documents and Records Relating to the Province of New Hampshire from 1738-1749* (Nashua, NH, 1871), *New Hampshire State and Provincial Papers* [hereafter cited as *NHSP*], Vol. V, 519.
14. "Records of the Council, Feb. 22, 1745," *NHSP*, Vol. V, 101.
15. "Francis Nicholson and Samuel Vetch to Council of Trade and Plantations, September 16, 1710," *Calendar of State Papers*, Vol. 25, No. 396.
16. "Minutes of a Council of War, June 21, 1711," *Calendar of State Papers*, Vol. 25, No. 893.
17. "Colonel Richard King to Mr. Secretary St John, July 25, 1711," *Calendar of State Papers, Colonial Series, America and West Indies, July, 1711-June, 1712* (reprint of 1925 edition, Vaduz, 1964), Vol. 26, No. 46.
18. Douglas Leach, *Arms for Empire: A Military History of the British Colonies in North America, 1607-1763* (New York: Macmillan, 1973), 266.
19. Gary B. Nash, *The Urban Crucible: The Northern Seaports and the Origins of the American Revolution*, abridged ed. (Cambridge: Harvard University Press, 1986), 46-47.
20. "Pepperrell to Shirley, 10 April, 1745," *Collections of the Massachusetts Historical Society*, 1st Ser., Vol. I (1794), 14-16.
21. "Pepperrell Papers," *Collections of the Massachusetts Historical Society*, 6th Ser., Vol. X (1899), 124-25.
22. Chandler E. Potter, *The Military History of New Hampshire from Its Founding until the Present Time* (Report of the Adjutant-General of the State of New Hampshire for the Year Ending June 1, 1866 (Concord, NH, 1866), 73-75.
23. "Pepperrell Papers," Vol. X, 348-49.
24. "Pepperrell Papers," Vol. X, 358, 365-66.
25. Francis Parkman, *Count Frontenac and New France under Louis XIV* (Boston, 1896), 245.
26. "Governor Joseph Dudley to Council of Trade and Plantations, November 15, 1710," *Calendar of State Papers*, Vol. 25, No. 491.
27. Fairfax Downey, *Louisbourg: Key to a Continent* (Englewood Cliffs, NJ: Prentice-Hall, 1965), 63.
28. "Thomas Cockrill to Council of Trade and Plantations, July 2, 1709," *Calendar of State Papers*, Vol. 24, No. 617; see "Charles Redford to Sir Edmund Andros, March 7, 1689," *Calendar of State Papers*, Vol. 13, No. 783.
29. Julian Gwyn, "War and Economic Change: Louisbourg and the New England Economy in the 1740's," *Revue de l'Université d'Ottawa*, 47, No. 1-2 (1977), 122. Gwyn indicated that "New England's trade with Great Britain, upon which so much of her American earnings depended, reached in 1745 the lowest point of the entire war. It is to the deflection of shipping to the Louisbourg expedition that this can be directly attributed."
30. Leach, *Arms for Empire*, 139.

31. "Canada Survey'd, July 27, 1708," and "Colonel John Higginson of New England, June 30, 1709," *Calendar of State Papers*, Vol. 24, Nos. 60, 609.

32. Leach, *Arms for Empire*, 139. Vetch had earlier been accused of trading with the enemy when sent to Nova Scotia to negotiate for the release of captives. For more about Vetch, see G. M. Waller, *Samuel Vetch, Colonial Enterpriser* (Chapel Hill: University of North Carolina Press, 1960).

33. "Canada Survey'd, July 27, 1708," *Calendar of State Papers*, Vol. 24, No. 60.

34. "Council of Trade and Plantations to Secretary of State Henry Boyle, August 4, 1708," and "Secretary Boyle to Council of Trade and Plantations, August 11, 1708," *Calendar of State Papers*, Vol. 24, Nos. 71, 85.

35. "Explanatory Supplement to Vetch's Canada Proposal, November 17, 1708," *Calendar of State Papers*, Vol. 24, No. 196.

36. "Samuel Vetch to Council of Trade and Plantations, November 29, 1708," *Calendar of State Papers*, Vol. 24, No. 217.

37. "Council of Trade and Plantations to the Queen, December 1, 1708," *Calendar of State Papers*, Vol. 24, No. 221.

38. "H. M. Instructions for Colonel Vetch, March 1, 1709," and "Francis Nicholson and Samuel Vetch to Earl of Sunderland, June 28, 1709," *Calendar of State Papers*, Vol. 24, Nos. 387, 604.

39. "Samuel Vetch to Secretary Boyle, June 28, 1709," *Calendar of State Papers*, Vol. 24, No. 602. Vetch first reminded Boyle that he had mentioned the possibility that Vetch would be named governor of Canada.

40. *Calendar of State Papers*, Vol. 24, Nos. 606, 612. News of this change in plan was sent to the colonies on July 27 and did not arrive until October 11. See "Memoranda Taken from Sunderland's book of Letters, July 1, 1709," *Calendar of State Papers*, Vol. 24, Nos. 658, 794.

41. "Governor Joseph Dudley to Council of Trade and Plantations, August 16, 1709," *Calendar of State Papers*, Vol. 24, No. 691.

42. "Samuel Vetch to Earl of Sunderland, August 2, 12, 1709," *Calendar of State Papers*, Vol. 24, No. 666.

43. Ibid.

44. Isaac Hammond, ed., *Miscellaneous Provincial and State Papers* (Manchester, NH, 1890), *New Hampshire Provincial and State Papers*, Vol. XVIII, 242–45.

45. "Governor Joseph Dudley, Francis Nicholson, Samuel Vetch and Samuel Moody to Earl of Sunderland, October 24, 1709," *Calendar of State Papers*, Vol. 24, No. 794; Douglas Edward Leach, *Roots of Conflict: British Armed Forces and Colonial Americans, 1677–1763* (Chapel Hill: University of North Carolina Press, 1986), 28.

46. "Account of Charges for Intended Expedition," *Calendar of State Papers*, Vol. 25, No. 81, iii. "The account broke down as follows: Wages and subsistence for 973 officers and men between May 18 and October 14—£12,973/18/8; Wages and subsistence for three ministers—£70/6/; Wages and subsistence for three doctors and assistants—£403/11/1; Coats provided the soldiers—£888/0/3; Hire of transports—£5272/10/9; Beer and water in casks put on transports—£669/4/10; Fitting transports—£467/7/1; 16 whaleboats—£160; Sloop equipped for war, wages and subsistence—£815/10/; Two vessels to guard coast in absence of *Province* galley—£1701/17/; Provisions with utensils—£5301/6/8; 38 drums with case—£83/12/; Building of barracks—£106/5/8; Clothing shipped for expedition—£1715/2/6; Ammunition—£120; 'Charge upon 6 Maquas that came down to see the fleet'—£109; Total—£30,811/12/6."

47. "Governor Joseph Dudley, Francis Nicholson, Samuel Vetch and Samuel Moody to Earl of Sunderland, October 24, 1709," *Calendar of State Papers*, Vol. 24, No. 794.

48. See "Treasury Minutes for February 13, 1712," *Calendar of State Papers*, Vol. 26, No. 308, for reference to compensation for the reduction of Port Royal in 1710. Julian Gwyn believed the compensation for Louisbourg was an "unprecedented action on the part of the British government," which "inaugurated a new policy by which colonies were partly reimbursed for their military expenses incurred on behalf of the Empire." But, actually, the precedent was established after the aborted 1709 expedition. Gwyn, "War and Economic Change," 126.

49. For example, the final authorization for payment of the large Louisbourg debt did not come until five years after the fall of the fortress. See Hammond, *NHSP*, Vol. XVIII, "Duke of Newcastle to Governor William Shirley," 323–24; "Warrant for re-imbursing New Hampshire for expenses of Cape Breton Expedition, 1750," 383.

50. "Thomas Savage to his brother in England, 1691," Vol. 3, 257.

51. "Pepperrell Papers," Vol. X, 144.

52. Ibid., 241, 266.

53. See chapter 6 for more about ammunition supplies.

54. Leach, *Roots of Conflict*, 51. See chapters 6 and 7 as well.

55. "Governor Joseph Dudley to Council of Trade and Plantations, November 26, 1704," *Calendar of State Papers, Colonial Series, America and West Indies, 1704–1705* (reprint of 1916 edition, Vaduz, 1964), Vol. 22, No. 679; Thomas Hutchinson, *The History of the Colony and Province of Massachusetts Bay* (London, 1768; reprint, Cambridge, MA, 1936), 53.

56. Parkman, *Count Frontenac*, 245.

57. Downey, *Louisbourg*, 59–60.

58. "T. W. Waldron and Jonathan Prescut to the Governor, Council and House of Representatives of New Hampshire, September, 24, 1745," in Hammond, *NHSP*, Vol. XVIII, 238.

59. Hammond, *NHSP*, Vol. XVIII, 105–6; "Francis Nicholson and Samuel Vetch to Earl of Sunderland, June 28, 1709," *Calendar of State Papers*, Vol. 24, No. 604. See chapter 7 for more about recruiting, provincial prejudice against garrison duty, and the consequences of extended duty.

60. "Explanatory Supplement to Vetch's Canada Proposal, November 17, 1708," *Calendar of State Papers*, Vol. 24, No. 196. Vetch wrote that seven hundred regulars were needed to garrison Quebec; two hundred for Trois Rivière; three hundred for Montreal; two hundred for Port Royal; and two hundred for Placentia.

61. "T. W. Waldron and Jonathan Prescut to the Governor [et. al.]," in Hammond, *NHSP*, Vol. XVIII, 238.

62. Henry Guerlac, "Vauban: The Impact of Science on War," in Edward Mead Earle, ed., *Makers of Modern Strategy: Military Thought from Machiavelli to Hitler* (1943; Princeton, NJ, 1971), 34. Most battles that did occur had at their origin the need to relieve a besieged fortress or city.

63. John Keegan and Richard Holmes, *Soldiers: A History of Men in Battle* (New York: Viking, 1985), 172–74; Guerlac, "Vauban," in Earle, *Makers of Modern Strategy*, 30–40; Archer Jones, *The Art of War in the Western World* (Urbana, IL, 1987), 280–81.

64. "Pepperrell Papers," Vol. X, 138.

65. Ibid., 151–53.

66. Ibid., 155; "Samuel Rhodes to William Pepperrell, May 7, 1745."

67. "Pepperrell Papers," Vol. X, 191.

68. Ibid., 166–68. See also Louis E. De Forest, ed., *Louisbourg Journals: 1745* (New York, 1932), 17, 18.

69. "Francis Nicholson and Samuel Vetch to the Council of Trade and Plantations, Sept 16, 1710," *Calendar of State Papers*, Vol. 25, No. 396, reporting the cost of the "company of gunners and mattrosses belonging to the [artillery] traine"; "Pepperrell Papers," Vol. X, 168, "Peter Warren to William Pepperrell, May 13, 1745."

70. "Board of Ordnance to Council of Trade and Plantations, August 8, 1704," *Calendar of State Papers*, Vol. 22, No. 499. The Board of Ordnance assigned the engineer "for H. M. service in New England, New York and neighboring Continent of America."

71. Romer requested a replacement because "he labours under a distemper not curable in those parts for want of experienced surgeons." "Council of Trade and Plantations to Board of Ordnance, Nov. 19, 1703," *Calendar of State Papers*, Vol. 21, No. 1287.

72. "Colonel Romer to Council of Trade and Plantations, March 28, 1705," *Calendar of State Papers*, Vol. 22, No. 983. The "calamityes" would continue for Romer. On the return voyage, eight years of work—all his papers and detailed sketches and drawings of the colonial fortifications he had built or maintained—had to be tossed overboard when his ship was captured by the French. Romer was held as a prisoner of war in France for a while until exchanged. See "Romer to Council of Trade and Plantations, August 30, 1708," *Calendar of State Papers*, Vol. 24, No. 123.

73. "Governor Joseph Dudley to Council of Trade and Plantations, July 25, 1705," *Calendar of State Papers*, Vol. 22, No. 1274.

74. "Captain John Redknap to Council of Trade and Plantations, February 20, 1708," *Calendar of State Papers*, Vol. 23, No. 1347.

75. "Lt-Governor John Usher to Council of Trade and Plantations, June 28, 1708," *Calendar of State Papers*, Vol. 23, No. 1592.

76. John Ferling, *Struggle for a Continent: The Wars of Early America* (Arlington Heights, IL: Harlan Davidson, 1993), 88.

77. Leach, *Roots of Conflict*, 64–66.

78. The only other English officers were the captains of the small Royal Navy warships supporting the operation. They apparently agreed with Redknap's assessment.

79. Leach, *Roots of Conflict*, 74.

80. Ibid., 69.

81. "Pepperrell Papers," Vol. X, 332–34; "Shirley to Pepperrell, July 7, 1745."

82. *Journal of Colonel John Storer of Wells, Maine in the Expedition against Louisbourg, 1745* (typewritten copy in the Maine Historical Society), March 19.

83. Samuel Adams Drake, *The Border Wars of New England, Commonly Called King William's and Queen Anne's Wars* (1897; reprint of 1910 edition, Williamstown, MA, 1973), 62–63.

84. "Journal of Benjamin Stearns," *Proceedings of the Massachusetts Historical Society*, Vol. 42, 137–44.

85. De Forest, *Louisbourg Journals*, 3.

86. "Storer Journal," April 8.

87. Ibid., April 23.

88. De Forest, *Louisbourg Journals*, 6.

89. "Storer Journal," April 8; De Forest, *Louisbourg Journals*, 9.

90. De Forest, *Louisbourg Journals*, 11.//
91. Hutchinson, *The History of the Colony and Province of Massachusetts Bay*, 126.//
92. "Narrative of Mr. John Wise, Minister of God's Word at Chebacco," *Proceedings of the Massachusetts Historical Society*, Series II, Vol. XV, 292.//
93. "Pepperrell Papers," Vol. X, 43, 50. Among the liquors mentioned were rum, Madeira wine, claret wine, cider, "(half pint of rum w/ beer & sugar (flip)," and "half pint of rum w/ water & sugar (punch)."//
94. "Storer Journal," April 23.//
95. Belknap, *History of New Hampshire*, 278.//
96. Hutchison, *The History of the Colony and Province of Massachusetts Bay*, 126.//
97. De Forest, *Louisbourg Journals*, 17.//
98. Drake, *The Border Wars of New England*, 63–65.//
99. Ibid., 234–35.//
100. Belknap, *History of New Hampshire*, 277.//
101. De Forest, *Louisbourg Journals*, 69. The provincial regiments at Cartagena were also used by the British as human pack mules. In one assault they carried no weapons, but they bore the scaling ladders and fascines to be used by the regulars. Leach, *Roots of Conflict*, 56. See also chapter 9.//
102. "Narrative of Mr. John Wise," 292–93.//
103. De Forest, *Louisbourg Journals*, 10.//
104. Downey, *Louisbourg*, 96.//
105. Hutchinson, *The History of the Colony and Province of Massachusetts Bay*, 126.//
106. Leach, *Arms for Empire*, 242. For more about disease and medical problems concerning provincial soldiers, see chapter 11.//
107. Parkman, *Count Frontenac*, 382–84.//
108. George F. G. Stanley, *New France: The Last Phase, 1744–1760* (Toronto: McClelland and Stewart, 1968), 17–18.//
109. Leach, *Roots of Conflict*, 164.

CHAPTER 6

1. John Keegan and Richard Holmes, *Soldiers: A History of Men in Battle* (New York: Viking, 1985), 221–25.//
2. Lee Kennett and James LaVerne Anderson, *The Gun in America: The Origins of a National Dilemma* (Westport, CT: Greenwood Press, 1975), 13; André Corvisier, *Armies and Societies in Europe, 1494–1789*, trans. Abigail T. Siddall (Bloomington, IL: Indiana University Press, 1979), 9–10.//
3. In 1670, the income was £150 per annum. Kennett and Anderson, *The Gun in America*, 22–23.//
4. Harold L. Peterson, *Arms and Armor in Colonial America, 1526–1783* (New York: Bramhall House, 1956), 7. See Patrick M. Malone, *The Skulking Way of War: Technology and Tactics among the New England Indians* (Baltimore, MD: Johns Hopkins University Press, 1991).//
5. Darrett B. Rutman, *A Militant New World, 1607–40* (New York: Arno Press, 1979), 744.//
6. "An Act for Regulating of the Militia, Nov. 22, 1693," Massachusetts Militia Laws, *Background of Selective Service* (Washington, 1947), Vol. II, 139.

7. "An Act for the Regulating of the Militia, May 14, 1718," New Hampshire Militia Laws, *Background of Selective Service*, 57; "An Act for Regulating of the Militia, Nov. 22, 1693," Massachusetts Militia Laws, *Background of Selective Service*, 45.

8. "An Act for the Regulating of the Militia, May 14, 1718," 51; "An Act for Regulating of the Militia, Nov. 22, 1693," 138.

9. Kennett and Anderson, *The Gun in America*, 45.

10. *American Antiquarian Society*, Mass. Col. 1629–1869, Box 3, Folder 11: Militia returns, Officers commissions and Misc. Papers 1696–1762: John Chandler's Report.

11. Herbert Milton Sylvester, *Indian Wars of New England* (Boston, 1910), Vol. III, 303.

12. Men who had three sons in the militia were exempt from training, but according to law the father was still required to possess a weapon and ammunition. See "An Act for Regulating of the Militia, Nov. 22, 1693," 139; "Petition of John Bowers and Others," in James Phinney Baxter, ed., *Documentary History of the State of Maine* (Portland, ME, 1897), *Collections of the Maine Historical Society*, 2nd Series, Vol. V, 52–53.

13. "An Act for Regulating of the Militia, Nov. 22, 1693," 140; "An Act for Settling the Militia, March 24, 1688," New Hampshire Militia Laws, *Background of Selective Service*, 13.

14. "The Journal of Dr. Benjamin Bullivant," *Proceedings of the Massachusetts Historical Society*, Vol. XVI, First Series, 107.

15. J. A. Houlding, *Fit for Service: The Training of the British Army, 1715–1795* (Oxford: Oxford University Press, 1981), 140.

16. "Joseph Dudley to the Board of Trade, Oct 27, 1703" in James Phinney Baxter, ed., *Documentary History of the State of Maine* (Portland, ME, 1907), *Collections of the Maine Historical Society*, 2nd Series, Vol. IX, 161.

17. "George Vaughn to Council of Trade and Plantations, March 1, 1709," *Calendar of State Papers, Colonial Series, America and West Indies, June, 1708–1709* (reprint of 1922 edition, Vaduz, 1964), Vol. 24, No. 393.

18. "An Act for Levying Soldiers, Nov. 23, 1693," Massachusetts Laws, *Background of Selective Service*, 146.

19. "Petition relative to a Slave of Theodore Atkinson who was in the Louisbourg Expedition," in Isaac Hammond, ed., *Miscellaneous Provincial and State Papers* (Manchester, NH, 1890), *New Hampshire Provincial and State Papers* [hereafter cited as *NHSP*], Vol. XVIII, 279; "Petition of Eleazer Young, Jr., Dec 14, 1744," in Isaac Hammond, ed., *Documents Relating to Towns In New Hampshire, "A" to "F" Inclusive, 1680–1800* (Concord, NH, 1882), *New Hampshire Provincial and State Papers*, Vol. XI, 514.

20. For examples, see Hammond, *NHSP*, Vol. XVIII, 245–50.

21. "Joseph Dudley to the Board of Trade, Oct 27, 1703," in Baxter, *Documentary History*, Vol. IX, 161.

22. Clayton Cramer reviews various studies in *Armed America: The Story of How and Why Guns Became as American as Apple Pie* (Nashville, TN: Nelson Currant, 2006), 51–55. While outside New England, Gloria Main found that 76 percent of young fathers in six Maryland counties owned firearms, including 50 percent of the poorest and 96 percent of the richest. See Gloria Main, "Many Things Forgotten: The Use of Probate Records in Arming America," *William and Mary Quarterly*, 3rd Series, Vol. LIX, Number 1, 213. This article was part of a forum that discussed Michael A. Bellesiles's controversial *Arming America: The Origin of a National Gun Culture* (New York: Knopf, 2000). Bellesiles made the claim that gun ownership in colonial America was uncommon, a claim that has been pretty thoroughly refuted.

23. John J. McCusker and Russell R. Menard, *The Economy of British America, 1607-1789* (Chapel Hill: University of North Carolina Press, 1985), 97.

24. "Council of Trade and Plantation to Governor Joseph Dudley, January 16, 1710," and "Ambrose Crowley to Arthur Moore, Council of Trade and Plantations," *Calendar of State Papers, Colonial Series, America and West Indies, 1710-June, 1711* (reprint of 1924 edition, Vaduz, 1964), Vol. 25, No. 34, 578; Arthur Cecil Bining, *British Regulation of the Colonial Iron Industry* (Philadelphia: University of Pennsylvania Press, 1933); Darrett B. Rutman, *The Morning of America, 1603-1789* (Boston: Houghton Mifflin, 1971), 61.

25. Kennett and Anderson, *The Gun in America*, 40; M. L. Brown, *Firearms in Colonial America: The Impact on History and Technology, 1492-1792* (Washington, DC: Smithsonian, 1980), 130.

26. Brown, *Firearms in Colonial America*, 130. By the last quarter of the seventeenth century the gunmaking industry in England had achieved a great deal of specialization as arms merchants contracted with gunsmiths who subcontracted with craftsmen who specialized in barrel forging or lock making. These parts were then assembled by the gunsmiths who basically "stocked" or carved the wooden stock to receive the metal parts, a common practice in the New World as well, when they could get the parts from England. London had been the principal center of gunmaking in England, but in 1683 Birmingham gunsmiths accepted a government contract. By 1690 they were producing 200 military muskets per month and were about to enter the commercial market.

27. "Answer to Sir Edmund Andros's Account of Forces raised, &c." in Baxter, *Documentary History*, Vol. V, 124; examples of appeals for weapons are numerous. For an example, see "Dudley to Council of Trade and Plantation, July 13, 1704," *Calendar of State Papers, Colonial Series, America and West Indies, 1704-1705* (reprint of 1916 edition, Vaduz, 1964), Vol. 22, No. 455, and "Dudley to Board, Oct 27, 1703," in Baxter, *Documentary History*, Vol. IX, 161.

28. "Council of Trade and Plantations to Queen, February 16, 1704," *Calendar of State Papers*, Vol. 22, No. 109. In this instance, the ship sent with goods to pay for the weapons was captured by the French. See "Council of Trade and Plantation to Queen, November 7, 1704," *Calendar of State Papers*, Vol. 22, No. 645.

29. "Enlistment proclamation for Port Royal, 1710," *Calendar of State Papers*, Vol. 25, No. 491 i.

30. Samuel Penhallow, *The History of the Wars of New England with the Eastern Indians* (Boston, 1726; facsimile reprint, annotated by Edward Wheelock, Williamstown, MA, 1973), 50: Hammond, *NHSP*, Vol. XVIII, 105.

31. Houlding, *Fit for Service*, 141.

32. "Letter Isaac Addington Secretary, to Joseph Prout," Nov. 14, 1689, in Baxter, *Documentary History*, Vol. V, 7; "Pepperrell Papers," *Collections of the Massachusetts Historical Society*, 6th Ser., Vol. X (1899), 95

33. "Dudley to Board of Trade, Jan. 31, 1710" in Baxter, *Documentary History*, Vol. IX, 285.

34. "William Shirley to Benning Wentworth, Oct 29, 1747" in Hammond, *NHSP*, Vol. XVIII, 325-27; "Joseph Dudley to Council of Trade and Plantations, December 2, 1712," *Calendar of State Papers, Colonial Series, America and West Indies, July, 1712-July, 1714* (reprint of 1926 edition, Vaduz, 1964), Vol. 27, No. 153.

35. Although the records are hazy, it does appear that Prescott may have been from Massachusetts. Myron O. Stachiw, ed., *Massachusetts Officers and Soldiers, 1723–43: Dummer's War to the War of Jenkins's Ear* (Boston: Society of Colonial Wars of Massachusetts, 1979).

36. "William Shirley to Benning Wentworth, Sept. 25, 1744," in Hammond, *NHSP*, Vol. XVIII, 211.

37. "Petition from Louisbourg Soldiers, 1745," "Soldiers Losses at Louisbourg," in Hammond, *NHSP*, Vol. XVIII, 245–49.

38. "An Act for Levying Soldiers, Nov. 23, 1693."

39. Bureaucratic mistakes were even common in the eighteenth century. On at least one occasion several soldiers were charged for the use of provincial weapons when they had supplied their own. See "Petition from Several Soldiers," in Hammond, *NHSP*, Vol. XVIII, 292–93.

40. "Pepperrell Papers," 6th Ser., Vol. X, Copies of Orders, May 26, 1745, 95.

41. Baxter, *Documentary History*, Vol. IX, 43.

42. Ibid., 66.

43. Ibid., Vol. V, 264.

44. Brown, *Firearms in Colonial America*, 279.

45. Dwight B. Demeritt Jr., *Maine Made Guns and their Makers* (Hallowell, ME, 1973), 1–2.

46. Ibid., 6.

47. Ibid., 3–4.

48. Ibid., 6.

49. William Blake Trask, *Letters of Colonel Thomas Westbrook and Others Relative to Indian Affairs in Maine, 1722-1726* (Boston, 1901), 111.

50. See Penhallow, *History of the Indian Wars*, 88.

51. "Minutes of Massachusetts Council, May 1, 1703," *Calendar of State Papers, Colonial Series, America and West Indies, December 1, 1702-1703* (reprint of 1913 edition, Vaduz, 1964), Vol. 21, No. 652.

52. "Minutes of the Massachusetts Council, August 21, 1703," *Calendar of State Papers*, Vol. 21, No. 1039. It is unclear how the weapons were actually to be repaired, but the specific precaution to attach the owner's name to each weapon indicates they were sent back to Boston.

53. "Robert Tufton Phibrook's Account, 1745," in Hammond, *NHSP*, Vol. XVIII, 241–42; George Gilmore, *Roll of New Hampshire Men at Louisbourg, Cape Breton, 1745* (Concord, NH, 1896); Rev. Charles Nelson Sinnett, *Richard Pinkham of Old Dover New Hampshire and His Descendants East and West* (Concord, NH, 1908), 23.

54. Peterson, *Arms and Armor in Colonial America*, 164–65; Brown, *Firearms in Colonial America*, 227; Houlding, *Fit for Service*, 138–39.

55. "An Act for the Regulating of the Militia, May 14, 1718," 51; "An Act for Regulating of the Militia, Nov. 22, 1693," 139.

56. Peterson, *Arms and Armor in Colonial America*, 45. The snaphaunce was an early form of flintlock that had frizzen separate from the pan.

57. See Patrick M. Malone, *The Skulking Way of War: Technology and Tactics among the New England Indians* (Baltimore: John Hopkins University Press, 1993), 40–45, for a further discussion.

58. George C. Neumann, *The History of Weapons of the American Revolution* (New York: Harper and Row, 1967), 5; John Ferling, *A Wilderness of Miseries: War and Warriors in Early America* (Westport, CT: Greenwood Press, 1980).

59. Peterson, *Arms and Armor in Colonial America*, 28–31.

60. Baxter, *Documentary History*, Vol. IX, 29; "An Act for Regulating of the Militia, Nov. 22, 1693," 139.

61. "Archaeology Comes to the Rescue of a 17th Century Shipwreck: Weaponry Recovered, 1996," http://www.mcccf.gouv.qc.ca/phips/wreck19b.htm.

62. Houlding, *Fit for Service*, 147.

63. *American Antiquarian Society* [hereafter cited as *AAS*], Curwen Family Papers, Box 3, folder 1. See chapter 10 for the effects of loading practices on firing speed.

64. Brown, *Firearms in Colonial America*, 70.

65. "An Act for the Regulating of the Militia, May 14, 1718," 51; "An Act for Regulating of the Militia, Nov. 22, 1693," 139.

66. Brown, *Firearms in Colonial America*, 138.

67. Ibid., 128.

68. Ibid., 13, 51.

69. Ibid., 86; Neumann, *The History of Weapons*, 114.

70. Brown, *Firearms in Colonial America*, 153; Neumann, *The History of Weapons*, 64; Charles E. Hanson Jr., *The Northwest Gun* (Lincoln: Nebraska State Historical Society, 1955), 2, 6–7.

71. Brown, *Firearms in Colonial America*, 140.

72. "An Act for Regulating of the Militia, Nov. 22, 1693," 139, 141; "An Act for the Regulating of the Militia, May 14, 1718," 51, 55; "Selectmen to provide full stock of Ammunition, Feb. 10, 1691," in Baxter, *Documentary History*, Vol. V, 176.

73. Brown, *Firearms in Colonial America*, 127.

74. Rutman, *A Militant New World*, 325; Kennett and Anderson, *The Gun in America*, 41.

75. "Dudley to Council of Trade and Plantations, July 25, 1705," *Calendar of State Papers*, Vol. 22, No. 1274; "An Act that the Duty of Tunnage of Shipping be Paid in Powder," passed on June 27, 1702 in Massachusetts Laws, *Background of Selective Service*, 156.

76. "Ten Single Rates to be Levied. March 14, 1690," in Baxter, *Documentary History*, Vol. V, 50.

77. "Answer to Sir Edmond Andros's Account of Forces raised, &c., May 30, 1690," in Baxter, *Documentary History*, Vol. V, 124.

78. "Report of the Lords of Trade and Plantations, June 12, 1690," *Calendar of State Papers, Colonial Series, America and West Indies, 1689–1692* (reprint of 1903 edition, Vaduz, 1964), Vol. 13, No. 941.

79. Richard R. Johnson, *Adjustment to Empire: The New England Colonies, 1675–1715* (New Brunswick: Rutgers University Press, 1981), 128.

80. Ibid., 130.

81. Baxter, *Documentary History*, Vol. IX, 111.

82. "Council of Trade and Plantation to the Queen, 1695," *Calendar of State Papers, Colonial Series, America and West Indies, May 1696 to October, 1697* (reprint of 1903 edition, Vaduz, 1964), Vol. 15, No. 1024.

83. See "Orders of Queen in Council, June 10, 1703," *Calendar of State Papers*, Vol. 21, No. 813.

84. See Jeremy Belknap, *The History of New Hampshire* (reprint of 1831 edition, New York, 1970) Vol. 1, 291; Sylvester, *Indian Wars of New England*, Vol. III, 370–75.
85. "Letter from Captain John Floyd to the Governor and Council, Jan. 27, 1691," in Baxter, *Documentary History*, Vol. V, 314.
86. Cotton Mather, *Decennium Luctuosum* (1699; reprinted in Charles H. Lincoln, ed., *Narratives of the Indian Wars, 1675–1699*, New York, 1913), 229, 268–69.
87. "New Hampshire Council and Assembly to the Queen, October 22, 1707 (received July 29, 1708)," *Calendar of State Papers*, Vol. 24, No. 65 ii.
88. "George Vaughn to Council of Trade and Plantations, July 15, 1708," *Calendar of State Papers*, Vol. 24, No. 45; "Council of Trade and Plantations to Charles Spencer, Earl of Sunderland, Secretary of State, July 19, 1708," *Calendar of State Papers*, Vol. 24, No. 54.
89. "Council of Trade and Plantations to Col. Romer, August 17, 1708," *Calendar of State Papers*, Vol. 24, No. 92; "Council of Trade and Plantations to Board of Ordnance, August 17, 1708," *Calendar of State Papers*, Vol. 24, No. 93.
90. "Board of Ordnance to Council of Trade and Plantations, August 24, 1708," *Calendar of State Papers*, Vol. 24, No. 114.
91. "Col. Romer to Council of Trade and Plantation, August 30, 1708," *Calendar of State Papers*, Vol. 24, No. 123.
92. "Council of Trade and Plantations to Queen, November 8, 1708," *Calendar of State Papers*, Vol. 24, No. 185.
93. "Orders of Queen in Council, November 25, 1708," *Calendar of State Papers*, Vol. 24, No. 205.
94. "Board of Ordnance to Council of Trade and Plantations, January 18, 1709," *Calendar of State Papers*, Vol. 24, No. 306.
95. "Order of Queen in Council, January 27, 1709," *Calendar of State Papers*, Vol. 24, No. 332.
96. "Council of Trade and Plantations to Governor Dudley, February 11, 1709," *Calendar of State Papers*, Vol. 24, No. 354.
97. "Governor Dudley to Council of Trade and Plantations, October 25, 1709," *Calendar of State Papers*, Vol. 24, No. 797.
98. See "William Vaughn to Council of Trade and Plantations, May 10, 1703," *Calendar of State Papers*, Vol. 21, No. 672; "Lt-Governor John Usher to Council of Trade and Plantations, May 16, 1703," *Calendar of State Papers*, Vol. 21, No. 698; "New Hampshire Council to Governor Dudley, November 11, 1710," *Calendar of State Papers*, Vol. 25, No. 507 i.
99. *AAS*, Curwen Family Papers, Box 3, folder 1
100. Thomas Church, *The History of the Great Indian War of 1675 and 1676 Commonly Called Philip's War, also, The Old French and Indian Wars, from 1689 to 1704* (1716; Hartford, CT, 1845), 160–70.
101. Ibid., 245–49.
102. Keegan and Holmes, *Soldiers*, 221.

CHAPTER 7

1. Kyle F. Zelner, *A Rabble in Arms: Massachusetts Towns and Militiamen during King Philip's War* (New York: NYU Press, 2009), 53–55, 68.
2. Harold E. Selesky, *War and Society in Colonial Connecticut* (New Haven: Yale University Press, 1990), 66.

3. *Background of Selective Service* (Washington, 1947), Vol. II, Massachusetts Militia Laws, 160–62; Chandler E. Potter, *The Military History of New Hampshire from Its Founding until the Present Time* (Report of the Adjutant-General of the State of New Hampshire for the Year ending June 1, 1866) (Concord, NH, 1866), 40. The quote is from the Massachusetts Levying Law of 1721. The devaluation and fluctuation of colonial currency during the French war period, especially its relative value to pounds sterling, is a subject too broad to go into detail here, beyond the immediate effects on the soldiers themselves. All references to currency in the text are colonial valuation, unless otherwise noted. For more about colonial currency and the effect on the economy, see Leslie V. Brock, "The Colonial Currency, Prices and Exchange Rates," *Essays in History*, Vol. 34, http://etext.virginia.edu/journals/EH/EH34/brock34.htm.

4. James Phinney Baxter, ed., *Documentary History of the State of Maine* (Portland, ME, 1897), *Collections of the Maine Historical Society*, 2nd Series, Vol. V, 24–25; "Massachusetts Council in Assembly, May 28, 1703," *Calendar of State Papers, Colonial Series, America and West Indies, December 1, 1702–1703* (reprint of 1913 edition, Vaduz, 1964), Vol. 21, No. 760. See also "Journal of the House, April 13, 1745," in Nathaniel Bouton, ed., *Documents and Records Relating to the Province of New Hampshire from 1738–1749* (Nashua, NH, 1871), *New Hampshire Provincial and State Papers* [hereafter cited as *NHSP*], Vol. V, 314.

5. "Minutes of New Hampshire Council in Assembly, October 1, 1703," *Calendar of State Papers*, Vol. 21, No. 1114.

6. "Gov. Shirley's Communication, Jan. 25, 1745," in Bouton, *NHSP*, Vol. V, 266; Massachusetts Militia Laws, *Background of Selective Service*, 160.

7. Massachusetts Militia Laws, *Background of Selective Service*, 146, 162, 174. The deduction for the use of firearms was reduced to three pence in 1721, but by 1745 the fee was increased to the earlier four pence. Other equipment, initially supplied by the soldiers but replaced because of wear or damage, was provided by the government and the cost was deducted from the soldiers' pay. See "Minutes of Massachusetts Council, August 19, 1703," *Calendar of State Papers*, Vol. 21, No. 1039.

8. H. C. B. Rogers, *The British Army of the Eighteenth Century* (New York: Hippocrene, 1977), 46.

9. "Samuel Vetch to Earl of Sunderland, August 2, 12, 1709," *Calendar of State Papers, Colonial Series, America and West Indies, June, 1708–1709* (reprint of 1922 edition, Vaduz, 1964), Vol. 24, No. 666.

10. "Shirley to Wentworth, November, 24, 1747," in Isaac Hammond, ed., *Miscellaneous Provincial and State Papers* (Manchester, NH, 1890), *New Hampshire Provincial and State Papers*, Vol. XVIII, 320.

11. "Letter of Jeremiah Moulton, 1724," in William Blake Trask, ed., *Letters of Colonel Thomas Westbrook and others Relative to Indian Affairs in Maine, 1722–1726* (Boston, 1901), 56.

12. "Pepperrell Papers," *Collections of the Massachusetts Historical Society*, 6th Ser., Vol. X (1899), 45.

13. "George Vaughn to Council of Trade and Plantation, July 6, 1708." *Calendar of State Papers*, Vol. 24, No. 19.

14. "The Comparative Value of Money Between Britain and the Colonies," Department of Special Collections, University of Notre Dame, http://www.coins.nd.edu/ColCurrency/CurrencyIntros/IntroValue.html.

15. Gary B. Nash, *The Urban Crucible: The Northern Seaports and the Origins of the American Revolution*, abridged ed. (Cambridge: Harvard University Press 1986), 36–37.

16. Quoted in William Pencak, *War, Politics and Revolution in Provincial Massachusetts* (Boston: Northeastern University Press, 1981), 17.

17. "Journal of Lieutenant John Burk," Stevens Family Papers, Special Collections, University of Vermont, entry for March 21; Brock, "The Colonial Currency," http://etext.virginia.edu/journals/EH/EH34/brock34.htm.

18. New England soldiers were never jealous of British redcoats. Although the New England currency was worth less than the sterling paid to English soldiers, the lack of deductions actually put the provincials far ahead.

19. "Gov. Shirley's Communication, Jan. 25, 1745," in Bouton, *NHSP*, Vol. V, 266.

20. "Pepperrell Papers," Series VI, Vol. X, 45.

21. Nash, *Urban Crucible*, 35–38.

22. See Ronald F. Reid, "New England Rhetoric and the French War, 1754–1760: A Case Study in the Rhetoric of War," *Communications Monographs*, Vol. 43, no. 4 (Nov. 1976), 259–86, for a study of war propaganda during the last French war.

23. Benjamin Wadsworth, *Good Soldiers a Great Blessing* (Boston, 1700), 6, 22.

24. Thomas Church, *The History of the Great Indian War of 1675 and 1676 Commonly Called Philip's War, also, The Old French and Indian Wars, from 1689 to 1704* (1716; Hartford, CT, 1845), 174.

25. Charles Edward Banks, *History of York, Maine* (Boston, 1931–1935), Vol. I, 335. See chapter 9 for more information about propaganda and its effect on fighting spirit.

26. Selesky, *War and Society*, 44.

27. James Phinney Baxter, ed., *Documentary History of the State of Maine* (Portland, ME, 1916), *Collections of the Maine Historical Society*, 2nd Series, Vol. XXIII, 251–52.

28. James Phinney Baxter, ed., *Documentary History of the State of Maine* (Portland, ME, 1907), *Collections of the Maine Historical Society*, 2nd Series, Vol. IX, 2; Baxter, *Documentary History*, Vol. V, 158–59.

29. See chapter 4 for more about these scalp hunters.

30. Samuel Penhallow, *The History of the Wars of New England with the Eastern Indians* (Boston, 1726; facsimile reprint, annotated by Edward Wheelock, Williamstown, MA, 1973), 39. The figures are by Penhallow; other sources indicate the initial reward was £40 for volunteers without pay and £32 for those with pay. See "Minutes of Massachusetts Council, December 2, 1703," *Calendar of State Papers*, Vol. 21, No. 1344.

31. "Governor Joseph Dudley to Council of Trade and Plantations, April 20, 1704," *Calendar of State Papers, Colonial Series, America and West Indies, 1704–1705* (reprint of 1916 edition, Vaduz, 1964), Vol. 22, No. 260; "Governor Joseph Dudley to Council of Trade and Plantations, March 1, 1709," *Calendar of State Papers*, Vol. 24, No. 391; Penhallow, *The History of the Wars of New England*, 94; James Phinney Baxter, ed., *Documentary History of the State of Maine* (Portland, ME, 1907), *Collections of the Maine Historical Society*, 2nd Series, Vol. X, 280.

32. The first figure is from Nash, *Urban Crucible*, 46. The second is quoted in Pencak, *War, Politics and Revolution*, 37.

33. On Lovewell's second raid, he and his men killed ten Indians, at £100 each, plus they sold most of the captured weapons for £7 a piece. Other plunder included blankets, moccasins, and a few furs. Penhallow, *The History of the Wars of New England*, 110. See also *Journals of the Rev. Thomas Smith and the Rev. Samuel Deane* (Portland, ME, 1849), 120–21.

34. Penhallow, *The History of the Wars of New England*, 42; "Captain John Redknap to Council of Trade and Plantations, February 20, 1708," *Calendar of State Papers, Colonial Series, America and West Indies, 1706-1708* (reprint of 1916 edition, Vaduz, 1964), Vol. 23, No. 1347.

35. "Samuel Vetch to Earl of Sunderland, August 2, 12, 1709," *Calendar of State Papers*, Vol. 24, No. 666; "Enlistment Proclamation, 1710," *Calendar of State Papers, Colonial Series, America and West Indies, 1710-June, 1711* (reprint of 1924 edition, Vaduz, 1964), Vol. 25, No. 491 ix.

36. Penhallow, *The History of the Wars of New England*, 50.

37. "Proclamation by Governor Joseph Dudley, June 12, 1711," *Calendar of State Papers, Colonial Series, America and West Indies, July, 1711-June, 1712* (reprint of 1925 edition, Vaduz, 1964), Vol. 26, No. 44 xb.

38. "Governor Joseph Dudley to Council of Trade and Plantations, December 2, 1712," *Calendar of State Papers*, Vol. 27, No. 153.

39. "Henry Norton to Council of Trade and Plantations, May 13, 1715," *Calendar of State Papers, Colonial Series, America and West Indies, August, 1714-December, 1715* (reprint of 1928 edition, Vaduz, 1964), Vol. 28, No. 408.

40. The quotes come from various reports, including *Calendar of State Papers*, Vol. 28, Nos. 173, 397, 411. The last complaint came from "John Mulcaster, Agent and Paymaster to the Garrison and Four independent companies [of provincials]"; see also Nos. 413, 423.

41. *Calendar of State Papers*, Vol. 26, No. 115.

42. Hammond, *NHSP*, Vol. XVIII, 105-7; Douglas Edward Leach, "The Cartagena Expedition, 1740-1742, and Anglo-American Relations," in Maarten Ultee, ed., *Adapting to Conditions: War and Society in the Eighteenth Century* (Tuscaloosa: University of Alabama Press, 1986), 46.

43. Hammond, *NHSP*, Vol. XVIII, 49; David Syrett, "The Raising of American Troops for Service in the West Indies during the War of Austrian Succession," *The Bulletin of the Institute of Historical Research*, Vol. 72, Issue 180 (Dec. 2002), 23.

44. Bouton, *NHSP*, Vol. V, 235, 266.

45. Hammond, *NHSP*, Vol. XVIII, 243.

46. "Enlistment Proclamation, 1710," *Calendar of State Papers*, Vol. 25, No. 491 ix; Hammond, *NHSP*, Vol. XVIII, 108.

47. Baxter, *Documentary History*, Vol. V, 60-61.

48. Francis Parkman also condemned Phips for his actions. He believed the plundering of the fort did "him no credit" and that he actually "displayed a scandalous rapacity." See Francis Parkman, *Count Frontenac and New France under Louis XIV* (Boston, 1896), 239.

49. "Proclamation by Governor Joseph Dudley, June 12, 1711," *Calendar of State Papers*, Vol. 26, No. 44 xb; Hammond, *NHSP*, Vol. XVIII, 105.

50. Bouton, *NHSP*, Vol. V, 266.

51. Louis E. De Forest, *Louisbourg Journals: 1745* (New York, 1932), 92; "Pepperrell Papers," Vol. X, 45.

52. "Curwen to W.G., 1745," in American Antiquarian Society [hereafter cited as *AAS*], Curwen Family Papers, Box 3, Folder 1.

53. *Journals of the Rev. Thomas Smith and the Rev. Samuel Deane*, 124, entry for June 20, 1746.

54. "Francis Nicholson and Samuel Vetch to Council of Trade and Plantations, September 16, 1710," *Calendar of State Papers*, Vol. 25, No. 396.

55. Quoted in Pencak, *War, Politics and Revolution*, 123.
56. Massachusetts Militia Laws, *Background of Selective Service*, 144. The quote is from the act passed in 1693–94; thus, the reference to "their majesties."
57. Douglas Leach, *Arms for Empire: A Military History of the British Colonies in North America, 1607–1763* (New York: Macmillan, 1973), 22–23.
58. Massachusetts Militia Laws, *Background of Selective Service*. See laws for the year 1693–94, 144–45.
59. Massachusetts Militia Laws, *Background of Selective Service*. See Laws for Levying Souldiers in 1699 (150), 1702 (158), 1721 (161–62), and 1746 (176).
60. Leach, *Arms for Empire*, 23.
61. Massachusetts Militia Laws, *Background of Selective Service*. See laws for 1699, 150.
62. "Lt-Governor Dummer to Timothy Dwight at Fort Dummer, Dec. 28, 1725," *Massachusetts Historical Society*, Miscellaneous Bound.
63. Baxter, *Documentary History*, Vol. V, 5; Massachusetts Militia Laws, *Background of Selective Service*. See laws for 1693–94, 144–45. The sentence was increased to six months in 1699.
64. Trask, *Letters of Colonel Thomas Westbrook*, 69.
65. Massachusetts Militia Laws, *Background of Selective Service*, 158. This would be an augmentation of the alarm list system. See chapter 1.
66. "Governor Joseph Dudley to Council of Trade and Plantations, August 5, 1703," *Calendar of State Papers*, Vol. 21, No. 996.
67. "Governor Joseph Dudley to Council of Trade and Plantations," in Baxter, *Documentary History*, Vol. IX, 180–82.
68. Massachusetts Militia Laws, *Background of Selective Service*, See laws for 1746, 176.
69. See James Kirby Martin and Mark Edward Lender, *A Respectable Army: The Military Origins of the Republic, 1763–1789* (Arlington Heights, IL: Harlan Davidson, 1982), 19; Lawrence Delbert Cress, *Citizens in Arms: The Army and the Militia in American Society to the War of 1812* (Chapel Hill: University of North Carolina Press, 1982), 5.
70. "Francis Nicholson and Samuel Vetch to Earl of Sunderland, June 28, 1709," *Calendar of State Papers*, Vol. 24, No. 604; "Enlistment Proclamation, 1710," *Calendar of State Papers*, Vol. 25, No. 491 ix; "Proclamation by Governor Joseph Dudley, June 12, 1711," *Calendar of State Papers*, Vol. 26, No. 44 xb. The printing of these proclamations constituted another of the little charges that increased the cost of the war. See Bouton, *NHSP*, Vol. V, 888.
71. Quotes taken from *AAS*, Curwen Family Papers, Box 3, Folder 1; Hammond, *NHSP*, Vol. XVIII, 215.
72. Rogers, *The British Army*, 58–80.
73. In this instance, the drummers of the company, if available, would probably be used to assemble the men, thus providing literal meaning to the "beating order."
74. Hammond, *NHSP*, Vol. XVIII, 215.
75. Church, *The History of the Great Indian War*, 251.
76. See John K. Mahon, *History of the Militia and the National Guard* (New York: Free Press, 1983), 21.
77. For more about recruits produced by economic crisis, see Pencak, *War, Politics and Revolution*, 121; Nash, *Urban Crucible*, 35, 104–5.
78. "Bartholomew Gedney of Salem to Bay government, Oct. 15, 1690," Baxter, *Documentary History*, Vol. V, 154–55.

79. Baxter, *Documentary History*, Vol. X, 150–51.
80. Ibid., 186–87.
81. Hammond, *NHSP*, Vol. XVIII, 119. The government of New Hampshire granted Eyre £20 for his trouble.
82. Baxter, *Documentary History*, Vol. V, 479–81.
83. Baxter, *Documentary History*, Vol. X.
84. "John Osbourne to William Pepperrell, Feb. 18, 1744," Massachusetts Historical Society, Pepperrell Papers, Belknap Papers.
85. "Moses Butler to William Pepperrell, February 21, 1745," Massachusetts Historical Society, Pepperrell Papers, Belknap Papers; Banks, *History of York, Maine*, Vol. I, 333–34.
86. Rev. John Emerson to Wait Winthrop, July 26, 1690," *Collections of the Massachusetts Historical Society*, Series V, Vol. I, 437–38. See also Baxter, *Documentary History*, Vol. V, 260–61, and "Letter dated November 25, 1691," *AAS*, Curwen Family Papers, Box 3, Folder 1.
87. "John Osbourne to William Pepperrell, Feb. 18, 1744," Massachusetts Historical Society, Pepperrell Papers, Belknap Papers.
88. "Edward Hartwell to Lt-Governor William Dummer, March 18 1725," *AAS*, Mass. Coll. 1629–1869, Box 3, Folder 11, Militia returns, Officers commissions and Misc. Papers 1696–1762.
89. *Annals of Lancaster, Massachusetts, 1643–1825* (Clinton, MA, 1884), 222. See also "Eleazer Tyng to Lt-Governor William Dummer, April 1, 1725," *AAS*, Mass. Coll. 1629–1869, Box 3, Folder 11, Militia returns, Officers commissions and Misc. Papers 1696–1762.
90. Baxter, *Documentary History*, Vol. X, 277.
91. Baxter, *Documentary History*, Vol. IX, 13.
92. Henry S. Burrage, *Maine at Louisbourg in 1745* (Augusta, ME, 1910), 99.
93. For some examples, see Baxter, *Documentary History*, Vol. V, 49–50, 53.
94. "Governor Joseph Dudley to Council of Trade and Plantations, January 31, 1710," *Calendar of State Papers*, Vol. 25, No. 81.
95. "Governor Joseph Dudley to Council of Trade and Plantations, November 15, 1710," *Calendar of State Papers*, Vol. 25, No. 491.
96. See chapters 2 and 3.
97. "Francis Nicholson and Samuel Vetch to Earl of Sunderland, June 28, 1709," *Calendar of State Papers*, Vol. 24, No. 604; Hammond, *NHSP*, Vol. XVIII, 106.
98. "Pepperrell Papers," Series VI, Vol. X, 30.
99. Ibid., 320–22.
100. Ibid., 339. Clashes with the Eastern Indians were growing throughout the summer. Shirley would declare war on the tribes in late August.
101. Ibid., 45.
102. Ibid., 47.
103. Quoted in Pencak, *War, Politics and Revolution*, 123.
104. "Pepperrell Papers," Series VI, Vol. X, 49.
105. With so many men at Louisbourg, finding replacements was not easy, as the government of New Hampshire found, "men being now more stragling that when the last volunteers were raised." "Journal of the House, June 20, 1745," in Bouton, *NHSP*, Vol. V, 341.
106. De Forest, *Louisbourg Journals*, 96.

107. John Shy, "A New Look at Colonial Militia," in *A People Numerous and Armed: Reflections on the Military Struggle for American Independence* (London: Oxford University Press, 1976), 29–30. For similar sentiments, see Cress, *Citizens in Arms*, 13; Mahon, *History of the Militia*, 21.

108. Martin and Lender, *A Respectable Army*, 18.

109. Ibid., 17.

110. Quoted in Fred Anderson, *A People's Army: Massachusetts Soldiers and Society in the Seven Years War* (Chapel Hill: University of North Carolina Press, 1984), 52.

111. Fred Anderson, "A People's Army: Provincial Military Service in Massachusetts during the Seven Years War," *William and Mary Quarterly*, 3rd Series, 40 (October 1983), 505.

112. Anderson, "A People's Army," 509, 520–21, 525.

113. Myron O. Stachiw, ed., *Massachusetts Officers and Soldiers 1723–43: Dummer's War to the War of Jenkins's Ear* (Boston: Society of Colonial Wars of Massachusetts, 1979), xiv–xv.

114. George Gilmore, *Roll of New Hampshire Men at Louisbourg, Cape Breton, 1745* (Concord, NH, 1896). The number of men from Dover is probably not complete because not all the men named on the roll of the New Hampshire regiment provided residence. For roll of the August patrol, see "Muster roll of Captain Joseph Hanson, August 5, 1745" in Isaac W. Hammond, ed., *Rolls and Documents relating to Soldiers in the Revolutionary War with an Appendix Embracing some Indian and French Rolls* (Manchester, NH, 1887), New Hampshire Provincial and State Papers, Vol. XVI, 904.

115. Vital data on the Dover men were obtained from various sources, including *Collections of the Dover, N. H. Historical Society* (Dover, NH, 1894), Vol. I; John R. Ham, "Dover, New Hampshire Marriages, 1623–1823" (manuscript, Dover Public Library); Rev. Dr. Alonzo Hall Quint, *Historical Memoranda concerning Persons and Places in Old Dover, N. H.* (Dover Public Library); John Scales, *History of Dover, N. H.* (Manchester, NH, 1923), Vol. I; *Descendents of William Dam* (Dover Public Library); Katherine F. Richmond, *John Hayes of Dover, New Hampshire: A Book of his Family* (Tyngsboro, MA, 1936); Rev. Charles Nelson Sinnett, *Richard Pinkham of Old Dover, New Hampshire and his Descendents East and West* (Concord, NH, 1908).

116. The records for Dover, like so many communities, are incomplete.

117. George Wadleigh, *Notable Events in the History of Dover from the First Settlement in 1623 to 1865* (Dover, NH, 1913), 141; Richmond, *John Hayes of Dover, New Hampshire*, 62–63.

118. *Collections of the Dover Historical Society*, 35; Wadleigh, *Notable Events in the History of Dover*, 141; Quint, *Historical Memoranda*, 6:295.

119. Stachiw, *Massachusetts Officers and Soldiers*, xxii–xxiii.

120. Ann M. Little, *Abraham in Arms: War and Gender in Colonial America* (Philadelphia: University of Pennsylvania Press, 2007), 15.

121. "Pepperrell Papers," Series VI, Vol. X.

122. Cress, *Citizens in Arms*, 13.

CHAPTER 8

1. Pressed men had little choice, except if they had the money to buy their way out of the service.

2. See below and chapter 7.

3. "Bulman to William Pepperrell, February 4, 1745," Charles Edward Banks, *History of York, Maine* (Boston, 1931–1935), Vol. I, 333–34.

4. Fred Anderson, *A People's Army; Massachusetts Soldiers and Society in the Seven Years War* (Chapel Hill: University of North Carolina Press, 1984), 48.

5. Jeremy Belknap, *The History of New Hampshire* (reprint of 1831 edition, New York, 1970), Vol. 1, 178; "Orders of Queen in Council, March 20, 1707," *Calendar of State Papers, Colonial Series, America and West Indies, 1706–1708* (reprint of 1916 edition, Vaduz, 1964), Vol. 23, No. 813.

6. William Blake Trask, *Letters of Colonel Thomas Westbrook and others Relative to Indian Affairs in Maine, 1722–1726* (Boston, 1901), 2.

7. Belknap, *The History of New Hampshire*, 271.

8. Ranz C. Esbenshade, "Sober, Modest Men of Confined Ideas: The Officer Corps of Provincial New Hampshire" (Masters thesis, University of New Hampshire, 1976), 37–38, 52.

9. "Petition of John Hammond," in Baxter, *Documentary History*, Vol. V, 333.

10. "Pepperrell Papers," *Collections of the Massachusetts Historical Society*, Series VI, Vol. X (1899), 308, 343–44, 345. Thomas Hubbard recommended the young man who delivered the letter to Pepperrell for him.

11. "Nathaniel Sparhawk to William Pepperrell, August 17, 1745," "Pepperrell Papers," Series VI, Vol. X, 361–62.

12. Baxter, *Documentary History*, Vol. V, 327–28.

13. Banks, *History of York, Maine*, Vol. I, 322–25, 333.

14. Chandler E. Potter, *The Military History of New Hampshire from its Founding until the Present Time (Report of the Adjutant-General of the State of New Hampshire for the Year ending June 1, 1866*, Concord, NH, 1866), 93–95.

15. John Gyles, *Memoirs of Odd Adventures, Strange Deliverances, &c.* (Boston, 1736; facsimile reprint in *The Garland Library of Narratives of North American Indian Captivities*, New York: Garland, 1977), 41–44.

16. Samuel Penhallow, *The History of the Wars of New England with the Eastern Indians* (Boston, 1726; facsimile reprint, annotated by Edward Wheelock, Williamstown, MA, 1973), 110; Charles E. Clark, *The Eastern Frontier: The Settlement of Northern New England, 1610–1763* (New York: Knopf, 1970), 235.

17. Fred Anderson, "A People's Army: Provincial Military Service in Massachusetts during the Seven Year's War," *William and Mary Quarterly*, 3rd Series, 40 (Oct. 1983), 506–7.

18. Trask, *Letters of Colonel Thomas Westbrook*, 35.

19. J. A. Houlding, *Fit for Service: The Training of the British Army, 1715–95* (Oxford: Oxford University Press, 1981), 100–104; Sylvia Frey, *The British Soldier in America: A Social History of Military Life in the Revolutionary Period* (Austin: University of Texas Press, 1981), 66.

20. Quoted in Douglas Edward Leach, *Roots of Conflict: British Armed Forces and Colonial Americans, 1677–1763* (Chapel Hill: University of North Carolina Press, 1986), 55.

21. "Lt-Governor Caulfield and Captain of the Garrison of Annapolis Royal to Governor Francis Nicholson, October 8, 1714," *Calendar of State Papers, Colonial Series, America and West Indies, August, 1714–December, 1715* (reprint of 1928 edition, Vaduz, 1964), Vol. 28, No. 411 i.

22. Leach, *Roots of Conflict*, 164.

23. Even Sir William Phips himself pointed this out in promoting an attack on Quebec in 1692. He informed the Earl of Nottingham that if he were placed in command, a sufficient number of men would volunteer without having to resort to a press. See James Phinney Baxter, ed., *Documentary History of the State of Maine* (Portland, ME, 1907), *Collections of the Maine Historical Society*, 2nd Series, Vol. X, 2–3.

24. Anderson, *A People's Army*, 44.

25. Ibid., 47–48.

26. Ibid., 44.

27. For the effect of such relationships on combat effectiveness, see chapter 10.

28. Henry S. Burrage, *Maine at Louisbourg in 1745* (Augusta, ME, 1910), 19.

29. "Moses Butler to William Pepperrell, February 20, 21, 23, 1745," *Massachusetts Historical Society*, Pepperrell Papers, Belknap Papers.

30. "The True State of Capt. Butlers Company, Louisbourg, Sept 17, 1745," Pepperrell Papers, Belknap Papers. In all fairness to Moses Butler, the exact reasons for his leaving are unknown.

31. Thomas Church, *The History of the Great Indian War of 1675 and 1676 Commonly Called Philip's War, also, The Old French and Indian Wars, from 1689 to 1704* (1716; Hartford, CT, 1845 edition), 210. Instructions for his third raid in 1692.

32. Baxter, *Documentary History*, Vol. V, 89–90.

33. Trask, *Letters of Colonel Thomas Westbrook*, 19.

34. Baxter, *Documentary History*, Vol. V, 262.

35. "Narrative of Mr. John Wise, Minister of God's Word at Chebacco," *Proceedings of the Massachusetts Historical Society*, Vol. XV, 283–303; Penhallow, *The History of the Wars of New England*, 114. See chapter 9 for more about military ministers.

36. American Antiquarian Society [hereafter cited as *AAS*], Curwen Family Papers, Box 3, Folder 1; "Journal of Lieutenant John Burk," Stevens Family Papers, Special Collections, University of Vermont.

37. "Levying Act of 1719," New Hampshire Militia Laws, *Background of Selective Service*, 58.

38. "Journal of Benjamin Stearns," *Massachusetts Historical Society Proceedings*, Vol. 42, 137–44.

39. Sylvia R. Frey, "Courts and Cats: British Military Justice in the Eighteenth Century," *Military Affairs*, 43 (1979), 7.

40. Louis E. De Forest, ed., *Louisbourg Journals: 1745* (New York, 1932), 6.

41. Frey, *The British Soldier in America*, 91. The British often used the gauntlet for first-time deserters; however, if the individual went through a three-hundred-man battalion, say, five times, he could possibly receive 1,500 blows.

42. De Forest, *Louisbourg Journals*, 102.

43. Leach, *Roots of Conflict*, 15.

44. Baxter, *Documentary History*, Vol. V, 20.

45. Ibid., 38–39. Jordan got no confession and had the soldier laid neck and heels for two hours more, then stretched him on a pole with his hands and feet tied behind him for another two hours.

46. Leach, *Roots of Conflict*, 18.

47. Church, *The History of the Great Indian War*, 210.

48. Trask, *Letters of Colonel Thomas Westbrook*, 11–12.

49. Baxter, *Documentary History*, Vol. IX, 474.

50. Massachusetts Militia Laws, *Background of Selective Service*, 151. In 1746, there was some doubt expressed by Governor William Shirley that the provincial officers could legally try soldiers who had enlisted in His Majesties' service for desertion without a commission from the crown. He felt an act should be passed to enable officers to hold a court-martial in such circumstances without necessarily having their Royal commission. "I don't otherwise see how the officers can mentain a proper command over the soldiers." The soldiers in question were those posted at Fort Atkinson. See "Shirley to Wentworth, Jan 27, 1747," in Hammond, *NHSP*, Vol. XVIII, 254–55.

51. Baxter, *Documentary History*, Vol. IX, 42. For more about this incident, see chapter 2.

52. "William Dudley to Joseph Dudley, July 17, 1707," in Baxter, *Documentary History*, Vol. IX, 245.

53. Hammond, *NHSP*, Vol. XVIII, 254–55; Belknap, *History of New Hampshire*, 285.

54. "Dummer to Wentworth, May 13, 1725," in Baxter, *Documentary History*, Vol. X, 270.

55. "Dummer to Tyng, May 13, 1725," in Baxter, *Documentary History*, Vol. X 270–71.

56. "Tyng to Dummer, May 14, 1725," in Baxter, *Documentary History*, Vol. X, 271–72.

57. "Complaint against Three Soldiers," in Baxter, *Documentary History*, Vol. V, 72–73; "Letter from Francis Hooke to the Governor and Council," in Baxter, *Documentary History*, Vol. V, 288. Hooke reported that "one Joseph Wheeler a prest soldier run away from his commander." See chapter 2.

58. "Letter to Governor from David Parsons, May 31, 1725," *AAS*, Mass. Col. 1629–1869, Box 3, Folder 11: Militia returns, Officers Commissions and Misc. Papers, 1696–1762. See chapter 2 for more about this issue.

59. "Joseph Prout to Isaac Addington, 1689," in Baxter, *Documentary History*, Vol. V, 10–11. See chapter 2.

60. "Letter from William Vaughn and Richard Waldron, July 5, 1689," in Baxter, *Documentary History*, Vol. IX, 9; "Letter from Major Samuel Appleton, July 14, 1689," in Baxter, *Documentary History*, Vol. IX, 13.

61. "Letter from William Vaughn and Richard Martyn to the Governor and Council, September 26, 1691," in Baxter, *Documentary History*, Vol. V, 292–93.

62. "Letter from John March to the Governor and Council, September, 27, 1691," in Baxter, *Documentary History*, Vol. V, 293–94.

63. Houlding, *Fit for Service*, 267.

64. Baxter, *Documentary History*, Vol. V, 424–25, 432–33.

65. "Letter by James Converse concerning a wounded soldier," in Baxter, *Documentary History*, Vol. IX, 98. For more about John Baker's problems, see chapter 11.

66. Penhallow, *The History of the Wars of New England*, 58.

67. Baxter, *Documentary History*, Vol. X, 268–69, 270.

68. John Keegan and Richard Holmes, *Soldiers: A History of Men in Battle* (New York: Viking, 1985), 261.

69. For more about this action, see chapter 2.

70. Penhallow, *The History of the Wars of New England*, 114.

71. Joseph Dow, *History of the Town of Hampton, New Hampshire: From Its Settlement in 1638, to the Autumn of 1892* (Salem, MA, 1893; reprinted, Somersworth, NH, 1970), 227.

72. Church, *The History of the Great Indian War*, 269.

73. Ibid., 282.

74. Ibid., 193.
75. "Joseph Sleepers Statement relative to the Trouble between Colonel Richmond and Captain Ladd at Louisbourg," in Hammond, *NHSP*, Vol. XVIII, 256-58.
76. "Pepperrell Papers," Series VI, Vol. X, 259-60.
77. "Lt-Governor Dummer to Secretary Willard, September 1, 1724," in Baxter, *Documentary History*, Vol. X, 218-19.
78. Ibid., 220.
79. Leach, *Roots of Conflict*, 64.
80. Ibid., 132.
81. "Supplement to Vetch's Canada Proposal, Nov. 17, 1708," *Calendar of State Papers, Colonial Series, America and West Indies, June, 1708-1709* (reprint of 1922 edition, Vaduz, 1964), Vol. 24, No. 196.
82. "Samuel Vetch to Earl of Dartmouth, June 24, 1712," *Calendar of State Papers, Colonial Series, America and West Indies, July, 1711-June, 1712* (reprint of 1925 edition, Vaduz, 1964), Vol. 26, No. 457.
83. Church, *The History of the Great Indian War*, 183, 191.
84. Ibid., 285.
85. Samuel Adams Drake, *The Border Wars of New England, Commonly Called King William's and Queen Anne's Wars* (1897; reprint of 1910 edition, Williamstown, MA, 1973), 227.
86. Penhallow, *The History of the Wars of New England*, 42.
87. Drake, *The Border Wars of New England*, 232, quoting William Dudley.
88. Ibid., 233-34; Penhallow, *The History of the Wars of New England*, 43-44; Belknap, *History of New Hampshire*, 174-75.
89. Thomas Hutchinson recorded that all the officers involved in Port Royal received some blame, but formal punishment of them all was impractical. "A court martial was judged necessary, and ordered, but never met. The act of the province, for the constituting courts martial, made so many officers requisite, that it was found impracticable to hold one. This must be owing to the great number of persons charged, the remainder be insufficient to try them." See Hutchinson, *History of Massachusetts*, 70.
90. See "Journal of Rev. John Pike," *Massachusetts Historical Society Proceedings*, Vol. XIV (1875-1876), 142. Even militia officers were not immune to censure if they failed in their responsibility to prepare their towns for defense. See "Vote in relation to Col. Saltonstall and Capt. Chubb, March, 1697," in Baxter, *Documentary History*, Vol. V, 481-82.
91. "Narrative of Mr. John Wise," *Massachusetts Historical Society Proceedings*, Vol. XV, 289-90.
92. Anon, "Phips Expedition to Canada," *Massachusetts Historical Society Proceedings*, Vol. XV, 315.
93. For Chubb's earlier service, see "Capt. Pasco Chubb and Lieut. Brackett to Lieut Gov. Stoughton, August 31, 1695," in Baxter, *Documentary History*, Vol. V, 426-27; "Major Charles Frost to Lieut. Gov. Stoughton, September 21, 1695," in Baxter, *Documentary History*, Vol. V, 431-32.
94. Mather, *Decennium Luctuosum*, in Lincoln, *Narratives of the Indian Wars*, 261.
95. Ibid., 262. To give Chubb the benefit of the doubt, both Thomas Hutchison and Francis Parkman believed he could not have held the fort against such overwhelming odds. See Hutchinson, *History of Massachusetts*, 70; Parkman, *Count Frontenac*, 381.
96. Baxter, *Documentary History*, Vol. V, 469-70.

97. Ibid., 481–82.
98. Drake, *The Border Wars of New England*, 134.
99. Carl von Clausewitz, *On War* (1832; Penguin reprint, 1985), 143.
100. Penhallow, *The History of the Wars of New England*, 43.
101. Esbenshade, "Sober, Modest Men of Confined Ideas," 52.
102. Penhallow, *The History of the Wars of New England*, 117. Wyman had little time to enjoy his fame and success. He fell ill and died while on a scout a few months later.
103. Herbert Milton Sylvester, *Indian Wars of New England* (Boston, 1910), Vol. III, 380–83. The town that grew up around the fort was named Charlestown to commemorate the gift.
104. "Governor Joseph Dudley to the Earl of Nottingham, December 10, 1702," *Calendar of State Papers, Colonial Series, America and West Indies, December 1, 1702–1703* (reprint of 1913 edition, Vaduz, 1964), Vol. 21, No. 30; Penhallow, *The History of the Wars of New England*, 19. The vote was not without opposition, however, as some felt the results of the raid left much to be desired.
105. "Governor Joseph Dudley to the Earl of Nottingham, December 10, 1702," *Calendar of State Papers*, Vol. 21, No. 30; "Minutes of the Massachusetts Council, March 11, 1703," *Calendar of State Papers*, Vol. 21, No. 433; "Minutes of the Massachusetts Council, September 13, 1703," *Calendar of State Papers*, Vol. 21, No. 1087.
106. Harold E. Selesky, *War and Society in Colonial Connecticut* (New Haven: Yale University Press, 1990), xiii.
107. Ibid., 72.
108. "French Captive Examination from Piscataway Co., March 19, 1689/90" in Baxter, *Documentary History*, Vol. V, 55–56. The Frenchman's interrogators were unclear if he meant Tyng of Merrimack River or Tyng of Casco Bay. The Tyngs of Dunstable had many men in provincial service. One who fell to the enemy in 1710 was Captain John Tyng, according to Samuel Adams Drake, "one of the best and bravest partisan leaders." Drake, *The Border Wars of New England*, 264. See also Hutchinson, *History of Massachusetts*, 106.
109. "Petition of Charles Frost, May 27, 1696," in Baxter, *Documentary History*, Vol. V, 434; Everett S. Stackpole, *Old Kittery and her Families* (Lewiston, ME, 1903), 168. Because this is the only account of Indians desecrating a grave during the early French wars, its veracity may be suspect.
110. Belknap, *History of New Hampshire*, 172, 178.
111. Penhallow, *The History of the Wars of New England*, 59; Drake, *The Border Wars of New England*, 263; Potter, *The Military History of New Hampshire*, 32–33.
112. Hamilton, *The French and Indian Wars*, 93; John R. Elting, *American Army Life: An Historical Portrait of the American Soldier from Colonial Times to the Present*, (New York: Charles Scribner's Sons, 1982), 9.
113. Clausewitz, *On War*, 144.

CHAPTER 9

1. Richard Holmes, *Acts of War: The Behavior of Men in Battle* (New York: Free Press, 1985), 36.
2. Ibid., 41–43.
3. Lawrence Delbert Cress, *Citizens in Arms: The Army and Militia in American Society to the War of 1812* (Chapel Hill: University of North Carolina Press, 1982), 8.

4. Carl von Clausewitz, *On War* (1832; New York: Viking Penguin, 1985), 258.

5. "An Act for Regulating of the Militia, Nov. 22, 1693," in Massachusetts Militia Laws, *Background of Selective Service*, Vol. II (Washington, 1947), 139.

6. "Instructions to the Governor, 1682," New Hampshire Militia Laws, *Background of Selective Service*, 5.

7. Cotton Mather, *Military Duties Recommended to an Artillery Company, 1687* (Boston, 1687), 23; Massachusetts Militia Laws, *Background of Selective Service*, 125.

8. Morrison Sharp, "Leadership and Democracy in the Early New England System of Defense," *American Historical Review*, 5 (1945), 253.

9. Samuel Adams Drake, *The Border Wars of New England, Commonly Called King William's and Queen Anne's Wars* (1897; reprint of 1910 edition, Williamstown, MA, 1973), 16.

10. Mather, *Military Duties*, 20.

11. Douglas Edward Leach, *Arms for Empire: A Military History of the British Colonies in North America, 1607–1763* (New York: Macmillan, 1973), 20–21.

12. "An Act for Regulating of the Militia, Nov. 22, 1693," Massachusetts Militia Laws, *Background of Selective Service*, 139.

13. Ibid., 138.

14. Ibid., 140.

15. "Samuel Vetch to the Earl of Sunderland, Aug. 2 & 12, 1709," *Calendar of State Papers, Colonial Series, America and West Indies, June, 1708–1709* (reprint of 1922 edition, Vaduz, 1964), Vol. 24, No. 666.

16. "William Pepperrell to Governor Shirley, April 28, 1745," *Collections of the Massachusetts Historical Society*, Vol. I, 22.

17. John Shy, "A New Look at Colonial Militia," in *A People Numerous and Armed: Reflections on the Military Struggle for American Independence* (London: Oxford University Press, 1976), 31; Harold L. Peterson, *Arms and Armor in Colonial America, 1526–1783* (New York: Bramhall House, 1956), 155.

18. Howard H. Peckham, *The Colonial Wars, 1689–1762* (Chicago: University of Chicago Press, 1964), 214.

19. Guy Chet, *Conquering the American Wilderness: The Triumph of European Warfare in the Colonial Northeast* (Boston: University of Massachusetts Press, 2006), 67.

20. John Keegan and Richard Holmes, *Soldiers: A History of Men in Battle* (New York: Viking, 1985), 27.

21. J. A. Houlding, *Fit for Service: The Training of the British Army, 1715–95* (Oxford: Oxford University Press, 1981), 261.

22. Ibid., 318; the confusion of battle could easily destroy the precision of such firing. The British would switch to a simpler version of platoon fire, called "alternate fire," later in the eighteenth century.

23. Houlding, *Fit for Service*, 262–63; Keegan and Holmes, *Soldiers*, 66.

24. Keegan and Holmes, *Soldiers*, 104–5, 167–72.

25. Cotton Mather, *Decennium Luctuosum* (1699; reprinted in Charles H. Lincoln, ed., *Narratives of the Indian Wars, 1675–1699*, New York, 1913), 223.

26. See Jeremy Belknap, *The History of New Hampshire* (reprint of 1831 edition, New York, 1970), 208; Fannie Eckstorm, "The Attack on Norridgewock: 1724," *New England Quarterly* (1934), 568.

27. Keegan and Holmes, *Soldiers*, 43.

28. Houlding, *Fit for Service*, 161.

29. Ibid., 266.

30. With the battalion dispersed in garrisons, the officers had no opportunity to practice the higher levels of firings and marching maneuvers. See Houlding, *Fit for Service*, 93.

31. *An Abridgement of the English Military Discipline* (Boston, 1690), 10–11. The first command refers to the necessity to blow away any loose "corns" of powder after filling the pan so the lighted match in a matchlock could not accidentally fire the weapon.

32. Bennett Cuthbertson, *A System for the Compleat Interior Management and Economy of a Battalion of Infantry* (Dublin, 1768), 163.

33. John Ferling, *A Wilderness of Miseries: War and Warriors in Early America* (Westport, CT: Greenwood Press, 1980), 22.

34. John Ferling, *Struggle for a Continent: The Wars of Early America* (Arlington Heights, IL: Harlan Davidson, 1993), 134.

35. There is no evidence of the term used by provincial soldiers in everyday use to refer to their weapons. While it appears in the militia laws as a term to distinguish a "flintlock" the various writings and petitions by soldiers concerning their weapons usually use the term "gun." Therefore it is possible that the reference here is tied to the use of that word in the European drill manual and should not be used to suggest the New Hampshire soldiers didn't know how to use a gun.

36. William Breton, *Militia Discipline: The Words of Command and Directions for Exercising the Musket, Bayonet, & Carthridge* (Boston, 1733; facsimile copy, East Winthrop, ME, 1975).

37. Houlding, *Fit for Service*, 281.

38. Breton, *Militia Discipline*, 45.

39. Updated versions of Bland were published in the colonies through the last edition in 1762.

40. Humphrey Bland, *An Abstract of Military Discipline* (Boston, 1743).

41. Indeed, Guy Chet has recently suggested that the printing of these European manuals in America proves the continued adherence to a European mode of warfare. He observed that "nothing in American military manuals published in the colonial era indicates that the men and institutions in charge of military training in the colonies were won over by a new philosophy of war through exposure to Indian tactics." However, there is no indication that either militia or provincial officers ever connected with publishers. Colonial publishers were simply copying English military manuals as the easiest way to publish and sell books, and they knew the demand as the population increased and militia companies multiplied. There was never any real thought connected to what was published. Nothing proves this more than the publishing of *An Abridgement of the English Military Discipline* in 1690 (mentioned earlier), which contained instruction for the coordination of pikes and musketeers. The pike had been given up as useless in America decades earlier, long before it was discarded in Europe. Chet, *Conquering the American Wilderness*, 56–60 (quote on 57).

42. Keegan and Holmes, *Soldiers*, 66.

43. Edward Pierce Hamilton, "Colonial Warfare in North America," *Massachusetts Historical Society Proceedings*, 80 (1968), 3. A participant in the battle, Malcolm Fraser of the Seventy-Eighth Regiment of Foot, called the Plains of Abraham "the first regular engagement that was ever fought in North America." C. P. Stacey, *Quebec, 1759: The Siege and the Battle* (Toronto: Macmillan, 1959), 153.

44. I. K. Steele, *Guerillas and Grenadiers: The Struggle for Canada, 1689-1760* (Toronto: Ryerson Press, 1969), 7.

45. W. J. Eccles, *Canada Under Louis XIV, 1663-1701* (London: McClelland and Stewart, 1964), 191.

46. Mather, *Military Duties*, 22.

47. Plymouth Colony Militia laws, 1634, *Background of Selective Service*, 10; Massachusetts Militia laws, 1677, *Background of Selective Service*, 124.

48. Houlding, *Fit for Service*, 262.

49. Ibid., 368; Stephen Brumwell, *Redcoats: The British Soldier and the War in the Americas, 1755-1763* (New York, Cambridge University Press, 2002), 248-49.

50. Church, *History of the Great Indian War*, 169.

51. Ibid., 266.

52. Ibid., 196.

53. Ibid., 247.

54. Samuel Penhallow, *The History of the Wars of New England with the Eastern Indians* (Boston, 1726; facsimile reprint, annotated by Edward Wheelock, Williamstown, MA, 1973), 110.

55. Richard Slotkin, *Regeneration Through Violence: The Mythology of the American Frontier, 1600-1860* (Middletown, CT: Wesleyan University Press, 1973), 154.

56. Keegan and Holmes, *Soldiers*, 44.

57. "Address to the House by Gov. Belcher, Feb. 1, 1740," Nathaniel Bouton, *Documents and Records Relating to the Province of New Hampshire from 1738-1749* (Nashua, NH, 1871), *New Hampshire Provincial and State Papers*, Vol. V, 11-12.

58. "House's Answer to Belcher's Speech, Feb. 15, 1740," in Bouton, *NHSP*, 18-20.

59. Keegan and Holmes, *Soldiers*, 39.

60. Holmes, *Acts of War*, 28.

61. Keegan and Holmes, *Soldiers*, 42.

62. Holmes, *Acts of War*, 237.

63. Clausewitz, *On War*, 254-55.

64. Quoted in Keegan and Holmes, *Soldiers*, 46.

65. Quoted in Steele, *Guerillas and Grenadiers*, 29-30.

66. Francis Parkman, *Count Frontenac and New France under Louis XIV* (Boston, 1896), 285.

67. Holmes, *Acts of War*, 139, 145.

68. Ibid., 147.

69. The account is contained in Samuel A. Green, *Groton During the Indian Wars* (Groton, MA, 1883), 98-101.

70. Holmes, *Acts of War*, 227-28.

71. "Wentworth to Dummer, May 28, 1725," James Phinney Baxter, ed., *Documentary History of the State of Maine* (Portland, ME, 1907), *Collections of the Maine Historical Society*, 2nd Series, Vol. X, 283-84.

72. "Dummer to Westbrook, September 24, 1725," in Baxter, *Documentary History*, Vol. X, 339.

73. "Westbrook to Dummer, October 1, 1725," in Baxter, *Documentary History*, Vol. X, 342.

74. Richard Slotkin, *Regeneration Through Violence*, 165.

75. "Governor Joseph Dudley to the Council of Trade and Plantations, March 1, 1709," *Calendar of State Papers*, Vol. 24, No. 392.

76. Church, *The History of the Great Indian War*, 187–89; Penhallow, *The History of the Wars of New England*, 46, 115; Francis Parkman, *A Half-Century of Conflict* (Boston, 1892), 255.

77. Penhallow, *History of the Wars of New England*, 87.

78. For the incident of Robert Rogers, see Mather, *Decennium Luctuosum* in Lincoln, *Narratives of the Indian Wars*, 207, and for William Moody, see Penhallow, *History of the Wars of New England*, 48–49.

79. Goody Webber was by no means the only pregnant women cut up by Indians. A woman at Oyster River in 1694 died in a similar manner. See Jeremy Belknap, *The History of New Hampshire* (reprint of 1831 edition, New York, 1970) Vol. 1, 138–39.

80. "Letter from John Hornabeck, 1703," in Baxter, *Documentary History*, Vol. IX, 178–79.

81. Penhallow, *History of the Wars of New England*, 6.

82. Church, *The History of the Great Indian War*, 244.

83. Mather, *Decennium Luctuosum*, 22.

84. Holmes, *Acts of War*, 360–66.

85. Richard Slotkin found that, in the literature of the period, the "exorcism of the Indians is likened to the hunting down and slaying of rapid beasts embodying all qualities of evil." Richard Slotkin, *Regeneration Through Violence*, 154–65.

86. John Prebble, *Culloden* (1961; reprint, New York: Penguin, 1981), 116.

87. For the early precedents for this arrangement, see Alden T. Vaughn, *New England Frontier: Puritans and Indians, 1620–1675* (Boston: Little, Brown, 1965).

88. Quoted in Penhallow, *History of the Wars of New England*, 88–89. Similar language was used in 1755 by the governor of New Hampshire, when he declared the Eastern Indians "to be Enemies, Rebels and Traitors to his most Sacred Majesty" ("Proclamation against some Indians, 1755," in Hammond, *NHSP*, Vol. XVIII, 427–28).

89. A third strike against the Eastern Indians involved their form of warfare. Richard Holmes has indicated that guerrilla warfare, the war of ambush and surprise, has always increased the intensity of feeling. See Holmes, *Acts of War*, 387.

90. Barbara Lambert, ed., *Music in Colonial Massachusetts, 1630–1820* (Boston: Colonial Society of Massachusetts, 1980), part I, 188–92.

91. Holmes, *Acts of War*, 367.

92. "Narrative of Mr. John Wise, Minister of God's Word at Chebacco," *Proceedings of the Massachusetts Historical Society*, Vol. XV, 288.

93. Church, *The History of the Great Indian War*, 265.

94. Ibid., 187–89.

95. Penhallow, *History of the War of New England*, 60.

96. Holmes, *Acts of War*, 368.

97. Ibid., 268–69; Keegan and Holmes, *Soldiers*, 268–70.

98. Charles E. Clark, *The Eastern Frontier: The Settlement of Northern New England, 1610–1763* (New York: Knopf, 1970), 117.

99. Cotton Mather, *Souldiers Counselled and Comforted; A discourse Delivered unto Some part of the Forces Engaged in the Just War of New-England Against the Northern & Eastern Indians* (Boston, 1689), 28.

100. Melvin B. Endy found that New England ministers were motivated by political rather than religious concerns. See Melvin B. Endy Jr., "Just War, Holy War, and Millennialism in Revolutionary America," *William and Mary Quarterly*, 3rd series, XLII (1985), 3-4. See also Drake, *The Border Wars of New England*, 226.

101. Ministers in frontier garrisons served the towns as well but were paid by the provincial governments. See James Phinney Baxter, ed., *Documentary History of the State of Maine* (Portland, ME, 1897), *Collections of the Maine Historical Society*, 2nd Series, Vol. V, 528-30; Clark, *The Eastern Frontier*, 83.

102. Drake, *The Border Wars of New England*, 41; "Narrative of Mr. John Wise, Minister of God's Word at Chebacco," *Massachusetts Historical Society Proceedings*, Vol. XV, 287-94 (14); Parkman, *Half-Century of Conflict*, 253.

103. "Narrative of Mr. John Wise," *Massachusetts Historical Society Proceedings*, Vol. XV, 288, 293 (14).

104. Holmes, *Acts of War*, 291.

105. Archer Jones, *The Art of War in the Western World* (Urbana: University of Illinois Press, 1987), 177.

106. Highlanders were told their names would be hung on the church door if they failed in their duty. For more, see John Prebble, *Mutiny: Highland Regiments in Revolt, 1743-1804* (1975; reprint, New York: Penguin, 1978), 98-102.

107. Thomas Pakenham, *The Boer War* (New York: Random House, 1979), 290.

108. "Levying Act of 1721," Massachusetts Militia Laws, *Background of Selective Service*, 160.

109. "Waldo to Pepperrell, May, 1745," "Pepperrell Papers," Series VI, Vol. X (1899), 213-15.

110. Holmes, *Acts of War*, 143.

111. Ann M. Little, *Abraham in Arms: War and Gender in Colonial New England* (Philadelphia: University of Pennsylvania Press, 2007), 15. Or what in the twenty-first century is often referred to as the "wimp factor."

112. William Hutchinson Rowe, *Ancient North Yarmouth and Yarmouth, Maine, 1636-1936* (Yarmouth, ME, 1937), 61.

113. Thomas Symmes, *Historical Memoirs of the Battle at Piggwacket or Lovewell Lament'd* (Boston, 1725), 4. Of course, Symmes was writing after the event, so this cannot be taken as a direct quote. But Symmes did apparently talk with the survivors and this probably captures the spirit of the conversation.

114. Keegan and Holmes, *Soldiers*, 56.

115. Ibid., 247.

CHAPTER 10

1. John Keegan and Richard Holmes, *Soldiers: A History of Men in Battle* (New York: Viking, 1985), 261.

2. Ibid., 263.

3. Ibid., 261.

4. For descriptions of seventeenth – and eighteenth-century battles, see Archer Jones, *The Art of War in the Western World* (Urbana: University of Illinois Press, 1987), chapters 4 and 5.

5. Louis E. De Forest, *Louisbourg Journals: 1745* (New York, 1932), 16, 17.

6. Samuel Penhallow, *The History of the Wars of New England with the Eastern Indians* (Boston, 1726; facsimile reprint, annotated by Edward Wheelock, Williamstown, MA, 1973), 40–41.

7. Ibid., 86–87.

8. Ibid., 121–22.

9. Fannie Eckstorm, "The Attack on Norridgewock: 1724," *New England Quarterly*, (1934), 568; see also Thomas Hutchinson, *The History of the Colony and Province of Massachusetts Bay* (London, 1768; reprint, Cambridge, MA, 1936), 235–37.

10. Charles Edward Banks, *History of York, Maine* (Boston, 1931–1935), Vol. I, 326–27.

11. See Cotton Mather, *Decennium Luctuosum* (1699; reprinted in Charles H. Lincoln, ed., *Narratives of the Indian Wars, 1675–1699*, New York, 1913), 191; William Hutchison Rowe, *Ancient North Yarmouth and Yarmouth, Maine, 1636–1936* (Yarmouth, ME, 1937).

12. Jeremy Belknap, *The History of New Hampshire* (reprint of 1831 edition, New York, 1970), Vol. 1, 134.

13. Mather, *Decennium Luctuosum*, 229.

14. Penhallow, *History of the Wars of New England*, 112–17; Belknap, *History of New Hampshire*, 210; George W. Chamberlain, "John Chamberlain, The Indian Fighter at Pigwacket," *Collections and Proceedings of the Maine Historical Society*, Second Series, Vol. IX; George Hill Evans, *Pigwacket* (Somerville, MA, 1939), 64–66.

15. "Act for Regulating the Militia, 1693," *Massachusetts Militia Laws, Background of Selective Service* (Washington, 1947), Vol. II, 139.

16. George C. Neumann, *The History of Weapons of the American Revolution* (New York: Harper and Row, 1967), 52.

17. See chapter 6 on weapons for more. See "French Captive Examination from Piscataway Co., March 19, 1690," James Phinney Baxter, ed., *Documentary History of the State of Maine* (Portland, ME, 1897), *Collections of the Maine Historical Society*, 2nd Series, Vol. V, 55–56.

18. "Thomas Savage to his brother in England, 1691" (London, 1691), in *Collections of the Massachusetts Historical Society*, Series II, Vol. 3, 257.

19. Thomas Church, *The History of the Great Indian War of 1675 and 1676 Commonly Called Philip's War, also, The Old French and Indian Wars, from 1689 to 1704* (1716; Hartford, CT, 1845 edition), 170. This is the battle where Church found that his spare ammunition was the wrong caliber. See chapter 6.

20. Sylvia Frey, *The British Soldier in America: A Social History of Military Life in the Revolutionary Period* (Austin: University of Texas Press, 1981), 100–101; J. A. Houlding, *Fit for Service: The Training of the British Army, 1715–95* (Oxford: Oxford University Press, 1981), 147–48.

21. Troops heading to Louisbourg were ordered "to make a form suitable to his gun and to choose out bullets suitable and to make as many cartridges as to fill their cartouch boxes with powder and ball and to allow as much powder in each cartridge as will be sufficient to prime too." See *American Antiquarian Society* [hereafter cited as *AAS*], Curwen Family Papers, Box 3, Folder 1.

22. M. L. Brown, *Firearms in Colonial America: The Impact on History and Technology, 1492–1792* (Washington, DC: Smithsonian, 1980), 11, 21.

23. "Journal of Capt. Eleazer Melvin," *New Hampshire Historical Society Collections*, Vol. 5 (Concord, NH, 1837), 209.

24. Frey, *The British Soldier in America*, 101.

25. Plains Indians used this technique when reloading their flintlock trade guns on horseback, because sprinkling powder in a small pan while being on the back of a galloping horse is not practical. See Charles E. Hanson Jr., *The Northwest Gun* (Lincoln, NE: Nebraska State Historical Society, 1955), 1.

26. Chamberlain, "John Chamberlain," *Collections and Proceedings of the Massachusetts Historical Society*, Second Series, Vol. IX, 8.

27. Penhallow, *History of the Wars of New England*, 114.

28. Chamberlain, "John Chamberlain," Second Series, Vol. IX, 8.

29. Penhallow, *History of the Wars of New England*, 46.

30. Mather, *Decennium Luctuosum*, 243–47. The inability of the Gloucester men to shoot any of these raiders convinced them that they were actually specters. Richard Slotkin felt the Gloucester incident was explained away as specters because the New Englanders could not believe the Indians could penetrate that close to Boston. See Richard Slotkin, *Regeneration Through Violence: The Mythology of the American Frontier, 1600–1860* (Middletown, CT: Wesleyan University Press, 1973), 119.

31. Richard Holmes, *Acts of War: The Behavior of Men in Battle* (New York: Free Press, 1985), 164.

32. Anon, "Phips Expedition to Canada," *Proceedings of the Massachusetts Historical Society*, Second Series, Vol. XV, 315.

33. Penhallow, *History of the Wars of New England*, 92.

34. Ibid., 100. See chapter 4. See Thomas Symmes, *Historical Memoirs of the Battle at Piggwacket, or Lovewell Lament'd* (Boston, 1725), vii.

35. Francis Parkman, *Count Frontenac and New France under Louis XIV* (Boston, 1896), 277.

36. Ann M. Little, *Abraham in Arms: War and Gender in Colonial New England* (Philadelphia: University of Pennsylvania Press, 2007), 37–42.

37. Mather, *Decennium Luctuosum*, 238.

38. Chamberlain, "John Chamberlain," Second Series, Vol. IX, 5.

39. *State of the British and French Colonies in North America With Respect to Number of People, Forces, Forts, Indians, Trade and Other Advantages* (1755; facsimile reprint, New York, 1967), 73–74.

40. The following account is quoted in Penhallow, *History of the Wars of New England*, 20–22.

41. Samuel Adams Drake, *The Border Wars of New England, Commonly Called King William's and Queen Anne's Wars* (1897; reprint of 1910 edition, Williamstown, MA, 1973), 31.

42. Ibid., 30–31.

43. Harold L. Peterson, *Arms and Armor in Colonial America, 1526–1783* (New York: Bramhall House, 1956), 7.

44. Belknap, *History of New Hampshire*, 127–28; Drake, *The Border Wars of New England*, 19, 218; Penhallow, *History of the Wars of New England*, 5–7, Notes, 11–13.

45. Cotton Mather, *Frontiers Well-Defended* (Boston, 1707), 22.

46. Belknap, *History of New Hampshire*, 145.

47. Keegan and Holmes, *Soldiers*, 206.

48. Francis Jennings, *Invasion of America: Indians, Colonialism and the Cant of Conquest* (New York: Norton, 1975), 150, 147.

49. Harry H. Turney-High, *Primitive War: Its Practice and Concepts* (Columbus: University of South Carolina Press, 1949), 147; Douglas Leach agreed with this assessment that primitive warfare was for individuals, see *The Northern Colonial Frontier, 1607-1763* (New York: Holt, Rinehart and Winston, 1966), 12. Leroy V. Eid attacked this notion somewhat by insisting Indians were capable of a "national war." Eid meant that large war parties were dispatched after discussions by leading chiefs. Eid may be correct because the Eastern Indians certainly were able to put together large war parties, but the individual motivation of the warriors, and their behavior in battle, did not differ remarkably from smaller raiding parties. See Leroy V. Eid, "'National' War among Indians of Northeastern North America," *Canadian Review of American Studies*, XVI (1985), 127-29.

50. Many studies have shown this; see in particular Holmes, *Acts of War*, chapter 6.

51. James Axtell, *The Invasion Within: The Contest of Cultures in Colonial North America* (New York: Oxford University Press, 1985), 16.

52. See chapter 2 for examples.

53. Belknap, *History of New Hampshire*, 293.

54. Drake, *The Border Wars of New England*, 119.

55. Jennings, *Invasion of America*, 168.

56. Mahon, "Anglo-American Methods," *Mississippi Valley Historical Review*, Vol. 45 (1958), 254-75.

57. Ibid., 271.

58. Ibid., 257, 255.

59. "Dummer to Westbrook, March 20, 1724," in William Blake Trask, *Letters of Colonel Thomas Westbrook and others Relative to Indian Affairs in Maine, 1722-1726* (Boston, 1901), 45.

60. Eckstorm, "The Attack on Norridgewock: 1724," *New England Quarterly* (1934), 568.

61. Now known as Lovell's Pond.

62. One Indian managed to escape momentarily but was seized by a dog. Belknap, *History of New Hampshire*, 208.

63. Turney-High observed that, for all their use of surprise tactics, American Indians rarely took steps to prevent a surprise attack on themselves. See *Primitive War*, 116.

64. Indians rarely pursued provincial soldiers for very long, fearing the individual might have reloaded and that they would lose their share of the plunder from the battlefield.

65. Mather, *Decennium Luctuosum*, 27-28.

66. Church, *The History of the Great Indian War*, 167.

67. Ibid., 185, 193-95. See chapter 7.

68. Ibid., 267-69.

69. Mather, *Decennium Luctuosum*, in Lincoln, ed., *Narratives of the Indian Wars*, 219; Drake, *The Border Wars of New England*, 50-51. Drake said the Indians rushed out and killed most of the others and only four made it back to the fort that night; however, Mather's account, given in the text, seems more reasonable.

70. Francis Parkman, *A Half-century of Conflict* (Boston, 1892), 253.

71. Mahon, "Anglo-American Methods," 260. See above.

72. Ibid.

73. For example, see John Gyles's account of the Pemaquid attack above.

74. See Penhallow, *History of the Wars of New England*, 113.

75. "Dummer to Westbrook, May 13, 1725," James Phinney Baxter, ed., *Documentary History of the State of Maine* (Portland, ME, 1907), *Collections of the Maine Historical Society*, 2nd Series, Vol. X, 270.
76. *Boston Newsletter*, May 20 to May 27, 1725.
77. Penhallow, *History of the Wars of New England*, 113.
78. "Melvin Journal," *New Hampshire Historical Society Collections*, Vol. 5 (1837), 207–11.
79. Houlding, *Fit for Service*, 261.

CHAPTER 11

1. The prevalence of gunshot wounds is revealed in the request of a Portsmouth doctor who indicated to the Bay government in January 1692 that he was "Altogather out of Medicens for gunn shott wounds." "Dr. Humphrey Bradstreet's Letter, January 26, 1692," James Phinney Baxter, ed., *Documentary History of the State of Maine* (Portland, ME, 1897), *Collections of the Maine Historical Society*, 2nd Series, Vol. V, 310–12.
2. "Petition of Richard Honnywell, March 18, 1697," in Baxter, *Documentary History*, Vol. V, 477–79.
3. "John Ellenwood's Petition, February, 1701," in Baxter, *Documentary History*, Vol. V, 522–23.
4. See also Cotton Mather, *Decennium Luctuosum* (1699; reprinted in Charles H. Lincoln, ed., *Narratives of the Indian Wars, 1675–1699*, New York, 1913), 268–69; "Eliezer Rogers' Petition, 1698," in Baxter, *Documentary History*, Vol. V, 512; "Certificate of Surgeon Humphrey Bradstreet, December 8, 1697," in Baxter, *Documentary History*, Vol. V, 494–95; Samuel Penhallow, *The History of the Wars of New England with the Eastern Indians* (Boston, 1726; facsimile reprint, annotated by Edward Wheelock, Williamstown, MA, 1973), Notes, 41.
5. "Thomas Westbrook to Lt-Governor William Dummer, May 28, 1725," James Phinney Baxter, ed., *Documentary History of the State of Maine* (Portland, ME, 1907), *Collections of the Maine Historical Society*, 2nd Series, Vol. X, 283–84.
6. Mather, *Decennium Luctuosum*, 221–22. For another example, see Jeremy Belknap, *The History of New Hampshire* (reprint of 1831 edition, New York, 1970), Vol. 1, 217.
7. Louis E. De Forest, *Louisbourg Journals: 1745* (New York, 1932), 16–18.
8. Penhallow, *History of the Wars of New England*, 27–28.
9. "Letter from Johnson Harmon, February 25, 1723," in William Blake Trask, *Letters of Colonel Thomas Westbrook and others Relative to Indian Affairs in Maine, 1722-1726* (Boston, 1901), 11–12; "Dummer to Harmon, March 8, 1723," in James Phinney Baxter, ed., *Documentary History of the State of Maine* (Portland, ME, 1907), *Collections of the Maine Historical Society*, 2nd Series, Vol. IX, 474.
10. Mather, *Decennium Luctuosum* in Lincoln, *Narratives of the Indian Wars*, 221–22.
11. Mather, *Decennium Luctuosum* in Lincoln, *Narratives of the Indian Wars*, 271.
12. "John White to William Dummer, May 9, 1725," *Annals of Lancaster, Massachusetts, 1643–1825* (Clinton, MA, 1884), 224–25.
13. "Petition of Joseph Bane, October 13, 1702," in Baxter, *Documentary History*, Vol. IX, 136.
14. "Pepperrell Papers," *Collections of the Massachusetts Historical Society*, Series VI, Vol. X (1899), 155, 166–69. See chapter 5.
15. De Forest, *Louisbourg Journals*, 18.

16. "Journal of John Lovewell, January 29 to February 27, 1725," James Phinney Baxter, ed., *Documentary History of the State of Maine* (Portland, ME, 1916), *Collections of the Maine Historical Society*, 2nd Series, Vol. XXIII, 151.

17. "Journal of Samuel Willard, September, 1725," *Annals of Lancaster*, 231–32.

18. "Journal of Lieutenant John Burk," Stevens Family Papers, Special Collections, University of Vermont, entry for May 10, 1748.

19. "Journal of Samuel Willard, September, 1725," *Annals of Lancaster*, 231–32; "Journal of Lieutenant John Burk," Stevens Family Papers, Special Collections, University of Vermont, entry for March 3, 1748.

20. John Keegan and Richard Holmes, *Soldiers: A History of Men in Battle* (New York: Viking, 1985), 143.

21. Samuel Adams Drake, *The Border Wars of New England, Commonly Called King William's and Queen Anne's Wars* (1897; reprint of 1910 edition, Williamstown, MA, 1973), 64–65.

22. Thomas Hutchinson, *The History of the Colony and Province of Massachusetts Bay* (London, 1768; reprint, Cambridge, MA, 1936), 126.

23. Douglas Edward Leach, *Arms for Empire: A Military History of the British Colonies in North America, 1607–1763* (New York: Macmillan, 1973), 218.

24. "Pepperrell to Shirley, January 28, 1746," "Pepperrell Papers," Series VI, Vol. X, 442.

25. Douglas Edward Leach, *Roots of Conflict: British Armed Forces and Colonial Americans, 1677–1763* (Chapel Hill: University of North Carolina Press, 1986), 74.

26. "James Convers to Governor and Council, November 3, 1690," in Baxter, *Documentary History*, Vol. V, 157.

27. "Samuel Moody to Governor Joseph Dudley, March 23, 1712," in Baxter, *Documentary History*, Vol. IX, 310; Hugh D. McLellan, *History of Gorham, Maine* (Portland, ME, 1903), 60.

28. "Westbrook to Dummer, April 2, 1724," in Baxter, *Documentary History*, Vol. X, 186–87.

29. Thomas Church, *The History of the Great Indian War of 1675 and 1676 Commonly Called Philip's War, also, The Old French and Indian Wars, from 1689 to 1704* (1716; Hartford, CT, 1845 edition), 195.

30. Quoted in Leach, *Roots of Conflict*, 74

31. See Keegan and Holmes, *Soldiers*, 143–44; Thomas Pakenham, *The Boer War* (New York: Random House, 1979), 403.

32. "Journal of Samuel Wheelwright, November to December, 1724," in Baxter, *Documentary History*, Vol. XXIII, 151.

33. "Richard Waldron to John Wentworth, July 31, 1725," in Baxter, *Documentary History*, Vol. X, 317. For more details on this scout, see chapter 4. The journal of the scout is printed in the *Annals of Lancaster*, 232–34.

34. White's widow's petition describing her husband's service is printed in the *Annals of Lancaster*, 227.

35. Penhallow, *History of the Wars of New England*, 114–15; Francis Parkman, *A Half-Century of Conflict* (Boston, 1892), 250–57; George Hill Evans, *Pigwacket* (Somerville, MA, 1939), 62–69.

36. "Letter from Jeremiah Swaine at Salmon Falls, October 15, 1689," in Baxter, *Documentary History*, Vol. IX, 65–66; "Capt. Simon Willard to Governor and Council, November 29, 1689," in Baxter, *Documentary History*, Vol. V, 14. See "Petition of William Arden," in Baxter, *Documentary History*, Vol. V, 55.

37. "King and March to Bay Government, July 12, 1691," in Baxter, *Documentary History*, Vol. V, 264–65.
38. "William Vaughn and Charles Frost to Governor and Council, July 11, 1691," in Baxter, *Documentary History*, Vol. V, 265–66.
39. "Governor and Council to Vaughn and Frost, July 13, 1691," in Baxter, *Documentary History*, Vol. V, 268.
40. "King and March to Governor and Council, July 17, 1691," in Baxter, *Documentary History*, Vol. V, 268–69.
41. Ibid., 270.
42. "Governor and Council to March and King, July 20, 1691," in Baxter, *Documentary History*, Vol. V, 270–71.
43. "March and King to Governor and Council, August 7, 1691," in Baxter, *Documentary History*, Vol. V, 282–83.
44. "Charles Frost to Lt-Governor Stoughton, September 21, 1695," in Baxter, *Documentary History*, Vol. V, 431–32.
45. Church, *The History of the Great Indian War*, 184.
46. "Lt-Governor William Dummer to Westbrook, October 1, 1723," in Trask, *Letters of Colonel Thomas Westbrook*, 38–39.
47. "Westbrook to Dummer, March 29, 1724," in Baxter, *Documentary History*, Vol. X, 183–84.
48. "Westbrook to Dummer, April 1, 1724," in Baxter, *Documentary History*, Vol. X, 184–85.
49. "Westbrook to Dummer, April 2, 1724," in Baxter, *Documentary History*, Vol. X, 186–87.
50. Banks, *History of York, Maine*, Vol. II, 397.
51. "Westbrook to Dummer, August, 1724," in Baxter, *Documentary History*, Vol. X, 216.
52. Banks, *History of York, Maine*, Vol. II, 324.
53. Ibid., Vol. I, 333–34.
54. "Mary Bulman to Husband, July 9, 1745," *Maine Historical Society Manuscripts*, Vol. I, 20.
55. De Forest, *Louisbourg Journals*, 140, 141.
56. Henry S. Burrage, *Maine at Louisbourg in 1745* (Augusta, ME, 1910), 99–100.
57. Louisbourg was especially hard on doctors. William Pepperrell reported to Governor William Shirley in January 1746 that two doctors had been lost when a ship sank. See "Pepperrell Papers," Series VI, Vol. X, 442. John Ladd petitioned the New Hampshire Assembly in 1746 concerning "his Son Jonathan Lad [who] went to Louisbourg in his Majesties Service in the Capacity of a Physitian and in his Return was taken Sick of the Distemper that Reigned at Louisbourge, and was landed in a verry weak and low condition." Ladd reported that his son died not long after his return. See "Petition of John Ladd relative to his Son, August 2, 1746," in Isaac Hammond, ed., *Miscellaneous Provincial and State Papers* (Manchester, NH, 1890) *New Hampshire Provincial and State Papers*, Vol. XVIII, 284.
58. De Forest, *Louisbourg Journals*, 98–107.
59. Fairfax Downey, *Louisbourg: Key to a Continent* (Englewood Cliffs, NJ: Prentice-Hall, 1965), 96.
60. "Journal of Lieutenant John Burk," Stevens Family Papers, Special Collections, University of Vermont, entry for March 4 and 5. Burk actually spelled it "grivd."

61. "Petition of Thomas Footman, March 29, 1692," in Baxter, *Documentary History*, Vol. V, 381–82.
62. "Petition of Jonathan Stanhope, relative to Indians, 1750," in Hammond, *NHSP*, Vol. XVIII, 379–80.
63. Plymouth Colony Laws, 1636, *Background of Selective Service* (Washington, 1947), Vol. II, 12.
64. "An Act for the Payment of Cure of Souldiers that are Wounded, July 23, 1696," New Hampshire Provincial Laws, *Background of Selective Service*, 58: "Levying Act, 1693," "Levying Act, 1744," Massachusetts Militia Laws, *Background of Selective Service*, 146, 174.
65. For an example, see Baxter, *Documentary History*, Vol. V, 177.
66. Provincial governments were flooded with petitions seeking compensation for almost everything imaginable from both soldiers and inhabitants. References have been made throughout this study to other grievances; however, this discussion will concentrate on wounded soldiers and death compensation to relatives.
67. "Petition of Thomas Footman, March 29, 1692," in Baxter, *Documentary History*, Vol. V, 381.
68. Petition of Samuel Drown, Wounded Soldier, May 28, 1747; "Bill for Nursing Samuel Drown," in Hammond, *NHSP*, Vol. XVIII, 307–8.
69. "Certificate of Edward Pratt, March 7, 1700," in Baxter, *Documentary History*, Vol. V, 525–26.
70. "John Baker's Petition, 1700," in Baxter, *Documentary History*, Vol. IX, 100–101.
71. "Letter John Baker to James Converse, March 6, 1700," in Baxter, *Documentary History*, Vol. V, 524–25.
72. Petition by James Converse in behalf of John Baker, 1700," in Baxter, *Documentary History*, Vol. IX, 99. For more about Converse and Baker, see chapter 8.
73. "John Baker's Petition, 1700," in Baxter, *Documentary History*, Vol. IX, 100–101.
74. "Petition of Charles Makarty," in Baxter, *Documentary History*, Vol. V, 366–67. It is unclear if Makarty received his compensation.
75. Cook eventually petitioned the government that because of his wound, he was "wholey rendred uncapable of performing any the souldiers worke . . . as also of doeing anything whereby to procure a livelyhood for his Subsistence." The assembly granted him an annual pension of £5.
76. "Journal of the Assembly, May 27, 1748," in Nathaniel Bouton, ed., *Documents and Records Relating to the Province of New Hampshire from 1738-1749* (Nashua, NH, 1871), *New Hampshire Provincial and State Papers* [hereafter cited as *NHSP*], Vol. V, 910.
77. "Levying Act, 1693," "Levying Act, 1744," Massachusetts Militia Laws, *Background of Selective Service*, 146, 174.
78. "Petition of Joseph Bane, October 13, 1702," in Baxter, *Documentary History*, Vol. IX, 136.
79. Baxter, *Documentary History*, Vol. 512.
80. William Prescott fell ill at Louisbourg and the "Humor fell into his Leggs and feet in Severe fevors Sores." Prescott eventually lost his right leg and two toes on his left foot, and he requested a pension. The New Hampshire Assembly paid him £30 "for loss of his leg &c." ("William Prescott's Petition," in Hammond, *NHSP*, Vol. XVIII, 282). Benjamin Thomas was granted £20 for an arm wound received at Louisbourg ("Petition of Benjamin Thomas, 1746," in Hammond, *NHSP*, Vol. XVIII, 261–62). Michael Whidden was hit in the right knee at Louisbourg and could not continue in his trade as joiner. He was paid £40.

81. "Louisbourg Soldier's Petition, Portsmouth Men," in Hammond, *NHSP*, Vol. XVIII, 263.

82. Gary B. Nash, *The Urban Crucible: The Northern Seaports and the Origins of the American Revolution*, abridged ed. (Cambridge: Harvard University Press, 1986), 105–6.

83. George Gilmore, *Roll of New Hampshire Men at Louisbourg, Cape Breton, 1745* (Concord, NH, 1896), 11.

84. Hammond, *NHSP*, Vol. XVIII, 286–88. This volume of the *New Hampshire Provincial and State Papers* is filled with petitions from soldiers and surviving families.

85. "Petition of Tabitha Cass, Widow of a Louisbourg Soldier, 1746," in Hammond, *NHSP*, Vol. XVIII, 270.

86. "Petition of Sarah Trefethen, February 18, 1746," in Hammond, *NHSP*, Vol. XVIII, 263–64.

87. "Petition of Hugh Montgomery, February 18, 1746," in Hammond, *NHSP*, Vol. XVIII, 260–61.

88. John F. Berens, *Providence and Patriotism in Early America, 1640–1815* (Charlottesville: University of Virginia Press, 1978), 14–34, quote on page 33.

89. Cotton Mather, *Military Duties Recommended to an Artillery Company, 1687* (Boston, 1687), 14.

90. Mather, *Decennium Luctuosum*, 259.

91. Samuel Penhallow, *The History of the Wars of New England*, iv.

92. Mather, *Decennium Luctuosum*, 272. Admittedly, it was Cotton Mather who related this story. This religious young man was killed a few minutes later.

93. "Mary Bulman to Husband, 1745," *Maine Historical Society Manuscripts*, Vol. I, 20.

94. Mather, *Decennium Luctuosum*, 214.

95. Anon, "Phips Expedition to Canada," *Proceedings of the Massachusetts Historical Society*, Second Series, Vol. XV, 317.

96. Louis E. De Forest, *Louisbourg Journals: 1745* (New York, 1932), 18; "Petition of Eleazer Young, Jr. Dec 14, 1744," in Isaac Hammond, ed., *Documents Relating to Towns in New Hampshire, "A" to "F" Inclusive* (Concord, 1882), *New Hampshire Provincial and State Papers*, Vol. XI, 514.

97. "Rev. George Burrough, et. al. to Governor and Council, January 27, 1692," in James Phinney Baxter, ed., *Documentary History of the State of Maine* (Portland, ME, 1897), *Collections of the Maine Historical Society*, 2nd Series, Vol. V, 316–17.

98. "Francis Hooke to Governor and Council, January 28, 1692," in Baxter, *Documentary History*, Vol. V, 317–18.

99. Drake, *The Border Wars of New England*, 131.

100. "Pepperrell Papers," Series VI, Vol. X (1899), 371–73.

101. Mather, *Decennium Luctuosum*, 7.

102. "Letter of Robert Pike, July 29, 1689," James Phinney Baxter, ed., *Documentary History of the State of Maine* (Portland, ME, 1907), *Collections of the Maine Historical Society*, 2nd Series, Vol. IX, 24.

103. Edward F. Bourne, *The History of Wells and Kennebunk* (Portland, ME, 1875), 209.

104. Penhallow, *History of the Wars of New England*, ii.

105. Ibid., vi.

106. "Letter William Lithgow, February 2, 1749," James Phinney Baxter, ed., *Documentary History of the State of Maine* (Portland, ME, 1916), *Collections of the Maine Historical Society*, 2nd Series, Vol. XXIII, 352–54.

107. "Samuel Denny to Governor, December 9, 1749," in Baxter, *Documentary History*, Vol. XXIV, 338–40.

108. "Committee Report, Dec. 13, 1749," in Baxter, *Documentary History*, Vol. XXIV, 340–42.

109. "S. Frost to Governor, Dec. 22, 1749," in Baxter, *Documentary History*, Vol. XXIV, 342–43.

110. "Joseph Blany to Spenser Phips, December 22, 1749," in Baxter, *Documentary History*, Vol. XXIV, 343. Blany said he thought he was entitled to the reward.

111. "House of Representatives, December 29, 1749," in Baxter, *Documentary History*, Vol. XXIV, 345–46.

112. Ibid., 347.

113. "Jabez Fox to Governor, January 1, 1750," in Baxter, *Documentary History*, Vol. XXIV, 347–49.

114. "Jeremiah Moulton to Governor, January 11, 1750," in Baxter, *Documentary History* Vol. XXIV, 349–50. See also *Journals of the Rev. Thomas Smith and the Rev. Samuel Deane* (Portland, ME, 1849), 141.

115. "House of Representatives, January 16, 1750," in Baxter, *Documentary History*, Vol. XXIV, 337; "Governor's Proclamation, January 22, 1750," in Baxter, *Documentary History*, Vol. XXIV, 350–52.

116. "Richard Saltonstall and Stephen Sewell to Governor, Council and Assembly, February 5, 1750," in Baxter, *Documentary History*, Vol. XXIV, 352; "Jeremiah Moulton to Governor, February 24, 1750," in Baxter, *Documentary History*, Vol. XXIV, 325.

117. "Letter William Lithgow, February 2, 1750," in Baxter, *Documentary History*, Vol. XXIV, 352–54.

118. "Lt. Jabez Bradbury to Governor, April 9, 1750," in Baxter, *Documentary History*, Vol. XXIV, 327.

119. "Indian letters, April 17. 1750," in Baxter, *Documentary History*, Vol. XXIV, 328–29.

120. "Governor's Message to Indians, August 8, 1750," in Baxter, *Documentary History*, Vol. XXIV, 335. The Rev. Smith wrote in his journal on June 15, "I rode to York. Albee was acquitted to the great surprise of the Court, who continued the other two prisoners to be removed for a trial elsewhere. This unhappy affair gives this country an ill name, and it is feared will bring on a war." *Journals of the Rev. Smith and Rev. Deane*, 143.

121. *Journals of the Rev. Smith and Rev. Deane*, 141 Note.

122. "Letter from Jabez Fox, January 1, 1750," in Baxter, *Documentary History*, Vol. XXIV, 349.

123. "Letter from Jeremiah Moulton, January 11, 1750," in Baxter, *Documentary History*, Vol. XXIV, 349–50. Ball's family had been in Maine when his father was killed, but afterward his mother and siblings returned "to the Westward in or about Dunstable where they first came from."

124. Douglas Edward Leach, *The Northern Colonial Frontier, 1607–1763* (New York: Holt, Rinehart and Winston, 1973), 120–21.

125. André Corvisier, *Armies and Societies in Europe, 1494–1789*, trans. Abigail T. Siddall (Bloomington: Indiana University Press, 1979), 4–6.

126. Francis Jennings, *The Invasion of America: Indians, Colonialism and the Cant of Conquest* (New York: Norton, 1975), 160, 162.

127. Corvisier, *Armies and Societies in Europe, 1494–1789*, 4.

AFTERWORD

1. Quoted in James Kirby Martin and Mark Edward Lender, *A Respectable Army: The Military Origins of the Republic, 1763–1789* (Arlington Heights, IL: Harlan Davidson, 1982), 19.
2. Martin and Lender, *A Respectable Army*, 19.
3. Ibid., 20.

Index

Abandonment of frontier communities, 36–37
Ammunition, 11, 28, 98, 100, 107, 109, 110, 119–127, 136, 201–202, 271n12, 292n21
Andros, Edmund, 3, 23, 51, 58, 159, 256n1
Anglo-American partnership, 92, 93, 94, 100–104, 108–109, 243
Artillery, 24–25, 100, 102, 198–199, 218

"Beating orders," 153
Brackett's Woods, Battle of (Falmouth/Portland, ME), 80, 126, 182, 194, 202, 211
Bulman, Alexander, 154, 226–227, 236
Burk, John, 62–63, 158, 220, 228

Cartagena expedition (1741), 92, 137, 138, 139, 144, 149, 186, 198, 199, 220, 232, 270n101
Chubb, Pasco, 65, 66, 75, 168–169, 192, 236, 285n95
Church, Benjamin, 30, 74, 77, 88, 90, 124, 134–135, 143, 144–145, 157, 160, 164–165, 170, 182, 188–189, 190, 192, 197, 202, 21, 221, 225, 241; raid of 1689, 80, 126; raid of 1690, 74, 166, 192, 221, 225; raid of 1692, 81, 165; raid of 1696, 81; raid of 1704, 75, 83, 164–165, 166, 182, 190, 192, 211; recommendations for scouts, 82–83, 126–127, 182–183
Clothing. *See* Provincial soldiers
Committees of war, 133
Converse, James, 45, 49, 81, 163, 164, 165, 170, 189, 205, 220, 230
Councils of war, 166
Coureurs de bois, 6, 89–90

Davis, Sylvanus, 32, 47, 64, 65, 67, 117, 120
Death. *See* Provincial soldiers
Deerfield, MA, 1, 12, 14, 22, 63; town fortification described, 57; 1704 attack, 2, 3, 4, 57, 245n2
Dehumanization of the enemy, 190. *See also* Provincial soldiers, hatred of Eastern Indians
Desertion. *See* Provincial soldiers
Doctors, 81, 217, 223–227, 230, 234, 297n57
Dover, NH, 3, 22, 34, 45, 47, 48, 72, 86, 136, 146, 149–150, 152, 162, 173, 222, 281n114
Drill and training: aiming at a target, 181–182; defined, 172–173; loading (*see* Weapons); militia training day (*see* Militia); types of marching drill, 179–180
Drill manuals, 178–180, 288n41
Dudley, Joseph, 52, 73, 75, 82, 84, 91, 99, 103, 112, 113, 114, 122, 125, 126, 142, 147, 161, 167, 258n33, 263n84
Dummer, William, 4, 30, 66, 118, 160, 161, 166, 188, 211, 219, 226
Dummer's War, 4, 5, 22, 23, 52, 61, 69, 75, 85, 117–118, 136, 141, 144, 149, 154, 155, 190, 221, 222, 225, 245n1
Dustan, Hannah and Thomas, 208–209, 214

Eastern Indians, 3, 4, 13, 14, 22–23, 51, 61, 69, 73, 74, 83, 85, 86, 92, 118, 124, 155, 170, 189, 204, 205, 207, 208, 209, 214, 237; attitude toward, 189–193, 236–237; as traitors, 190–191, 290n88
Economy: bills of credit, 133; disruption on frontier, 36–37, 145; New England, 10, 98, 100, 108, 113–114, 127, 131, 133, 146–147, 173, 217, 266n29, 276n3, 277n18

302

English regular soldiers, 6–7, 28, 64–65, 96, 98, 101, 108, 132, 159, 177, 186, 190–191, 194–195, 202, 210, 215, 221, 250n33, 270n101, 277n18
Equipment. *See* Provincial soldiers
European warfare, 7–8, 175–177, 179, 184–185, 186, 198, 208–209, 241
Expeditions, 15, 91, 152, 154, 174, 194, 243, 267n46; described, 92–93, 247n49. *See also* Montreal; Port Royal, Nova Scotia; Quebec

Falmouth (Portland, Casco), ME, 3, 41, 42, 44, 61, 65, 85, 117, 126, 135, 139–140, 145, 162, 167, 221, 225, 237, 238, 240
Fighting spirit: *See* Provincial soldiers
Flints, 98, 120–122, 126
Food. *See* Provincial soldiers
Forts, 16, 132, 135, 152, 231, 243; Castle William (Boston, MA), 52, 132, 231; Fort Andros (Pejepscot, ME), 80; Fort Atkinson (Lake Winnipesaukee, NH), 64, 161, 284n50; Fort Dummer (Brattleboro, VT), 52, 60–61, 63, 141, 155, 199, 202, 213; Fort Frederick (Pemaquid, ME), 52, 59; Fort George (Brunswick, ME), 52, 55, 225; cost of, 58, 61; Fort at Gorham, ME, 55, 57; Fort Loyal (Falmouth/Portland, ME), 3, 32, 47, 51, 64, 67, 80, 120, 211; Fort Mary (Saco, ME), 51, 52, 55, 66, 117, 219; Fort Massachusetts (North Adams, MA), 4, 55, 62, 63, 66, 67, 68, 123; Fort at Number Four (Charlestown, NH), 52, 55, 61, 62, 66, 68, 77, 155, 158, 220, 228; Fort Pelham (Rowe, MA), 55, 63; Fort Richmond (Richmond, ME), 52, 86, 226; Fort Shirley (Heath, MA), 52, 55; Fort St George (Thomaston, ME), 23, 52, 61, 66, 67, 68, 85, 239; Fort on West Hoosic River (Williamstown, MA), 55; Fort William Henry (Pemaquid, ME), 15, 52, 55, 58, 62, 65, 67, 117, 167, 168, 192, 231; Fort William and Mary (Portsmouth, NH), 52, 59–60, 64, 124–125, 133; "Lovewell's Fort" (Ossipee Lake, NH), 55, 161, 223, 225; "New Casco Bay Fort" (Falmouth/Portland, Maine), 52, 62, 65, 66, 117, 256n4; Fort at Winter Harbor (Maine), 52; construction, 55–59; families at, 62; garrisons, 61; life in, 62–65; method of attack on, 65–67; significance of, 51, 67–68
French, superior at war, 6, 8, 13, 91
"Frontier town," designation as, 38
Frost, Charles, 36, 77, 170, 224, 225, 236

Garrison houses, 1, 13–14, 15, 29, 162, 231, 253n30; defense of, 49, 211; described, 39–40; led to overconfidence, 47–48; living conditions, 40–41; psychological advantage, 48–49, 208
Glorious Revolution, 3, 11, 32, 46, 51, 64, 94, 117, 122, 141
Goffe, John, 87–88, 89, 135, 155, 156, 157, 245n1
Guides. *See* Pilots
Gunners, 92, 102, 218, 235
Gunsmiths (gun repair), 61, 64, 117–118, 272n26
Gyles, John, 25, 61, 155, 206–207

Harmon, Johnson, 75, 77, 84, 85, 86, 90, 135, 157, 160, 189, 196, 199–200, 219
Hassell, Benjamin, 161–162, 164, 211, 236
Hilton, Winthrop, 83–84, 90, 154, 163–164, 167, 170, 199
Hunniwell, Richard, 75, 217

Illness. *See* Provincial soldiers
Interpreters, 61, 72, 155

Jacques, Richard, 196, 200

King George's War, 4, 22, 38, 45, 67, 87, 108, 155, 221, 237, 240
King Philip's War, 8, 15, 79, 117, 131, 173, 193, 209, 229
King William's War, 3, 8, 11, 22, 25, 32, 37, 43, 51, 58, 61, 69, 79, 82, 90, 119, 123, 132, 135, 141, 144, 155, 224, 229, 230, 234
Linear tactics, 175–176, 180–181, 182, 184–185, 243
Louisbourg, Cape Breton Island, 4, 9, 15, 23; siege of 1745, 88, 95, 96, 97, 100, 101, 102, 105, 106, 107, 108, 116, 120, 123, 132, 133, 135, 138, 139–140, 145, 146, 147, 149–150, 152, 154,

Index | 303

Louisbourg, Cape Breton Island (*continued*), 157, 158, 165, 16, 175, 178, 186–187, 195, 196, 198, 199, 218, 219, 220, 224, 227, 231, 232, 233, 235, 236, 239, 247n52, 268n48, 280n105

Lovewell, John, 76, 86–87, 89, 155, 156, 157, 161–162, 164, 189, 200, 209, 210, 219, 225, 277n33

Lovewell's fight, 4, 86–87, 124, 146, 161–162, 164, 169, 188, 194, 196, 200, 203, 205, 211–212, 214, 218, 222

March, John, 21, 30, 46, 62, 65, 75, 76, 82, 83, 163, 167, 168, 169, 192, 224

March-King raid, 1691, 30, 46, 75, 76, 80, 117, 163, 164, 200, 224–225

Mather, Cotton, 25, 36, 40, 41, 168, 173–174, 177, 190, 193, 204, 205, 207, 211, 218, 219, 234, 235, 236

Melvin, Eleazer, 87–88, 155, 202, 213–214

Military engineers, 92, 101–103. See Redknap, John; Romer, Wolfgang W.

Militia: committees of, 21, 31, 131; system, 26–29, 250n36; training days, 173–174, 182, 183

Ministers, 134, 190; accompany soldiers, 194, 223. *See also* Mather, Cotton; Religion; Wise, John

Montreal, 91; expedition of 1690, 11; expedition of 1747, 92, 132

Moulton, Jeremiah, 71–72, 86, 135, 155, 199–200, 210, 239–240

Native American warfare, 66–67, 183, 205–210, 294n64; aversion to hand-to-hand combat, 207, 209, 215, 243

Norridgewock, 69, 72, 73, 81, 85, 90; 1724 raid, 75, 86, 135, 191, 193, 196, 199–200, 210, 234, 264n88, 264n93

Notification of Attacks, 24–26

Oyster River (Durham), NH, 3, 24, 27, 48

Palisade walls, described, 55–57

Patrols, 16, 69, 70, 132, 149, 152, 153, 164, 168, 174

Pejepscot Proprietors, Company of, 37, 52, 57–58, 61, 135, 260n86

Pemaquid, ME, 3, 12, 15, 51, 117, 206, 258n33

Pepperrell, William, 9, 96, 97, 100, 102, 104, 106, 116, 135, 139, 146, 147, 154, 155, 157, 165, 166, 195, 220, 227, 236

Pequawket, 69, 72, 73, 78, 82, 86–87, 90, 146, 203, 222

Petite guerre, la, 13, 16, 65, 69, 89, 175, 176–177, 181, 182, 187, 190, 199

Phips, William, 3, 12, 27, 51, 91, 97, 101, 105, 106, 112, 117, 138–139, 166, 168, 198, 220, 235, 283n23

Pilots (guides), 75–76

Plunder, 134, 138–140, 277n33

Portland, ME. *See* Falmouth (Portland, Casco), ME

Port Royal, Nova Scotia: expedition of 1690, 3, 15, 91, 92, 101, 106, 138, 139; expedition of 1707, 3, 4, 12, 91, 92, 94, 95, 103–104, 106, 107, 108, 136, 138, 154, 160–161, 167, 220, 285n89; expedition of 1710, 3–4, 15, 92, 96, 97, 101, 106, 108, 138, 139, 140, 152, 198

Portsmouth, NH, 43, 45, 52, 60, 76, 80, 81, 220, 221, 224, 226

Pursuit (of raiding parties), 32–34

Pressing (impressment): exemption from, 138; of food and clothing, 43–45; of soldiers (*see* Provincial soldiers); of tailors and shoemakers, 97; of weapons, 114

Provincial officers, 69, 70, 82, 132, 142, 152, 153, 155, 158; animosity between officers and with governors, 165–167; English officers' opinion of, 156, 166; pressure and presence in the field, 164–165; punishment, 167–169; recruiting methods, 143–144; reputation, 157; rising from ranks, 155–156, 163; supporting soldiers, 163

Provincial soldiers, 69, 70, 75, 82, 83, 88, 90, 101, 104, 133, 139, 141, 142, 151, 153, 172, 173, 175, 182, 183, 184, 191, 198, 208, 210, 215, 217, 234, 240; accidents, 160, 219–220; bounties, 136–138; charging in battle, 209–215; definition of, 29; desertion and panic, 64, 160–162, 187–188; English officers' opinion of, 2, 8–10, 175, 180, 183, 221, 242–243; equipment, 44, 76, 81, 82, 114, 119–121, 136–138, 201–202; fighting spirit, 195–197; food and clothing,

42–46, 63, 76, 82–83, 92, 94–97, 105–106, 107, 110, 132, 136–137, 148; as frontier garrison troops, 38, 41, 46–47, 62–65, 132, 136, 152, 174, 220, 231; hatred of Eastern Indians, 189–193, 236–237; historians' opinion of, 2, 5–7, 8, 10, 175, 183, 184, 242; illness and death, 63–64, 77, 105, 106, 108, 217–219, 220–223; infractions and punishments, 158–160, 284n50; killing of prisoners, 192–193; length of service, 147–148, 152; pensions and compensation, 229–233; pressed, 131, 140–142, 162, 281n1; psychological damage, 237–241; recruiting, 131; soldier's life, 105; training and drill (*see also* Drill and training; Weapons), 99; treatment of wounds and illness, 227–228; wages, 131–134

Quebec, 92; expedition of 1690, 3, 4, 10, 12–13, 91, 94, 100, 105, 106, 107, 120, 123, 133, 139, 166, 167, 186, 192, 194, 198, 202, 204, 205, 220, 247n42; expedition of 1709, 92, 94, 95, 98, 101, 108, 112, 136, 140, 166, 174; expedition of 1711 (*see* Walker Expedition); expedition of 1746, 92, 108
Queen Anne's War, 3, 22, 23, 44, 52, 61, 69, 73, 75, 79, 81, 85, 88, 90, 95, 118, 132, 133, 136, 147, 154, 190, 231

Raids, 14, 16, 69, 152, 153, 154, 156, 164, 168, 174
Rale, Sebastian, 4, 85, 86, 191, 196, 200, 235, 264n88
Redknap, John, 59, 103, 167
Religion, 105, 134, 151, 158, 193–194, 217, 234–237
Rogers, Robert, 155
Romer, Wolfgang W., 52, 59–60, 103, 124, 269n71

Scalp bounties, 84–85, 131, 136, 263n84, 277n30, 277n33
Scouts, 14, 133, 136, 194, 219, 220, 224, 235; best soldiers used for, 77; definition of, 69–70; effectiveness, 88–90; intelligence gathering, 72–73; living on, 70–72; operations, 77–79, 210; search and destroy, 72, 73–74; weather, 70–71, 77; winter, 83–84
Seven Year's War, 11, 15, 94, 149

Shirley, William, 23, 97, 100, 111, 115, 116, 139, 220, 284n50
Shute, Samuel, 5, 23, 85, 144, 191
Siege warfare, 175, 176, 198
Snowshoemen, 85, 264n87
Snowshoes, 83
Stevens, Phineas, 66, 77, 170
Storer, John, 105, 111, 152, 157
Storer Garrison (Wells, ME), siege of (1692), 49, 164, 205

Training. *See* Drill and training; Provincial soldiers; Weapons
Two-Pronged attack strategy (Quebec and Montreal), 92, 98, 108

Usher, John, 27, 47, 52, 84, 125–126

Vetch, Samuel, 98, 99, 101, 166, 174

Walker expedition to Quebec, 1711, 4, 13, 92, 94, 95, 137, 139
Walley, John, 107, 168, 169, 194, 235, 236
Warren, Peter, 104, 139, 221
Weapons, 11, 28, 98, 100, 109, 110, 111–22, 132, 136, 174, 175, 203, 210, 213, 235, 271n12, 272n26, 273n39, 288n35; loading procedure and firing rates, 119–120, 178–179, 202–203; value, 112, 106, 276n7; variety, 118–119, 126–127, 273n56
Wells, ME, 3, 22, 24, 37, 42, 45, 48, 49, 71, 105, 111, 152, 157, 236, 248n14, 253n30
Westbrook, Thomas, 30, 46, 48, 66, 75, 76, 117–118, 144, 145, 154, 156, 166, 188, 211, 221, 225, 226, 245n1, 264n88
Wheelwright Pond, Battle of (Lee, NH), 75, 200, 228
Wise, John, 107, 168, 192, 194
Women, attacks on as incentive for soldiers, 134, 189–190, 241
Wyman, Seth, 76, 77, 79, 164, 169–170, 187–188, 200, 203, 204, 211, 222

York, ME, 3, 4, 12, 14, 22, 24, 33, 40, 42, 71–72, 86, 117, 225, 226; 1692 attack, 38, 40, 84, 117, 124, 154, 236, 238

Index | 305

About the Author

STEVEN EAMES is a retired professor of history who lives in North Berwick, Maine. He is the author of *Sacrifice of Self: Nahant and the Civil War*.

www.ingramcontent.com/pod-product-compliance
Lightning Source LLC
Chambersburg PA
CBHW020354080526
44584CB00014B/1014